Jesus and the Religions of Man

Jesus
and the
Religions
of Man

David Marshall

Kuai Mu Press

Jesus and the Religions of Man

Copyright © 2000 David Marshall

ISBN: 0-9702278-0-9

Cover Illustration by Elizabeth VanDijk

Published by

KUAI MU PRESS

6765 37th SW, Seattle, WA, 98126

Dedication

THIS BOOK has been more than fifteen years in the making, and I have doubtless forgotten many whose assistance and suggestions were helpful in its formative and early development stages. It has always seemed to me that one of the chief benefits of public speaking is what the speaker learns from the audience, and the ideas presented in this book would not be what they are apart from the input of intelligent and thoughtful participants in various seminars and discussions. Thanks to Pastor Ivan Raskino for the information on the Rig Veda, Paul Chang for the book on Lao Zi and Jesus, and Elaine Colvin for various input. I also appreciate the people, including kind Internet strangers, who tracked down references.

Five people in particular put a great deal of effort into this project, and it would be much poorer without their help. I'd like to express my special gratitude to Ron Rice for going over the manuscript between flights, and during flights, to Africa. Your suggestions were invaluable, and always reasonable. To David Steinmetz for spending many hours reviewing the manuscript with your sharp eye and "which-hunting" expertise. To Laurel Fullington, who first gave me the seed of the idea that ultimately evolved into this book, and whose help in research, no-nonsense criticism, and just about everything else over the years, was always appreciated. Finally, to my parents, John and Patricia Marshall, to whom I dedicate this book. Thank you for being the kind of people who are always helping others, and that you have never gotten tired of helping your grown-up children.

Table of Contents

CHAPTER 1

Notes from the Underground

THE GREEK philosopher Plato told of a group of slaves who had been held captive in a cavern all their lives. Born in darkness, the only hint of the life beyond came from a fire that projected shadows on the wall. One day, an escaped slave found his way back into the cave. He told his fellows tales of a world of wonders, filled with light and beauty outside. Thinking he was mocking them, in a fit of rage, they put him to death.

Plato seemed to be goading the citizens of Athens with his parable. "Is the material world all that is?" he was asking. "And do you remember my Master Socrates, the community gadfly with the temerity to question what you took for the certainties of life, whom you forced to drink the deadly hemlock?"

The pattern of a hero who descends into the earth to rescue those trapped in darkness, facing death to deliver those without hope, appears again and again in both ancient and modern mythology. Orpheus crossed the River Styx and entered Hades in search of his lost love. Miao Shan, a patron saint of Chinese Buddhism, was murdered by her jealous father, but when banished to the underworld, chains fell off prisoners and captives went free. Egyptian civilization traced its origins to the time Osiris, god of the Nile, was killed by a jealous Set, god of shriveled harvests, and his sister-wife Isis brought him back to life. James Bond let himself be captured and led to the underground base of Spectre to rescue his flame of the hour and save the world. Indiana Jones entered the temple of Doom to free a village of enslaved village children.

The same pattern also appears in contemporary history. A frail Hindu lawyer fasts the British empire into submission while in jail. A Baptist preacher shakes prison dust off his suit and wins African-Americans the right to be treated with respect. Both heroes, like Socrates, pay for their ambitions with their lives. A Filipino senator, imprisoned, then exiled, returns home and dies for the liberty of his island nation. An African statesman emerges from decades in prison, shaky and pale, to overthrow apartheid and bring racial reconciliation to a nation on the verge of civil war. An army officer turned novelist is released from the Gulag and prays God to "make me a sword to smite the forces of evil." He strikes the Evil Empire with his pen, and it withers and dies like a dragon in a fairy tale. These epics of national death and resurrection did not occur in an obscure corner or in a Hans Christian Anderson tale; they defined the twentieth century. They remind us that sometimes, myths come to life. And when they do, society itself may be reborn.

Two thousand years ago, a rumor spread that a prophet had died for the sins of the world and come to life again. Some said the story had "turned the world upside down." Over the centuries, tremors continued. A measure of this story's continuing revolutionary potential is the fact that many of the principles in these modern fables—Gandhi and King, Aquino and Solzhenitsyn—were each deeply influenced by some aspect of the life and teachings of Jesus.

The story of the cave is the story of the dilemma that religion seeks to solve. For Christians, not one nation or race, but every one of us is in the dark: a gloom not just of political repression, nor illusion or dream, but frustration of our true nature and potential. We are princesses wearing rags in an attic, butterflies stuck in our cocoons. The purpose of life is to find *mukti,* to use a Hindu term, liberation, as the Marxists put it: freedom from the confines of sin and death to the discovery of what Jesus called the "Kingdom of God." Through the birth of the Son of God into this world, his death on the cross, and resurrection from the dead, we realize a humanizing and empowering fellowship with our Creator.

What relation does the Christian story bear to other solutions to the problem of the cave? (The "religions of man," as Huston Smith called them in a popular book comparing the spiritual paths of humanity.) Should the life of Jesus as it appears in the Gospels be classified among mythologies like Osiris or Miao Shan? The date on today's newspaper reminds us that human experience is divided into two eras by the Gospel story. Does that tale merit the centrality in our lives the calendar gives it in history?

The question of how Christianity relates to other religions has never been more important than in today's shrinking world. Presbyterian churches house Taoist study centers. Jewish rabbis go on pilgrimage to India. Zen devotionals, sermons by the Dalai Lama, and books about "conversations with God" and "spiritual tourism" jostle for space with volumes on the brotherhood of Christ and Buddha and stories of how Jesus learned exorcism in the subcontinent. Humanists and neo-Marxists use the methods of higher criticism to deconstruct the Gospels. The church is polarized between those who think every religion not born in the Holy Land came from the pit of hell, and those who think all roads lead to Mount Zion.

Why believe in Jesus over those thinkers and sages whose insights laid the cornerstone for great non-Western civilizations—Buddha, Confucius, Gandhi, Moses, or Zoroaster ? Or that clamoring crowd of hustlers, revolutionaries, and madmen who channel voices from other worlds, promise freedom from inhibition and neurosis, bring salvation to the working class, or offer release from the bonds of ego if we chant their name or follow their regimen—Rousseau, Yogananda, Baba, Marx, or Bishop Spong?

And which Jesus should we believe? "Very God from very God"? The Jesus who was "born of the virgin Mary, suffered under Pontius Pilate, the third day rose again"? The Jewish avatar who went to Ladakh to study under Hindu Masters? The radical who fomented trouble for the imperialists of first century Palestine? Or the ghostly enigma from whose life early church fathers allegedly patched a pious portrait to meet social needs and ambitions?

Which ideals are projections cast by the flickering light of wishful thinking? Which can stand inspection under the light of day? How can we tell the difference? Or is the best solution to live and let live? Let each seeker find his or her own path to the Godhead, if that is where he or she wishes to go?

The latter solution carries the force of conventional wisdom in our day. Many feel religion is not about objective reality, a God "out there" who watches over Creation, but an experience "in here." They believe each of the tales tradition passes down contains much to admire and learn from: the story of the man who heard the voice of God in the desert, and taught his people the unity of God and the brotherhood of man; of the rich young prince who realized the impermanence of material existence; of ascended pilgrims who find Godhood within, and pass their attainment on to those who seek higher states of consciousness. Many hold that all these tales are projections of truth from the collective unconscious, the thousand faces of a universal heroic archetype we are called to become: Christ-conscious, self-realized humanity.

To others, the search for God is not a search for any reality in the phenomenal world, but a kind of poetic license. Karen Armstrong, in a volume called *History of God,* described religion in terms of artistic creation:

"Other rabbis, priests and Sufis have taken me to task for assuming that God was—in any sense—a reality 'out there:' they would have warned me not to expect to experience him as an objective fact . . . in an important sense God was a product of the creative imagination, like the poetry and music that I found so inspiring."[1]

I will argue that while each faith community says something about Jesus that can add to the conventional Christian understanding of him, Jesus is more than the sum of these parts. I will make the case that the more honestly we examine human faith traditions, the clearer it is that Jesus is from *outside* the system. Paradoxically, one way Jesus shows this is that the call he makes to people of all faiths to follow him comes from *within* each tradition.

I think Plato's parable gives us a useful key to the problem of faith. We should be *sympathetic,* because all of us, no matter what our gender, race, creed, or class, are born into the same mysterious yet confined world. We should be *critical,* because it is easy to get turned around in the dark. We can be *personal* at times, because where can we start but our own experience? But we should also be *empirical, b*eginning with facts believers of all faiths and skeptics share in common, rather than dogma or subjective experience. That, at least, is the approach I intend to follow.

The moral of Plato's story is that we should listen to the gurus of man with a critical ear, not as a music aficionado, but like a fox caught in a trap, listening for a friend among the hounds. We should hunger and thirst for righteousness, but be skeptical when we find it. Why? Because this world can be a dark place. Furthermore, many who promise to bring us to the light, only made it darker.

And It Was Night

One person who took a close look at the darkness in the modern world was Nobel Prize-winning Jewish author Elie Wiesel, whose perfectly titled little book *Night* describes how he lost family and faith in Buchenwald.

> "Never shall I forget that night, the first night in camp, which has turned my life into one long night, seven times cursed and seven times sealed. Never shall I forget that smoke. Never shall I forget the little faces of the children, whose bodies I saw turned into wreaths of smoke beneath a silent blue sky. Never shall I forget those flames which consumed my faith forever. Never shall I forget that nocturnal silence which deprived me, for all eternity, of the desire to live. Never shall I forget those moments which murdered my God and my soul and turned my dreams to dust. Never shall I forget these things, even if I am condemned to live as long as God Himself. Never."[2]

Here are two challenges all face within the cave. First, in its attempt to open the doors of heaven, does faith create hell? The Nazis and Marxists were not unique in turning this trick: inquisitions, holy wars, and caste oppression have always followed in the wake of messianic programs like buzzards in the train of an army. It is not only that some people twist the words of God to further their own mean ends. That happens often enough. What is worse, religious ideas themselves often cast the human drama into deeper shadow.

And in the end no matter what their cause, such dark episodes in history constitute an even deeper challenge to faith. Where was God while children were suffering in Buchenwald? It is often a difficult question to answer.

My epiphany on this subject came fourteen years ago in Taiwan, in a red light district called Snake Alley, a colorful night market street in old Taipei.

I walked down a dark road, past a venereal disease clinic with a graphic, full-color menu of diseases on a board out front that, by all rights, should have scared the customers away from neighboring establishments. I had the chance to exchange a few furtive words with a sad-looking young woman nearby, using pidgin Chinese and hand signals. "Why did you come here?" She asked, realizing I was not a customer. "I came to pray." I replied, bringing my hands together. She crossed herself. "This is not a place for good people," she replied.

Indeed it was not. Gangsters ran the district in cooperation with a police station a block away. In these blocks one might come across drug addicts, gay bars, and the snakes that gave the district its name, hung up from hooks and their blood, thought to have aphrodisial properties, draining into cups. As if there were a tacit agreement that those who bare bodies to strangers had best keep souls hidden, no one looked you in the eye there. I was surprised when the girl made the sign of the cross, but I shouldn't have been. She'd probably been surrounded by religion all her life. Traveling to little tribal Tairoko and Taya villages from where many such girls came, I often found three or four churches. Up to a fifth of the young women in these towns, many taught to sing worship songs and pray as children, were sold as prostitutes by their own parents. The church sometimes wrung its hands, and sometimes sat on them, but did little to rescue these girls.

Snake Alley also enjoyed the auspicious presence of the most historic Buddhist temple in Taiwan, Dragon Mountain temple. Beautified by stone pillars and scenes from the *Tale of Three Kingdoms,* and tables laden with sumptuous fruits, the interior softened by the play of candles on incense, the 200-year-old temple was dedicated to the Goddess of Mercy. The Bodhisattva Guan Yin, too, seemed to sit on her 10,000 hands and do nothing for the teenage prostitutes a stone's throw away.

The local Taoist temples were worse. Every back alley seemed to have one or two, and I sometimes came across ten foot figures of Taoist gods parading in back alleys, practicing for temple dramas. Popular Taoism was involved in the oppression of these girls both ideologically and practically. Ideologically, because one popular element in the Taoist tradition, exemplified by a book called the *Secret Instructions of the Jade Chamber,* encouraged Chinese men to seek long life by mixing yin and yang by intercourse with teenage girls. The theory was that the woman's loss would be the man's gain. Practically because, as an ex-gangster later told me, gangs that controlled the brothels formed around Taoist temples. This was nothing new: temples have doubled as brothels for thousands of years.

This is one reason I intend to balance sympathy with a more critical approach than is usual in discussing faith. The Jewish prophet Micah said, "He has declared to you, O man, what is good, and what does the Lord require of you but to do justice, to love mercy and to walk humbly with your God?" (Micah 6:8). But religion does not always increase the stock of the world's justice, mercy, and humility. Nor do base spiritual impulses always blow themselves out in church politics, animal sacrifice, or esoteric rituals of questionable effect. Spirituality is power—a power that has more potential both to save and to harm than any other human force.

Comparing Figs and Lotus

There are several useful ways of sorting religions, though no other as simple and elegant as the picture Plato painted of the cave.

Some compare faiths by listing them *horizontally*. Huston Smith's *Religions of Man* takes this approach, describing Hinduism, Buddhism, Confucianism, Taoism, Islam, Judaism and Christianity in order, like fruits arranged on a shelf. Sometimes the same approach is taken by writers with a hostile intent, lining up the competition like ducks in a row, to point out errors of wrong religions more efficiently.

Others list faiths *chronologically*. Many Asian sects take for granted that the further back a lineage traces its origin, the closer it must be to the taproot of true spirituality. Modern sects influenced by the Enlightenment, such as Humanism and Marxism, take the opposite tack, assuming that later is better, that modern sects are more progressive and scientific than the superstitions of the past.

Another common way to look at faiths is *vertically*, according to the stage a religion or person has reached along a checklist of spiritual insights. Popular holistic guru Deepak Chopra describes seven stages of understanding God, each of which stage he says "are found in every spiritual tradition:" a punishing God, rule-making God, God of peace, of intuitive knowledge, creation, miracles, and for him the highest stage, unity with the Godhead, cosmic awareness. The Tian Tai and Hua Yan sects of Buddhism also represent a cataloguing approach to spirituality. *Tian* means heaven and *tai* means level or stage, so the name itself refers to stages through which we must go in our approach to God. In this arrangement, common to Hindu and Buddhist sects, one tends to see followers of competing sects not as wrong, but as less mature or "evolved."

Probably the most popular way to compare beliefs is *geographically*. Christianity and Islam are "western" faiths. Hinduism, Buddhism, Taoism, Bon, and

Shinto belong to the East. This is the understanding Karen Armstrong assumes in her books on what is usually called "western monotheism."

If each of these approaches were not useful, it would not be so popular. However, Plato's story hints at another possibility. We are in a cave. The light of eternity casts images of another world, of trees and meadows and running brooks. Then a man appears. He reminds us of those images, but his outline is sharper and his gestures more urgent than any we have seen. He tells us he has come to bring us out. We must be "born again." Yet we hesitate. How can we tell image from reality? How can we be sure we can trust him? Others have called before, leading those who followed down dark paths and into hidden crevices.

"I Have Come to Fulfill the Law and the Prophets"

We might call the Christian solution to the puzzle of world religions the *fulfillment* model. Jesus told his disciples, "Do not suppose that I came to annul the Law or the Prophets. I did not come to abolish, but to *complete* (or, in some versions, *fulfill*) them" (Matt. 5:17). It is true he was referring to Jewish moral law. However, from the earliest days, Christians like St. Paul, John, Augustine, Dante, and it seems St. Patrick, believed the Gospel completed other cultures as well. Jesus was not "of" the cave, the darkness and light of human despair, they said. He is not merely a shadow or a brilliant interpretation of one of the shadows, nor a figure we see when we strain our eyes. He was the savior from outside foreshadowed in these images of gods, bodhisattvas and revolutionary martyrs, the "Light of the world" (John 8:12) that "illuminates every person who comes into the world" (John 1:9).

The most powerful modern proponents of this view were three popular Christian writers: C. S. Lewis, G. K. Chesterton, and Don Richardson.

Lewis, one of the best writers and perhaps the best reader of the twentieth century, communicated his enthusiasm for mythology in all his many books. For him, religion was not an apple-or-orange ultimatum: divine truth should not only contain or transcend lower-level truths, but deepen them and bring out hitherto unrealized meaning even in the "queerest" belief systems. "The question was no longer to find the one simply true religion among a thousand religions simply false. It was rather, 'Where has religion reached its true maturity? Where . . . have the hints of all Paganism been fulfilled?'"[3]

Among Chesterton's many insights he threw off, almost parenthetically, an interesting analysis of beliefs. He suggested that religion in all cultures contained four elements, which he called God, gods, philosophers, and demons. Jesus operated with what Nicholas Wolterstorff spoke of as a "unique dialectic of affirmation, negation, and redemptive activity"[4] to create a synthesis that *fulfilled* the truest elements within mythology and philosophy.

Don Richardson made a theme that was implicit in Lewis and Chesterton historically explicit. Having worked as a missionary in New Guinea, he showed how the success of Christian missions was often attended by a remarkable phenomena. In tribe after tribe, the local people acted like they knew about the Christian God and had been waiting for the message the missionaries brought. Peoples around the world saw Christianity as the fulfillment of prophecies handed down from generation to generation. With the Gospel, the remote Sky God whom they worshiped came suddenly near, and told them: "This that is coming is my truth. Listen and follow this path." That is one of the reasons the Gospel of Jesus has spread throughout the world.

According to this view, the religions and ideologies of humankind are images flickering on the wall. Jesus is not different in being utterly unlike those pictures. On the contrary, the world he brings us to is the culmination of the insights of sages and myth-makers: constricting and narrow because, like the entrance to a cave, it leads to freedom. Jesus was not denying glimmers and sparks of truth within each tradition. But he was claiming some unique relation to the ultimate source of light. He was claiming that he would fulfill pagan mythology by bringing all races, tribes and tongues into the kingdom of God. Jesus told his disciples on one occasion, "Many prophets and upright men have longed to see what you see" (Matt. 13:17). In this view, Jesus had in mind not only Elijah and Moses, but Socrates, Confucius, Lao Zi, Indian sadhus and African medicine men, seekers for truth and wanderers beyond number who never found a home, and never stopped looking for one.

"I Am the Way, the Truth, and the Life"

Jesus said, "I am the Way, the Truth, and the Life; no one comes to the Father except through me" (John 14:6). When understood in the sense he intended, the words "I am" were an implicit claim to a unity with the Godhead that was unprecedented and threatening to the Jews of his day and no less to the religions of our day. As a modern Chinese philosopher has pointed out, the ancient Jewish name for God, Yahweh, "I am that I am," is essentially the same as *Zizaizhi,* the self-existent and non-dependent source of being—what Lao Zi called the Tao.

The purpose of this book will be to argue in the context of world belief systems that we can trust Jesus, that he is who he said he is.

Jesus said, "I am the Way." Marxist, Sexual, and Aquarian revolutions have shaped modern history by claiming to provide a better way than the path Jesus took. What was at the heart of Marx's appeal? And why did the movement he founded fail so abruptly? What did that failure have to do with Marx' attitude towards Jesus? And what warning does his failure hold for those of us who are not Marxists?

The Sexual Revolution also tried to liberate men and women from the confines of orthodox religion. We will see why this attempt was a prescription for loneliness and heartache. We will see that Jesus, more than anyone, taught humanity what it means for a man to love women, and vice-versa.

The Aquarian Revolution encourages us to turn from narrow reliance on the "intolerant Western concept of God" and look to the great spiritual traditions of Asia and tribal peoples for inspiration. Having lived in many Asian and tribal cultures, I am convinced there is much Westerners can learn from these sources. But the modern world tends to overlook two elements in "pagan" religion that are most universal of all. First, as Chesterton suggested, the devil has been haunting other Edens beside the one in Genesis, and his most potent weapon against humanity has always been our desire to "be as gods." Second, there are hints scattered among pagan religions of a Savior too much like Jesus to call the resemblance chance.

Next, we will look more closely at Christian morality. Are the teachings of the Gospels patriarchal, anachronistic dogma? Or do they provide a reasonable balance to enhance the welfare of family, church, society, and state? Has the church blown its mission to represent Christ in the world? Or has God used those who try to follow Jesus to transform the world in ways we seldom recognize? What about shameful episodes such as the Inquisition, the Crusades, pogroms against Jews, and the Salem witch hunts? Was the Bible to blame? I will suggest that the Gospel shows an uncanny theoretical ability to balance the complex demands of human relationships: freedom and responsibility, the collective and the individual, the *yin* and *yang* in each of us. In practice Jesus has transformed life on this planet for the better in a tremendous way. As for the sins of the church, there is much we can learn from them. The chief lesson, I will argue, is that Christians should stick to the Bible.

Jesus said, "I am the Life."[5]

An ancient prince looked down from his palace at the city he had built and asked, "Is this not Babylon the Great, which I have made for the glory of my own majesty?" A second prince looked up at the stars and asked, "what is man, that you take thought of him?" A third looked within, and loosed an enigmatic smile on the world. Under the motto of "self-actualization" or "self-realization," modern society interprets the Christian idea of humility as masochism or self-loathing that frustrates healthy human pleasure. Society generally prefers the first, or more recently the third, of these paths to happiness. But I will argue that worship of a God who is other than ourselves is the basis of the truest satisfaction even in this life, salve to the self-inflicted wounds of our spirits, and a key to delight in the beauty that surround us.

Jesus said, "I am the Truth."

Was *Yahweh* a stranger to Gentile humanity? Or were Chesterton, and the apostle Paul, right in saying that all humanity is aware on some level of our Creator? I will argue that the concept of a holy but distant Creator who loves people is a universal and surprisingly consistent, though widely suppressed, awareness among "pagan" cultures in every part of the world.

Are miracles impossible or, on the other hand, a universal phenomena that do not mark out the Christian Gospel as anything special? Is the devil a public relations ploy by the church to undermine "pagan" competitors? Or is the occult a legitimate way of attuning oneself to the rhythm of nature? I will propose that miracles, while rare, do happen, and are a clue to understanding our universe. They confirm that picture of the Creator's character that the Bible and nature both reveal to people around the world. By contrast, the occult shows a character radically different from Gospel miracles.

Was the "historical Jesus" a first century humanist, a primitive revolutionary, or a Jewish reformer, around whom the church added garbled tales about Osiris, Mithras, or even Buddha? Skeptics dissect the Gospels, and materialists and spiritualists stake claims to the tattered bits that remain of Christ's legacy, as the Romans gambled for the scraps of his clothing. Certainly he did not work any miracles or claim to be the Son of God, they say, let alone rise from the dead. Or maybe he did claim to be God in a mystical sense—and we are all gods in that, attaining Christ-consciousness, we too can share in the cosmic divinity. Some say he learned his miracles in India as a young man.

Skeptics often draw attention to the affinity of the Gospels with some ancient myths. "Doubtless the Gospel is just a fantasy like these," they say. "Perhaps the Gospel writers were even influenced by pagan stories." I will admit the similarities, and even point out some peculiar similarities skeptics do not seem to have noticed. But if A and B are alike, it does not follow that A caused B. Their similarities may be accidental. B may have caused A. Or C may have caused both. Gospel and myth may be copy of something else: Jung's collective unconscious, or the plan of God for mankind. It does not follow that A and B even belong to the same category. If C is a human being and A and B are his works, then they can be alike as two ball bearings, or as unlike as the statue of Liberty and the statute of limitations. If C is the Holy Spirit, then A may be all the myths in the world, and B that historical consummation of mythology by which God has determined to save the human race. In Lewis' words, "where have all the hints of paganism been fulfilled?"

"In Jesus" is the answer I suggest best fits the facts.

I will consider pictures of a Savior like Jesus that appear in sacred Scriptures such as the *Analects, Dao Dejing, Rig Veda,* and *Qur'an.* I will also present glimpses from "folk religion" of "the true light that illuminates every man who comes into the world."

I will argue that Jesus does not merely affirm our belief systems. Nor does he simply deny them. Nor does he pick and choose useful items, as if at a buffet. He does not merely pose with ascended masters at religious dialogues in a colorful robe from first century Palestine, alongside the Dalai Lama, the Pope, and Billy Graham. Rather, he does something much more threatening: he brings truth within each doctrine to life, and shows us what it really meant all along.

The slaves in Plato's story preferred shadows over light. Why? The man from outside threatened the status quo, the tolerant compromise they reached with each other and with their own hearts. Likewise, it has always been dangerous, even in "Christian" countries, to walk too closely with Jesus. Religious leaders have usually seen him the way the rabbis of his day did: as a threat to their power. Nowadays they often wield a weapon even more powerful than persecution to contain that threat: literary reconstruction. Apocryphal Gospels remake Jesus in the image of each religion—a Hindu Christ, Buddhist Christ, Muslim Christ, Marxist Christ, even Presbyterian and Catholic Christ. The most popular of these is the "historical Jesus" of higher critics and Jesus seminarians. Each of these is an attempt to make Jesus at home among shadows. But he calls us outside, and bids us be born again.

---

[1] Karen Armstrong, *History of God*, Ballantine Books, New York, 1991, Introduction

[2] Elie Wiesel, *Night*, Bantom, 1960, p. 32

[3] C. S. Lewis, *Surprised by Joy*, Harvest, 1956, p. 235

[4] *The Grace That Shaped My Life*, in *Finding God at Harvard*, Kelly Monroe, editor, Zondervan, Grand Rapids, MI, 1996, p. 154

[5] Christians often interpret this in terms of eternal life. I suspect the doctrine of eternal damnation is, along with sex, one of the most common objections people have to Christianity. But Confucius said, "to know what you know, and know what you don't know, that is knowledge." Not having seen into heaven or hell, I discuss Jesus' claim to bring "abundant life" primarily in its psychological aspect.

CHAPTER 2

The Middle Path of Truth: The Marriage of Faith and Reason

I CLIMBED from the south, ascending slopes that took my breath away in more than one sense, over stairs carved into what might mildly be called cliffs. I slept at the hostel by the Welcoming Pine, a symbol of hospitality reproduced in vivid color on tiles and paintings at inns across China. Mao Zedong's poetry was etched in his reckless calligraphy onto a cliff beside the tree. The next day I scrambled under and through boulders to the top of the next peak, then down to a trampled alpine meadow called Beijing Park. I met two philosophers from The Academy of Social Sciences, who had clambered up the bamboo cleats that temporarily covered the northern trail while workmen did repairs. That night we sat in the meadow under the stars: a naive young American Christian and two Chinese Marxists old enough to have had their lives, like the rock, etched indelibly by the violent poetry of Chairman Mao. We talked about the routes we had taken the day before, and the ways we would go the next. We also compared where we had come from in life, and where we were going, arguing about God and life and human destiny.

We might have enjoyed a less-threatening chat by looking at the stars and comparing the way various cultures interpreted them. The ancient Chinese saw one constellation as a lock. It looked like a stinging desert insect to the Greeks, while the Polynesians were reminded of the god Mani, who drew up the island Tongarera from the depths of the sea. The Egyptians looked in one part of the sky and saw the car of Osiris; but the Sudanese saw a hippo. The Iroquois Indians, looking at the same stars, saw the Great Bear, followed by the hunter birds:

chickadee, blue-jay, owl, saw-whet, and robin, the last of whom was red with the blood of the bear and scattered the colors of fall across the forest floor.

As far as I know, no one has ever fought a war over the stars, or gotten into a barroom brawl. With such conversation we could have passed the hours of the night, but never come closer to the mystery of where the stars come from, or where we are headed along the "Silver River," as the Milky Way is called in China. Still less would such conversation have given us a plan for the next day's journey. The stars on Yellow Mountain were beautiful, but did not illuminate anything besides themselves.

I had arrived at Beijing Park late in the afternoon, and I looked forward to the dawn, when I could see the landscape and get some idea where the trail would take me the following day.

About six the next morning I scrambled over futons in the dark, splashed cold water on my face, and groped my way to a spot near the edge of the clearing. Soon, the silhouette of pine trees stood out against a glow in the east, and I realized that many branches above me were filled with people watching. Wild and turbulent peaks appeared against the morning light. Around the clearing people watched in rapt attention, then cheered, as the sun rose through a high overcast.

Why climb a mountain? Not only because it is there, but because more of the world can be seen from its summit.

Why swap notes with travelers along the way? No one can see everything for himself, and even that which we view in common, we seldom see quite the same way. For example, my friends had bought a book of old legends about the rock formations on Yellow Mountain. Where I saw only oddly-shaped stacks of granite, they now saw monkeys and mysterious women, adding an exotic new dimension to hiking.

But we also talked because we shared a real environment in common. We were on top of a mountain. Trails were steep, and our bones fragile. No matter what romantic stories had been told about the rocks we walked across, a careless step could put us in the hospital—if we could reach it.

The first question that concerns us when we consider religions is the need for a common starting point. What questions, facts, experiences, fears and desires do all of us share, which provide a base from which we can consider the shape of our spiritual environment? The second question is the need for a common methodology, and the third, for a common goal. Are we only after mutual understanding and respect, a cheerful borrowing from one another's astrology charts a reality that seems "real" but corresponds to nothing objective in our common environment? Or do we want to find truth? If the former is all we want, we can exchange experiences, "give personal testimonies," if you will, and part as we met. The latter, on the other hand, may involve confrontation, disagreement, raised voices; in a word, debate.

The intellectual timidity of our era arises from an error about faith: that is, about vision. It arises from the assumption that faith has to do with star-gazing, with fancy and imagination, rather than looking at a landscape so we can ascend to heaven and go home in one piece. Faith and reason are thought of as separate checking accounts, ships that pass in the night, mutually exclusive or at least separate compartments of a person's life. A buffer zone between intellect and spirit lends us a sense of comfort—the religious, because it allows believers to build a wall within which "intensely personal" and "deep" beliefs and experiences can grow unthreatened by contrary evidence; the non-religious, because they perceive a threat to the institutions of free society, free thought, or at least free sex from religions that intrude upon the "public domain." People look askance at those who would trespass the no-man's land between the two. The Buddhist monk Thich Nhat Hanh expressed typical fears: "People kill and are killed because they cling too tightly to their own beliefs and ideologies. When we believe that ours is the only faith that contains the truth, violence and suffering will surely be the result."[1]

But I have come to the conclusion that this separation is both wrong and costly. Faith and reason should not be thought of as enemies, even less as strangers, but as lovers to whose union truth is born. To vary the metaphor, reality is like light, composed of both particle and wave. To search for truth without both faith and reason combined in an objective and mutually-correcting unity is as mad as wandering mountain cliffs by starlight.

With the sunrise, individual dreams fade and humankind shares an environment with fixed and provable features. It is at this point that faith of a kind that is little understood by the modern world becomes necessary, a method of finding truth that can serve as common ground between skeptics and believers of all kinds. This faith is the faculty to look and see, rather than trust to imagination alone. Reason is the cold water that wakes us and allows us to exercise faith rationally, and the light by which we test the reality of what we see. The union of faith and reason, I believe, is what empirical science and the teachings of Jesus share in common.

Four Levels of Faith

One of the most awesome sights I have seen on screen was an IMAX movie simply called *Everest*. Avalanches seemed to sweep us from our seats as we watched. Crevasses opened at our feet. My four-year old son said, "I'm afraid" and "I want to go home." But for months afterwards, he lobbied to see the film again.

The movie told the story of the ascent of Mt. Everest in 1996 by Ed Viesturs, two team-mates, and their hard-working Sherpa guides, who carried the IMAX camera gear to to summit. It showed the rigorous, and photogenic, training the team undertook climbing sea stacks and bicycling along the edge of red sandstone cliffs. It followed the team to base camp, and recorded their tension as they helplessly monitored cell phones when another party was trapped in a storm high on the mountain, and nine climbers, some of them friends, tragically succumbed to the elements. Finally, it showed their awesome ascent of the great mountain, beginning in morning darkness lit by torches. Even to watch the climbers ascend to the roof of the world one felt something of the "dread, distress, and paradox," with which Kierkegaard insisted we must understand faith.

A mountain climb involves a marriage between faith and reason. Trust is a serious thing on a mountain, not lightly given. On rock faces, or glacial icefalls, each step must be tested and planned in advance. Yet without trust, in one's eyes, muscles, partners, equipment, the pilot of the craft that ferries you to the base camp, and the people who have been there before and made the maps, no one could approach the roof of the world on foot. In religion, as in mountain climbing, faith is the most necessary and the most foolish thing. When divorced from the rules of logic and evidence that rule all other fields of human endeavor, we have seen, in the camps of Stalin, Pol Pott and Jim Jones, that nothing is more dangerous. Every step is a step of faith, but any step of blind faith may be the last. When a leap is required, the ground that it will cover should be tested with every faculty at our disposal, with utter concentration and will to know what is there.

"I think, therefore I am," wrote the philosopher Descartes. Nothing can be thought until the validity of thought in general is taken on faith. By "take on faith" I do not mean "taken without reason," but "taken with reason, and with something else." Any argument in favor of arguments begins with that which is its goal. You cannot build the second story of a house until the first floor is framed. Faith (not blind faith) is always the lower floor on which reasoning must rest.

Most of us would feel insulted if asked to prove the trustworthiness of our minds. But it was precisely this problem that drove the philosopher David Hume and, later, the logical positivists, to a radical skepticism that in effect closed the door on intellectual endeavor. Hume argued that nothing could be proven from experience—the fact that A followed B yesterday does not prove that it will again today. In this regard western existentialists came close to reinventing radical Zen skepticism. It was out of fear of the implied threat Hume's theories posed to science that Kant wrote a book whose title says it all: *Critique of Pure Reason*. Mind by itself is deadly to mind. As Chesterton pointed out, not only is it possible to reason oneself into the asylum, those already there are often, on their own terms, persuasive reasoners. "There is a thought that stops thought. That is the only thought that ought to be stopped. . .Descartes said, 'I think, therefore I am.' The philosophical evolutionist reverses and negates the epigram. He says, 'I am not; therefore I cannot think.'"[2] The first step of faith is to close our minds to the possibility that our minds are wholly delusional.

The second level of faith is trust in our senses. I hear the computer hum as I write. I see snow blowing in from the hills to the north of campus, which, unfortunately, is not sticking. The small of my back faintly reminds me that my posture is bad, and I had better change positions. The linings in my nose, the hairs on the back of my hands, relate data to my brain: I had better open the window before the heater comes on and change the air.

"How do you know this is not all an illusion?" ask mystics, the world's most determined logicians. "Can you prove that which you see, hear, smell, touch and taste exists outside your own mind?" India has developed lifestyles that cultivate detachment from the material. By lying on beds of nails or sitting in one spot for years without speaking, the sadhu shows he is drawing close to a world of which the senses know nothing. In East Asia, on the other hand, Zen used the same logic to come to an opposite conclusion: "In the chopping of wood, there lies the wonderful *Tao*." If the world is an illusion, why not simply live a normal life, sleep on an ordinary bed, work at a productive job, and play along? Just remember it is all a game.

On a practical level, most people who have not studied Zen koans or the *Bhagavad Gita* may see the debate as a quaint eccentricity of Eastern mystics and Western philosophers with too much time on their hands. "No, I can't prove the reality of the world around me," they might admit. "Maybe I am stuck, like Arnold Schwartzeneggar, in a 'total recall' universe that some corporation has implanted in my brain, or like Jim Carey, in a scripted TV series overseen by some god-like producer. But why do I even think such lunacy? I have work to do." With virtual reality and designer heavens beckoning like a cloud on the technological horizon, and scientists like Richard Dawkins arguing that thought itself is no more than a mechanical by-product of evolution, however, this question of what we know and how we know it has gained new urgency. I have on occasion found myself toying with the thought, "how do I know that I am really here?" And then common sense, perhaps inspired by the voice of Descartes reaching across the centuries, provides half an answer. "Well, I think I am." Laughing at solipsism, we choose to live by faith in this second sense, and in so doing, touch the world of phenomenal reality.

The third level of faith is confidence in other people.

It has been suggested that the landing on the moon was staged in a Hollywood studio. How can we know otherwise, except by faith?

Faith in our teachers is increasingly open to verification as we grow older. As a child, I relied on "what people say" for almost every fact I called my own, from where I was born to who my parents were, the existence of leptons (not to say Leprechauns), Labrador, and my own liver. In high school biology I dissected a turtle and found a purplish object that resembled diagrams of the liver. After graduation, I flew to Europe over a land of twisted bedrock and hidden lakes that lay where

Labrador appeared on my map. I saw the world (a small part of it) for myself, and thus confirmed, and sometimes refuted, what my teachers had told me.

For a mountain climber, the question of whether faith in other people is reasonable is far from academic. Were densely concentrated contour lines that signified a cliff drawn in the right place? Did the Nepali colonel who piloted the big Russian helicopter over glaciers and serrated peaks check the mechanics of his craft that morning with adequate care, or had he been drinking the night before?

Only madmen live without faith, but only fools live by blind faith, faith that cares nothing for external verification. We cross-examine witnesses, sip before we swallow, cut cards and check phone bills. Yet even taking a bus we entrust our lives to armies of strangers: engineers, factory workers, the driver, the drivers of oncoming vehicles. As Chesterton said of natural law, we don't count on the mental stability of our neighbors, we bet on it. The bet doesn't always pay off: ten minutes after I crossed a bridge in North Seattle on a bus, a passenger shot to death the driver of a bus coming the other way, plummeting the bus forty feet to the ground from the same bridge. I continue to get on buses and cross bridges, not because I have a death wish, nor because I have scientifically proven that my fellow passengers are trustworthy, but because I am sane enough to take a reasonable chance. (A sanity based, in my case, on an ultimate trust in God.) Anyone who determined to believe only what he had seen for himself would walk to work, walk up the stairs (carefully checking for loose joists) and look for tacks on his seat as he sat down—or stay home all day and worry about burglars. Such a complete reliance on reason and the lower levels of faith is the mark not of scientific genius, but of a mental breakdown.

As Chesterton put it, we say that the insane have "lost their mind," but in reality, it is not reason they have lost. They often have excellent reasons for mistrusting people, often as a result of a stormy childhood. It is faith they have misplaced.

Together these three levels of faith constitute the foundations of life: faith in our reason, trust in our senses, and confidence in other people. They are the ground on which we stand, the light by which we see the world, and the legs which allow us to walk down the street and live our lives in a dangerous world.

The fourth level of faith, religious faith, is not then a separate form of consciousness or an eccentricity of peculiar people. Nor should it involve suspension of critical thinking. It is part of a natural human continuum which we accept every day. And, like lower forms of faith, religious belief can and must be tested by reason.

How Do World Religions Relate?

As technology continues to give humankind an increasing sense that the world is becoming a single race or "global village," the question of how the various faiths of humankind relate, has become of paramount interest. At the end of his thought-provoking introduction to the subject, Huston Smith posed this question. "How do these religions fit together? In what relation do they stand to one another?"[3] Smith argued that three solutions were feasible, which we might summarize as, "my religion is the only way," "all religions are paths up the same mountain," and, "learn what you can from each and then blaze your own trail."

Smith formulated the first as follows:

"The first (answer) is that in the midst of all the religions of man there stands one so incomparably superior that no significant religious truth is to be found in any of the others which is not present in equal or clearer form within this religion itself . . ."

Pope John Paul seemed to argue such a position:

"Christ is absolutely original and unique . . . He is the one mediator between God and humanity."

Thich Nhat Hanh responded:

"Of course Christ is unique. But who is not unique? Socrates, Muhammad, the Buddha, you, and I are all unique. The idea behind the statement, however, is the notion that Christianity provides the only way of salvation and all other religious traditions are of no use. This attitude . . . does not help."[4]

But the Pope did not invent the idea that "Christianity provides the only way of salvation." In identifying the way to God, a gulf does yawn between Jesus and mortal sages. The great leaders of humanity, at their boldest, say, "This is the Way. Follow in it." Jesus said, "I am the Way."

Many people feel more comfortable with Buddha's report that there are 80,000 paths to enlightenment. And yet Buddha only spoke of one goal, which all sentient beings must attain eventually, whether they wish to or not: nirvana, the snuffing out of the candle. (A goal most Asians did not really look forward to.) Is it more narrow-minded to say there is only one means of arriving than to say there is one destination? Thich, a big believer in dialogue, suggests his Christian dialogue partners redefine God before the dialogue begins. "God did not create man in the same way a carpenter creates a table . . .God is not a being in the phenomenal world . . . It would not be difficult for Christians and Buddhists to agree on this."[5] Yes, and if Buddhists defined Buddha in terms that agree with the Christian idea of God, that would not be difficult either. But the point is, religions as they are now disagree. Tolerance is a poor title for the pretense that they don't, a pretense than can mask an underlying dogmatism.

If we share a common real environment, all religions and ideologies but one (at most) must be false to some degree, because they disagree. While each

might be partly right, they can't all be right on matters on which they take radically different positions. *A* excludes non-*A*. All religions and ideologies are
"exclusive" in this sense. Christianity gets the most criticism partly because it is
up-front about this, and partly because Jesus' claims about himself are more
extreme and inherently divisive. But that is not to say that to Christians, other
religions must be "of no value."

"One Mountain, Many Paths"

One of the most popular metaphors of the modern world is that religions
are like different paths up the same mountain.

The second approach, Smith said, lies in saying the major religions are "in
all important respects" the same. But sameness is itself not the same. Plotted on
paper, the remarks, "She looks like Marilyn Monroe" and, "Women! They're all
the same!" might appear parallel. But they do not sound parallel to the women
who hear them. Edward Gibbon wrote that the people of ancient Rome looked
at human faiths as "equal," but in different ways: "Philosophers saw all religions
as equally false, common people saw all religions as equally true, and politicians
saw all religions as equally useful." In our day, too, the idea that faiths are equal
can express cynicism, democratic solidarity, gullibility, or some combination of
the three.

Religion is the opiate of the people, said Marx, used by the exploiting classes to dull the senses of working men and women. Religion is a neurotic projection of our fathers, said Freud. Religion, Nietzsche argued, is a cowardly
flight from the demands of heroism.

It is not hard to feel sympathy with philosophers who say all religion is
equally false. "Heaven and earth treat men like straw dogs," Lao Zi noted. Isn't
it just our vain imagination to suppose some divine figure really cares for us and
pursues us into this heart of darkness? How many times have those around us
called out the name of some savior who will rescue the working class and build
paradise on earth or heaven, the vision of some bodhisattva or diva, only to
guide their followers into a wall or over an abyss?

Yet who can deny religion has, in many ways, elevated humankind? The
stark war on heaven waged by the nineteenth century atheists led to even stark-
er images of secular hell in the twentieth. Buddhism, by contrast, created civilizations in the wilderness of Central Asia and Japan. Islam prompted a rag-tag
collection of desert tribes into founding a great civilization. And where would
human culture be without Christopher Wren, Dostoevsky, St. Francis or Mother Theresa? While religious and anti-religious ideologies still compete for followers, a second commonality of thought has grown up within each community that parallels the emergence of a kinder and gentler secular humanism.

Today one notes an assumption that spirituality in general is a psychologically useful part of the good life. Religion is a search for meaning and is valuable to the extent that it causes people to do good. "Where Mercy, Love, and Pity swell, there God is dwelling also," wrote William Blake.[6] "Kindness is my religion," said the Dalai Lama. On this point a serendipitous ecumenism has coalesced among creeds, a union of outlook that joins the secular and the religious. In *Jew in the Lotus,* Roger Kamenetz chronicled the journey of a group of Jewish leaders who dialogued with the Dalai Lama in India. Passing familiarity with esoteric Buddhism bred not contempt, but recognition: here were a people, like the Jews, who had been exiled from their homeland and sought to make religion serve as rallying point for preservation of a way of life. What value were squabbles over the existence of God or the nature of the afterlife compared to the solidarity and friendship one may find by interpreting beliefs as expressions of community solidarity? A Jewish American, Harold Kurshner, wrote, "If believing in the Resurrection makes my Christian neighbor a better person, more loving and generous, better able to cope with misfortune and disappointment, then that is a true belief, whether historically true or not."[7]

The concept that tolerance and good will is itself the highest goal of religious devotion has been embraced by religious leaders of all traditions. Within the *Bhagavad Gita,* Jesus' *Sermon on the Mount,* and Tolstoy's *The Kingdom of God is Within You,* Mohandas Gandhi found inspiration for a vision of tolerance and good will upon which he hoped to unite all the religions of India. Martin Luther King Jr. borrowed from Gandhi to lead black Americans to equal rights with an ideal that people of all or no religions may relate to, expressed that ideal in a brilliant rewording of the prophet Isaiah:

> "I have a dream that one day men will rise up and come to see that they are made to live together as brothers. I still have a dream this morning that one day every Negro in this country, every colored person in the world, will be judged on the basis of the content of his character rather than the color of his skin, and every man will respect the dignity and worth of human personality . . . I still have a dream today that one day war will come to an end, that men will beat their swords into plowshares and their spears into pruning hooks, that nation will no longer rise up against nation, neither will they study war any more . . . ."[8]

What did Huston Smith mean by describing the great faith traditions as "religions of men?" He meant that he appreciated religions as human creations, as attempts by mortals to come to grips with the world around them. That is the operating assumption of many who love and respect religion as much as those who disparage it.

What do secular Humanists, Marxists, liberal Christians, Jews and Muslims, intellectual Buddhists and Hindus share in common? Many agree that the fire of human imagination and the warmth of human kindness should light corridors still black with hatred. They share a vision of the world united rather than divided by bonds of religious commitment. They line the walls of our lives with books and video screens, images of green fronds and pink lotus, feeling free to share one another's holy relics as symbols of a human search for "deeper meaning." They share unease at wild-eyed "fundamentalists" and their talk of another world that is more than myth or symbol, that can be reached by following a certain path and not others.

"Choose the Best of Each Tradition"

Smith introduced his third and preferred solution to the problem of how our paths to the divine relate as follows:

> "A third possible answer . . . does not find all religions saying the same things, though the unity is in certain respects both striking and impressive. But neither, in the presence of differences, does it assume that all Important truths can be found in any single tradition. If God is a God of love, it seems most unlikely that he would not have revealed himself to his other children as well."[9]

Smith made it clear elsewhere that this was his own approach: "If we take the world's enduring religions at their best, we discover the distilled wisdom of the human race." He admitted that a balanced look at religion would have to consider human sacrifice, persecution, crusades, and holy wars. Smith picked from the major religious traditions what he liked, justifying this procedure by noting,

> "Probably as much bad music as good has been written in the course of human history, but we do not ask that a course in music appreciation give it equal space. Time being limited, we expect no apology for spending it with the best."[10]

One problem with this approach is not only that it allows subjectivity and self-deception, as Smith admitted, but it often boils down to mere "appreciation" for religion, rather than the "hunger and thirst for righteousness" that has so often served as the fuel for social progress. Such an appreciation can easily degenerate into mere aesthetics.

An ex-Catholic compared the spirituality he arrived at to a banquet or potluck dinner, at which one may choose one's favorites from among many tasty dishes. He noted that he was still a Catholic in the sense that he liked to drop into churches, and felt a special closeness for some of the saints, such as Saint Francis of Assisi and Theresa of Avila. But why confine oneself to the faith of one's fathers, when before us, like a great banquet, a "spiritual smorgasbord," lay the combined spiritual heritage of the human race?

It's not hard to see why such a view of religion is popular. If faith is poetry, then while we can criticize our neighbor's religion for bad taste, if it "works" for her, we need not sit in judgment and say she's "wrong." Anthropologist Emile Durkheim described how a society's concept of the divine derives from the social structure. Indeed, this idea of religion sits well with a democratic people. Having become accustomed to thinking that political authenticity must derive from the people, we tend to think God is up for election too, and that our "right to believe" must elicit a corresponding freedom from contrary evidence on the part of the universe.

Why should a spiritual seeker settle for unchanging dogmas in a world that is a whirl of change? Faith is a muse, an odyssey of the spirit, bringing to our inner sense exotic sights, smells, and tastes to sample and enjoy. We are a generation, as journalist Mick Brown described himself, of "spiritual tourists." Our slogans are "not all who wonder are lost" and "to travel hopefully is better than to arrive."

But to speak in such terms is to betray the limits of this approach in particular, and Smith's way of framing the debate about religion, in general.

What is a tourist? Someone who has his snapshot taken by a pyramid and forgets that he will lie in the ground one day, too. One who climbs temples in the Yucatan, or takes tours of isolation cells at the Lubyanka Prison in Moscow, but does not know the fear of the zek who suffered there, or the rage of the priest or comrade about to propitiate his deities with blood. He passes through the desert leaving only jeep tracks, taking only pictures. He does not fast on Mt.Hira to come face-to-face with Allah. (In a documentary Huston Smith once made on Islam, in his erudite enthusiasm, he almost forgot to use the word "God.") He puts picture books of Tibetan monasteries on the coffee table and speaks of past lives as Cleopatra or an Indian princess, but does not feel the weight of transmigrations behind Siddhartha's smile. He chants "OOOHMM!" but does not know why karma would drive a man to take a vow of silence and never speak to his only child. He tours the world without ever feeling the force of the words, "vanity of vanities!" Nor of the words, "I thirst."

For a spiritual tourist, the first step toward understanding Jesus sometimes comes when he really enters into the spirit of a non-Christian religion. Perhaps when one cries to the goddess Guan Yin with the desperation of a fisherman in the foam of a South China sea typhoon; shudders at the thought of rebirth as an insect; feels with terror the coming of the avenging angel of Allah; or rages against God and the universe like an atheist who has seen the depths of hell in a concentration camp.

In each of Smith's three solutions, we find part of the solution, yet the whole escapes us. That is because (like Smith) we commit the error of civility. We tend to think religion is like star-gazing, which can be done in the dark, rather than mountain-climbing, which is more wisely attempted under the harsh and illusion-dispelling light of day.

Consider Abraham, by contrast, whom God told to sacrifice his son, Isaac, on a mountaintop.

Abraham climbed Mt. Moriah in agony, because he believed God was not an artistic creation of his own, but real, and had called him to give up what he valued the most. Soren Kierkegaard said about Abraham's mountain-climbing expedition: "That in which all human life is united is passion. And faith is a passion." You might even say that when you have found what a person is passionate about, you have found his true religion. Religion always involves passion, because it is, before all else, a sacrifice and a risk of our lives. In Pascal's words, life is a "gamble." The dice are falling to the table, and we must choose before they fall.

Smith asked, "If God is a God of love, it seems most unlikely that he would not have revealed himself to his other children as well." This is a great insight, which it is one purpose of this book to develop. But it must be balanced by another question that the study of the world's religions forces on any honest observer. "If God is a God of truth, can 'divine revelations' that contradict one another or contradict the laws of logic be divine?" And a third as well: "If God is a good God, would he reveal himself through 'saints and prophets' who start expansionist wars, steal wives, and live in mansions while followers sleep on streets and sell carnations in airport lobbies?"

The greatest barrier to truth, and even to true mutual respect between those who disagree, is a terrible politeness that goes by the name of tolerance. Tolerance seems to mean not merely a determination to treat those with whom one disagrees politely, but the assumption that all religious beliefs are equally valid. It treats beliefs about God and life and death as if they were like the arbitrary stories, of only psychological or literary interest, we tell about the patterns stars impress on our imaginations.

As in ancient Rome, today, too, the masses tend to see religions as equally true, intellectuals as equally false, and politicians (including ecclesiastical statesmen) as equally useful. Both secular humanists and that class of believers vaguely called "fundamentalists" appear partly to blame for this schizophrenic flight from argument. Influential materialists in the nineteenth century thought society could do away with faith. The post-modern world said in reaction, "thus far (as far as science and technology) reason may go, but no farther." It has become an essential tenet of our neo-romantic age that faith, unlike science, need not tamely conform to some predetermined pattern ("dogma," rumor has it, has been run over by "karma") anymore than we should all dream the same dreams or see the same images in the fire. Faith is of value, or danger, according to the qualities it brings out in the individual, not according to any external validity: kindliness or pigheadedness, pity or anger, surliness or good cheer. Paul Hollander, in his book

Political Pilgrims, criticized western intellectuals who wrote glowing reports from Cold-War era Russia and China in terms that have become typical of such discussion: "While the suspension of disbelief has its place, it belongs to the artistic or religious sphere, rather than the political sphere, of life."

When Jesus called himself "The Way, the Truth and the Life," he was summarizing not only who he was but what we need as human beings. The goal of religious dialogue should be to break out of a world of self-referential idolatry and mutual back-slapping and find the moral, existential, and intellectual food our souls hunger for.

The darkness around us should not discourage us from looking for answers, but show the seriousness and urgency of the questions we must bring to the search. Wherever we have come from as human beings, we share our most important struggles and desires in common. Stars might romance our imagination with a thousand points of distant light, but in the end they reveal only themselves. The dawn illuminates the world as well. Just as light is best understood as neither wave nor particle alone, but as both simultaneously, so truth is best pursued by both faith and reason at the same time.

Christianity is often charged with crimes against the worshippers of other gods, intolerance, crusades, witch-hunting, and persecution of native religions. It is said, "People who live in glass houses shouldn't throw stones." Let us not live in glass houses, then, or in halls of mirrors. It is no service to honest dialogue or truth to gloss over such charges and "accentuate the positive" in the interest of getting along. It is reasonable to make distinctions between what authoritative sources command and what people take upon themselves to do, and between acting for personal gain in the name of God and acting from a sincere even if deluded desire for God's glory. But if we gloss over human sacrifice, the Inquisition, widow burning, and the Gulag Archipelago simply as "bad music" not worth considering, we are not paying true respect to the spiritual traditions of humanity. We are patronizing those who disagree with us. Evil, too, is a part of human religious experience, and must be considered in any solution to the question of how belief systems relate.

My approach will be critical, but ultimately, I hope, sincerely respectful, of the "religions of man." The first question to ask is not, "what relation do the various faith traditions bear to one another?" It is rather, "what relation do they bear to reality?" Rather than comparing paths, we should look at the mountain, and plot the routes men and women take up (or down) as each relates to that rock. While the answer to that question may be considerably harder, and the criticism involved may appear intolerant or irreverent at times, I believe it is more sincerely respectful to place truth at the center in this way. When we do so, a fourth solution to the problems of how Jesus and other faiths relate emerges, a middle path that combines both the empirical need to disprove what is false, and the insight that all human cultures hint at the truth of God, in a more harmonious and holistic whole than merely patching together insights we happen to like from different traditions. And that solution lies in the words of Jesus, "Do not suppose that I came to annul the Law and the Prophets. I did not come to abolish but to complete them" (Matt. 5:17).

Reason and Religious Faith

The Hebrew prophet Elijah was once involved in an inter-religious dialogue that, like mountain-climbing, involved an existential experience of faith fraught with danger. He stood before the Jewish people as representative of Yahweh while 400 priests of an opposing sect stood opposite, and proposed an experiment of rigid empiricism. Both camps would set up an altar, and the god who sent fire from heaven would be the true God. Elijah gave his experiment the following build-up:

> "How long will you lean to both sides? If the Lord is God, follow him;
> but if it is Baal, follow him" (1 Kings 18:21).

Elijah's solution to the problem of how religions relate may strike us as intolerant. In modern terms, he was saying, "Those who wander are lost, if they do not know what they are looking for, or are looking for what is not there. Seek truth, not what appeals to you personally. If extinction is the path to freedom, then renounce the material world and follow Buddha. If Mohammed truly met God in the desert, burn your idols and pray toward Mecca five times a day. If God is merely a father figure, and our consciousness no more than a lucky pattern of subatomic particles, then eat, drink, and be merry; and go into the void with a smile."

Few religious leaders are so willing to see their claims tested. Confucius was a rare exception, perhaps because his claims were modest. "I can describe the civilization of the Hsia dynasty, but the Ch'i does not furnish adequate documentation,"[11] he noted about one historical question. He approached spiritual questions with the same caution. Asked about the meaning of the sacrifice to God, the supreme religious ceremony of his time, he was not ashamed to simply admit, "I don't know."

The esoteric Buddhist Master Lu Sheng-yen, by contrast, was once asked about divine entities by a pair of journalists. He related the conversation:

> "'There are an innumerable, limitless, immeasurable, and unfathomable number of gods,' I answered.
> "'What proof do you have?'
> "'I am the proof.'
> "'One person is not sufficient proof. Give us some other proofs!'

"'There is no Dharma outside the mind. If one says there is Dharma out
side the mind, then it is not Buddhadharma . . . . If I myself am not a
sufficient proof for what I know, then there is nothing else in the world
that can serve as proof.'"[12]

A Zen teacher explained that reasoning is actually an impediment to progress:

"Be without thoughts - this is the secret of meditation . . . An ancient
says: 'In Zen the important thing is to stop the course of the heart.' It
means to stop the workings of our empirical consciousness, the mass
of thoughts, ideas, and perceptions . . . A great master said: 'Try to cut
off thought. By this alone eight or nine out of ten people will attain
the Way.'"[13]

It would not be true to say mystical and charismatic religious teachers provide no evidence for their claims, however. Supernatural proofs such as miraculous healings and magic talismans are an integral part of folk religion the
world over. As we will see, on other occasions sect leaders like Master Lu are
more than willing to provide evidence, of a sort.

Many popular arguments for religious faith are, however, too arbitrary to
be called empirical. For example, many religions, such as Islam, Mormonism,
and Marxism, explicitly put a lot of stress on their success in a version of what
is called the "bandwagon fallacy." (Other sects and denominations do so
implicitly.) "We are the world's fastest-growing religion—the wave of the
future," they say. "Does not our success represent the seal of approval from God
(or history) on our movement?" Not necessarily. Religions go through periods
of expansion and contraction. And there are always other reasons one can point
to for the growth of a religion—a high birth rate, due to poverty or religious
conviction, a strong missions program, social benefits, revolutionary morale,
and quite often, political coercion.[14]

Mohammed, when asked to work miracles to prove his claim to be a
prophet, refused. The *Qur'an* itself was proof of his office:

"If you doubt what We have revealed to Our Servant, produce one chapter comparable to this book. Call upon your idols to assist you, if what
you say be true. But if you fail (as you are sure to fail) then guard against
that fire whose fuel is men and stones prepared for the unbelievers."[15]

This is a challenge non-Arabic speakers find hard to meet, especially since
translation of the *Qur'an* is said to be impossible. However, Muslim apologists also
provide at least two more verifiable arguments: they often make the claims, first,
that the *Qur'an* embodies scientific wisdom beyond the capacity of a seventh century man, or second, that the Bible prophesies the coming of Mohammed.

Physical healing is one of the most common proofs offered of spiritual truth. Faith-healing often seems stagy, and has been proven often enough to have in fact been staged that intense skepticism lingers about the phenomena. In some sects, improved health is linked to a daily regimen of spiritual exercise; meditation, chanting, mantras, visualization of one's guru, or a sacred diet. The trouble (or beauty) of this method compared to more dramatic healing is that you can't tell for sure if the cure is the result of spiritual agents, dieting, suggestion, or mere time plus chance plus the healing propensities of the body.

Another common variety of evidence often given involves the appearance of divine talismans or stigmata: stones from the stomach, holy ash, pieces of the cross, odd marks on the teacher or leader's body. Rebellions are led by peasants who have find divine swords or hear voices from heaven. Golden books are found in caves or buried in fields.

Others prove the transcendent value of their message through other-worldly self-control: sitting on beds of nails or on pillars or staring at walls for years. The Chinese People's Liberation Army conducted a heroic and death-defying trek across thousands of miles of hostile territory. The legend of this "long march" lent a kind of divine sanction or inevitability to their quest for national liberation.

Many try to transfer prestige attained in mundane matters to metaphysics: Bertrand Russell earned a reputation as a logician, Arthur C. Clarke and Carl Sagan as scientists, Mao Zedong as a military strategist, each thereby earning a platform for speculation on diverse matters, including metaphysics and religion. Hitler cleaned up the streets and got Germany working again, parlaying success in mundane matters into a quasi-religious campaign to conquer the world.

Some offer an even bolder and in some ways more convincing reply to the request for proof: no proof. Or, "I am the proof." Or, "You have to experience it yourself." Or, "Prove yourself as my disciple. Only after years of faithful discipleship and obedience to my wishes will you be ready for such divine secrets as I can offer."

Such a multiplicity of often suspicious evidence and shaky reasoning seems bewildering. The truth is out there, we hope and believe: someone must be right about something. But how can we sort it out? The survival and continued popularity of the world's great faith traditions suggests that there must be a kernel of truth in each of them, and perhaps more than a kernel. But at the same time, we should also remember that those who followed Hitler and Jim Jones also found reasons to believe.

How did Jesus verify his message?

We are sometimes reminded that Jesus said, "Blessed are those who have not seen, yet believe" (John 20:29). This would seem to agree with those who say no proof of the truth is need, or that "you have to bite the apple to know what it tastes like." And certainly inner experience is part of what makes for

Christian belief. But as skeptics often admit, the Gospels were written in part to provide believers with an empirical basis for faith. Jesus said that the Jewish prophets spoke of him. He also publicly backed up his claims with miracles. We will see in later chapters how the miracles of Jesus differ both from legends and from magical tricks.

Jesus called his miracles "signs." What is a sign? It is a marker that orients one to objective realities. The Bible does not ask us to naively accept claims to absolute truth on face value. "Taste and see," commands Yahweh. (Ps. 34:8). "Come and let us consider together" (Isa. 1:18 pph.). "Thrust your hand into my side," said Jesus. (John 20:27). "Do not despise prophetic utterance, but test it," said Paul. (1. Thess. 5:20-21). "Put the spirits to the test," advised John. (1 John 4:1).

Many otherwise orthodox Christians assume that Biblical faith is opposed to reason. Martin Luther once referred to reason as "the devil's whore." Tertullian (*De Carne Christ*) said that "Faith must trample underfoot all reason, sense and understanding . . . to know nothing but the Word of God." But to Christians who do know the Word of God, revelation of all kinds, whether from an angel or our seventh-grade geography teacher, should be a means of finding truth that supplements, rather than ignores, reason. Most people fail to notice that when the New Testament uses the word "faith," it uses it in an empirical and experimentally falsifying sense. The *Book of Acts,* the earliest history of Christianity, is full of dialectic verbs like "argue," "persuade," "bear witness" and "prove." Modern Christians emphasize their "personal testimonies," but the earliest Christian preachers always directed the attention of their audience to evidence that they knew or could know, not merely a subjective burning in the bosom, but faith verified from the public record. Paul and his co-workers criss-crossed the Mediterranean world, suffering beatings, imprisonment, shipwrecks, muggings, and attacks by wild animals, not out of a glassy-eyed fanaticism worked up through drugs, sleight-of-hand or suggestibility, but because of what they claimed to have "seen with our eyes and touched with our hands" (1 John 1:1).

A passage in Hebrews that describes faith as "the evidence of things not seen" is often quoted to prove the subjective basis for Christian belief. (Heb. 11:1). But I do not think the author was advocating mystical "confidence in confidence alone." Rather, such passages remind us of the inherently risky response life requires. They remind us of what Kierkegaard meant when he emphasized the drama and risk involved in faith, and Pascal when he called faith a "wager." That is how one feels when one climbs a mountain. Yet one does not betray the adventure to climb in the daytime. Christian faith does not mean wandering in the dark or by the light of some subjective vision, eyes closed to the character of the world around us: it means looking carefully, and having looked, taking bold steps. Christian thinkers like Paul, Augustine, Aquinas, Chesterton, C. S. Lewis, and Pascal left a mark on history by stressing that Christian faith admits and indeed insists upon external verification.

So long as his questions aren't rhetorical, the nihilist who advises us to "question everything" stands firmly in the Biblical tradition. Driven to distraction by the mysteries of life, Solomon asked, "what advantage has the wise man over the fool? " (Eccl. 6:8) and, "who takes note that the breath of man goes upward and the breath of animals goes downward to the earth?" (Eccl. 3:21). Job impertinently challenged God, "why do you hide your face and consider me your enemy?" (Job 13:24 pph). Thomas insisted, "unless I see in His hands the print of the nails, and thrust my hand in His side, I will not believe" (John 20:25).

It is true that, as we ascend from simpler to more complex levels of faith, the object of our trust becomes less directly accessible to mind, and the quality of faith does subtly change. The initiative begins to shift from believer to object of belief. If I study mathematics, I do not need to leave the room. If I study rocks, I need to leave the room, but the rocks will not run away from me, unless I study volcanology. If rabbits are my field, I need to either stand very still or run very fast—or outsmart them by breeding or trapping them. If I study people, as a psychologist in a free society, if they do not choose to reveal themselves, I will never know them. Even if they do, it will take time to get beyond the normal defenses we all build against betrayal. They can and will psychoanalyze me, in return, before permitting me to get so close.

Some people talk of "Western scientific reasoning" or the "dawn of antithetical thought" as if the categories of "true" and "false" and how we decide them were some rather parochial concept dreamed up by a clever but eccentric Greek in his spare time. In fact, antithetical thought and dualistic categories are built into the structure not just of the universe, but of all possible existence.

Religion is the study of God. It is for this reason, not because Christian faith is irrational or pre-scientific, that there are limits to how useful scientific methods can be in verifying it. If scientists discovered that prayer heals people in some kind of double-blind, statistically-significant experiment, as some have claimed to do, I wonder if this wouldn't tend to slightly disprove, rather than prove, Christianity. A God who can be manipulated by science is, by definition, not the God of the Bible. Is God such a fool that he does not know what people are up to? Jesus refused to give a sign to some who demanded one, not because he despised reason—he had just healed a number of people—but because the questioners were confused about who was doing the testing, and who was being tested, in this experiment called life. Our lives, not God's, are on the line. He makes the mountain; we choose our paths. Jesus himself did not shy away from the "dread, distress, and paradox" faith forces upon us, but like Isaac, carried wood up a hill to gamble his life on the power and love of God.

What is the best way to verify or falsify a claim to transcendent truth? There may be as many ways of doing so as people in the world: through astronomy, AIDS, alcoholism, bee-keeping, meditation, prison camp, or Sunday School. The way of Jesus is not just a set of propositions about human nature or the First Cause of the cosmos that we are called to affirm. It is a relationship. And any relationship, whether between boy and girl, cat and dog, king and wine-taster, is individual, and must be tested primarily not through science but through history. Love is proven over a lifetime of meeting challenges together.

Jesus did give supernatural evidence: healing, casting out of demons, fulfilled prophecy, power to endure martyrdom, voices from heaven.

But first, Jesus said, "You will know them by the deeds they do" (Matt. 7:16). Grapes do not grow on briar trees, nor does fresh water come from a salty well. Don't be fooled by cleverness or sleight of hand. Look at the lives of the gurus. Do they do good? Do they treat people around them, their wives and children, the people closest to them, with ennobling respect and true compassion?

Second, Jesus warned, "All those who came before Me are thieves and robbers" (John 10:8). I do not take this to mean an blanket repudiation of other religious teachers; in fact, Jesus affirmed the words of Moses and the prophets in even stronger terms. Rather, he was repudiating those who make claims as ultimate objects of faith that conflict with his own; those who point to themselves rather than to the truth.

The Bible unapologetically puts all religions in a single category, and the Gospel in another. Not that all faiths are simply true, that "all roads lead to the top of the mountain," or that there are 80,000 distinct paths to nirvana. Not that all faiths are simply false, a delusion, wish-fulfillment, or projection of our fathers. Nor again that all religions are simply useful, as Eisenhower supposedly said, "Our government makes no sense unless it is founded on a deeply felt religious faith—and I don't care what it is." Nor equally useless, an "opiate of the people" by which the ruling class distracts the poor from their real concerns. Rather, non-Christian religions are the same in just the sense Smith implicitly admitted, in being the religions *of man.* To this point, Christianity agrees with Freud, Feurbach, Marx, Smith, and Armstrong.

Paul said, "we have these treasures in earthly vessels" (2 Cor. 4:7 NASB). That is, Christianity is also a "religion of man" in the sense that it is ordinary mortals who appropriate it over the centuries, and therefore it is interpreted through ordinary human glories and madness. Christianity is also "of man" in the sense that it usually comes to us through human beings who "see in a mirror, dimly" (1 Cor. 13:12 NASB).

But it is the contention of this book that Jesus is not merely "of man." One of the proofs of this, paradoxically, is that he affirms and deepens our humanity and the truths within the religions we create.

[1] Thich Nhat Hahn, *Living Buddha, Living Christ*, Riverhead Books, 1995, p. 2

[2] G. K. Chesterton, *Orthodoxy*, Doubleday, 1959, p. 33,35

[3] Huston Smith, *Religions of Man*, Harper and Row, 1958, p.350

[4] *Living Buddha, Living Christ*, p. 192

[5] Thich, *Going Home, Jesus and Buddha as Brothers*, Riverhead Books, 1999, p.7

[6] William Blake, *The Divine Image*, p.36

[7] From *When Bad Things Happen to Good Religion*, Richard John Neuhaus, *National Review*, November 10, 1989, p.52

[8] Martin Luther King, *Trumpet of Conscience, Christmas Sermon on Peace*

[9] *Religions of Man*, p. 353

[10] Ibid., p.5

[11] Confucius, *Lun Yu*, 3-9

[12] Master Lu Sheng-yen, *Encounters With the World of Spirits*, p.134-5

[13] *Buddhist Scriptures*, Penguin Classics, 1959; Rosen Takashina, *Controlling the Mind*, p.139

[14] A Nigerian scholar, discussing the fact that northern Nigeria, like much of sub-Saharan Africa, traces its religious heritage to jihad, or holy war, noted to a friend of mine, "It's hard to refuse conversion to Islam when you've just seen your brother's throat slit."

[15] From Colin Chapman, *The Case For Christianity*, William B. Eerdmans, 1981, p. 156

CHAPTER 3

Where Did Marx Go Wrong?

"TO INSURE food for humanity by forcing part of it to work was after all a very human expedient; which is why it will probably be tried again." G. K. Chesterton, 1925

"Thousands of epidemics and natural catastrophes are to be preferred to the slightest notion of a god." Vladimir Lenin[1]

Our sixth floor dorm was hot in June, and I'd been at my books for hours. We had been watching the epic drama of the "democracy movement" beamed via satellite across the Strait of Taiwan, and the restlessness growing in the city of Taipei seemed to weigh on me along with my studies. Thousands of students were pouring into Beijing day by day to swell the throng of protesters on Tiananmen Square. On the island of Taiwan, where Nationalist civil servants and soldiers and their children had been building in miniature their alternative interpretation of what it meant to be Chinese, people could talk of little else. I attended a mass rally in support of the mainland students in the spacious park around General Chiang Kai-shek's mausoleum. The Nationalists had been predicting the imminent fall of the "communist bandits" from grace since the 1920s. Was this finally it? Was Chiang Kai-shek to be vindicated from his grave? But even if the Marxist regime collapsed, as many expected, what would come next? Civil war? A long, painful period of economic restructuring?

One evening someone rented a video called *The Mission.* I'd seen the film, but to get my mind off my studies and the political tension, I slumped on the couch and watched it again. Rather than a cheap escape, though, the film seemed to echo and amplify what I was feeling inside. The movie told the story of idealistic missionaries who build a Christian Shangri-la among the Indians of the South American highlands. A world-weary old bishop unsuccessfully tried to negotiate a peaceful annexation of paradise. But in the end, colonial and church authorities seized the Indian's land by force and enslaved the survivors, with much bloodshed. Explaining to his superiors in Rome, the bishop pronounced a somber and paradoxical benediction on the fate of the respective participants in the conflict: "Now your priests are dead and I am left alive. But in truth it is I who am dead, but they who live."

As I went to bed, my eyes remained glued to the bunk above me. My mind was racing with the climactic images of the film: Spanish soldiers advancing across a river on an Indian village, cannon booming, muskets firing. Young warriors fighting bravely with crude weapons till they fell, blood pouring from their wounds. A priest with a cross around his neck falling next to a mother with a baby in her arms. Houses burning, children running for the river. What did soldiers think about when they looked in the eyes of mothers and children they were about to kill? How did they quiet their conscience as they bombed a defenseless village?

I did not realize it, but as these images and thoughts were keeping me awake, at that very moment on the other side of the Straits, the real-time drama I'd been watching over the preceding weeks was reaching a similar climax. Peoples' Liberation Army soldiers were lining up and pointing rifles. Tanks were moving on Tiananmen Square.

In a few months, however, the world would witness a surprising reversal in which, as Lao Zi put it, strength would be conquered by weakness. The configuration of political forces across Eurasia changed on an autumn tide, and the "Evil Empire," which the West had opposed with nuclear warheads, collapsed through people power, unless prayer power is a better name for it. A tide of proletarian humanity, led by a Polish electrician, a Czech playwright, and a Romanian pastor, overthrew the governments of Eastern Europe. As Christmas lights went up, the Berlin Wall came down. Pieces of it were sold in Western shopping centers as stocking stuffers. Before long even Russia itself was tearing down statues of Lenin. Since then in China, too, capitalism, freedom, and the rule of law increased, along with corruption. The communist party never recovered from its victory of June 6, 1989. The students died and gained a certain immortality, while the idea that killed them survived but suffered a fatal wound of the spirit.

Three great moral revolutions, social, sexual, and spiritual, like massive storm systems, were born in the sea of nineteenth century Enlightenment thinking, and tracked across our era to bring tremendous changes in their wake. Many praised those changes as escapes from feudal superstitions and the bondage of the church. Others blasted them as the thoughtless abandonment of thousands of years of insight. Both sides assumed that these changes represented a break with "premodern" views, and what some would nostalgically call "traditional morality." But on close inspection, none of these revolutions was really so revolutionary.

The history of Marxism defined the twentieth century. More than a third of the world was recruited into helping fashion an Eden of the cities, a vision for a communal society based on one particular strand of Enlightenment ideals. Countless intelligent men and women saw this vision as the hope of the human race, and millions laid their lives down to bring it about. The rise and fall of Marxism was the most spectacular spiritual experiment of the twentieth century, unleashing passions, inspiring martyrs, winning a third of humankind, radically transforming the consciousness of entire cultures—sacrificing the lives of 100 million men, women, and children along the way.

Whodunit? Why did so many people find the Marxist faith a cause worthy of pouring out blood, sweat and tears? Why didn't it work? Was the failure of communism the fault of particular personalities? Was it Stalin's fault? Or Lenin's? Was Marx simply not a good enough economist? As his mother is said to have complained in a letter, "I wish Karl would stop writing about capital and start earning some?" Were Russia and China just not ready for the radical changes Marx's theories heralded?

Or did communism fail because it was "godless?" Alexander Solzhenitsyn, the unauthorized historian of the Soviet period who I suspect knows as much as any man alive about the rise of the Soviet Union, compassed his decades of research with a concise four-word explanation: "Men have forgotten God." It may that be Solzhenitsyn's rich "inside experience" as a slave laborer in Stalin's camps robbed him of objectivity. And no one accuses the Spanish lords of South America of forgetting at least the *name* of God.

The world never held war crimes trials or any other kind of post-mortem to help us bring closure to the fall of Marxism. We have heard, from the principals, that no one is to blame. Everyone seems to have a good alibi. The people who planned revolution were merely social theoreticians distressed by the suffering around them, it is said. The mobs who carried them out were caught up in the moment, and misled by self-serving leaders. The leaders themselves are equally unrepentant. Even Pol Pott stated, before death, that his conscience was untroubled by the one million people who died in his "killing fields." Nor have many of the intellectuals in the West who supported the cause of Marxism stood up to accept blame.

But what does it matter now? For better or worse, the thing is dead and gone. Times have changed. Shouldn't we move on?

The quick readiness of some to let bygones be bygones reminds me of the expression on the face of the villain in a Colombo mystery, when the detective goes out the door and then returns saying, "oh just one more thing . . . " In this new era of Western triumphalism, when technology is making the ancient dream of humanity as god more and more attainable, I think the failure of Marxism is not only relevant, but pressing. Because I believe Russian and Chinese society sickened of a virus they caught from the West. And we're not just carriers: we're showing signs of coming down with the same bug, a spiritual bug, that has been around for a long time.

Was communism godless? No. In many ways, communism represented the joining of two ancient streams of spiritual thought that flow out of the garden of Eden. The first is what we might call religious revolution, and includes such movements as Islam, the Tai Ping Rebellion, and hundreds of what have been called the "religions of the oppressed." The second is the Enlightenment.

It is an old debate whether the life of humankind is best described as cyclical (as the ancient Greeks and Chinese thought) or linear (as the Hebrews, Romans, Norse, and modern Westerners tend to see it). The debate is never settled, because history progresses dialectically, with characteristics of both qualities. Who can deny the progress we have seen in the past 200 years, not only in medicine and technology, but even in the concepts of freedom and human rights? History is certainly not just "one darn thing after another." Yet it often shows a dramatic trick of restating old themes, of revisiting prior acts, of haunting us with patterns that look familiar, and even some of the same lines again. Thus the failure of Marxism can be retold as the original "whodunit:" the story of the Garden of Eden and the apple. We hear again from many quarters, as from the lips of Adam and Eve, "it wasn't our fault. This failure has nothing to do with us!" I will argue that the failure of Marxism has everything to do with us, and I don't just mean atheists. What is it in human nature, and therefore also in the religions of man, that starts with nice ideas and ends shooting children in the back? That is the nature of our inquiry.

While the words "new," "revolutionary," "bold," and "progressive" are scattered across their literature like cherry blossoms on the lawn after a May shower, none of the radical moral innovations of the modern world are really new. Revolutionary ideologies make up part of the common, seasonal pattern of human history. The moral ideas at the heart of each rebellion are, in fact, old-fashioned, conventional, and bound in ancient tradition. Revolution is one of the of the poles between which history oscillated since the snake and Eve formed a united front against Yahweh in the Garden of Eden. This story, which is the oft-told tale of the human race, has been called "paradise lost," but for Marx, it began in a concrete jungle.

Garden in the Jungle

Like Thailand or India at the beginning of their Industrial Revolutions, for the lower classes, England in the mid-nineteenth century seemed to combine the worst of all worlds: the poverty of subsistence farming with the soot and inhumanity of the machines that drove the peasant off his farm and the blacksmith and seamstress from their shops. Dickens described the "cold, wet, shelter-less midnight streets of London: the foul and frowzy dens, where vice is closely packed and lacks the room to turn; the haunts of hunger and disease, the shabby rags that scarcely hold together." A young Jewish scholar from the western German city of Trier wandered those streets. To him it seemed that the gap between the Ebenezers and the Cratchits was widening. "It is true that labor produces for the rich wonderful things," he wrote, "but for the worker, hovels. It produces beauty—but for the worker, deformity." While the rich got richer, the poor got old, choking on coal dust and unsanitary conditions, a cog in a wheel more impersonal than fate, unable to "affirm himself" or "develop freely."

Surveying the history of humankind under the influence of progressive thinkers like Darwin and Hegel, Marx thought he spotted a promising pattern, however. Over the ages, society could certainly be said to progress. This progress came not in a gradual and steady manner, though, but in a series of surges and storms, like a salmon making its way up a stream from pool to pool. Just when conditions within society worsened beyond bearing, a revolution occurred in means of production, leading a new and broader class to power. Thus society progressed from slavery to serfdom to capitalism. The next stage, he argued, would be socialism, and following that, communism. Workers would become their own masters. People would share fairly, each contributing their labor according to ability, and receiving benefits from the common store according to their need. There would be no room in this system for those who merely made use of other people's talents and hard work, who sucked up the lifeblood of common men and women, and gave nothing back.

Of course, you need to break eggs to make an omelet, as one of Marx's disciples later put it. Revolution, said another, was not a dinner party. The apathetic needed to be awakened, oppressors overthrown, and private property— here was the key, said Marx—needed to be "abolished." None of this could be expected to happen apart from a violent, bloody reaction from the Powers-That-Be. Marx welcomed such a conflict, and often seemed to exult in the bloodshed and violence which would accompany it.

Karl Marx and his followers believed the human race would get along better without religion, too. The old myths relegating Eden to another world, and telling slaves to submit to their masters, had been refuted by Enlightenment thinkers like Darwin, Feuerbach and Tylor. The angels guarding the entrance to paradise were paper mercenaries, scare crows of the ruling class. "The abolition of religion, as the illusory happiness of man," he wrote, "is a demand for their real happiness." Laugh, and the world laughs with you: Marx proved that the principle holds for sneering, too. Pouring scorn on the idea of supernatural powers and hope in

another world, he gained for his own intensely spiritual and highly speculative theories a certain exemption from the debunking spirit loose in Europe at the time.

Marx's theories were first tried in Russia.

The Holy Russian Empire was caught at an awkward moment. Russia had
been industrializing rapidly for decades. She revealed a surprising potential as a
breadbasket to the world when, in the late nineteenth century, her grain output
climbed and challenged that of America. Her artists were creating opera and epic
that would amaze the world for a hundred years. But when Prussian troops
counterattacked against a hasty Russian defense of their "brother Serbs"[2] across
the border, the Russian Army was caught flat-footed and this fragile progress was
fractured. With the royal family mesmerized by Rasputin, a mystical guru of
"salvation through sin," and her generals short on both the kind of intelligence
that figures out where the enemy is and the kind that knows what to do about
it, the Romanov state was no match either for the German war machine, nor for
the fire and spiritual force of revolution following in its wake.

The leader of the revolutionaries, who called himself Lenin, had an acid
tongue, a pen sharper than any bayonet, and a practical plan for realizing the
vague prophecies of his guru. He invented a tool of ideological and social control called the Communist Party, and used it to reorder and tame Russia. He
didn't live to extend Marx's vision much beyond the borders of Russia, however. That duty fell to a lieutenant: Joseph Stalin, a man of "steel," which is what
the name means, from the mountains of Georgia.

Some say the times were hard and called for a hard man to lead the nation.
Strong guidance was needed to force independent-thinking farmers to work for the
greater good, build a modern economy, take Russia through the Great Depression,
defeat the Nazi armies, and challenge the capitalist world. All this Stalin provided.

Stalin wasn't given to sarcasm like his predecessor. He came across to many
Western visitors as humble, efficient, even fatherly. But the angel of death hovered over Stalin's vast realm like a malevolent cloud, descending with the force
of a whirlwind to snatch away those whose deeds or thoughts were deemed
impure. This one died in a car crash, that one was tried for treason, a third was
found in Mexico with a pick in his back. Stalin skillfully cultivated contradic-
tions among more flamboyant rivals. When the dust settled, his companions
and rivals were gone, and so were whole populations: physicians, Red Army
officers, Ukrainian peasants.

Mother Russia was giving birth to a new world order. It seemed to be a
painful delivery; you could hear muffled cries from the delivery room. But few
among the Western intelligentsia jumped to hasty condemnation. On the contrary, one leading English publisher, Victor Gollancz, nominated Stalin as
"Man of the Year" at the height of the Great Purges.[3] George Bernard Shaw,
Jean-Paul Sartre, and many others, praised the Soviet Union in extravagant

terms long after horrible details came to light. "We have seen the future, and it works!" said one star-struck visitor to the Soviet Union.[4]

Marx's vision caught fire in more and more countries. The Baltic Republics were handed Russia in a deal with Adolf Hitler. Stalin took Eastern Europe as spoils of war. Mao Zedong, a librarian and student of Chinese military history from the hills of Hunan Province, liberated China after a long and complicated struggle between many armies. Rice patty revolutionaries outwit and outfought "imperialist" armies in Korea, Cuba, and Vietnam. One by one, newly independent states in Africa shook off the chains of their colonial masters and declared themselves for liberation.

By the mid-1970s waves of revolutionary idealism lapped even at the gates of European and American campuses.

Whodunit?

But just as socialism was being praised by young students as the wave of the future, its past began to catch up with it. The early work of Solzhenitsyn appeared in the West about this time. Official Soviet literature had degenerated to the level of works like *Cement,* a book historian Donald Treadgold described in a lecture as "the world's first boy-girl-tractor love triangle." But here, of a sudden, appeared meat for the soul in the best tradition of Russian literature. Solzhenitsyn's passionate yet sardonic description of the horrors of police-state terror in the Soviet Union gripped the imagination of Western thinkers and helped them visualize formerly faceless victims, bringing to fruition a "neo-conservative" reaction against Marxism.

Had the classes melted away in terror? Yes, it had, for a few moments. But then a new class of bullies rushed into the void. What had they constructed behind the barbed wire? The truth came out in a form the world could no longer ignore. True, as Edmund Burke noted, "those who destroy everything will remove some grievance." A rising tide lifts all boats, and the new society was organized in a military fashion that marshaled resources for health care and education that greatly increased life expectancy and, by some measures, the standard of living. But no one could look at these dismal forests of flaking high rises where toilets didn't flush, neighbor feared neighbor, coal dust choked the lungs, and official lies choked the spirit, and confuse them with utopia. And then there were the mass graves.

Whodunit? The detectives have drawn lines on the ground. The press has arrived with cameras and microphones. The coroner has appeared in white coat with scalpel. Court psychologists are at hand. Let us consider the suspects.

"It Was the Snake's Fault"

"Joseph Stalin is the reason communism failed," some say. "He wormed his way into the apple and spoiled it."

It would be hard for Central Casting to come up with a more plausible villain.

Stalin's were the thick, mustached lips that sent millions to labor camps and death. His fingers squeezed the life from Russian culture and commerce. He set the example for the communist parties of the world of what a socialist state ought to be. Stalin has certainly earned the prominent spot given him in Madame Tussaud's House of Horrors.

Before his arrest in 1945, as a Red Army officer at the front in Prussia, Solzhenitsyn agreed with those who fingered "The Leader." While Marx and Lenin remained objects of adoration and near-worship for him, a cutting descriptions in a personal letter of the "man with the mustache" earned him his prison term. But while in prison Solzhenitsyn ran into some of Stalin's revolutionary rivals, and decided he'd been naive. These Trotskyites and Octobrists, imprisoned for their ideals, surrounded by men who were suffering unjustly, still could not refrain from speaking with great ruthlessness, and showed little mercy to fellow-prisoners.

Dostoevsky showed, with his Grand Inquisitor, how a church can begin with "love your neighbor" as its premise and, after 1200 years of rationalization, come to torture as a conclusion. But what if "thou shalt hate thy neighbor" is your original premise? This was the problem among the Marxist oligarchy. None of Stalin's rivals could bring himself to openly denounce terror and murder as instruments of the state. Even those who may have been repelled by Stalin's bloody methods couldn't find a Marxist rationale to object. After all, Marx himself said the use of terror was "historically inevitable." Compared to some of his comrades, Stalin *talked* like a moderate.

Phnom Penh and Lima are a long ways from Moscow. Yet the cruelty of the Khmer Rouge and Sendero Luminoso would I think have embarrassed some of the rulers Stalin picked for Eastern Europe.

In China, many who terrorized neighbors during the Cultural Revolution now blame Mao for what they did. "We were deceived," I have heard some say. "It wasn't our fault."

But as French sociologist Jacques Ellul says, propaganda can only exploit what is in a person, not what is not. Who gained a new apartment when a neighbor was denounced in a secret letter, or ate imported sweets while everyone else was standing in a line for bread, because he was willing to shoot at shadows slipping westward into no-man's land? Not Stalin alone. The devil can't make us do what we don't want to do. Personal responsibility is at the heart of traditional morality common to the traditions of humanity.

"Wrong Apple"

Others, mostly scholarly Western Marxists, remind us that Karl Marx never predicted revolution in backward places like Russia or China. Marx described the evolution of advanced industrial societies like Germany or the United States. What were those uproars in Eastern Europe and unpronounceable countries of Asia and Africa? Either a clumsy attempt to kick-start the engine of history that instead slid primitive economies into the swamp of feudal tyranny, or else a virulent form of capitalism masquerading as socialism, to deceive if possible the very elect.

Marxist theorists call the first "Asiatic despotism." Ancient empires like Mesopotamia, Egypt, India and China grew up around rivers, as despotic rulers "mobilized the masses" of previously free peasants to build irrigation projects. Rather than allowing the common people to enjoy the fruit of their labor, however, rulers channeled the capital thus created towards projects that reflected their growing power and arrogance: pyramids, Taj Mahals, treasure-filled tombs. They seldom stopped to count the slaves buried in the rubble.

Communist regimes, some say, slipped into the mold of the Pharaohs and the Khans. And little wonder. Haven't the countries they ruled been under the thumb of one tyrant or another since before the days of Nero?

A second way some admirers of Marx explain away the failure of communism is by the term "state capitalism." Imagine a conglomerate so big it owns the government. Bureaucrats run the factories, and resources are allocated by office politics and bribery. The press is the conglomerate's marketing division, the police force its salesmen. What you have, now, is not socialism or any derivative thereof, but Marx's worst nightmare run amuck. Welcome to the U.S.S.R.

Both of these solutions carry a certain explanatory power. Communist rulers did share something in common with Xerxes and Genghis Khan, and something else with Bill Gates.

But we shouldn't let the purists return to their ivory towers or soap boxes too quickly. It may be that when Joseph Stalin built "New Siberia" in the frozen taiga on the corpses of his countrymen, he cackled like Ivan the Terrible. Perhaps Chairman Mao was a reincarnation of his illustrious predecessor, Emperor Qin, who sacrificed thousands of workers to bury clay horses under mounds of dirt. Maybe Pol Pott and Kim Il Sung were dancing to the muse of ancient Assyrian tyrants. But Mao was once a poet and an idealistic young man with a thirst for knowledge. Pol Pott was a teacher, and Abimael Guzman Reymoso, shadowy head of Peru's sinister Shining Path, taught philosophy at the university level. Even Stalin once risked life and limb for his ideal and the future of the human race. What such rhetoric tends to obscure is that what Stalin and Mao shared in common with the rulers of the past, is something they also share in common with us: their humanity.

Human Nature and the Ship of State

Governing a nation is often compared to the sailing of the "ship of state" across a rough body of water. This metaphor is implicit in the title communist regimes often gave their leader, the "Great Helmsman."

On old sailing ships, sailors made allowance for bad weather. The ship would come about and face the wind and waves. Sailors would tie the helmsman to the bridge, and someone would stand by so that even if the pilot went overboard, the ship wouldn't founder.

Democracies allow that, due to the vicissitudes of human nature, government, like the sea, is a dangerous place. Voting "ties" leaders to their promises. Parliaments, judges, churches, and the press keep an eye on politicians and provide alternative leadership should the president "go overboard" in his or her policies. Such institutions were built into democracy out of a particular, some say cynical, religious view that government is "for men, not angels," as James Madison (author of the American Constitution) put it.

But to Marx all human flaws were by-products of the old order. Much has been written about the economic aspect of this assumption, and how "all for one and one for all" led to mass starvation by taking away the ordinary worker's "selfish" desire to make good for his family. But if communism wreaked havoc by ignoring the self-centeredness of those at the bottom, this damage was exponentially increased by a corresponding naivete towards those at the top. Communist government was designed for angels, not men, but given to men whose vanity and narcissism was more than ordinary, to put it mildly. Each new communist ruler, as he emerged in dashing red bandanna or egalitarian Mao jacket from the pack of idealistic teachers and students who formed the manpower base of most revolutions, was greeted by a chorus of wild popular applause. Success breeds success. The popular enthusiasm by which the masses merged their enthusiasm with that of the regime helps explain why many in the West remained in denial long after survivors had begun to creep across no-man's land with signs of torture on arms and testicles.

But how could such widely read, intelligent people as Karl Marx and the intellectuals who to this day admire him, convince themselves that iron workers in Kiev would want to put in extra hours for wood cutters in Yakutsk once factories were unionized? Or that men who have gained power with bombs and lies will wield power with restraint? How could Marx deny the sense inherent in Burke's prophetic criticism of the French Revolution?

> "Criminal means once tolerated are soon preferred. They present a shorter cut to the object than through the highway of the moral virtues. Justifying perfidy and murder for the public benefit, public benefit will soon become the pretext, and perfidy and murder the end."[5]

"It's Just One Branch–The Rest of the Tree is Solid"

How far should the buck be passed for the failure of Marxism? Many say to Marx and his followers, and no further—except, perhaps, to the church. "It was the lack of democratic controls that made this ideology dangerous," they say. "Marx and Lenin made communism into a kind of state church. Marxism imbibed its crusader mentality, its need to be right and make everyone agree, from the Christianity of the Dark Ages. Tolerance and separation of church and state are important precisely to prevent such a dominant ideology, a fundamentalism, if you will, from forcing its will on society again."

The Cold War was an ecumenical struggle, with Christians, Muslims, Buddhists, and Humanists cooperating to oppose communism. Since the Iron Curtain came down, some Humanists have argued that Marxism was merely another chapter in the long and cruel story of ecclesiastical dogmatism. Robert Meneilly, pastor of the Village Presbyterian Church, one of the largest churches of his denomination in the United States, wrote in a *New York Times* article that the "Religious right confronts us with a threat far greater than communism."[6] If you consider Marx's ideas, however, it is clear that Marx's theory of "cracking eggs" derive not from the Christian tradition, but from Enlightenment concepts like "survival of the fittest," the Promethean struggle against God and bondage to conventional morality, and human perfectibility, which ran like a current through nineteenth century humanist thought. "Abolish all religion" is a pretty fundamental break with the West's religious heritage, after all. While it may be reasonable to trace the iconoclastic, evangelistic fervor of his followers in part to the revivalist spirit of Christianity, there is no reason to suppose Stalin or Mao were directly influenced by the church as to how many eggs they chose to crack or how they cracked them.

At the same time, one can trace the effect of these same concepts on the writings of other Western moralists: Peter Singer, who justifies the murder of infants, Joseph Fletcher, whose influence we will discuss in the next chapter, and many others. Marx drank his barbarism from a well that has not run dry 150 years later. He began *Communist Manifesto* with the words, "A specter is haunting Europe." While the body of Marxist ideology has died, the barbaric and cruel spirit that animated it does indeed seem to be with us still.

"Marx Cut Down the Tree of Good and Evil"

Yet it would not be fair to say, as some Christians have, that all atheists or all of those who ignore God are somehow implicated in the cruelty and moral abandon of the KGB. An Indian-born Christian, Ravi Zacharius, wrote a book entitled, *"Can Man Be Good Without God?"* and answered in the negative. If we define "good" in the ordinary sense, I would answer in the positive. We defy credibility as Christians if we deny that people almost as skeptical of our faith as Marx often make excellent neighbors, colleagues and spouses. (True, there is a deeper meaning of the word "good" of which Jesus spoke, and many psychologists deal with, at which these appearances may be deceiving. But more on that later.)

Marx wrote, "communism abolishes all morality, all eternal truths, and all

religion, instead of constituting them on a new basis." Some say Marx took his
false step here, not in his war against God, but in his assault on the common
moral heritage of all religions.

For this, too, a case can be made.

Traditional morality said, "honor your father and mother." Marx, Engels, and
Mao were each on terrible terms with one or both parents. Stalin's father was a
drunk who beat his sons and died in a brawl. Mao learned dialectic strategy arguing with his tight-fisted father. Once, he persuaded his father to not beat him by
threatening suicide. Burke noted that the French revolutionaries felt that, "It is a
sufficient motive to destroy an old scheme of things, because it is an old one."[7]
The Chinese communists, their spiritual descendants, mounted campaigns
against "the Four Olds." Mao stood on Tiananmen Gate and called teenagers
from around the nation to go home and struggle against their parent's generation.
Teachers suffered in particular. Confucius, Moses, or Freud might have made the
same point: what else would you expect from children who hated their parents?[8]

The *Tao* said, "thou shalt not steal," and "thou shalt not covet thy neighbor's house, wife, or goods." Rousseau initiated a modern rebellion against this
universal standard when he traced all human heartache to the instant the first
man drew a circle around a plot of land and said, "this is mine." Karl Marx
agreed possessiveness was the fatal error. The Bolshevik Party financed its early
struggles by bank robbery. When it seized power, it took everything it had overlooked in its previous heists, from kitchen cutlery to the Ural Mountains.

Traditional morality said, "thou shalt not murder." For what will the twentieth century be best remembered? Perhaps for the fact that, even with all its
bloody wars to end all war, almost as many people died at the hand of their own
governments as those of enemies. Disciples of Karl Marx were responsible for
even more deaths than those of Adolf Hitler.

The theory that Marx's gravest error lay in "abolishing" traditional morality is, therefore, plausible on the surface. The eloquence of Burke's rhetorical
fire scorches the French revolutionaries for the harm a relativized morality can
cause: "Kings will be tyrants from policy when subjects are rebels from principle."[9] "Criminal means once tolerated are soon preferred."[10] But if you talk
with a modern revolutionary, or an older person in Russia or China who looks
back with fondness on the more fervent period of rebellion, what they remember is often not the criminal means, but a nostalgia for the moral principles by
which those means were justified. While Marx often claimed to "abolish" religion or morality, he is also remembered as a moral pioneer, a Moses coming
down from the mountain with words of thunder written in stone. In fact Marx
did "reestablish morality on a new basis." Marx's value system was built not one
new basis, but on three. And none of them were new, but three familiar ideas,
"alternative moralities" as old as Cain and Abel. Traces of Marx's three "old

moralities" can be found like fingerprints across the history of the twentieth century, indeed of every era.

Classes, Masses, and the Enlightened

Marx applied the first standard to the "oppressors," to members of the old society he blamed (often correctly) for injustice. Some scholars say Marx used words like "oppression," and "exploitation" in a technical, scientific, non-moralistic sense. But when you talk with real Marxist revolutionaries, you find them full of righteous anger. When you read Marx, you see where it came from. Thus the *Communist Manifesto* speaks of the "slothful indolence" of the ruling class and their "naked, shameless, direct, brutal exploitation" of the poor. Marx shakes his finger and rants, "The bourgeois sees in his wife a mere instrument of production."[11] He piles on moralistic sarcasm: "Do you charge us with wanting to stop the exploitation of children by their parents? To this charge we plead guilty."[12]

Moral passion and indignation against oppression were always the first weapon every Marxist revolutionary drew against the ruling classes. Later, a second weapon would be unsheathed on the proletariat.

A month after the Tiananmen massacre I visited southern China. On many street corners, magazines with amateurish photos of half-naked women were displayed openly. Prostitutes seemed to be using some of the rooms of the otherwise respectable hotel I stayed at. In mainland China, this came as a shock. On my first visit, in 1984, one could hardly tell Chinese were sexual beings, apart from numbers! Husbands and wives didn't even hold hands as they crossed the street.

After the massacre, the "left," diehard Marxists, took some time to reconsolidate power. When they had done so, they conducted a campaign against "spiritual pollution." By my next visit, pornography was gone again, and thousands of prostitutes had been arrested. Human sexuality was not as invisible as in 1984, but sex was off the streets, temporarily.

For an ideology that abolished morality, when it came to power Marxism turned out surprisingly straight. Not just in regards to sex, either. Wall posters and ads sprang up urging people to work hard, keep sober, don't spit, take thought for your fellow man. (And woman: the Marxist regime made real strides in reducing gender inequality in China.) Big Brother had a side to him not unlike a strict but well-meaning grandmother.

As with other forms of what might be termed social dualism, such as radical feminism and the Nation of Islam, socialism shows reality through a polarizing lens. The classes were a dark, malevolent mass like a cloud, bound to spend themselves and be carried away on the winds of history. The masses were a layer of air polluted by the old system, ready to be scrubbed clean by the rain of revolution. The weaknesses of the common people were due to enemy intrigues (said Stalin) or to lack of sufficient ideological training (said Mao).

What about revolutionaries themselves? What moral absolutes did the "glorious, shining, illustrious, irradiant" communist party adhere to? (as the authors of my Chinese dictionary, printed in Beijing a few years after the Cultural Revolution, described it.) What about the supreme leaders themselves? How should a man guide his life whose thoughts were, like Mao's, such that the same dictionary could think of nothing better to illustrate the meaning of the word "radiance"? One does not light candles to guide the sun across the sky. Nor was legalistic conformity to puritanical moral codes expected of great communist teachers. (Any more than it is of those in esoteric Asian sects who have attained enlightenment.)

C. S. Lewis wrote, "I am very doubtful whether history has shown us one example of a man who, having stepped outside traditional morality and attained power, has used that power benevolently."[13] Revolutionary religions tend to breed a double standard. Mohammed, Jim Jones, and Hong Xiuquan received special revelations allowing them to marry many wives, while restricting the common believer to a few, or, in the case of Hong and many other cult leaders, none at all. In the same way, Mao Zedong separated families across China for the good of the revolution, while forming a harem for himself.

Can we count up dachas and swimming pools and consider the riddle solved? Was old-fashioned hypocrisy responsible for the failure of Marxism?

I cannot read the writings of the communist elite and convince myself of the Machiavellian theory of Marxist morality. It seems to me that, for all their hypocrisy, the elite did hold itself to a moral standard. This is what Joseph Fletcher called "situation ethics": that the end, the "greatest good of the greatest number," justifies the means. Communist apologists reconstruct Marx' contradictory writings on morality in different ways. But the fact is, from the Paris Commune to the Peruvian Andes, no matter how they might bend the rules of "bourgeois morality," not even when they denied "right" and "wrong" meant anything, did revolutionaries stop trying to convince themselves they were right by this standard. In his brilliant novel *First Circle*, Solzhenitsyn pictures Stalin plotting murder at night while dreaming in the abstract of how he was offering mankind happiness like a man giving a bowl of milk to a puppy. Such a picture, it seems to me, is true to human nature and to the history of Marxism.

Churchill called the Soviet Union "a riddle wrapped in a mystery inside an enigma." The Bible says "The heart is deceitful . . . who can know it?" (Jer. 17:9). Karl Marx and his followers did away with morality, and spoke in its place of historic necessities, the inevitable enmity of classes, and the hypocrisy of the bourgeois morality. Yet they could not attack enemies, inspire masses, or write memoirs, without at each stage appealing to one or another version of what they claimed to have abandoned, preaching the *Tao* with bullhorns from street corners, when they rose up and when they sat down.

Here, again, the story of Adam and Eve helps us makes sense of Karl Marx. Remember what the snake said to Eve?

"You will not surely die, but will be as gods, knowing good from evil."

Adam and Eve also abandoned the command of God in search of a revolutionary, autonomous "knowledge of good and evil." Their story also ended with eviction from paradise and a pointing of fingers. The story of the Garden of Eden does not allow us to ignore that in a sense, we are all to blame, when we make ourselves as gods.

The God Within

In the end, I do not entirely agree with Solzhenitsyn that Marxism failed because "men have forgotten God," nor with Dostoevsky's statement that, "If there is no God, everything is permitted." I don't think the human heart allows either the complete freedom from moral law Dostoevsky and Orwell feared, nor complete atheism, as we will see in a later chapter.

Marx wrote that "Religion is only the illusory sun around which man revolves, until he begins to revolve around himself."[14] You can get dizzy, doing that. In a nutshell, I believe this attempt to revolve around an immortalized and omnipotent projection of oneself, individually and collectively, is what made world communism lose its balance and fall down.

This is also the lesson the failure of Marxism holds for children of the Enlightenment, students of revolutionary religions, Christian believers, and gurus who claim unity with ultimate reality. Not that we forget God, but that we try to be God.

Consider what observers said about the character of three great Marxists: Marx himself, Vladimir Lenin, and Leon Trotsky:

"Never have I seen anyone whose manner was more insufferably arrogant. He would not give a moment's consideration to any opinion that differed from his own. He treated with open contempt everyone who contradicted him. Arguments that were not to his taste were answered either by mordant sarcasms upon the speaker's lamentable ignorance, or else by casting suspicions upon the motives of his adversary."[15]

"(Ivan Plekhanov, the 'father of Russian communism') "Was the first and last of Lenin's contemporaries to whom he deferred in wisdom, and that only for a few years."[16]

"It is not true that (Trotsky) was modest, but that his vanity consisted in seeing himself as the instrument of never clearly-defined historical and class forces."[17]

Undoubtedly it takes a person with more than the average quota of *chutz-pah* to suppose he can take over from a functioning government and make things run better. American politicians are hardly known for their humility, either. Yet the essential sanity of the divine calling that social revolutionaries who operated within the *Tao*, such as Gandhi, Confucius, Wilberforce and Aquino seemed to feel, was validated by other aspects of their personalities, such as self-forgetfulness and curiosity, a willingness to learn and an awareness of limits. Such humble qualities seem utterly foreign to religious revolutionaries like Lenin, Mao, Hong Xiuquan, Adolf Hitler, or Jim Jones; men who could never get enough of themselves. They littered the squares of their cities with statues, like an invading army of patriarchal gray giants.

George Orwell understood the spirit that pervaded Marxism. His villain, O'Brien, explained to his victim Winston Smith in the satire *1984:*

> "The Party seeks power entirely for its own sake. We are not interested in the good of others; we are interested solely in power. All the others, even those who resembled ourselves, were cowards and hypocrites. The German Nazis and the Russian Communists never had the courage to recognize their own motives. Power is not a means, it is an end."[18]

It may seem unfair to call such men "cowards" and say they had no interest in the common good. Facing torture and death, intrigue and betrayal, they charted the course of the twentieth century, and brought about reforms that more politically-timid religions never accomplished. They were the rugged warriors of China's Long March, veterans of Siberia and the Ho Chi Mihn trail. Yet bullets can be easier to face than the truth about oneself.

Few would defend Stalin or even Lenin today. But were they the only ones to blame? Were the leaders the only ones who cheered and swelled with pride when East Germany struggled to train a corps of athletes to bring home as many Olympic medals as countries ten times their size and a hundred times their wealth? Did only the masters gain a vicarious pleasure from reports of the colossally inefficient canals and model cities in the tundra, or endless figures about tractors and hydroelectric projects and record grain output? And isn't the appeal of collective self-idolatry the true reason wild prophecies could pass as "social science," and serious people could talk of "abolishing" morality? "Take a bite of the apple, and be as gods."

Marxism was not about quality of living. Marx took little care of his own family, or his own body. Marx succeeded by making the common man and woman feel the franchise of godhood was also within their grasp. Communism was about seeking cosmic power in the collective self, of whom the supreme leader was image and model.

The failure of Marxism does not represent collective guilt (we've had enough of that for a while), so much as symptomatic guilt. The human weakness responsible for the Gulag is something common to capitalists, Zen Buddhists, Zoroastrians, and Baptists.

Marxism and Spirituality

I believe Marxism should be seen primarily as the greatest religious experiment of the twentieth century. Why? First, a person's faith is not only what he believes about the afterlife or God. It is how we see our world, our "ultimate concern," to use philosopher Paul Tillich's widely-accepted term: the object of our highest level of trust.

Second, Marxism created what in other contexts would be called a "faith community." Religion is in part a socially-conditioned behavior concerned with ultimate values. Thus a Hindu or a Buddhist may be atheist, pantheist, or monotheist, but is looked on with respect by their peers so long as he practices the rites of his caste. A typical example is the Sikhs. Guru Nanak, the founder of modern Sikhism, deliberately created outward symbols (comb, hidden knife one always wears, hair one is not to cut) so that male followers would stand out and find solidarity. "Western" monotheistic religions are often also primarily concerned with outward conformity, especially communities which struggle to preserve themselves in the face of larger numbers. Among Reformed Jews, and many liberal Christian congregations, purity of belief is less important than shared community. One can hide a multitude of heretical thoughts in a sea of men praying *Allahu Akbar* outside a mosque. While communism did its utmost to change people's minds as well, Marxism created a community of ritual, a cult as well as a culture, even aside from its influence on human thinking.

Third, even on a superficial level, communist governments created the ceremonial paraphernalia of traditional religion: relics of saints, holy Scriptures, confession, repentance, liturgy, hymns, prayer, and even tales of the supernatural. (In *Modern Times*, Paul Johnson quotes Kim Il Sung as claiming to have "worked countless legendary miracles," for example.)

Fourth, even from the beginning, Marxism borrowed and expanded on religious archetypes. In his dissertation, Marx discussed a religious theme: the war of Prometheus upon the gods. Mao Zedong was equally fond of the Monkey King, who literally waged "guerrilla warfare" against the ruling classes of heaven.

Marxism represented the merging of two great rivers of human spiritual experience. Theologically, Marxism is one of a class of "ultimate concerns" which derive from the Enlightenment. Socially, it can be looked at as one of a class of religious revolutions, in common with early Islam, Mormonism, and peasant rebellions throughout Asia and Europe. These have as their defining characteristics a willingness to blend church and state, aggressive social reform, a tendency to mix ideas from disparate sources, and the philosophy that, whether or not there is an afterlife, the role of government is to promote God's Kingdom in this world.[19]

Marx and his followers consciously drew on the experience of various religious communes in Europe and America, such as the Quakers. Mao Zedong also freely admitted his debt to a long Chinese tradition of messianic "grass-roots bandits." From this point of view, communism should be viewed as a classic expression of the same impulse that fired Mohammed, Joseph Smith, Hong Xiuquan, and modern cults. At the heart of such revolutionary movements is always some new revelation.

There is nothing particularly shocking that Marx used the terminology of the budding social sciences to frame his philosophy. Revolutionary religion borrows from diverse sources, but builds psychologically on the strongest passions of the hour. Islam borrowed a stone and polygamy from Mohammed's pagan neighbors, political institutions and the veil from the Persian empire, a view of God and most of the prophets from the Jews, and Jesus and a few more prophets from the Christians—meeting felt needs to unify the Arab tribes. Joseph Smith also borrowed from all quarters: Indians, Masons, popular spiritualism, and of course Christianity. Hong Xiuquan, the great nineteenth century Chinese revolutionary, also ignored spiritual boundaries by brilliantly synthesizing diverse and hitherto distinct traditions: Old Testament iconoclasm, village shamanism, ancient Chinese monotheistic poetry, and Qing Dynasty Confucianism.

Marx was a spiritual entrepreneur with the same eclectic habits. He built upon the philosophical premises shared in common by the people of his class and era, especially skepticism and social evolution. He borrowed biology from Darwin, a general pattern of history from Hegel, religious evolution from Tylor, social ideals from Rousseau, and revolution from Robespierre. Having brought in a touch of Methodist fervor, Quaker communalism, and a prophet's staff from his Jewish ancestors, he cobbled together a revolutionary ideology that shared much in common with other such syncretic and violent religious movements.

A London newspaper once sponsored an essay contest on the subject, "What is Wrong with the World?" G. K. Chesterton sent in his concise reply: "I am"

The failure of Marxism should not allow religious believers to pat each other on the back and say, "see what crimes godless heretics can commit? See how important religion is?" (Although it wouldn't hurt godless heretics to consider such questions.) It should serve as a warning shot across all our bows. For it was not so much Marx's denial of God that led to his crimes. The Old Testament prophets also denied the socially-indifferent construct that the upper classes tend to designate as their deity, after all. The real harm was done by the gods Marx served, in particular, the god within.

---

[1] Richard Wurmbrand, *From Suffering to Triumph*, Kregel, Grand Rapids, MI, 1991, p.140

[2] In tones eerily reminiscent of more recent sentiment, Russian newspapers warned that, "Over the head of little Serbia the sword is pointed as mighty Russia." Alexander Solzhenitsyn, *August 1914,* Bantom, 1974, p.64.

[3] Paul Johnson, *Intellectuals*, Harper and Row, 1988, p.277

[4] Actually, "I have been over to the future, and it works." (Lincoln Steffens, from Paul Johnson, *Modern Times*, HarperCollins, p. 88.

[5] *Reflections on the Revolution in France*, Penguin, 1969, p.177

[6] Robert H. Meineilly, *Government is Not God's Work, New York Times*, August 29, 1993

[7] *Reflections on the Revolution in France*, p.184

[8] I think psychologist Paul Vitz makes this point most persuasively, however. In *Faith of the Fatherless: the Psychology of Atheism*, Paul Vitz reverses a standard Freudian syllogism by arguing, with admirable compassion and restraint, that male atheists tend to come from the ranks of those who have lost fathers or had abusive fathers. He discusses Marx, Stalin, and Mao briefly, as well as Hitler, and philosophers who have influenced modern totalitarianism, such as Rousseau, Nietzche and Sartre.

[9] *Reflections on the Revolution in France*, p.172

[10] Ibid., p.177

[11] *Marx-Engels Reader*, Edited by Robert Tucker, W. W. Norton & Co., 1978, p.488

[12] Ibid., p.487

[13] C. S. Lewis, *The Abolition of Man*, Macmillan Co.,1947, p.78

[14] *Intellectuals*, p.56

[15] Civil War general Carl Schwarz, on meeting Marx, from Lewis Feuer, *Marx and the Intellectuals,* p. 42-3

[16] Donald Treadgold and Herbert Ellison, *Twentieth Century Russia*, 1995.

[17] Hugh Seton-Watson, *From Lenin to Krushchev: The History of World Communism,* Westview Press, 1985, p. 90.

[18] George Orwell, *Nineteen Eighty Four*, Harcourt Brace Jovanovich, 1977, p. 217.

[19]Marxism shares many characteristics with a class of belief systems that I would describe as "social dualism." This class of faiths includes both secular ideologies like radical feminism and Marxism, and religious sects such as the Nation of Islam, most Messianic cults throughout history, and many New Age sects. It is typified by (1) An emphasis on history. (Technically, historicism.) (2) A pre-historic fall

from grace. (3) The idea that oppression arises from the social structure. (4) The belief that the struggle between good and evil is primarily a social struggle (black vs. white, male vs. female, rich vs. poor). (5) The hope that the future utopian community will be ushered in by drastic changes to the social structure. (6) And that human nature will reach a new innocence through such a historical process.

CHAPTER 4

The Sexual Revolution

"I WANT to go back to Owhyhee / Where the sea sings a soulful song, Where the gals is kind and gentle / And they don't know right from wrong." —James Michener, *Hawaii*

"If we had been in on the Creation, and God had asked us whether or not He should make two sexes and put a great urge into both of them for each other's bodies, we would have advised Him not to."[1]—*Thomas Howard*

"Caught between these voices, the sirens and the Sage One too many choices, for the victims of the age."—*Mark Heard*

The most popular image of paradise today may be an island rather than a garden. But if we picture Eden with sand and a tropical breeze, this image has also been tainted with visions of paradise lost. William Golding, in his masterful parable, *Lord of the Flies,* described a planeload of English school boys left on an island who ran wild and turned to human sacrifice. Golding's story was a mild retelling of the actual fate of paradise in the modern world. Shiploads of lusty Spanish sailors land on Caribbean islands populated by natives so backward they grab the blade of swords; after decades of cruelty, the Spanish are forced to bring in African slaves to repopulate paradise. In the Pacific, sailors swim ashore for trysts with native girls, and mutiny when it's time to sail home. Adventurers drop sailors sick with smallpox off among native tribes in a primitive version of germ warfare. The moral seems to be that if you want to know the worst that is in a person, send him to Eden with firepower, and watch.

In 1923, a young anthropologist named Margaret Mead arrived in Samoa. Her research methods were informed by a lax empirical philosophy and the ideas of her mentor, Franz Boas, who believed that "much of what we ascribe to human nature is no more than a reaction to the restraints put upon us by our civilization."[2] Mrs. Mead, who had not brought her husband along, cast off any such restraints. She claimed virgin status, which allowed her to move among and interview young women on the island, but had an affair with an 18-year-old school teacher. She was only on the island a few months, not long enough to learn much of the language, which did not stop her from claiming to have conducted her interviews exclusively in Samoan. But the book she wrote from her research, *Coming of Age in Samoa*, proved a sensation, and she became "mother goddess" of anthropology. She reported that among Samoans, romantic love was not "bound up with ideas of monogamy, exclusiveness, jealousy and undeviating fidelity" as in the West.[3] Samoans had accepted Christianity, but found the idea of chastity "absolutely meaningless," as young people practiced casual "love under the palm trees" with friends of either sex.

Armed with pen rather than sword or pathogen, Margaret Mead had power only to irritate the Samoans.[4] But her tales of the South Pacific contributed to the second great moral revolution of the twentieth century: the sexual revolution, an attempt to regain paradise through the act of love. While Marx called humankind to free itself from bondage to capital-owning classes, the sexual revolution was a call to free ourselves from the archaic and restrictive norms of "Victorian" Christianity.

It is, perhaps, arbitrary how we date the start of the Sexual Revolution. "Saint Rousseau," as George Sand, the nineteenth century's Madonna, called the French philosopher Jean-Jacques Rousseau, with his doctrine of "natural" living and the casting off of "artificial" modern prudery, was in a sense the father of three waves of revolution: the French, the communist, and the sexual.[5] By George Sand's time the theory of evolution provided a new intellectual foundation for a call to "natural," that is, free and unrestrained, sexuality. Aldous Huxley frankly noted, "we all jumped at (Darwin's *Origin of the Species)* because the idea of God interfered with our sexual mores."[6] In the twentieth century, the *Humanist Manifesto II* echoed a sentiment that had become the consensus of progressive intellectuals long before: "In the area of sexuality, we believe that intolerant attitudes, often cultivated by orthodox religious and puritanical cultures, unduly suppress sexual conduct."

B. F. Skinner's utopian *Walden II* provided a new model as a hundred free-love communes were launched across America in the 1960s. The Roussean and Taoist ideal of getting "back to nature" was interpreted by an urbanizing western society as a call to natural foods and relaxed sexuality, while the invention of the pill and relatively safe abortion provided the technological basis for the revolution.

Ethicist Joseph Fletcher helped popularize a "new morality" based on what he called "situation ethics:" "Any sexual act—hetero, homo, bi, or auto—is good if it is done with loving concern; otherwise it is evil and morally wrong."[7]

Others thought it better to drop the pretense of morality altogether. Why be ashamed of our bodies? We are animals. Why repress what comes natural?

Time magazine recently ran an article reporting scientific studies of primate sexual behavior. Among some species, the researchers found, half the babies were born to males other than the "official" mate. "While some species of primate may appear monogamous, genetic tests on their offspring show that the females play the field more than we thought." The article seemed to imply that it is "natural" for primates, including human beings, to fool around.

Sensual pleasure should be liberated from the piety of any moral system, some argued. Simon and Schuster editor-in-chief Michael Korda wrote that the Sexual Revolution took sex out of the hands of "self-appointed moralists and clinicians" and put it "where it belongs—in the realm of normal pleasurable human instinct." He added with great enthusiasm: "The Sexual Revolution was a success! . . . We all won it!"

Oh, the enthusiasm of the convert. In fact, the Western sexual revolution was nothing new: in many ways, it merely returned us to the status quo of many exploitative pagan cults. Condoms, pills and new abortion methods make promiscuity less costly, but in all other regards the world has "been there, done that" countless times before. A "new" solution to the ancient quandary "can't live with 'em, can't live without 'em" is among the selling points of almost every new ideology. Each age calls us to the isle of our idyllic fantasy, whether a Platonic retreat, like Augustine's bachelor commune, or the staging grounds for Rajneeshian orgies. Yet most sects create sex from which civilization in its resilience recovers, rather than profits, and the same, I will argue, is true of the modern sexual revolution. But Jesus, I will argue, is the true liberator of our sexual nature, freeing men, women, and children, straight and gay, to be more fully human and to truly love those around them.

The Legacy of the Sexual Revolution

We all won the Sexual Revolution? How about our children?

In 1930, Bertrand Russell advised doing away with the family as an obsolescent and "uneconomical" entity. He said people who "understand the modern scientific attitude towards children" must take upon themselves "a grave responsibility of propaganda" for the rearing of children by an enlightened state. "At present the state," he added, "except in Russia is in the grip of moral and religious prejudices which make it totally incapable of dealing with children in a scientific manner."[8]

The Russian experiment in "scientific" child-rearing ended badly. Sergei

Kourdakov was raised by the state in a Soviet orphanage, and his experience seems to have been typical:

> Ivan Chernega, my good friend, was to spend years in prison, and Alexandre Lobuzhov had been shot by a firing squad. I was shocked to realize how many of the boys and girls in the home at Barysevo turned out to be criminals, gangsters, or prostitutes. The weak, like Sasha Ognev, died or committed suicide."9

A similar link between the breakdown of the family and the rise in crime in America has often been suggested, though hotly debated. One criminologist suggested that based on his profile of the typical serial killer, that kind of murder was likely to increase as children of divorced parents grow to adulthood. At a meeting I attended in Vancouver, B.C., black preacher and social development pioneer John Perkins told of an informal survey he conducted at a jail in Fort Worth. He asked the men in the institution who had come from a broken home in which their father "was not there for them" to stand. "Of those eighty-four men, eighty stood up."

No doubt divorce is better than sharing a house with a homicidal maniac. Yet a more common model for family breakup is probably the kind of situation Robin Williams and Sally Fields portrayed in the sad and funny comedy, *Mrs. Doubtfire.* After yet another argument, an irresponsible but loving Dad, Robin Williams, is asked by his straight-laced wife to move out. Williams does everything he can to bring his family back together. Failing that, he finds refuge as a children's television host passing on philosophical lessons he learned: "Sometimes Daddies and Mommies get along together better when they're not living together."

To which any smart child will respond, "Hah! You tell me to get along with my sister. You don't accept my excuses when we fight. Now you're moving out and tearing my world apart because you can't get along with Mommy."

Actions speak louder than words. We pass the consequences of our lack of commitment on to our children's children. No longer is it the judge who frightens mothers by threatening to cut their children in two, as Solomon did. Mothers and fathers do that themselves, by abortion, and by divorce.

Childhood innocence was not the only loser of the Sexual Revolution. Intimacy and romance also took a body-blow.

As early as the 1960s, psychologist Rollo May described how the sexual freedom of the era (which he called the "new Puritanism,") had begun to undermine romantic passion and alienate the sexes. "The old Puritans repressed sex and were passionate; our new puritan represses passion and is sexual."10 Even sexual rhetoric had become violent. "The new Puritanism brings with it a depersonalization of our whole language. Instead of making love, we 'have sex,'; in contrast to intercourse, we 'screw'; instead of going to bed, we 'lay' someone or (heaven help the English language as well as our-selves) we 'are laid.'"

"It is not surprising that the new Puritanism develops smoldering hos-tility among the members of our society. And that hostility, in turn, comes out frequently in references to the sexual act itself. We say, 'go f— yourself' or f— you' as a term of contempt to show that the other is of no value whatever beyond being used and tossed aside. The bio-logical lust is here in its *reductio ad absurdum.* Indeed, the word f— is the most common expletive in our contemporary language to express violent hostility. I do not think this is by accident."[11]

Even psychologists, he noted, were telling their married patients to use the same term to describe the sexual act, for fear that a more human term would be "dissimulating." (We wouldn't want to deceive ourselves by pretending we are more than monkeys!)[12]

Can anyone claim that the thirty years of sexual license that have followed Rollo May's remarks have re-humanized or re-romanticized the sexual act? Is it sexual repression which encourages a "gangsta rappa" to talk about "bitches" with the attitude of a Bolshevik terrorist contemplating a rich landlord who has fallen into his hands? Anger and hatred are the fuel of every revolution, and the sexual revolution has proven no exception.

One of the first casualties of war is truth. The world averts its gaze, and repeats the party line. "The sexual revolution has been won! We all won it!"

Is Sex Just an Instinct?

The sexual revolution, like the communist revolution, was greatly influenced by an urge that has grown as the West industrialized and urbanized to "get back to nature." But what is natural to human beings? If monkeys play the field, does it follow that we have no recourse but to do likewise, or that it is healthy to do so?

It seems odd to me that no one at *Time Magazine* would have thought of this, but the mating rituals of monkeys and men do differ in significant respects.

Baboons don't sing about how "love will keep us together," nor write songs about how to "slip out the back, Jack" when it doesn't. Chimpanzees don't walk down aisles in churches and vow, before relatives and God, to be faithful "till death do us part." Nor do we have any evidence that God holds them respon-sible for doing so. The Bible says, "Thou shalt not commit adultery," but ani-mals can't read, and it's reasonable to suppose God knows that.

Monkeys may realize that infidelity leads to violence. But do they also know it leads to venereal disease, unstable relationships, lack of mutual trust, divorce, less educational and economic opportunity, psychological maladjust-ment in the next generation leading to higher rates of crime, and immune deficiency syndromes? Do they carry out comparative studies which tie the stability of civilization to the success of long-term family covenant relationships? For that matter, do they create civilizations?

However it may be for animals, for us, fidelity and infidelity are not merely something we find programmed into our genes, but something we choose. We choose as individuals, and we choose as cultures.

In a book entitled *Sex and Culture,* printed in 1934 (a few years after Margaret Mead's "pathological lies" caught the public eye), Joseph Unwin surveyed the history of the choices societies had made in regard to sex, and the effects those choices had on later generations. He concluded that sexual promiscuity, especially among young women, inevitably led, within a few generations, to a breakdown of the productive vitality of that society. Young men channeled their energies into "getting laid," to use the modern slang, rather than creating things of value for the good of their families. He argued: "Any society in which prenuptial sexual freedom has been permitted for at least three generations will be in a zoistic (primitive, unproductive) cultural condition."

Modern society, being mad about sex, has accepted the argument from instinct without noticing how insulting and untrue to life the assumptions behind it are. Only now, millions of deaths and ruined lives later, are we beginning to notice how absurd this facile slavery to instinct is, and admit that "I want" need not imply "I may" or "I must."

An electric cord is sheathed in plastic. A power line that lights a city is draped from metal pillars hundreds of feet in the air, and the forest cleared around it. A nuclear power plant is confined behind concrete walls and billions of dollars worth of technology. Who can deny that the sexual instinct is a powerful, and potentially dangerous force? More people have died of misdirected passion than of leaking radioactive waste. More have fallen from venereal disease than lightning strikes and even nuclear holocausts. Every powerful force, whether human or natural, can only be harnessed productively and safely by restraining it. Am I the only one to whom "casual sex" sounds like "casual electric wiring" or "casual nuclear engineering?"

Having said that, fear, while useful at times, admittedly lacks staying power to discipline our sexuality on a long-term basis. After all, if salmon knew they were going to die when they swam up the river, would they still go? I think, after a few last, sorrowful bites of luscious ocean shrimp, and a heady drought of intoxicating river water, they would. And I think the evidence shows people will too.

The Bible says, "Perfect love expels fear" (1 John. 4:8). Compassion is stronger than death. Love is gift-giving and self-sacrificing. Our love for our mate and children, present or future, while imperfect, may be enough for most people to maintain purity. "I will do this for her," we can tell ourselves. In addition, Jesus said, "The pure in heart will see God" (Matt. 5:8). Christianity does not propose to direct the flood of passion merely through rules, but through a stronger passion—a higher love, a motive for purity that remains, however trampled or ambivalent human relations become. "I will do this for Him."

Genghis Khan had instincts. Lemmings have instincts. A cat that has drunk a full bowl of milk, sitting on a Persian carpet, has instincts. Civilization is a collection of individuals who live productive lives through the discipline of instinct. The Tang Dynasty of China was the most glorious and balanced period of Chinese history, and poetry her greatest pride. That poetry is full of husbands thinking of wives and children far away, of women looking at the river or moon and thinking of husbands: the productive love in restraint in action. Isn't that also the secret to the energy of the Puritans and Victorians? Unwin claimed that civilizations only remain productive for two generations after abandoning sexual restraint.

The Bible takes away our "freedom," barges into bedrooms with whips (like Jesus in the temple), sending furniture flying and lovers leaping into the streets with towels around their midsections. "This is a holy place," it affirms with passion, against the mating calls of the world. "One man, one woman, one life. Those who are not ready to make the commitment—stay out."

"Puritans!" The world sniffs. Who has reckoned the cost of those sneers? But ironically, pleasure was another thing we lost in the revolution.

Monogamists Make Better Lovers

Recently a survey appeared which canvassed attitudes of Central Americans in regard to adultery. In Costa Rica, adultery was nearly ubiquitous: 90 percent of men and more than 80 percent of woman reported having had an affair at least once. The report went on to note, with an air of having passed on to an interesting but rather mystifying piece of data, that while the people of Costa Rica were the most promiscuous, they enjoyed the act of sex less than any of the other peoples surveyed. Intercourse only lasted a few minutes, occurred less frequently, and was felt as least pleasurable.

Studies in the United States show the two are related. Monogamously-committed married people do derive more pleasure from sexuality than "swinging singles." The studies which prove this have not been widely reported or entered into the national consciousness as have famous (and spurious) surveys purporting to prove the opposite, such as Margaret Mead's South Sea island fantasy. (As the saying goes, a lie can get half way around the world while the truth is still putting on its boots.)

Glenn Stanton, *in Why Marriage Matters,* showed that, according to the most comprehensive research data in the United States, the National Health and Social Life Survey (NASLS), people who stick to their marriage vows have better quality and frequency of sexual relations than anyone else. "Conservative

Protestant married women" were happiest of all with their sexual life.[13] The authors of the survey summarized:

> "The public image of sex in America bears virtually no relationship to truth . . . in real life, the unheralded, seldom-discussed world of married sex is actually the one that satisfied people the most."[14]

Stanton argued that free physical expression was easiest in a long-term atmosphere of mutually-verified trust. He noted that only three percent of marriage partners who never had sex before marriage had extramarital affairs. Divorce and venereal disease were more common among those who cohabited before marriage than among those who had not. Live-in lovers had quarrels more often and more violently than married couples. He concluded, "The best sex—wild, passionate, real sex—is reserved for the couple who experiences it exclusively within the safe harbor of a lifelong, monogamous relationship. Only in this relationship are there no dangers, and the married partners can abandon themselves to each other."

Hollywood appears to be wrong: John Walton knows more about having a good time than James Bond. The Enlightenment philosophers were even more wrong, as Paul Johnson describes in a critical series of snapshot (or drive-by) biographical sketches entitled *Intellectuals*. Rousseau, prophet of the natural life, was one of the most pathetic creatures to ever crawl the earth: he treated his mistress like a slave, and while writing popular theories of child-rearing, sent his own five children at birth to an institution where, on average, two out of three young inmates died within the first year. Shelley, Russell, and Sartre treated every promise they made, and nearly every woman they met, with the same contempt, leaving wrecked lives in their wake as they traveled the world telling it how to improve on the *Tao*. The Bible was right even in insisting that the rewards of right living are not limited to the couple but spread out as a blessing to society and future generations:

> "First-time, lifelong, monogamous marriage is the relationship that best provides for the most favorable exercise of human sexuality, the overall well-being of adults, and the proper socialization of children. Marriage has no close rival. It stands independently above any other option singleness, cohabitation, divorce, and remarriage."[15]

By contrast, as another observer put it, "The sex-obsessed society unhesitatingly breaks both divine and human laws, . . . Like a torpedo, it leaves in its path a legion of corpses, a multitude of wrecked lives, an untold amount of suffering, and an ugly debris of broken standards. It destroys the real freedom of normal love, and in lieu of enriching and ennobling the sexual passion, it reduces it to mere copulation."[16]

East Meets West

How does the Sexual Revolution relate to the teachings of other religions on sexuality?

Growing up in the Sixties, I found myself caught between two competing ways of viewing human sexuality. One was the religion of my parents, which taught that sensual love is a matter between a man and a woman, who forsake all other bonds to "cleave" to one another "for better or for worse, richer or poorer, sickness and health, till death do us part." But our church seemed embarrassed by sex. As Thomas Howard put it, if God asked us our advice, we would have warned against putting such thoughts in peoples' heads. The youth pastor, a lively preacher, was found to have had a series of affairs with the girls in the junior high school group, after which the subject became even more embarrassing.

The world and the church both seemed to associate sex with "wickedness." I found myself caught in the middle. Pretty girls didn't *look* evil. Nor did the accessories the world tried to associate with passion, whiskey, whips, or snake blood, look sexy. G. K. Chesterton wrote that "no restriction on sex seemed so odd and unexpected as sex itself . . . Polygamy is a lack of the realization of sex; it is like a man plucking five pears in mere absence of mind."[17] I never felt that absence of mind: I felt intensely grateful for the existence of beautiful women. But while the restrictions made clear sense, I still felt inclined to pluck.

In the Far East, I discovered four things about sex. First, my own, often half-hearted attempts at purity seemed at times to meet with a cosmic affirmation. Second, I found a certain sexual restraint built into most cultures, even those on whom more "civilized" peoples liked to project their fantasies. Third, this restraint was not a stable thing, but was subject to waves of often religiously-justified sexual liberation. Fourth, almost everywhere Christians were actively helping victims of the sexual oppression which tended to follow in the wake of these revolutions.

One time, I sailed to the tropical island of Hainan alone. The Chinese on Hainan island, like those in other parts of Southern China, cherished a mystique about the tribal peoples around them much like Margaret Mead and her Samoans. "The Li are wild and have no morality," a Han Chinese man told me with a leer. "Be careful with the Li girls—they'll slip poison in your tea cup when you're not looking."

I was worn out from three weeks of travel in the mountains of mainland China. During the ferry ride from Hong Kong, I spent the time chatting with a couple attractive local girls. I arrived at the bus station in the city of Haikou, bought a ticket for a town down the east coast of the island, and sat down, ready to let hormones simmer down. A pretty girl got on the almost-empty bus, looked at her ticket, and sat down next to me. We talked a bit. Then we set off as a tropical storm lashed the darkness around us, bolts of lightning lending a shimmering life to the countryside and reflecting off sheets of rain that poured across the road.

After a while my neighbor began to get sleepy, and leaned on my shoulder. Gravity, or some other force, slowly moved us closer. I began to feel the motion of the bus in two ways, through the motion of my seat and through the motion of the girl. The electricity inside started to match that outside. I shrugged and looked towards the ceiling. (which was being lashed by squalls of rain.) "If I had-n't flirted with those girls on the ferry, I'd have more power of resistance right now. " I prayed. "Still, look at the situation. I don't know another person on this island, and I'll be here for eight days. I didn't ask her to sit here, but here she is."

On top of the bus was a ventilation window flush with the ceiling. It was closed, and filling with water. It suddenly sprang open, spilling a bucket of water on the girl. She looked sheepishly at me and moved to a dry seat a couple rows back. By the time we got off the bus and shared a pedicab to my hotel, the storm was still raging around us, and we both got soaked, but inside I'd dried out and regained control. [18]

Such was the affirmation. I discovered both restraint and revolution among the hill tribes of Asia.

The Chinese of Taiwan also nursed a fantasy about "uninhibited" natives—the Polynesian "hill tribes" who occupied the islands before them. Before industrialization some of these tribes had fairly strict codes about sexu-al conduct, like the virgin cult Margaret Mead exploited in Samoa. (They are in fact related to the Samoans.) But tribal girls were much in demand for broth-els, and many tribal villagers, morally debilitated by the breakup of the old community system and by drink, proved willing to oblige.

When I first moved to Taiwan, a missionary took me for my first visit to "Snake Alley," which I briefly described in the first chapter. Young ladies, many tribal, stood in rows outside several dozen storefronts, with pink neon framing their figures and the bars on the windows, and beckoned at crowds of milling men. The traditional Chinese triad of organized crime, religion, and police (a precinct a block away collected bribes) worked in harmony as they offered the "owners" of the girls their respective forms of protection.

I traveled to the beautiful mountain villages where these girls had been born. I got to know the depressing, dehumanizing alleyways of sex factories where they worked, interviewing relatives, gangsters, and a public health official. I also wrote a series of articles for a Chinese newspaper about the spread of AIDS. I went to Thailand, where I interviewed Christian workers who looked after young prosti-tutes. "In Thailand it's not at all identifiable with homosexuals or drug abusers." They told me. "It's whole villages The girls come down and work as prostitutes and then go home . . . They're afraid of dying. They're terrified of dying."

As a result, while I was as interested in the opposite sex as any young man, the calls and posters in the Red Light district had a different effect on me from that intended. Some days these faces seemed to call into question the whole enterprise of sex. Cheap sex was not, in this neighborhood, the product of any modern sexual revolution, but part of the ambivalent religious and social heritage of Asia.

Let us take a closer look at that heritage.

The Sexual Revolutions of Man

Karen Armstrong thinks the ideal of the "guru" in Hinduism, a man who is "higher than the gods," was a "remarkable assertion of the value of humanity" and "the great religious insight of the subcontinent." Many feminists have taken up Hinduism and Buddhism, or worship of "the goddess" in her various eastern and western incarnations (Kali, Aphrodite, Yao Chi Jin Mu, etc.), to express their rejection of "patriarchal" western religion. Yet India, land of the god-men, has the distinction of being one of the only countries in the world where life expectancy is lower for women than for men.[19] While some female gurus, like Mother Meera, have done well, and may help to feminize Indian religion, some western women who came to India as spiritual pilgrims have been disappointed. One remarked caustically after visiting Sai Baba: "Have you ever noticed that during *darshan* only 10 percent of Sai Baba's time is spent among women? And you never see women up on the platform with the all-important men."[20] Another complained at the Dali Lama's retreat in the Himalayas, "for many women practicing today, one of the greatest obstacles remains the absence of clear female role models and foremothers in the Buddhist literature and scripture. It is still a truism that all major teachers, lineage holders, and masters down the ages have been men."[21]

This seems naive to me. Those who have taught reincarnation generally viewed women as less-evolved beings. Why should anyone condescend to learn from someone not even spiritually advanced enough to be born as a man? Buddha himself is said to have demanded that "A nun, though she be a hundred years old, must reverence a monk, rise on meeting him, salute him with clasped hands and honor him with her respects, although he may have been received into the order only that day."[22]

A chapter in the Buddhist sutra *Book of Discipline* pointedly called *Defeat* reflects the fact that rather than channeling the river of sexuality into productive modes, early Buddhism tried to dam, if not damn, it altogether. The chapter tells how a monk named Sudinna went to visit his wife and parents. Worried about not having any heirs to carry on the family name, her parents told her to adorn herself with two piles of gold, and try to seduce him. This she did, and after a long and tedious temptation, she conceived a son. In remorse, he became "haggard, wretched, of bad color, yellowish, the veins showing all over his body, melancholy, of sluggish mind, miserable, depressed, repentant, weighed down with grief."[23]

Buddha upbraided his disciple as follows: "Foolish man, is not *dharma* taught by me for the waning of passion . . . the destruction of the pleasures of the senses . . . It were better for you, foolish man, that your male organ should enter the mouth of a terrible and poisonous snake, than that it should enter a woman . . ."[24] The author, of a cataloguing turn of mind, then put a long and (one hopes) exhaustive list of sexual taboos in the mouth of Buddha. Other than masturbation, which earned a slightly lighter punishment, every other sexual act of the author's diverse and perverse imagination earned precisely the same painful penalty as making love to one's wife.

After more than a thousand years of compromising with the culture around them, and with human nature, under the influence of Tantric Hinduism, some Buddhists adopted a radical "new" sexuality which intentionally went to the opposite extreme from that of primitive Buddhism. Tantric gurus claimed enlightenment could most effectively be attained through "consort practice," a ceremonial union of male and female that connected one to the source of all power in the universe. (Founders of esoteric cults, such as Rajneesh, David Berg, and Lu Sheng-yen, continue to follow in their footsteps.) In Tibet, the sexual revolution brought about by esoteric Buddhism got out of hand, however. Medieval Tibet re-interpreted bizarre acts described in tantric scriptures as symbolic, and returned in theory to the doctrine of monastic celibacy. I say in theory, because hundreds of years later, the Chinese complained about religious orgies among powerful Tibetan priests in the capital. Even in modern times, it has been reported that venereal disease was the biggest medical problem in monastery-dominated pre-communist Tibet, and young women were at the mercy of men. The pendulum set in motion by Siddhartha's radical rejection of sexuality swung back and forth throughout the centuries, seldom coming to a point of balance.

The *Analects* of Confucius have little to say about women. Confucius clearly saw girls as a distraction from more important things: "I have never met a man who cares as much for virtue as for beautiful women."[25] But I do not think Confucius should be blamed, as he often is, for the double standard which sprang up in his name in later centuries.

Lao Zi used gender as a metaphor for and example of his paradoxical philosophy of the weak overcoming the strong. "Keep to the role of the female," he advised, and called the *Tao* the "Mother of the myriad creatures." But Lao Zi and Zhuang Zi, the founders of Taoism, had even less to say than Confucius explicitly on the subject of relations between the sexes. One extremely popular sexual ideology usually related to Taoism was a theory similar to Tantric Hinduism and Buddhism, trying to lengthen life through sex with as many young women as possible. Other Taoist sects went to the opposite extreme, and forbid even the sin "to speak or walk about with a woman alone."[26]

The *Qur'an* proposed a sexual morality which was neither especially strict nor especially lax for its day, yet did not strike a very attractive balance, either. One shouldn't force one's slave girl to act as a prostitute. The God of Mohammed demanded modesty, and that one marry women (the reader is assumed to be male) who are Muslims or at least not hostile to the faith. "And let those who find not the means to marry be abstinent till God enriches them."[27]On the other hand, Allah makes it clear that men should "manage the affairs of women, for God has preferred one of them over another . . . Righteous women are therefore obedient . . . And those you fear may be rebellious admonish, banish them to their couches, and beat them."

It is striking that men with as diverse theologies as Mohammed (a monotheist), Joseph Smith (who taught a modified polytheism), and Hong Xiuquan (who called himself the younger brother of Jesus) all said God directly and specifically revealed they were to marry more wives than their followers. Some revolutionary sects, under the charismatic force of the leader's personality, go to both extremes at once: absolute chastity for the masses, and unbridled pleasure for the leaders. Hong segregated foot soldiers in his army and penalized fraternization between the sexes. Mao Zedong, Jim Jones, and David Berg are among the cult leaders who have emulated him in these regards in the twentieth century.

The book *Tread Upon the Lion* tells the story of the stocky young pioneer missionary from Canada, Tommy Titcombe, who worked among the polygamous Yagbas in Nigeria. Once, traveling to a new village to preach his message, he invited the villagers to meet at the chief's hut. After a long wait, he looked at the crowd of men who had gathered, and asked the chief. "We invited all the people. Where are your women?"

"We are the people," the chief replied with casual arrogance. "The women are just animals."

It seems to me there is some causal relationship between polygamy and such disrespect for women. Polygamy creates a vicious cycle. Rich men despise women. Women pass their frustration to children. The only recourse for poor men without families is bloodshed. It is striking how young men in the inner cities, who share the same "winner-take all" and matriarchal approach to mating, recreate the rituals and violence of primitive tribes.

The Biblical book of beginnings, *Genesis*, describes how God created man and woman "and the two became one." A couple chapters later it relates that a character named Lemech married two wives. The Old Testament allowed but did not encourage polygamy. The New Testament restored monogamy as the standard, not only to Christendom, but indirectly to the whole world.

Jesus, the Sexual Liberator

More than words, the essence of leadership lies in actions. One's life creates an aura of influence over one's followers, whether in a temple, cabinet, or family.

Feminists leaders often support politicians who affirm "women's issues" (especially abortion) no matter how shabbily they treat their wives and lovers. One wonders when such women are going to connect the dots and see the pattern. This is bad strategy, as well as bad ethics, because people are more influenced by a leader's actions than by his words. The second great philandering American president of the twentieth century was a great admirer of the first; why are we surprised he treated his wife so poorly? It is as reasonable for a philandering politician to favor abortion as for a burglar to favor the manufacture of quality gunny sacks.

Jesus did not propose any very radical sexual innovation. He affirmed marriage as the foundation of society. He agreed with Jewish interpretations of the *Song of Solomon*, the poetry of the prophets, and tantric Indian religion, by saying that sex could be a symbol of the union between the soul and God. But pointing to Old Testament precedent, he argued that only the lifelong union of man and woman (not sex alone, as in the tantric ritual) was a valid symbol of that union. Asked about divorce, he quoted *Genesis'* "the two shall be one flesh," and explained, "What God has joined, let not man divide" (Mark 10:8-9). He did not argue with his religion's strictures on adultery or homosexuality. Even when he warned against lust, he was echoing the patriarch Job.

Nevertheless, Jesus radically improved human sexuality. How? Mostly by the power of example. Jesus didn't patronize women. Nor did he fear them. He didn't hide their faces to save himself from temptation and claim it was because the opposite sex couldn't control themselves, as Mohammed did a few centuries later. He didn't betray his followers' trust. Nor did he use spiritual authority to establish a harem. Most remarkably, Jesus didn't even ignore females in the interest of propriety. In the New Testament, one finds instead a remarkable series of dignity-enhancing encounters between Jesus and the women of Palestine. He confronts loose-living women he met, as well as encouraging and forgiving them. He challenges the faith of a mother who lost her son as well as having mercy on her. He allows a repentant women to stoop while the Pharisees (and, no doubt, the feminists in the crowd) scoffed at them both. He praised her for doing "something beautiful for God." (A phrase Mother Theresa took to heart.) He shocks his disciples by talking with immoral women, and shocked the women even more by looking them in the eye and lovingly but firmly calling them to God. He mourns for pregnant women even as he carries his cross, and remembers the needs of his mother while he is dying.

M. Scott Peck points out that because his role as a psychiatrist is like that of a parent, if he were to enjoy sexual gratification with one of his patients, he would forfeit the parenting role required of a healer. He said he could not conceive of a situation in which such contact would be helpful to his patients. Jesus treated every woman he met with an ennobling and therapeutic love.

The Marxist complaint that religion is the "opiate of the people" has been retooled by contemporary feminists and applied to the church. "What the Bible has to say about women is horrendous," one person argued, pointing to passages in the apostolic writings which say women should stay quiet in church, that woman was created "for man," that women should submit to their husbands. Karen Armstrong asserts that while Jesus and Mohammed allowed women more freedom than they enjoyed before, church fathers made their teachings a tool of misogyny and patriarchy later. While feminists ascribed eastern misogyny to particular gurus, in the case of Christianity, Armstrong thought she saw the link between theory and practice: "A religion that teaches its followers to regard their humanity as chronically flawed" is naturally going to be harmful to sexual expression.[28] According to both Marxists and feminists, it was the Enlightenment and the modern humanist spirit that finally brought true emancipation of women.

It seems to me the opposite complaint, made by Nietzche, is more plausible: the Bible was on the whole an instrument not of the strong against the weak, but of the weak against the strong. More often, women used the New Testament to keep men in *their* place—for the good of society.

Paul, who never married, proposed a near equality of the sexes, and affirmed married sex, in a way which was quite radical for the Roman and even the Jewish world. The Bible has a great deal to say against sex before marriage and outside of marriage, but in only one place does it talk about sex within marriage: "Do not deprive each other" (1. Cor. 7:5). Thomas Cahill suggests that Paul was the first person in history to insist on the basic equality of the sexes. In passing, Paul noted that most of the other apostles of Jesus were married and took their wives with them on the road.

According to sociologist Rodney Stark, Christianity won the West largely because of its dramatically kinder treatment of women. Stark argued that Christian women married later and had more choice in their marriages than most Roman women. (The same contrast has been noted between Christians and Muslims in modern Africa.) Christianity rejected the Roman double standard whereby women were expected to be chaste, but men allowed to play the field. Christian women were not forced to abort or abandon their babies, as was common in the Greco-Roman world. "By prohibiting all forms of infanticide and abortion, Christians removed major causes of the gender imbalance that existed among pagans."[29] The ratio of women in the church increased both through birth and because of the attraction Christianity held for women because of the "far higher" status they held in the Church. "Women held positions of honor and authority within early Christianity,"[30] unlike contemporary Roman or even (which was already better) Jewish culture.

It is true European Christianity was later influenced by a pagan view of the body as prison-house of the soul, which may have ultimately derived from Buddhism. St. Augustine, after repenting of the licentiousness of his youth, seemed to assume that a serious Christian was a celibate Christian. He left mistress and lovers and founded a bachelor commune, which acted as prototype for Western monasteries.

By nature men have this power over women: not so much that men are physically stronger, but that women are bound more closely to children. The fathers of the Enlightenment also tended to be fathers of illegitimate children. The humanism these men created, by loosening the bonds between men and women, and between women and children, sometimes put women back in the shackles from which Jesus came to free them.

In 1988 a survey of the status of women around the world was published by the Population Crisis Committee. The survey revealed wide differences in the position of women in various countries. In Marxist-feminist fashion, the cause of those differences was interpreted in the press, and to a degree in the paper itself, as owing to economic disparities:

> "The status of women varies enormously from one part of the world to another . . . In the least developed countries of Africa, the Middle East, Asia and Latin America, crushing poverty (and) discrimination create living conditions for women almost too harsh to imagine for women in Western industrialized countries."[31]

But what really determines the status of women more: economics, or belief? The survey solicited information in regard to four categories: employment, education, marriage and children, and health. Of the countries that ranked among the ten highest in any of these four categories, all but one (Taiwan, third highest in the category of "marriage and family"), thirty-nine out of forty, had a Christian heritage. Among the countries near the bottom of the scale in any category, not a single one with a Christian heritage appeared.[32] The twelve countries for which the cumulative scores were highest, all had a Christian background, including five relatively-poor Eastern-Bloc countries. Among the twelve countries with the lowest scores, three, Saudi Arabia, Libya, and Kuwait, were rich but Muslim. The data was consistent to a rare and striking degree. All the countries appraised as assigning women the highest status had been deeply influenced by the teachings of the New Testament. This was true of none of those which treated women the most shabbily.[33]

Muslim states have rejected Christian influence more completely than any others. The bastion of Islam, Saudi Arabia, one of the richest countries in the world, where Christianity is completely prohibited, came second to last, right before poor Bangladesh, on the Population Crisis Committee's list.

Even the relative positions of non-Christian countries could be explained in terms of the degree to which each culture resisted or accepted the social input of nineteenth and twentieth century Christian missions. While thinking it odd that one of the world's most wealthy and socially-aware societies, Japan, was not on any of the "good" lists, one might suppose the nation escaped all the "bad" lists by virtue of 120 years of economic progress. But how in fact did the position of women improve in Japan? Schools for women were introduced to Japan by missionaries. Before Christian influence, Japanese women had so few rights that if a prostitute ran away from her brothel, the police brought her back. In 1900, William Booth's Salvation Army led a parade of believers and journalists through the red light district in Tokyo, pounding drums and singing songs. Three hundred gangsters attacked them, beat them up, and smashed their musical instruments. The press printed the story, and that was the straw that broke the camel's back and led to increased freedom for Japanese geisha girls. But even a hundred years later, confronted by the fact that Japan had become the world's leading producer of child pornography, it took the threat of international embarrassment and the prodding of a Catholic priest for Japan to take any action.

Confucius was among the kindest and most sensible of philosophers, but what we call "Confucianism" increasingly became a tool by which the powerful oppressed the weak, even within families. In the early twentieth century, the great Chinese reformer Hu Shi noted with bitter hyperbole the role Christianity played in liberating Chinese women:

> "'Let women serve as oxen and horses.' This saying is not sufficient to describe the cruelty and meanness with which Chinese have treated women. We 'let women serve as oxen and horses,' put on yokes, wear saddles, and as if that were not enough, spurs and horse shoes, then chased them out to work! Our holy Scriptures were of no saving value. For a thousand years, Confucian philosophers talked about love and benevolence day after day, yet never noticed the cruel and inhumane treatment of their mothers and sisters.

> "Suddenly from the West a band of missionaries arrived. Besides preaching, they also brought new customs and new ways of looking at things. They taught us many things, the greatest of which was to look at women as people."[34]

Some might reply that Western missionaries were simply representatives of a culture which had embraced the Enlightenment. They were proselytizing not so much Christian values, as values which had become common to progressive Europeans and Americans. But I think this argument underestimates the influence of the Bible on such reform, and also the quickness with which that consciousness has sometimes been lost without input from the Bible.

I well recall the day that served as an epiphany for me on this subject. I'd just come out of a prayer visit to Snake Alley, and was feeling disoriented and tired. I'm not much of a shopper at the best of times, and found Taiwanese markets in

PART II: THE WAY

flesh even worse. Nobody smiled in that neighborhood. As I exited the alley, I saw two healthy-looking young American men, carrying big black books. I was hoping they were Bibles. Even if they were not Christians, I thought they would at least share enough of the chivalry of Western culture to see these girls as human beings, so I went up to talk with them.

One asked, "Aren't those girls pretty?"

Pretty? With those vacant eyes? Or maybe he hadn't looked at their eyes. "Don't you know some of these girls were sold by their parents when they were fourteen, and have to have sex with thirty men a day?" I asked.

"Oh, yes," he replied, not at all put out. "Some are even younger."

The fact that he could look me in the eye and cheerfully affirm the crushing and betrayal of a little girl, made short work of my racial bigotry. At that moment, for all our shared cultural history, I realized they were one with the degraded environment.

Mormonism gives us another reason to see the sexual freedom of the West as a precarious thing. Besides reintroducing polygamy, Joseph Smith proposed that women would be pregnant in heaven eternally. That is if their husbands (busy with other wives) let them in: women needed male permission to enter paradise.

The survey did show, however, that not all sexual revolutions in the West entirely jettisoned the higher view of women Jesus modeled for us. Stalin and Mao were predators in the sexual as well as political sense. But in the East communist revolutionaries took over the role of liberating prostitutes and combating foot binding and widow-burning from the missionaries they evicted. In India the communist party allied itself with Christians and enlightened Hindus in a fight against widow burning and child prostitution which continues to this day.

It may still be possible to build a case that the Christian church is inherently misogynist. In most conservative Christian churches, women are not allowed to serve as priests. One can trace this restriction to Paul's infamous admonition against women speaking in church, whatever he meant by it, since he also spoke kindly of colleagues who were female. The fact that Jesus chose only male disciples is often brought up in this context. But this strikes me as proof of how misguided and petty the whole argument is, no matter the merits of the specific points feminists or misogynists may make. Jesus chose only male disciples, true, but it is a far greater and more enduring fact that Jesus treated women with a dignity, respect, and understanding that no other religious figure has ever shown. Plato thought women half the value of men. Mohammed, Bagwan Shree Ragneesh, Joseph Smith, Rasputin, and David Koresh created theologies to justify sexual exploitation. Martin Luther King Jr. had difficulty treating women with respect in his personal life. Even the great Mahatma Gandhi was in the practice of sleeping with twelve year old girls (only sleeping) so as to develop sexual discipline. Was sharing a bed with an old man, no matter how saintly, really the ideal discipline for developing the spiritual and social health of the young women involved? Or a good example for those with less restraint?

Observe, by contrast, the extraordinary balance, sanity and courage by which Jesus interacts with the women in his life. Jesus' love was of the healing kind. He was not afraid of women, nor was he afraid of himself around women. Whenever the common people have been able to read the records of his life, women have enjoyed the benefits of his liberating and ennobling love, teaching and elevating, setting women free from the evils of suti, footbinding, polygamy, and forced prostitution . . . and most of all, setting an example of what it really means for men to love women.

"Did God Make Gays?"

To many it seems arrogant and cruel that orthodox Christians, Buddhists and Muslims continue to insist that a sexual act between two people of the same sex is a sin. Homosexuals tell us their "sexual preference" is a fact about themselves they can't change, like skin color or personality. In fact, many deny homosexuality is their preference in the first place. Mel White, who worked as ghost writer for several well-known Christian leaders until he came out as gay, tells how he tried to deny his sexual nature in conformity with what Christians told him was right, trying to "cast out" evil desires, cure them through "inner healing," fast them away, get married and hope a "normal" sex life would drive those demons away or smother them. When none of this worked, he tried to kill himself.[35]

When a Washington state legislator tried to institute a law against promoting homosexuality in schools, one "appalled" observer wrote to the Seattle Post Intelligencer complaining that the man "hasn't a clue about what drives a person's sexuality."

> "Sexuality, like ethnic origin, skin color, hair color, eye color, net value of parents' estates and place of birth, is not one of those things about which a person has a choice."

But of course, while I can't call in a computer programmer and have him rewire the sexual circuitry of my brain, I do have a choice about what I input on a day-to-day basis. To put it in Buddhist terms, at every moment I can "create karma" by my views, aspirations, speech, conduct, mode of livelihood, effort, mindfulness, and what I take pleasure in. I have a choice what I watch. I have a choice where I live. I have a choice with whom to make friends, where to entertain myself, with whom to spend the evening, where to touch, what to take off or leave on, and when to go home at night.

"Sexuality" is the sum total of our choices and the raw material it acts upon. As for the raw material, it no doubt is a complex phenomenon, influenced by genetics (whether or not there is a single "gay gene") as well as upbringing, environment, and emotional needs. But we must not forget this distinction between desire and behavior, for it is the basis for all clear moral and psychological thinking.[36]

Dr. Nada Stotland, head of the American Psychiatric Association's board, explaining the board's reversal from an earlier position favoring the treatment of homosexuality, argued, "All the evidence would indicate this is the way people are born. We treat disease, not the way people are. The very existence of therapy that is supposed to change peoples' sexuality is harmful because it implies that they have a disease."[37]

With all respect, I find this false to my own experience as a sexual being. Behavior can be modified, mental and social habits can be trained and channeled, and even sexual feelings are in part malleable. And if Dr. Stotland is right, why should anyone go to a psychiatrist with any sexual or other addiction? A pedophile, or rapist could just as easily say, "This is the way I was born. It's not a disease—it's the way I am."[38] Or someone like me, who is married to one woman but may find himself attracted to others at times, or anyone else whose appetites are not affirmed by moral majoritarianism. The gay-bashing murderers of Matthew Shepherd could hire a psychiatrist to say the same, no doubt. "This is the way they were born. The human animal, especially in its young male form, is aggressive and violent by nature." And the psychiatrist would be right. In a sense, we are all "natural born killers." But not all of us are guilty of murder.

Religion begins with the premise that we are not robots. If we are going to justify homosexuality, let us at least do so in such a way that allows us to remain human. The point of spiritual exercises, whether walking across burning coals in bare feet or fasting on a mountain top, is not to be mastered by our bodies, but to learn to master them. From any responsible point of view, "I want" need not imply "I may."

The gay community tends to picture the world as containing two kinds of people, "straight" whom society affirms, and "gay" whom it commands, "go and be celibate." But reality is both more complicated and more simple.

Our sexual natures are more complex, because there are all sorts of temptations besides homosexuality. Many religious people never marry, and remain celibate. Others lose a spouse. Many feel attractions nearly every day for beautiful members of the opposite sex. Every human being has sexual desires which, if they want to live a productive life, they need to suppress or divert most of the time.

The universality of sexual temptation also makes the problem simpler than the contrast between straight and gay would have it. In the end, we're all in the same boat. There are no "straights" and "gays," we're all human beings, and therefore somewhat crooked. Men who want men, or women who want women, or men who want someone else's woman, aren't special cases. Other people have desires too. The person who "needs" children or gets a kick out of using force may also say, truthfully enough, that the warp in his spirit was caused by forces beyond his control. Every one of us is responsible for living a life of purity. Whether to unload bad karma, keep out of jail, or please God, we squelch most of our desires most of the time. Such "repression" does not destroy us, though it may feel like a kind of death at the time, but keeps us alive.

We are responsible for what we do. No matter how many times we fail, the only path to liberation and self-command lies in holding onto this truth. Whether making passionate love, taking an extra chocolate, or robbing my employer of a million dollars, if the light goes on in the next room, I suddenly discover the power to pull my hand back from the cookie jar. This proves I had that power all along, though I didn't want to admit it. Even in this life, our normal, healthy instincts destroy us if we let them. So we tell them to pipe down. Take a cold shower. Walk away. "Just say no." Whatever it takes to keep out of the hospital and in the good esteem of our friends. We may not be able to change our desires, but we can change both what we think about and what we do, if we really want to.

Regardless of the psychological origins or comparative strength of homosexual feelings, Christianity tells us the act is wrong. It is wrong biologically, for the obvious reason. It is wrong medically, because even before AIDS, sexual acts between men (especially) were an epidemiologist's nightmare.[39] It is wrong psychologically. The release and sense of freedom a person may feel when they come "out of the closet" may be exhilarating. So might Buddha have felt when he walked away from his father's palace, or a soldier from a sentry post. But abandonment of responsibility works against true spiritual growth in the end.

Also, homosexuality is wrong, Christians believe, because God forbids it.

Is this fanatical? Cruel? Hateful? Certainly many gays can tell horrendous tales of the cruel way their families, sometimes with Christians at the lead, have treated them after they "came out." People talk about the cruelty with which Christians have treated homosexuals, and who can help but cringe that feels the heart of Christ? But people forget the other side of the coin. People forget that the moral strictures of the Bible had a public health as well as an ethical function. Not all of us "won" the sexual revolution; it had casualties. Now that the crest of the wave has passed, I think about those who so nonchalantly swept aside the old standards and persuaded those with homosexual feelings to "come out of the closet"—the Fletchers, the Gordas, the Cantors. I realize this is not itself a strong argument against homosexuality—the world suffers many diseases, and not all of them pick on sinners more than saints. But do they ever permit themselves to reflect that if the old prejudices had been given more respect, thousands might be alive today who are now dead or dying? Mel White admitted he had seldom been treated with anything but love by Christians, yet in his autobiography he compared the religious right to Nazis, and spoke wistfully of the lost sexual pleasures of his youth. Is it insignificant to him that apart from the moral strictures of his church, he would probably be dead by now? There are thousands of people like White who are alive who would not be apart from the Christian teaching on homosexual practice. And there are thousands now dead who would not have died had they not accepted the teaching of the sexual revolutionaries. America will have proven to have paid a higher price in young lives for this great new liberty than for any other—a liberty not mentioned in the Constitution, nor by any of the great religions. Who speaks with anger on behalf of these martyrs?

I talked with a woman who had helped start a church in the gay district of San Francisco before the AIDS epidemic. I don't think I'll ever forget what she said.

"When I think about it, it scares my socks off. I can picture faces . . . they are no longer alive. I can think of people who we ministered to who went back into that lifestyle—they're almost all dead. We were there just before it began. The ones who came out of it are still alive."

I know in today's America the idea of saying "no" to one's desires seems very strange. I know we prefer to invent insatiable appetites; it is the basis of our economy. But most of the world has always recognized self-denial as the beginning of what it means to be human. I bet there are many homosexuals who wish with all their hearts that the world around them would support rather than undermine them as they try to "just say no," who have been trapped by the tolerance and encouragement of society in a pit that seems to have no exit. Society tells them, "if it feels good, do it," and when they dropped like flies, society cried crocodile tears and built quilts for the martyrs.

Jesus had a warning not just for gays or for those who sleep around, but for anyone who "looks lustfully at a woman" (Matt. 5:28). People laughed when President Jimmy Carter admitted to this "sin." But here too, the Christian standard, while hard, shows reason and consistency. A weed isn't gone until its roots are dead. Jesus reminds those to whom the straight or restrained lifestyle comes naturally, the so-called "moral majority," that they, too, need divine help and forgiveness from a God who demands "purity in the inmost part." Christianity picks a path between promiscuity and abstinence, between chauvinism and feminism, between loneliness and loss of self in the group. It's a tough path, one which we need the help of God to walk.

A Christian should be the last to divide people into a "moral majority" and an immoral minority. One Christian responded to a doubter's demand that he define the Christian message in ten words or less with a more Biblical aphorism: "We're all bastards, but God loves us anyway."[40] The true Christian scheme is a vast immoral majority and a moral minority of one. We ride on his coat tails.

I cannot afford to look down on any human being. Few days pass that I do not break the strict standards of Jesus. At the same time, I cannot deny those standards. I can't simply say, "Nature has evolved a tremendous desire to perpetuate the species. This is the way I am because God made me this way. I've tried to cast the demons out, but they keep coming back. It's the woman's fault. It's the snake's fault. It's God's fault." Neither the Bible, nor society nor reason allows excuses on these grounds, for the simple reason that we know we are not animals or robots. Even our excuses prove our own humanity; animals don't need them.

Pragmatic Western society finds the teachings of more "practical" moralists like psychologist Pamela Cantor more to its taste:

> "This is the kind of worthwhile information I would want my daughter to hear: Sex without feelings . . . is fairly worthless . . . Making out is often just as much fun as having sex . . . If you do have sex with someone, protect yourself from disease and pregnancy . . . Avoid anyone who might hurt you, and do not hurt or use anyone else."[41]

At that, I can only shake my head and, paraphrasing the old-fashioned professor in C. S. Lewis' *Lion the Witch, and the Wardrobe,* "What are they teaching them in psychology schools these days?" Making out is as much fun as sex? Making out is sex, in the early stages, and serves the sole biological function of preparing body and mind for what is to come. Do not "use" anyone? But if you're only having sex for "fun" and warm "feelings," you are using the other person. Getting what you can with no commitment and the kind of feelings that turns to contempt the morning after, when you find yourself faced with a human being instead of a fantasy, how do you avoid hurting him or her?

Sex is the passion that causes salmon to swim up waterfalls. It builds civilizations and tears them down. It causes men and women to risk both body and spirit. "Making out is almost as fun as sex!" Try containing a forest fire with a garden hose!

Maybe the West needed a breath of the more cheerful sort of paganism to yank us out of a Manichean loathing of the body. Unlike our grandparents, we are not obliged to swim in clothing down to our ankles. Human sexuality can be discussed freely. Even Reader's Digest prints the word SEX in large letters so near-sighted Republican housewives shopping at Safeway will pick it up. Who really wants to go back to the days when the word was taboo? But in significant ways, we all lost the Sexual Revolution. We lost as a civilization, as families, as individuals trying to sort the elements of our being into an integrated and coherent whole. We lost as romantics and as sexual beings. People with aberrant desires lost. And women stand to lose most of all. Well, I'll take that back; our kids are losing even more.

One man came out of the desert teaching that men may marry five wives so long as they treat them with equal kindness, except for himself, called to marry fourteen. He is hailed as a prophet. Another left his wife and young son, leading disciples in a "great renunciation" of all earthly passion. He is called the Enlightened One. Another holed up in his palace with a thousand wives. He is remembered for his wisdom—in other things. The "great American religion" of Mormonism revolted against monogamy, with its founder marrying fifty or more women, teaching that women will be permanently pregnant in heaven. Gurus from the subcontinent migrate westward, some gathering harems and Rolls Royces and teaching free love, others taking vows of silence and raising children without a single kind or even harsh word.

It is said all roads lead up the same mountain. It is striking how many and diverse are the sexual paths great religious teachers beat to domestic hell. Chesterton said that when it comes to sex, "Men are born mad." The modern sexual revolution, like those that have gone before it, serves mostly to prove him right. By contrast, the Gospel offers a balanced freedom and healing.

Another tale of the Pacific comes to mind: the true story of *Mutiny on the Bounty*. After the crew rebelled against Captain Bligh and took over the ship, they recruited some Polynesian women, and a few men, and set out for a remote island called Pitcairn. Fletcher Christian founded an egalitarian society. There they spent their days reveling in freedom from authority, sexual license, and the natural state: drinking, fighting, murdering one another, and oppressing the Polynesians so badly that they finally rose in revolt. After four years, only four of the nine mutineers remained alive. Then one fell off a cliff drunk, another was put to death for his violent ways, and a third died of asthma. When it looked as if they were going to accomplish everything the harshest British justice might have and more, the last remaining Englishman began to read the ship's Bible. This was the beginning of a new life for the little English-Polynesian society. So, one hopes, it might be for us as well.

---

[1] Thomas Howard, *Christ the Tiger,* Ignatius Press, 1967, p.85

[2] Margaret Mead, *Coming of Age in Samoa*, William Morrow & Co. 1961, from foreword by Franz Boas

[3] Ibid. p.105

[4] Which she did. In 1983, Derek Freeman published a book which argued Meed knew almost nothing about Samoa and had done a shoddy and inaccurate piece of field work. Later he wrote a second volume arguing that her information had been based on a hoax by two teenage girls, one of whom recanted. Australian Hiram Canton Griffitt, while agreeing the work had been largely a product of fantasy, argued the fantasy was her own: she was a "pathological liar" who betrayed her hosts, not to mention her husband, and patched together her report from the "pillow talk" of her young lover and her own bisexual imagination. One clever Amazon.com reviewer, while not disputing that her study was "questionable in terms of facts," gave the book four (out

of five) stars and recommended it on the grounds that it had "caused the anthropological world of the time to rethink itself." One wonders if he would praise the Catholic Church's treatment of Galileo for a similar accomplishment.

5 Also of five illegitimate and cruelly-abandoned children.

6 James Kennedy and Jerry Newcombe, *What if the Bible Had Never Been Written*, Thomas Nelson, Nashville, 1998, p.26

7 Joseph Fletcher, *Situation Ethics*, Westminster Press, Philadelphia, p.139

8 Bertrand Russell, *Why I Am Not a Christian*, Simon & Schuster, 1957, p. 163.

9 Sergei Kourdakov, *The Persecutor*

10 Rollo May, *Love and Will*, New York, 1968, p.34

11 Ibid., p.48

12 By contrast, Cotton Mather, one of the old Puritans, argued that for "a man to beat his wife was as bad as sacrilege." Elizabeth Pleck notes that the Puritans made laws against wife-beating, and in general, "sided with the weak, the dependent, and the helpless." *Domestic Tyranny: The Making of Social Policy Against Family Violence From Colonial Times to the Present*, Oxford University Press, 1987

13 Glen Stanton, *Why Marriage Matters*, p.193

14 Ibid., p.41

15 Ibid., p.11

16 Ibid., p.53

17 *Orthodoxy*, Doubleday, 1909, 1958, p.57

18 Interestingly, Gandhi noted in his autobiography that several times in his youth he was saved from adultery by what he interpreted as divine intervention.

19 For example, see *Women in the World: An International Atlas*, Simon and Schuster, 1986 in *World Encounter* No.2 1989. This atlas lists mortality rates as being ten percent higher for girls as opposed to boys in India compared with a poor Muslim country, and twenty percent higher than in Peru or Panama, two poor Christian countries.

20 *Spiritual Pilgrims*, p.77

21 Lenore Friedman, quoted by Rodger Kamenetz, *The Jew in the Lotus*, p.219

22 J. Isamu Yamamoto, *The Buddha and What He Taught*, *Christian Research Journal*, Spring/ Summer 1994

23 *Vinayapitaka*, Suttavighanga (Parajika), p.243

24 Ibid., p.244

25 *Analects*, IX-17

26 *San Yuanpin*, from Livia Kohn, *The Taoist Experience*, State University of New York Press, 1993, p.103

27 *The Koran*, translated by Arthur Arberry, Oxford U. Press, 1964, p.356

28 Karen Armstrong, *History of God*, Ballantine Books, 1993, p.124

29 Rodney Stark, *The Rise of Christianity*, Harper San Francisco, 1997, p.99. Stark makes a case that the position of women in a culture or sub-culture is a function of

gender ratio: the early church treated women well, he thinks, because women were in the majority, fueling a virtuous cycle. But he admits this attitude goes back to the earliest New Testament documents, the writings of Paul. It may comfort him to have a sociological explanation at hand, but you only have to read the Gospels to see the source from which Christianity's radical attraction to women really came. Similarly, one might explain the increasing patriarchal character of the church after 400 A. D. as owing to more even demographics in the church, but it was also at this time that the church was diluted by a mass of nominal believers who accepted Christ for ulterior motives and only very indirectly influenced by the example of Jesus.

[30] Ibid. p.109

[31] *Population Briefing Paper, Population Crisis Committee, Country Rankings of the Status of Women; Poor, Powerless and Pregnant,* No.20, June, 1988

[32] War-torn Mozambique was the most ambiguous case. The South-African country, which is fairly evenly divided between Christians and animists, with a tithe of Muslims, ranked fourth highest in the "employment" category, but seventh lowest in the "health" category.

[33] One might quibble with a few of the criteria by which the data were evaluated, that may have shown a feminist or Western bias. Is absolute equality of the work men and women do really the ideal for all women? I am not sure even most women would agree wholeheartedly with this criteria. This detracts little from the overall drift of the data, however.

[34] Gu Weiming, *Jidujiao yu Jindai Zhongguo Shehui*, People's Publishing Co., 1996, p.313

[35] Mel White, *Stranger at the Gate: To be Gay and Christian in America*, Plume, 1994

[36] Another basis for clear and compassionate Christian thinking about the subject of homosexuality is Thomas Schmidt's excellent book, *Straight and Narrow?* Schmidt does an excellent job of applying Paul's admonition to "speak the truth in love" to this subject.

[37] *Seattle Post Intelligencer*, December 12, 1998

[38] And have in fact begun to echo these arguments. See Jeffrey Satinover, *Homosexuality and the Politics of Truth*, p.63

[39] See Jeffrey Satinover, M.D., *Homosexuality and the Politics of Truth*, Baker Books, 1996, chapter 3.

[40] Will Campbell, *Brother to a Dragonfly*, Continuum, 1977, p.220

[41] Pamela Cantor, *USA Today*, January 5, 1990

CHAPTER 5

The Aquarian Revolution

SUNLIGHT FILTERED softly through rustling bamboo and the boughs of graceful poinsettia trees, as saffron-clothed monks padded silently along stone corridors. Hundreds of golden statues of Siddhartha Gautama rose in ascending rows, with a baleful sixty-foot figure at the top which would have overlooked the rest, were his eyes not closed in the bliss of nirvana. The main temple of Light of Buddha Mountain featured thousands more Buddhas contributed by believers, including an enormous seated Buddha facing the entrance. The crowds who came to gawk and worship and the bright lights and gentle music gave the complex something of the atmosphere of a theme park for fairies, a Magic Kingdom where tourists came to meet Maitreya rather than Mickey.

My visit as a young missionary to this center of the Buddhist faith in southern Taiwan revealed a curious blend of the familiar and the exotic, the commanded and the forbidden. A nun ushered me into a reception room where a list of ten rules hung on the wall. "Do not lie . . . do not steal . . . do not commit adultery . . ." Translate it into English and add a call to worship the Supreme God and a proscription on idols, and you could have called it the Ten Commandments and hung it in my church at home. But there was no such call or proscription.

I was introduced to an American graduate student from Berkeley who handed out incense in the main temple and taught students English in the sect's high school. I wondered how an American, indoctrinated from childhood against idolatry, had adjusted to the company of so many "graven images." She found them too few, I learned, as we entered her room, and she knelt in front of a stone figure at the foot of her bed and prayed silently. She'd studied Buddhism in California with other Americans. Some had been reluctant to bow to an idol, not because it was *un-Christian*, but *too* Christian. "They thought it was like worshiping God," she noted apologetically. But, she insisted, those who accurately understood Buddhism realized the idol was only a symbol. "When I worship Buddha I'm really worshiping myself," or, more accurately, the Buddha within. The Light of Buddha lifestyle had begun to feel confining, though, and she was thinking of leaving the temple to study Taoism. "I miss sex and drugs," she told me a bit coyly.

Feeling outnumbered by the idols and her revealing shirt, I left without asking any very critical questions.

On the way out, I noticed blueprints for a new facility planned for the Los Angeles area. It would be called "Come to the West" temple, invoking the intuition on the part of many Asian Buddhists that the Western world was ripe for Asian spirituality.[1]

That belief has been well-corroborated in years since. Within a few minutes walk of a home I lived in when I returned to the United States thirteen years later, I could drop in at a Tibetan Buddhist temple, Hindu ashram, yoga center, Zen meditation class, or Taoist study center. (Conveniently housed in the auditorium of a church of my own denomination.) Bumper stickers on cars in front of me proclaimed, "born-again pagan," "the goddess is alive and magic is afoot," and "my other car is a broom." Both Christian bookstores in our part of town closed, while stores specializing in mystical, New Age, eastern philosophical and occultic topics ran an apparently flourishing business. Works by the Dalai Lama, Daisetz Susuki, Yogananda, Thich Nhat Hanh, Deprek Chopra, and Chuang Zi were filling a mainstream spiritual void.

Interest in socialist paradise evaporated after the fall of the "Evil Empire." The sexual revolution has begun to occasion cautionary reflections in some quarters. But the third revolution against the West's Judeo-Christian heritage, the Aquarian Revolution, has reached a new peak of popularity. As I write this, "Religion and Spirituality" on *Amazon.com* features a selection of books which reflects the same search for a spirituality unfettered by Christian dogma that I had seen among many travelers in Asia: "*God's Funeral,*" by A. N. Wilson, about the fading of Christian orthodoxy in England; a new edition of the *Dao De Jing*, the short, pithy, but enigmatic Taoist classic whose translation seems to serve as a kind of a coming-out exercise for scholars of classical Chinese; a devotional reader for Zen Buddhists; a book on Zen for Jewish readers; a book immodestly called "*The Magic Power of White Witchcraft: Enjoy a life of profound happiness, unbelievable riches, and long-lasting love with the secrets of white witchcraft.*"[2] Finally, "*Spiritual Tourist.*"

The latter might serve as the *Odessey* of the Aquarian generation. Brown gives an intensely introspective tour, "half believing, half doubting" as the Chinese put it, of divine gurus and sacred communes currently in vogue around the world, from Sai Baba to the Divine Mother to the Dalai Lama. In the end, Brown comes to rest in a personalized merger of western skepticism and Buddhist philosophy: "I do not believe in a Redeemer. We must save ourselves, and have faith in that belief . . . Joy is non-attachment. Joy is to be found only in the moment. And in the moment, I feel giddy with joy, knowing even as I feel it, that this, too, will pass."[3]

Unlike Odysseus, and more in tune with most modern seekers, however, while Brown traveled hopefully, his hope seemed to consist less in the arriving than in the journey itself.

The third moral revolution of our time no longer appears as a few pin-pricks of interest on the part of one or two left-over hippies or eccentric scholars, but a vast and still growing shift in Western consciousness.

Thousands of years ago, a ribbon of commerce across Central Asia called the Silk Road brought East and West together. Today, a Silicon Highway, and 747s in place of camels, bring the world together in a dramatic new way. Humankind is becoming one, if not politically, at least as a market of spiritual concepts and philosophical categories. Even in the Middle Ages, Europe vacillated between a dogmatic view of a holy, majestic and distant God, the Sky God transformed into an engine of orthodoxy like Islam, and a mystic view of God revealed through nature and the heart of men and women in a manner not unlike Hinduism or Buddhism. Now we have direct access, in translation and easy travel, to a wealth of interpretations of life which have developed in isolated and "pure" forms for thousands of years as someone else's orthodoxy.

Why are young Westerners attracted to the mystic traditions of Asia as against, say, Islam or Confucianism? Some of it has to do, perhaps, with aesthetics: if opposites attract and familiarity breeds contempt, it is not surprising that westerners find delight in pillars of winding dragons and ponds of blooming lotus, while Japanese scholars sketch cathedrals of Europe. Moralistic Confucianism and dogmatic Islam seem too familiar and confining to serve as a locus of neo-romantic attraction. Our generation may feel a reaction against Marxism and other brands of reductive materialism. We seek a transcendent link to the rest of humankind and current models of nature, a universal cosmology which allows us to connect with truth beyond the confines of our tribal deities. To many, nineteenth century materialism and monotheism both seem narrow, lifeless and anti-scientific. And while we have lost hope of establishing Shangri-la through political or military action, or through free love, many hope to find an escape for their souls from globalized commercialism in some hidden valley, secret ceremony, or ancient lineage of Gnostic teachings.

For the past fifteen years I've indulged a bit of Mick Brown's spiritual tourist fantasy: visiting temples, living among tribal peoples, reading the works of religious revolutionaries, even studying an ancient sacred language or two. I interviewed hundreds of Asians, asking questions like,

"What is the purpose of life?"

"What is the most important virtue and the worst vice?"

"What happens after death?"

I went, though, not as a tourist, but as a missionary. I had doubts but also an underlying belief that the Truth was "out there." Chesterton said the ideal philosophy should allow us to "feel the universe at once as an ogre's castle, to be stormed, and yet as our own cottage, to which we can return at evening."[4] I wanted adventures, but also to come home in one piece afterwards.

A wise traveler prepares before setting out on a trip. He buys a guide-book. He compares hotel prices. He asks if he can drink the water. He gets shots. If he is traveling to unsettled regions, he pays attention to reports of terrorist activity or civil war, and alters travel plans if need be. Why? Because despite a growing permeability of cultural boundaries, the world can still be a complex and sometimes dangerous place.

So can the world of the spirit.

If I met the girl at the Light of Buddha mountain again, I would like to ask her three questions, questions any tourist should consider before going abroad. First, "What are you looking for?" Do you want a pretty postcard, a mandala, a jade Buddha to impress visitors? A heroic adventure? Firm truths on which to settle your heart? Or to somehow combine the adventure of faith with the stability of reason? My second question is, "What dangers are out there?" Considering the history of the twentieth century, let us not dismiss this question too quickly. Third, a practical matter which guidebooks address by printing a list of embassy phone numbers. "Who can you call if you get in trouble?"

Things to Look for in Buddhism

What is the faith that caused an advanced and scholarly civilization to blossom from a warlike kingdom 14,000 feet up on the Tibetan plateau? What power made the Japanese warrior class artists, without ceasing to be warriors? What ideal gave Thich Quang Duc courage to burn himself alive during the Vietnam War to protest the destruction of his land?

Buddha's life story pulses with eternal personal as well as social relevance. Leaving his father's palace, Buddha first saw a sick man. We hear through the media how AIDS is spreading like Black Death in Africa, leaving millions of orphans in its wake, and malaria is making a worldwide comeback. Next, he met an old person. This is hard for any young person to fathom. Will a day come for me "when the watchers of the house tremble, the strong men are bent, the grinders cease for they are few, and those looking out the windows are darkened?" (Eccl. 12). Then he saw a corpse. The "silver cord severed, the golden bowl shattered." One day, the fingers that type these words will be bleached bones. Siddartha's final sight startled him in a different way: a monk, begging for a meal. Here's someone who lives by different rules. He has opted out of the rat race. What has he have gained in return?

From his renunciation, Buddha is said to have gained a great deal that the modern world finds attractive. Peace. Detachment. Mindful attention to the beauty of each moment. A fellowship of monks seeking after the same goals, cultivating their spirits in unity. Many who have joined ashrams or temples have sought for and, to a degree, discovered such treasures.

One perennially-attractive ideal eventually rose above all others in the Buddhist tradition, and captured the hearts of the Asian masses: the bodhisattva of compassion. Guan Yin, they called her in China, Kannon in Japan, Avolokitvara in India. Her 1000 raised arms symbolized the hope of the common people for a salvation from outside themselves. She was the heavenly Queen who conquered the Monkey King, and having conquered him, made him a loyal vassal. Her figure adorns hot springs and fishing harbors in Japan, and a thousand temples throughout China. She rescues drowning fishermen, turns bad people into good, and blunts the blow of swords.

Such were the ideals by which Buddhism enticed East Asia. But Asians with a skeptical turn of mind note that for all its beautiful ideals, Buddhism accomplished less in a practical way for the common people of China than, for example, Mao Zedong. And the Chinese revolution was a muddied channel diverted from a purer source, from a river that rose in the West, a story of a God of compassion who walked in Palestine.

Taoism

Taoism, even more than Buddhism, is a hodge-podge of historical influences and religious ideals which are interpreted in a variety of contradictory ways.[5] The term "Tao" itself (pronounced "dow" as in Dow Jones) originally referred to a road or path, and seems to have first been used in a metaphorical sense by Confucius. It came, in both philosophical and religious Taoism, to mean the ultimate principle in the universe, the "way" which serves as essence and origin of all things. Lao Zi, the enigmatic philosopher who is taken as founder of the school, spoke of *Wu Wei*, "lacking action." Success can be accomplished by "going with the flow." For some Taoist philosophers, this meant accepting the course of nature. For Taoist believers, this meant trying to prolong one's life by exploiting secret cross-currents of nature, often through alchemic potions, magic cures, and a prolonged search for the herbs of immortal fairies who were said to dwell on remote mountain peaks. But this search also encouraged the stirrings of something akin to experimental science. The greatest of China's discoveries, the compass, gunpowder, and printing press, helped lay the technological foundations for the industrial revolution in the West.[6]

The girl at the temple expressed a common western perception that among "Eastern" religions, Taoism was most likely to provide an escape from Puritanical sexual morality. But this perception may tell us less about Taoism, than about what she was looking for.

The *Secret Instructions of the Jade Chamber* does give love advice (if we can call it that) startlingly unorthodox by Christian or even secular Humanist standards:

> "According to Pengzu the long-lived, if a man wishes to derive the greatest benefit, it is best to find a woman who has no knowledge of (these techniques), between fourteen and fifteen and eighteen or nineteen. In any event, they should never be older than thirty. Even those under thirty are of no benefit if they have given birth. My late master (!) handed down these methods and himself used them to live for three thousand years. If combined with drugs, they will even lead to immortality."[7]

The text advises the disciple to "not limit yourself to just one woman . . . the more the better!" One should deceive young partners so as to draw sexual energy and life force from them; leaving them sick, but adding to one's own life span. Women of means could profit from the same techniques: the text notes that the Queen Mother of the West (a deity identified with the Indian Kali, the Greek Aphrodite, and the Canaanite Asheroth) "attained the *Tao* by cultivating her *yin* energy. As soon as she had intercourse with a man he would immediately take sick, while her complexion would be ever more radiant . . ."

But it would be a mistake to take Taoism in general as proof of cultural relativism. On the contrary, one thing we can learn from the history of Taoism is just how universal and stubborn moral absolutes tend to be.

Lao Zi advised us to be rid of the moral rules of the sages. "When the great way falls into disuse, kindness and righteousness appear."[8] "Put an end to compassion and be done with right action, and the people will become loyal and kind again."[9] I think like Jesus, Lao Zi was disputing not so much the goals of the sages, as the legalistic means by which they hoped to attain them. The Queen Mother certainly "put an end to compassion," but it is clear from the *Dao De Jing* as a whole that that is not what Lao Zi had in mind. Still, it is remarkable that within a few hundred years, mainstream Taoism was rather pedantically interpreting Lao Zi's rebuke to mean not that rules are bad, but that you have to follow the right (Taoist, not Confucian) rules. Not long after, schools of Taoism invented their own "Ten Commandments," modeled on the Buddhist version, to which one sect added the symmetrical and auspicious count of 180 rules. This list of proscribed sins makes fascinating reading for anyone interested in what human beings share between cultures:

"The sin to pick a fight with a good fellow . . .
The sin to transmit scriptures to the wrong people . . .
The sin to speak nicely while thinking something bad . . .
The sin to burn the mountainsides in order to hunt . . .
The sin to abort children or harm the unborn . . .
The sin to speak or walk about with a woman alone . . .
The sin to get too close to members of other clans . . .
The sin to ridicule the poor and humble . . .
The sin to worship ghosts and spirits . . .
The sin to proudly claim to be special or call yourself a perfected . . .
The sin to accumulate superfluous clothing instead of distributing it to
the needy . . .
The sin to idly set up taboos . . . ."[10]

The greatest apologist of the twentieth century, C. S. Lewis, believed no ethic could be valid if the whole world did not affirm it (at least in theory) already. When it comes to morality, innovators should not be trusted. In *Abolition of Man*, though he did not limit it to that meaning, he borrowed the term *Tao* to describe the morality all peoples share in common. I think the Bible agrees. Even the New Testament book of *Romans*, which Christians who emphasize the "total depravity" of man apart from the Gospel tend to emphasize, speaks of Gentiles who "naturally practice the Law," written on their hearts, and whose thoughts "defend" as well as "accuse" them. (Romans 2).

Lao Zi described the self-effacing humility of one who lives by the *Tao*. "The sage, the holy man, abandons himself (lit. 'puts himself to the back') and so find himself. He loses his life ('puts himself outside') and so preserves his life" (*Dao De Jing*, 7:2,3). Jesus described his Way in similar terms: "If anyone wants to come after Me, he must deny himself, take up his cross day by day, and follow me. For whoever . . . loses his life on my account. . .will save it" (Luke 9:23-24). One who follows the *Tao* succeeds through weakness rather than force. We don't know how Lao Zi practiced his philosophy or even *if* he did. With Jesus, however, the *Tao* appeared not only in words, but as records of a life lived in public, among crowds and critics.

Chinese Christians have written provocative essays comparing John's concept of "*Logos*" to the Chinese term "*Tao*." Both terms refer not only to morality but to that which is the source of all things, from which all life comes to being. The *Gospel of John* in Chinese begins, "In the beginning was the *Tao*. The *Tao* was with God. The *Tao* was God. All things were made by Him" (John 1).

And then, John makes a quantum leap and confronts us with a stupendous claim. "The *Tao* became flesh and dwelt among us."[11] Indeed, how did a blue-collar Jewish laborer with no official position, program, weapons, or political ambition, change the world in three years more than any emperor or general? Taking time along the way to talk to bag ladies, hookers and madmen? Yuan Zhimin, a philosopher whose ideals influenced the democracy movement in China, has recently written a book called *Lao Zi and the Bible*, (*Lao Zi Yu Sheng Jing*) in which he argued that Jesus fulfilled the ancient ideals of Lao Zi better than any other human being.

Tribal Values

When I lived in Taiwan, I sometimes stayed in the homes of the original inhabitants of Taiwan, descendants of the Polynesians. I spear-fished with tribal families in a mountain creek, hitched a ride with a Taya tribal man in a pickup heading up to the hills with a dog to hunt pigs and with Ami young people on a holiday from the city, out to dig roots.

Before the government coaxed the tribes down to the lowlands for schooling, they lived in thatch homes in the mountains, in a simple, natural, community-based lifestyle. When boys played with matches and burnt down a house, villagers pitched in and rebuilt it in a few days. While many "civilized" Asians scorned such "primitive" tribes, in many ways these people knew more about the country they lived in than my professional friends who worked for Texas Instruments or trading companies. Young men and women learned to survive on what they found growing and moving around them. "From this fruit you can make soap," they knew, "but this one is poisonous." To this day, the older generation of Taiwanese tribal men can survive for years in the jungle. That knowledge stood one tribal man well who, during the Japanese occupation, was inducted into the Japanese army, and survived in the hills of Malaysia for forty years after the war.

Sports are an attempt by civilized peoples to recapture some of the physical challenge and solidarity of the hunt our ancestors enjoyed as an everyday part of life. It is no coincidence that ethnic groups with a tribal background, whether black, Native American, or tribal Taiwanese, tend to excel in sports. I suspect "back to nature" cults derive their attraction as much from yearning for community as for connection with the natural world.

It is hard not to admire the courage of the tribal warriors. The religion the Taya once practiced enshrined that courage in a ritual of headhunting. One Taya explained to me, "A Taya was not a man until he had killed a man from the plains." This quality made mountain tribes like the Apache, the Burmese Wa, the Montegnards of Vietnam, formidable adversaries even against enemies equipped with modern weapons.

In an attempt to revive communal action, courage, and closeness to nature, the men of the Makah Indian tribe in Washington State re-instituted a hunt for whales in 1999. White Americans angrily denounced the tribe for the "greed and ignorance" of its "war on whales." "If the tribe wanted to revive its culture, why did it use high-powered guns and power boats?" "Shouldn't they row out and throw the harpoons by hand?" Came sarcastic comments, over the Internet, Faxes and other traditional Norwegian messaging systems from the McDonalded™ suburbs of Puget Sound.

I had lived on the Makah reservation for five months, and did not view the Makah attempts to revive their culture with such cynicism. I remember strolling outside one frosty January morning to meet a Makah fisherman who labored all night on a frozen river to catch a single salmon. It wasn't the Indians who wiped out the marine mammal and fish runs. They were ruthless and unsentimental when necessary, as nature is ruthless and unsentimental, but with a fundamental respect and understanding more attractive to me than the cheap sentiment of weekend John Muirs who hunt their meat at Costco™.

In *Journey to the Western Islands of Scotland*, Samuel Johnson described how isolation encouraged the development of clans and tribes in hidden valleys of the Scottish highlands, and how already in the eighteenth century, this way of life was threatened by modernization. His description of the Highlanders—distinct, quarrelsome poverty-stricken, given to theft, among whom "the quality of highest esteem is personal courage," the reigning vice mutual suspicion, "every Highlander can talk of his ancestors, and recount the outrages which they suffered from the wicked inhabitants of the next valley"—could be word-for-word what lowland peoples of modern Asia say of modern hill tribes. The Highlanders were already feeling the draw of a larger capitalist culture, which in the twenty-first century threatens to consign proud mountain cultures around the world to oblivion. This is the wind of change against which the Makah Indians, having lost language and lifestyle, were proud enough to spit.

It is understandable that those who admire tribal cultures feel animosity towards Western culture, which has done so much to destroy native cultures. Christian missionaries have sometimes contributed to the mayhem. Yet the wisest leaders among tribal peoples are not, for the most part, seeking isolation, which is in any case impossible, but to save the particular within the universal. This is the central problem modernization sets for tribal peoples.

Beyond all this, one finds three spiritual commonalities among tribal peoples that many politically-correct observers seem slow to notice. I will discuss these later: an almost universal concept of a Supreme God, an equally universal fear of evil spirits, and the repeated notion, that unites a thousand mountain tribes with Jewish, ancient Indian Vedic, and three millennia of Chinese custom, that sin can only be dealt with through atoning sacrifice.

Code of the Rebel

The *Water Margin* records episodes in the struggles of 108 Chinese brigands, heroes according to the view of the book, in a long epic of swash-buckle and chaos, a bloody, and occasionally supernatural *Robin Hood* or *Three Musketeers*. The leader of these rebels is Song Jiang, scholar, though scholarship alone does him no good, and a man of action. The anti-hero Li Kui described the code of honor by which he acted as follows: "Song Jiang is not a common man. We are not old friends, and yet he immediately advanced me this money. He is a hero who despises wealth and stands for justice—of that there is no shadow of doubt."[12] Song, like other Chinese rebels and tribes of Asia, claimed kinship to the gods by marriage, pledged comrades with wine mixed with blood, and received a sacred stone from heaven with the names of the rebels written on it, vowing to "uphold justice." The band's spirituality lent it high morale, compared with unruly bands of common thieves: "His followers help the poor, and the old, and are welcomed by all the people."[13]

Communism is not usually thought of as "eastern" or "religion," but many of its key concepts found deep root in this Asian tradition. The young Mao Zedong was deeply influenced by these semi-tribal ideals of heroism and solidarity:

> "What I enjoyed were the romances of Old China, and especially stories
> of rebellions. I read the . . . *Water Margin* . . . and *Journey to the West* . .
> . while I was still very young, despite the vigilance of my old teacher, who
> hated these outlawed books and called them wicked. I used to read them
> in school, covering them up with a Classic when the teacher walked past.
> So also did most of my classmates. We learned many of the stories almost
> by heart, and discussed and re-discussed them many times. We also
> knew more of them than the old men of the village, who also loved them
> and used to exchange stories with us. I believe that perhaps I was much
> influenced by such books, read at an impressionable age."[14]

Few would claim this tradition moved Mao entirely to kindness. In fact, reading the random acts of cruelty of the *Water Margin*, including cannibalistic "heroes" who ran the original "Hotel California," I am inclined to agree with Mao's teacher: the book *is* wicked. Having met Chinese who starved in prison and lost their loved ones to Mao's continuing resentment against teachers and other authority figures has not changed my mind. Still, it would be unfair to dismiss the genuine heroism of the quest for justice, or the courage and egalitarianism at the heart of the revolutionary ideal. Mao's "brotherhood" rid China of opium, taught prostitutes new trades, and brought about medical revolutions which prolonged the lives of millions. One missionary in a remote mountain post wrote of her admiration after meeting an idealistic young communist girl:

> "You have been a real challenge to me. You have deliberately stripped
> yourself of privileges you might have had in order to come down to
> the level of the Lisu people. You walk their trails—thirty miles you did

yesterday, and that is superb. You sleep on their board beds, eat their course food without a murmur, never asking for anything better. I've been disgruntled sometimes lately because living conditions continue to be so rough—that old ladder, the smoke, the drafts, and so on. But I see now it was the Lord's kindness to me, so that I might not have to blush in your presence."[15]

Secret societies were a poor man's Kiwanas Club, a gnosticism of the lower classes that retained many elements of good sense which the religious clubs of the upper classes found expendable. The heroes of the *Water Margin*, like the heroes of the kung fu movies which copy it, did not show contempt for the body by shaving their heads and putting on formless robes, but implicitly affirmed the goodness of creation through weightlifting. While the religious clubs of the rich existed to exclude, outcasts of the *Water Margin* affirmed, with a call that echoed down the centuries, "all men are brothers." They sealed that brotherhood in blood sacrifices often similar to communion.

Jackie Pullinger, who has worked with gangsters in Hong Kong for thirty years, notes that sometimes she also finds honor among thieves, and is moved when she meets gangsters who pimp and steal yet at a crucial moment reveal for "little brothers" that greatest of all loves, the love Jesus said prompts a man to "give his life for his friends."[16] She tells them about a Savior who reveals the characteristics of their own ideal "big brother": Personal strength. An authority figure alienated enough from temporal authority to stand against injustice. ("You brood of vipers! How will you escape the flames of hell?"; Matt. 3:7 pph). A leader with the strategic wit to outflank stronger opponents. ("Who's likeness is on this coin?"; Matt. 22:20 pph). One who does not merely manipulate those who follow him for his own ends, but has the welfare of followers truly in mind. ("If you're after me, let the others go"; John 18:8). Who teaches that "all men are brothers." Who knows that there may come a time for shedding blood, and is not paralyzed by the possibility that it may be his own.[17]

Hinduism

There is also much the world can gain from the insights of the subcontinent.

Dr. Paul Brand, who was born in India and made pioneer contributions to the rehabilitation of lepers as a missionary doctor, notes that one of the medical innovations he used in plastic surgery was invented by a brilliant Indian physician 500 years before Christ.[18] Dr. Brand grew up in the hills of southern India, and has said that apart from the lack of modern medicine, his ideal lifestyle would be that of Indian villagers. Among other things, he noted that in contrast to the protected, ulcer-driven, pain-drugging, entertainment-saturated West, he is impressed with the ability of Indian patients to endure pain without complaining.

In *Pain: The Gift No One Wants,* he related that skill to Indian religion and to what modern medicine had discovered of the dynamics of pain receptivity:

"First as a child, then later as a physician in India, I was fascinated by the fakirs and *sadhus* who had exquisite command of their bodily functions. They could walk on nails, hold a difficult posture for hours, or fast for weeks. The more advanced practitioners even managed to control heart rate and blood pressure. Hindu "holy men" were known for their asceticism, and esteem for that high cultural value percolated down to the society at large. From an early age, the Indian people learned to respect discipline and self-control, qualities which helped them to cope with suffering. . .According to Eastern thought, human suffering consists of "outer" conditions (the painful stimuli) and "inner" responses that take place in the mind . . . As I became acquainted with these philosophies, I could not help noting the parallel to the signal-message-response stages of pain I had learned in medical school. In effect, Eastern philosophy affirms that stage-three pain, the response in the mind, is the dominant factor in the experience of suffering, and also the one we have most control over."[19]

Hinduism is a rich and complex matrix of sects, values and beliefs. The ideals the most popular sects share in common may be reduced to five: caste obligation, monism (all is one), karma (what goes around, comes around, so what comes around, must have gone around) tolerance (in theory and often in practice), and the centrality of the guru.

Karen Armstrong admires the religion of India for what she sees as the humanistic quality of this latter emphasis. "The greatest religious insight of the subcontinent," she argued, is that a religious teacher is "higher than the gods."[20] The chronicles of spiritual tourists often cause one to question such optimism. Mick Brown tells the story of a brilliant Oxford fellow named Andrew Harvey. Harvey had become an enthusiastic disciple of a young woman named Mother Meera, a supposed incarnation of the Supreme Mother. Brown described his conversion story, *Hidden Journey,* as "one of the most remarkable spiritual testaments of all times." "There was no self in her; only a Presence like the red-gold sunlight and warm wind." After following this "sunlight" for *ten years,* he succumbed to her divinity in a blinding and bedazzling series of psychic experiences. "Her life force seized me and began to pour itself into me. I felt as if the lid of my head and my entire face had been peeled off and molten radiance was being poured directly into my heart and mind."[21] Aware of similarities between this experience and those of more sinister cults, Harvey was reassured by Mother Meera's lack of pretension: "There is no cult of adoration around her . . . She is the only normal human being

I've ever met . . . And her message is very simple. We must live in harmony with the environment and with each other."

But within a few years, Harvey had changed his mind. He described ashrams as "lunatic asylums" filled with "jealous and needy people." He no longer believed in Mother Meera, and suggested we "do away with the guru system." "A lot of those we now call 'enlightened gurus' are nothing of the sort," he wrote bitterly. "They are . . . extremely powerful occult manipulators . . . Mother Meera simply wanted me to remain her devotee and to go on 'using' me, and her lies prove she is not enlightened (to say the least)."[22] Mick Brown, having interviewed a remarkable sample of the world's gurus, seemed nearly as disillusioned.

Certainly, manipulative Messiahs belong on the short list of items to be avoided in our spiritual tour. But I think there is something positive to learn from such an experience as well. Could an idea which attracts people so strongly contain no important element of truth? Abstract philosophy is all very well. But one thing Hindu religion teaches us, is that people need a *human* face to follow. Faiths which make cosmic principles rather than personalities ultimate (dialectic materialism, Theraveda and Zen Buddhism) tend to reverse course before long and mold idols, proving this law of human nature. Perhaps the problem lies in the refusal to discriminate among gurus and imposing a monistic oneness on the dissimilarities of spiritual leaders. What we need is a guru who, like Gandhi, stoops to conquer, and illustrates the humility of God.

In one sense like sadhus who walk on coals or allow fingernails to grow through their hands, Dr. Brand's missionary parents embraced a lifestyle that involved a great deal of pain. The couple lived in remote and disease-ridden mountains. His father died of black-water fever as a young man. His mother, "Granny Brand," rode mountain trails on mules and lived in the hills to the age of 95. But the pains they suffered were not self-inflicted assertions of mastery. They suffered only to heal. This is the ideal Dr. Brand and his missionary colleagues embraced, which they learned not from abstract philosophy, but from the "man of sorrows" who was *their* guru.

China's First Teacher

The lifestyle of the Confucian sages was grounded in an assumption about the body opposite to that of the Indian fakirs and tribal warriors. To Confucius, willful self-harm was an act of ingratitude to one's parents. At the core of Confucius' teaching were loyalty and a love which begins at home but extends towards all the world. Within that context, many of the ideas Confucius and his disciples bandied about were surprisingly modern: God as love, (hundreds of years before St. John), empiricism, environmentalism, even supply-side economics! All these concepts were part of knowing one's limits.

In our progressive and self-confident age, perhaps it is not surprising that these ideas seem tepid to many Western pilgrims. Nor was Confucius a rebel. Like Edmund Burke or Samuel Johnson, he built on traditions of loyalty to family, state and the Supreme Deity.

China's "First Teacher" did show a wistful side, however. Like Bono, he "Still hadn't found what he was looking for." His ideal was a "holy man," a *Sheng Ren,* who would incarnate the kindness of heaven and bring blessing to all mankind. He knew of no one who lived up to his ideal in the past, and did not expect to see such a person in his own life. According to Mencius, Confucius' greatest disciple, a sage could be expected to appear once every 500 years. Confucius died in 479 B.C.

The more we study the ideologies of humankind, the more we see the dialectical quality of revolution that is needed: a revolution which takes us back to our roots. Which affirms authority and attacks it. Which tell us to save ourselves, and promises a savior who will leave paradise and enter the phenomenal realm to save those in need. A leader with courage and wit who affirms the body and teaches us to embrace and fulfill our humanity, yet "puts himself to the rear" and is willing to die for his brothers. Who overcomes by weakness. Who stoops to conquer. One who makes all men—and women—one family. A bodhisattva. A filial son. A sacrifice whose death will "coerce an abrogation of death itself."

Let us not, at this point, jump to conclusions. I am not saying, at least not yet, "Jesus is the man." We will later look in more detail at the way Jesus fulfills the ideals of humankind. For now let us only leave it as an open question, as we take a look at the other side of the account: elements in world religions we best avoid.

What Should We Look Out For, Out There?

After a firefight broke out in the local media between Christians and New Agers, an affable skeptic wrote to the *Seattle Times* advocating a cease-fire. "So what if people want to commune with crystals, get guidance from rocks, consult channelers? What is it that we're afraid of in all that?" Is it only our own petty egos, our need to be right, that leads Christians to bad-mouth other religions?

Well, it was a strange century. Our ancestors were afraid of devils. Our mothers worry instead we'll "join a cult:" follow some teacher who hides a grim spirit behind sunglasses, manipulates followers with flattery, has them shave heads and sell carnations in airports, and tells them what to think. A few have earned special infamy through mass murder or suicide. But just as every natural disaster wounds ten for every fatality, so only a minority of the casualties of modern religion can be counted in the fields of Magadan or jungles of Guyana.

Only fools are never afraid. Perhaps such wariness is a sign of health.

Yet it may be that we are too eager to project danger onto an external object, whether human or demonic. Jesus said that from within, out of the inner person, comes all manner of evil (Mark 7:15). Perhaps the greatest danger "out there" arises from something "in here." But at the same time, the role occult religion plays in bringing it out is not, I think, arbitrary.

The Great Divorce

The first danger of many forms of monism is disattachment of faith from reason. Mystics have claimed for millennia that people have untapped mental powers which aid us not only in overcoming pain, but in allowing us to escape the confines of personal attachment. When we "realize our true selves," our identity with Universal Mind, we realize the distinction between self and others, between spiritual and material, is an illusion. When we realize this, we will be free, not just to believe, but to accomplish, all we desire. Indian guru Sai Baba once claimed, "I have the power to change the earth into the sky and the sky into the earth."[23]

George Orwell showed that skeptical monism could lead to the same conclusion. In *1984* his villain O'Brien, who believed in the supernatural no more than Orwell himself, told his hapless victim, Smith,

> "We control matter because we control the mind. Reality is inside the skull . . . I could float off this floor like a soap bubble if I wished to."[24]

Orwell called this kind of thinking "goodthink," but the traditional philosophical term for believing reality is "in the mind" is "solipsism." The most horrible episodes of the Chinese, Cambodian, North Korean and Soviet revolutions did in fact occur when leaders of godlike status attempted to recreate their nations, in effect, through mental energy and the power of mantra-like slogans. They believed, as Neale Walsch put it in *Conversations With God*, "Whatever you shall choose, so shall it be . . . To the degree that it is fervently held as truth, to that degree will it be made manifest in your experience."[25] The exercises in Goodthink they conducted swept up millions in mass-enthusiasm and faith; people who starved to death or were thrown out of windows a few months later. Philosopher A. J. Ayer, an old-fashioned materialist, wrote,

> "Admittedly, the philosophical problem of justifying one's confident belief in the existence and contents of other minds has not yet been satisfactorily solved . . . even so . . . no philosopher has acquiesced in Solipsism."

The "problem" of faith in the external world ("dualism" as pantheists call it) can never be "solved," because the mind organizes data, rather than gathering it. Faith is the faculty which allows us to input data. Reason is the faculty that enables us to sort it wisely. One danger of New Age thinking is that is can encourage Westerners who never came within a thousand miles of India to think, as one New Age enthusiast put it: "The entire physical universe itself is nothing more than patterns of neuronal energy firing off inside our heads . . . There is no physical world 'out there.'" Complete skepticism and complete gullibility have this in common: whether all religions are equally true, or equally false, in both cases empirical data, and the critical thinking and argument which rely upon it, are rendered superfluous. Both, in the end, throw the mind back on its own resources.

The Magic Eye

Another hazard of monist faith is the power of feelings detached from moral absolutes.

Consider the seductive appeal of gurus like Rasputin and Rajneesh. If there is an argument for reincarnation, extant photographs of those two lust-haunted faces has to be it. Rasputin seduced court ladies and gained a following in early twentieth century Russia by the healing touch of his hands, the magnetic attraction of his eyes, and his teaching of "salvation through sin." The infamous "Guru to the rich," Shree Bagwan Rajneesh, preached the same message, and recruited disciples from the same strata of the bored rich. Why did so many intelligent people follow them both? Their smiles would make a dog growl. Believers explained, as one of Rajneesh's disciples wrote,

> "Many people have asked me how a sensible, independent person could be mesmerized by someone like Bagwan. The answer . . . is that once you had been affected by his energy and experienced the sensation of being touched by it, you knew that there was nothing like it, no bliss to compare with it. Once you had experienced it, you had to go back for more, to try and regain that feeling of harmony and being at one with the universe."

Marx called religion the "opiate of the people." This disciple of Rajneesh' certainly sounds as if he were addicted to something, or a spell had been cast upon him, with a narcotic rather than an opiate effect on his senses, however.

Jim Jones had a similarly mesmerizing effect, as his long-term disciple, Deborah Layton, described in her aptly-titled autobiography, *Seductive Poison*: "His firm voice was consoling. It called out to me to trust him. His eyes told me he had waited almost his entire life to meet me. He leaned over and kissed my forehead. I felt weak, swooning in his intense and wholly focused attention . . . My forehead, where he had kissed me, remained extraordinarily warm. I was convinced that this man truly and unconditionally loved me."[26]

Andrew Harvey recounted his psychic experience in Mother Meera's presence in almost exactly the same terms:

> "She was looking at each person so attentively. She was all there. The room itself was like a force-field, dense with peace and sweetness . . . then I became aware that she was looking at me. And what I felt was, she

knew everything; she knew me entirely; she knew me better than I knew myself, and she could see my goodness. . . . I felt a pure unconditional love streaming into me. I knew she really cared for me."[27]

If all is one, and there are no firm categories, right or wrong, heaven or hell, true or false, and no "thou shalt nots," what can we hope for but feelings? You can analyze a feeling, what it symbolizes, whether the states which give rise to it correspond to mundane material appearance. But you can't argue with it. And like any other stimulant, arbitrary spiritual thrills are not only addictive, they are subject to a law of diminishing return. Thus Chesterton wrote of those who, "seek stranger sins or more startling obscenities as stimulants to their jaded senses . . . They try to stab their nerves to life, if it were with the knives of the priests of Baal."[28]

The defining moment in Huxley's *Brave New World* was a virtual reality experience called the "Feelies." Before attending, participants got high on the ancient Indian sacred drug *soma*. The state of oneness with the universe, which is the goal of mysticism, has indeed often been attained through physically-harmful drugs. One of the authors of the Rig Veda, one of the oldest Scriptures in the world, writes drunkenly: "The two world halves cannot be set against a single wing of mine. Have I not drunk Soma? In my vastness, I surpassed the sky and this vast earth. Have I not drunk Soma? Yes! I will place the earth here, or perhaps here. Have I not drunk Soma? . . . I am huge, huge . . ."[29] To give a modern example, Elliot Miller wrote:

> "The drugs themselves led me to pantheism because on them I experienced a loss of ego or self-image boundaries. I began to feel intrinsically connected to the universe as my larger and more real self—an infinite consciousness into which my finite consciousness was merging . . . I was God! With very little outside help I'd seemingly gone through all the classic mystical experiences and come to all the standard pantheistic conclusions."[30]

Surely that ought to give us a clue to the anti-rational and unhealthy character of such experiences! How could the origin of personhood and the Creator of the human mind be the source of "insights" arrived at by assaulting the brain with destructive chemicals?

The Angel of Death

Unreason. Emotional seduction. What else should we be wary of? The devil, perhaps?

I met a tall, stocky young man in a park in a suburb of Taipei. "Zhang" told me about a voice that often talked to him. Sometimes it claimed to be Jesus, sometimes the "Son of Matsu," Chinese goddess of the sea. This voice first came to him, he said, while playing *Dian Chi,* an occult game like Ouija. Zhang bragged his neighbors were afraid of him. He told me matter-of-factly that he sometimes felt as if the spirit were compelling him to jump in front of a car. We rode a train to visit a pastor friend I hoped would be of help. We stood between carriages so he could smoke. The countryside whizzed by with nothing between it and me but the cool night air.

"I've heard people in his state can be as strong as several men," I thought. "He's bigger than me anyway. He could push me off this train if he wanted." Zhang looked over at me, as if he guessed what I was thinking, and gave me a grin rather like that of Rasputin or Rajneesh. "Are you afraid of me?" he asked. He seemed to hope I was.

I do not know, to this day, what was the matter with that young man. Maybe the "Son of Matsu" was "merely" a psychosis. It hardly matters. It did not seem Zhang was much interested in being cured. He was trying to start a cult of his own, using the mysterious powers at his disposal to recruit followers. I know he picked up his illness through practice of the occult, and that this "projection" or "complex" influenced him towards destruction of himself and others. I had the chance to note on more than one occasion in Taiwan an association between spirit possession and depression, self-delusion, and suicide. Anthropologists have written field studies of mutilation that would curdle the blood of anyone with blood in their veins instead of ink.[31]

When I say it doesn't matter whether such occult powers are "real" or contrived, let me give an example from Western history which will also throw light on the universal character of the psychological phenomena involved in channeling. The Salem witch trials, a series of episodes in which superstition worked on public opinion and resulted in the public execution of twenty innocent persons in colonial Massachusetts, occurred when a group of adolescent girls began to act in a strange way. One historian of the period relates, "the Salem hysteria had its rise in a small gathering of young girls who met one evening a week to learn what magic a West-Indian slave woman could teach."[32] Soon, they began to accuse members of their society of satanically hoaxing them. They barked like dogs and purred like kittens. They "frothed at the mouth, vomited pins, threw their legs and arms and necks out of joint, were constantly pinched and bitten—they could always show the marks of the accused of the moment." It was on the testimony of these girls that, first those generally held in suspicion in the community, such as a Catholic woman, then those who stood up to the girls, were accused and executed.

There is much that is peculiar about these trials, conducted as it is supposed in the interests of Biblical orthodoxy. I'll save the bulk of that discussion for an appendix. But perhaps the most peculiar aspect of the trial was this. If we define "black magic" as "the attempt to use occult arts to exert power over and harm one's enemies," then the only magicians in the case were the girls on the witness stand. They took the initiative to study magic. They manifested signs of spiritual possession which other cultures relate to the presence of malevolent powers. The parties most guilty of all in these strange cases, usually blamed on overly-fervent Christianity, were wanna-be sorcerers' apprentices! Why were they believed, and their enemies put to death?

The hysteria of the witch trials was not unique. If these girls had lived in a modern democracy, they might have accused their enemies of rape or ritual Satanic abuse. If they had lived in the Soviet Union, they might have gained equal power and attention by calling their neighbors "counter-revolutionaries."

What caused them to act as they did? We are protective of our children, and sometimes loath to admit the depths of cruelty to which teenagers can descend. The use of occult forces to pursue power over other people is almost the definition of witchcraft, and that is what those girls in Salem did. Whatever the devil is, part of the human personality, emanation of the collective unconscious, hungry ghost from the underworld, or fallen angel; if you travel to certain regions in the spirit world, an exorcist seems as practical an accessory as malaria pills or a motion sickness bag.

Skeptics have laughed long and hard at medieval believers. "So. You believe in witches, do you?" Actually, the Bible doesn't believe in the kind of witches Cotton Mather preached against. But then society moved in the blink of an eye from laughing at the idea there were once witches to the realization that there are thousands of witches (practicing white magic) in our midst, and frowning on past Christian intolerance. And no doubt many of the modern priests and priestesses of Wicca see themselves as healers, men and women in pursuit of the rhythms of nature. But the occasional appearance of a Charles Manson or Jim Jones reminds us of bodies discovered in the bogs of pre-Christian England, blood-stained skulls in museums, little corpses in charcoaled pits in Canaanite villages, and Aztec stones coated with blood. Many of the great villains of modern Western history, Marx, Hitler, Jim Jones, and Rasputin, also showed an interest in spiritualism, and seemed to work on the same assumption as Tantric operators who taught that human sacrifice was a key to gaining power over the spirit world. If we note the premises of the New Age that Ascended Masters are undying, and good and evil ultimately aspects of the same Oneness, where were these spirit guides when the innocent were sacrificed to immortal cosmic spirits of an earlier age? The issue may sound ludicrous to some, but for those who are interested in spiritual tourism, it seems to me a very practical question. I wonder that more people have not asked it.

Start a religion and make a fortune, advised Ron Hubbard, who founded Scientology. Isn't that really what most cults are about? cynics ask. Bagwan Rajneesh accumulated dozens of Rolls Royce (defining status symbol of the Indian maharaja), and had beautiful women at his beck and call. A sucker is born every minute. Who needs any more explanation?

George Orwell understood the pleasures of such people as something more subtle and spiritual. His villain, O'Brien, asked his hero in the belly of the state torture chamber:

> "How does one man assert his power over another, Winston?"
> "By making him suffer."
> "Exactly."

Tal Brooke noticed that Sai Baba's favored apostles expressed a bemused contempt for lesser disciples who punished themselves to gain enlightenment. The tantric interpretation of Asian religions is, in essence, "Sin and grace will abound." By reversing the moral commandments of Buddha, one could gain power over beings in other spheres of existence, that can aid in pursuit of both mundane (healing, making money, cursing an enemy) and supra-mundane (spiritual) goals. But is power means or end? The sadism and masochism inherent in the means is, I suspect, the key to understanding the goal. Ability to inflict suffering shows power.

Tibetan scholar David Snellgrove notes that, "a young generation of Western Buddhists, much attracted by the Tibetan form of this great religion" objects to "the most natural translations" of ancient tantric literature "because they suggest the kinds of superstitious and magical practices such as were prevalent in our own 'unenlightened' Middle Ages."[33] It may be dishonest of these scholars to distort ancient texts in this Way. But it may also be a sign of health.

Rudyard Kipling tells the story of a shy but hard-working Englishman who returned from three years at a remote outpost in the Indian jungle addicted to secret drink. He met a woman whom he took to be a paragon of kindness, and fell in love. Everyone knew this woman was cruel, and cultivated such friendships to enjoy her power over men, but being shy, he did not hear the opinion of society. In order to make himself worthy of her, he conquered his inner demons and stopped drinking. Later, happily married to another and better woman, he ended a friendship rather than allow someone to cast doubts on the goodness of his previous "benefactress."

The history of religion tells many such tales. Malcolm X transformed himself from petty criminal to honest man to make himself worthy of a con man named Elijah Mohammed. Many Marxists laid down their lives with an idealism Marx lacked. It is often said modern believers fail to live up to the ideals of the founders of their religions. But many respectable religions were founded by scoundrels who preached noble ideals followers live up to better than they themselves.

Huston Smith's desire to focus attention on the good in religion may also be a sign of a healthy innocence, too. But has its dangers. If we ignore the down side of religion, we ignore something which, if not "out there" waiting to get us, expresses something inside the human psyche. There is a famous photograph of California Democratic Congressman Ryan in Jonestown the night before he was murdered. On the crossbeam behind him a sign reads, "those who do not remember the past are condemned to repeat it."

How do we oppose the "dark side of the force?"

Don Richardson tells how he discovered, to his horror, that Yali head-hunters who had begun to accept Christianity, maintained a custom called *gefam ason,* or *"touching the stench."* When a loved one died, his body was tied into a tree and left to rot in the tropical heat for nine days. Mourners caked in mud surrounded his body, "shrieking like banshees," reached out as if to touch his corpse. One began to dance beneath the rotting remains as maggots rained down on him. Another worked up his courage and plunged his hand into the body, then ate sago from the contaminated hand.

Richardson considered. "I knew it would not be enough simply to tell them: 'Look here! Stop doing this! It's not nice!' They already knew it wasn't nice. Obviously the very unniceness of it was somehow related to its purpose." Then he thought of another practice in the Sawi culture, called a *waness* bind in which a man would manipulate a person by humiliating himself before her. "Could the custom called *gefam ason* simply be a way of trying to impose a massive *waness* bind . . . on not just an individual, but on the whole supernatural world? . . . But what could be the purpose of such a large-scale *waness* bind, carried out by unnumbered Sawi over aeons of time? Could it be to coerce an eventual abrogation of death itself?"[34]

Witchcraft which arises from such a deep fear and need cannot be overcome by preaching platitudes, as Richardson realized, or with imprecations to "be nice." Ordinary evil may be opposed with platitudes. But Dracula is only vulnerable to a cross.

I also wonder what it really means to worship "the Buddha within."

"The Buddha, the goddess or idol, is merely a symbolic representation, while the true object of worship is the Buddha within." The woman at the True Buddha temple correctly understood orthodox Buddhist doctrine. As C. N. Tay wrote, "when self nature is awakened, we are Buddhas." The goal is to realize unity with all things, and the means is worship of an external object which represents the higher self, beyond duality, in one of its guises. But how does one distinguish between transcendence of ego boundaries which is pride, and transcendence of ego-boundaries that is mystical unity with the Absolute?

In practice, this distinction does not always seem as obvious as many spiritual tourists seem to assume. Even a creepy guru to the rich, like Bagwan Rajneesh, can preach emptiness:

"You have to peel your being the way one peels an onion . . . You will find layers within layers and finally when all the layers are discarded or eliminated you will find in your heads pure nothingness . . .

emptiness . . . Shunyata (a Buddhist term for emptiness) is your essential (being)."35

Empty yourself. Realize your identity with the godhead. You are a divine being. You will be a scorpion in your next life. Why do so many gurus want us to accept as our "essential being" everything except our humanity?

We are told to tear down the walls which divide us from the universe and embrace Infinity. But walls exist for protection. A bacteria dies when its cell wall is ruptured. The Starship Enterprise is blasted by the Klingons when it lowers its shields. Worship opens the front door of the soul. Letting someone into one's heart is a perilous hospitality. Surely if one is selective about whom one allows into one's bed, and body, we should be most cautious and careful of all, deciding whom to worship. The Bible equates the two, warning us against "spiritual prostitution," and telling us God is "jealous," not I think for his sake, but for ours. The world within, like the world without, is a hazardous country.

"Who Can We Go To When We're In Trouble?"

My third question was asked 2500 years ago by an Assyrian general with a tactical interest in comparative religions. Sennacherib, emperor of Assyria, sent troops marching on Jerusalem. The valley dark with his warriors, the general in charge approached the city gate to negotiate with, or at least taunt, the ants trapped in their little monotheistic hill. Sending an ultimatum to the pious king Hezekiah, he asked a series of questions he thought his enemies would chew over for a few hours, but still seems worth consideration 2500 years later.

The envoy began by needling the officials sent to meet him with the weakness of the Jewish position. He spoke loudly and in Hebrew, so the people manning the walls—who would have to "eat their own excrement and drink their own urine" if the king refused to surrender—could hear. "The emperor wants to know whom King Hezekiah is depending on in defying him," he asked. "Do you think empty words can take the place of military power? Do think Egypt, that reed that breaks when you lean on it, is going to come to your aid now?" The general stopped and considered what he knew of the spiritual inclinations of the Jewish people. "Or maybe you think your God, Yahweh, whose altars Hezekiah has been destroying, is going to save you? Actually it was God who sent me here to punish you." (The general had, perhaps, not been fully briefed on the iconoclastic nature of the Jewish God; but it's always worth an effort to stir up internal antagonisms.) He offered carrot as well as stick: "Surrender, and we'll lead you to a land not so different from this, and give you 2000 horses if you can provide the cavalry to make use of them."

Finally the general made an appeal to skeptics in his audience by asking the

$64,000 question. "Come, now. What god have you seen ever save any nation from the hands of the Assyrian army? Where now are the gods of Hamath and Arpad? Where are the gods of Sepharvaim, Hena, and Ivvah? Where are the gods of Samaria? Did they save Samaria from me? Among all the gods of the nations, can you name a single one who saved his land from me? Do you really think this Yahweh is going to save Israel?"

Modern man, who prides himself on being scientific, talks of spirituality as a "potluck dinner," or calls himself a "spiritual tourist." Here, by contrast, was a man who approached questions of faith in a scientific and serious manner. "Does ivory soap float?" "Which god answers prayer of a people about to be swallowed?"

The Jewish historian says Yahweh gave an answer through the prophet Isaiah. "Do you not know? Can you not understand? Long ago I planned it. But now I am going to shield this city from you."[36]

But the general's largely rhetorical question remains historically interesting. Where are the gods of the states he envoy mentioned—Hamath, Arpad, Sepharvaim, Hena, and Ivvah? Where, for that matter, are the people of those states? Or even Assyria? Swallowed up without a trace into larger or more vigorous ethnic identities.

The Jewish people, however, survived Sennacherib. The Hebrews came back from exile in Babylon, as prophesied by Jeremiah, while greater nations were absorbed. They survived the rise and fall of Alexander the Great. The Romans sacked Jerusalem and sent them into exile, where they remained for 2000 years, keeping their identity intact through shared worship of this "tribal" god who was now identified as Creator by half of humanity. They survived the Grand Inquisitor, the Russian patriarchs, and Adolf Hitler, whose thousand-year Reich fell in thirteen. Then the Jewish state was resurrected, as the prophets predicted 2500 years before. Jews trickled into Tel Aviv from places as far afield as Hangzhou, China and Lima, Peru, and again survived "weapons of mass destruction" and promises to push them into the sea.

"What other god has ever done that?" Among the thousands of people groups which inhabit the earth, I can think of—none.

In a broader sense, (to get ahead of myself a bit) Yahweh saved the poor, orphan, and widow for centuries from sacred prostitution and religious exploitation. He saved families from sexually-transmitted diseases and divorce. The prophets mandated a systematic program of social justice that allowed the poor a dignified opportunity ("sweat equity") to glean the fields, saving them from both hunger and the dependent status of beggars.

By contrast, consider India, land of monism and tens of millions of gods. A land that has the distinction of being about the only country in the world where the life expectancy for women is lower than for men. Which of India's

gods saved widows from being burnt with their husbands? Which allowed out-
castes to escape from social animosity or Brahmins from self-sufficiency?
Which protected girls from temple prostitution? Kali? Shiva? Ram? Agni? Forgive my intolerance. But I happen to think a god that, rather than protecting
children, demands them as an object of pleasure and sacrifice, ought to be
smashed to crumbs and fed to the crocodiles of the Ganges River.

Did any of these millions of gods accomplish the moral revolution and
social cleansing India needed? Or were monism and tolerance precisely the problems? Could it be that mythology and philosophy are powerless against the
demonic apart from a God who makes boundaries and takes sides? Which god
shook up the caste system and rescued the poor and helpless in India and around
the world? For the spiritual traveler, I think it is a question worth considering.

What should a Christian say to an idealist setting out on a journey? Seek
the good in every spiritual tradition and cherish it; but don't be naive. Allow
yourself to become desperate enough to be heretical, and even desperate
enough to be orthodox. Give credit where credit is due, but also blame where
blame is due. Take ideals seriously enough to live by, even die for. But be careful to whom you open your heart. Follow each star to the place where it leads.
Then come and look again in a town called Bethlehem.

What is it you are looking for? Look, then, for a god among the gods of
humanity. Look for a guru among the gurus of humankind at whose feet to
find enlightenment. Wear tennis shoes out upon the holy hills of the Incas.
Shake clouds of dust from ancient manuscripts of the sacred libraries of Lhasa
and Alexandria. Ponder every sect, tribe and teacher from Tierra Del Fuego to
Tibet. Then come, open the New Testament. Look again at the life and teachings of the man who said of the Jewish writings, "You investigate the Scriptures,
because you suppose you have eternal life in them, and yet they bear witness to
me" (John 5:39).

---

[1] Built for $25 million in Hacienda Heights, California, the temple seems to
cater primarily to overseas Chinese. Vice President Al Gore got in trouble here years
later when he accepted surprisingly generous donations from clergy who, in theory,
had renounced the world.

[2] Disclosure seems to be a trend in esotericism, no doubt reflecting the general
world-wide movement towards democratization. Master Lu Sheng-yen, whose True
Buddha movement I studied, has devoted more than 130 volumes to "leaking the
(esoteric Buddhist) secrets of heaven" to his audience.

[3] Mick Brown, *The Spiritual Tourist*, Bloomsbury, 1998, p. 306-7

[4] Chesterton, *Orthodoxy*, Doubleday, 1908, 1959, p.72

[5] In Chinese there are two terms: the philosophical school called *Dao Jia*, and the religion called *Dao Jiao,* whose teachings are in many ways opposite. Intellectuals, both Chinese and Western, tend to praise the virtues (and vices) of the first, and denigrate the vices (and virtues) of the second, which I will discuss in the context of folk and secret society religion.

[6] Francis Bacon spoke with a touch of hyperbole of three "recent" discoveries whose origin "is obscure and inglorious: namely, printing, gunpowder, and the magnet. For these three have changed the whole face and state of things throughout the world, the first in literature, the second in warfare, the third in navigation . . . no empire, no sect, no star, seems to have exerted greater power and influence . . . " *Novum Organum,* from Joseph Needham, *Science and China's Influence on the World,* in *The Legacy of China,* Oxford U. Press, 1964, p. 242

[7] *Yufang Bijue (Secrets of the Jade Chamber),* from Livia Kohn, *The Taoist Experience, An Anthology,* State University of New York Press, 1993, p.156

[8] *Dao Dejing,* 18

[9] Ibid., 19

[10] *Chishu yujue and Sanyuan pin,* from *The Taoist Experience,* Chapter Four

[11] One early Platonist reportedly advised Christians to inscribe these words in letters of gold and set them in the most prominent place in every church. Augustine, *City of God,* translated by Henry Bettenson, Penguin, 1984, p. 417

[12] *Water Margin,* p. 523

[13] Ibid. p. 854

[14] Edgar Snow, *Red Star Over China,* p.127

[15] Isabel Kuhn, *Stones of Fire,* Moody Bible Institute, 1960, p. 184

[16] Jackie Pullinger, *Chasing the Dragon*

[17] During the nineteenth century, a school teacher in the Chinese countryside, calling Jesus his "big brother," started a rebel movement which almost overthrew the Qing Dynasty. He drew on a social environment in which the categories of "rebel" and "bandit" were closely intertwined, and many of his followers had been members of secret societies like the famous "Heaven and Earth" society.

[18] Personal correspondence, 1999.

[19] Paul Brand and Philip Yancey, *Pain: The Gift No One Wants,* Harper Collins Zondervan, 1993, p. 234

[20] Armstrong, *History of God,* Ballantine Books, 1993, p. 16-17

[21] Quoted by Marc Brown, *Spiritual Tourist,* p.169

[22] Ibid., p.182-3

[23] Tal Brooke, *Riders of the Cosmic Circuit,* Lion Publishing, 1986, p28

[24] George Orwell, *1984*

[25] Neale Walsch, *Conversations With God, An Uncommon Dialogue,* G. P. Putnam's Sons, 1995, p.12

[26] Deborah Layton, *Seductive Poison*, Doubleday, 1998, p. 43

[27] Mick Brown, *The Spiritual Tourist*, p. 179

[28] Chesterton, *The Everlasting Man*, p.160

[29] *The Soma-drinker praises Himself,* from *The Rig Veda*, Penguin Classics, 1981, p. 131

[30] Elliot Miller, *A Crash Course on the New Age Movement*, Baker Book House, 1989, p. 213-4

[31] See Jordan, *Gods, Ghosts, and Ancestors*, Chapter 4

[32] Ralph and Louise Boas, *Cotton Mather: Keeper of the Puritan Conscience*, Harper and Row, 1928, p. 105

[33] David Snellgrove, *Indo-Tibetan Buddhism: Indian Buddhists and Their Tibetan Successors*, p.130, Shambhala, 1987

[34] Don Richardson, *Peace Child*, Regal Books 1974, p. 259

[35] From Tal Brooke, *Riders of the Cosmic Circuit, Lion Publishing*, 1986, p. 28

[36] I have condensed and paraphrased this story from 2 Kings 19.

CHAPTER 6

Is Jesus a Fundamentalist?

I ARRIVED in New Delhi, India the day before Indira Gandhi was assassinated by Sikh gunmen in the fall of 1984. For several nights, we heard the shouts of mobs taking revenge on the city's one million-strong Sikh community. An unnatural silence would be punctuated by distant rifle fire or the explosion of a bomb. Then "tap-tap-tap" came the sound of our neighborhood's impromptu night patrol.

After the army was called out and the streets reclaimed, I walked for miles through the city, past bombed-out taxis and children playing cricket beside the blackened hulls of buses. As in our neighborhood, everywhere residents of New Delhi had strung hand-made gates and barriers across alleyways to repel rioters. A Sikh told me how he stood side-by-side with Hindu neighbors and pitched Molotov cocktails at attacking mobs all night long. I saw a banner strung across one downtown boulevard. "We thank our Hindu brethren who saved the lives of their Sikh brethren."

An idealistic young Jewish professional once asked Jesus how to inherit eternal life. Jesus replied by telling him, "Love God with all your heart, mind, soul, and strength" and "Love your neighbor as yourself" (Luke 10:27 pph). But who is my neighbor? The man asked. Jesus responded with one of his most famous stories, about a fellow from the outcast region of Samaria who stopped and helped a man of a different race and denomination on a dangerous mountain road. Who is our neighbor? Anyone we come upon who needs our help, Jesus implied. Since the bipolar confrontation between Russia and America ended, the world has been increasingly fractured by tribal violence, and has come to appreciate anew those of any faith willing to treat the person who lives next door as a neighbor.

But in many cases, religion appears to be the cause of the violence, rather than its solution. And in many countries, such as Indonesia, Northern Ireland, Nigeria, and Serbia, one of the mobs marches under the banner of the cross, recalling ancient armies that devastated Byzantium and Jerusalem, and tore Europe apart for the seat of Peter and the sermons of Paul. In America, some Christians speak in a loaded metaphor of a "cultural war" to reclaim Western culture for Christian morality.

No book talks about love so eloquently and with such power as the Bible. Love ennobles the sexual instinct: "Arise, my love, my beauty, and come along with me. The winter is past, the season of rains is over and gone" (Song. Sol. 2:10). Love raises comradeship to the level of the heroic: "Love one another as I have loved you. No one has greater love than this: to lay down his life for his friends" (John 15:12-13). Love alone validates faith: "Even though I speak in human and angelic languages, and have no love, I am as a noisy brass or a clanging symbol" (1 Cor.. 13:1). Love "is from God" (1 John. 4:7 NASB). Heaven remembers even the smallest act of kindness: "Anyone who gives a cup of water in my name, will not lose his reward" (Matt. 10:42 pph). Charity is the heart and soul of Christian morality. It's a lonely world, and news of a transcendent love from beyond time sounds like a cool spring to a person lost in the desert.

But it is also a suspicious world. Understandably so. As we saw in the last chapter, totalitarian cults pamper potential disciples with sexual indulgence or a sweet facade of unconditional love like honey to attract flies. Some thinkers— Feurbach, Freud, and Sartre for examples—have seen the Christian "love of God" as an intrinsically unhealthy, even neurotic, metaphysical dependency. Did Jesus, with his talk of a God who is like a Father, and of a church whose commanding principle was "love one another," set the greatest trap of all? Over the past two centuries, skeptics have developed an entire vocabulary to say yes. Feminist, gay, and other skeptics pepper a harsh critique of the church with words like "patriarchal," "authoritarian," "repressive," "sexist," and "puritanical." Christian morality, they say, serves the interest of the rich, male, ruling classes. It stifles freedom and represses spontaneity. The church is so busy trying to force society to live by petty and arbitrary standards that it allows greed, injustice, and rape of the environment to go unchallenged. And most of all, the Gospel's exclusive claims—which trace to Jesus' "I am *the* way"—encourage a partisan and uncooperative spirit, and allow the Church to isolate itself from and marginalize other people of good will—a dangerous tendency in a world as small and mutually-dependent as ours has become.

I will make the case, on the contrary, that the Way described by Jesus and his early followers is wise and balanced to a degree that is nothing short of uncanny. I have already discussed the family and sexual relations, so I will focus now on the Christian attitude towards four other institutions: worship, the church, state, and society.

Loving God: Where it Begins

"Love the Lord your God with all your heart, and with all your soul, and with all your minds, and with all your strength" (Mark 12:30). This is where Jesus began. But what does it mean to love a being we cannot see or touch, who does not seek shelter in our Skid Row mission or eat and drink the milk and cookies we leave on the fireplace mantle?

In some Asian countries worshippers parade a god through crowded urban streets on its birthday. With firecrackers exploding all around them, the especially devout cut themselves with swords. Muslims express devotion to God by fasting during the daytime for the forty days of Ramadan. Hindus bring goats to be sacrificed in the beautiful Kali temple of Dakshineswar in Calcutta. People in every religion offer the gods fruit, animals, or money, on the theory that whether or not divine spirits enjoy such goods, they will at least appreciate the sacrifice involved.

Jesus said "All the law and the prophets" could be summarized as, "love God" and "love your neighbor." Empathy among humans has not always followed automatically from worship of the divine, however. Through history, appeasing the powers of nature often involved cruelty to human beings lower in the pecking order. Joseph Campbell bizarrely contended the people of the Indian subcontinent practiced human sacrifice because they did not see it as evil. When buried alive, their victims died with a smile. He admitted, however, that when the community could not find a volunteer, they "honored" criminals and thieves instead. The Aztecs had a legend that a god had given its life to save the world, and now they must cut out the hearts of captives to repay him. I suspect we see the same psychological force operating on the minds of the founders of secular ideologies as well, when modern tyrants propitiate the spirit of History or the Master Race with blood.

It was the work of the great sages to tie cosmology to morality as Jesus said the Old Testament did. Where do we experience the *Tao* more directly than when we care for another person? Mozi, a radical Chinese thinker who lived 300 years before Christ, taught that because Heaven loved humankind impartially, our love much be like his, without regard for conventional ties or tribal alliances, but unfettered and universal. "To obey the will of Heaven is to be universal (in love)."[1] Those we call sages argued that knowledge of the ultimate comes not by self-mutilation or cruelty, but by embracing others in the universal love of God. The prophet Micah made the case for this point of view with shattering simplicity:

"'With what shall I come before the Lord? Shall I come with burnt offerings? Will the Lord be pleased with ten thousand rivers of oil? Shall I give my first-born for my transgression?' He has shown you, oh man, what is good, and what the Lord requires of you: to do justice, to love mercy, and to walk humbly with your God" (Micah 6:6-8).

Why worship God? Is God egotistical, that he needs our affirmations and applause? No, if that were the case, those who blaspheme really would be struck by lightning, like in the cartoons. Worship orients our hearts to reality. Through worship, we learn what Paul called "the things that remain:" faith, hope and love.

For the Christian, love is not primarily what we give God, but what he gives us. The Old Testament book of *2 Samuel* tells how King David decided to build a showcase temple for his God. "I have been living in my new cedar palace, but the dwelling place of God is still that tattered tent we brought from Egypt several hundred years ago," he reasoned. Doubtless Yaweh would appreciate more comfortable quarters. God did not respond to David's proposal with the derision of a modern skeptic or philanthropist, but neither did he accede to the limited horizons of his feudal vision. Rather, he gently affirmed the motivation behind David's naive proposal, and allowed him to begin the project. But then he reminded him who was building a house for whom. To paraphrase: "I called you when you were still out in the fields whistling for sheep, and made you who you are. And I'm going to keep on watching over you, and your son, the dynasty that follows."

Christians worship God not because we have made him in our image and like our craftmanship. We worship not because the cathedrals, epic poems, paintings, and symphonies dedicated to his name have become defining symbols of Western civilization, or the repositories of moral and psychological insight— or because God needs them. Worship proceeding from such grounds alone would constitute a form of idolatry. The essence of Christian love is not that we love God, but that God loves us. We are "his people and the work of his hands."

The doctrine of Creation creates a certain tension in the heart of any sensitive believer, which is where faith and hope come in. Jesus told us "God pours rain upon the just and the unjust" (Matt. 5:45). Does he send rain, then, on those who have lost their homes in a flood in Bangladesh? Does he shine his sunlight on those who are dying of thirst in the Taklimakan desert? Upon Burmese regiments waiting for the dry season to launch an attack upon independent mountain tribes?

Why do bad things happen to good people? To Christians, because we are not making up our God, and because we are not Masters of the universe, the first and wisest answer may be, "I don't know." But the Christian "I don't know" is not the nihilist "I don't know," which assumes there is no answer. Nor is it the "I don't know" of blind faith, which simply determines to believe in a loving heart behind the universe despite all evidence to the contrary. Rather, "I don't know, but I have met God, and I choose to trust him. One day, 'God will wipe away all tears from their eyes' (Rev. 7:17). One day, 'the river of the water of life" will flow "from the throne of God" with trees beside it whose leaves are "for the healing for the nations' (Rev. 22:1-2). Until then, there is only one thing I can do: trust God." For every Christian, there comes a time to echo the words of the young Jewish believers: "The God Whom we serve is able to save us. But whether He does or not, we will not worship the image you have set up" (Dan. 3:17-18). Such faith is rational but risky, like climbing a mountain.

Christianity also offers a second, and, if possible, even more difficult, answer to the problem of pain, yet one that is the source of much adventure.

A little girl, trying to be grown-up, digs up her mother's tulips, spreading compost and clay over the sidewalk. Her mother barks, "clean up that mess!" But then she sees her daughter's tears. She crouches down to her toddler's level. "The dirt has to stay in the flower bed, honey," she explains. "The worms will get sick if they're left on the sidewalk, and then they can't make flowers." She shows her daughter which side of the bulb goes up, how deep to dig, and how to pour water on the replaced earth. She could clean up the mess in half the time on her own. Why go to all this fuss? Because she has conceived a vision of a girl competent and caring enough to make rather than destroy. She teaches her daughter the pleasure of creation and allows her to cleanse herself from the shame of destruction.

The purpose of life, Christians believe, is to learn to garden with God. That is part of what the Bible means when it says we are created in his image.

"Affecting Godhood, and So Losing All"

While we are called to realize and develop the likeness to God with which we were endowed, according to Christianity our downfall comes when we try to take his place. That is the "original sin," and not only for mortals. John Milton described the devil "affecting Godhood, and so losing all . . . " Even while technological genius creates civilizations which reveal the god-like creative nature of humanity, self-infatuation has caused the human race to "lose all" not once but many times. We see it in large events, like the failure of Marxism and the sexual revolution, and also in small matters, the isolation and paranoia of the individual who "affects godhood" in their daily relations. "Pride comes before a fall," warned Solomon. Slapstick comedy gives a literal twist to this basic theme of Christian theology: a businessman in an expensive suit and his nose in the air walks towards a banana peel and a manhole.

Language is often one of the modes of affectation. The ancient Greeks identified the ultimate principle behind the universe with language—*Logos* means "word." So did the Chinese—one of the earliest meanings of *Tao* is "to speak." But while the *Tao* is part of God's universal revelation, we often use words to cover rather than reveal.[3] Priests revel in obscure terminology which reminds the rank and file who holds the keys to heaven: the Church Slavonic of the Russian patriarchy, Joseph Smith's "Reformed Egyptian," New Age blends of pseudo-scientific and ancient Sanskrit jargon, deliberately obtuse social science terminology. The monkeys in Rudyard Kipling's *Jungle Book* created a Gnostic mix of animal sounds over which they gave themselves similar airs:

"All the talk we have ever heard
Uttered by bat or beast or bird
Hide or fin or scale or feather —
Jabber it quickly and all together!
Excellent! Wonderful! Once Again!
Now we are talking just like men!"[4]

The New Testament, by contrast, was written in work-a-day Greek. Pentecost allowed the disciples to suddenly speak the humble vernacular languages of a diverse Mediterranean world. The *Book of Revelation* speaks of a crowd of "all tongues" worshiping God. By these striking images, the Bible makes a statement that God's salvation is not about a select company of priests showing they speak the language of heaven, but about heaven speaking the language of earth.

Why love God? Worship is in part therapy for a race imprisoned in the shadow of its own love. "Mirror, mirror, on the wall," we ask. "Who's the fairest of them all?" If when we ask this question all we see is our own long, sad faces, peering back, one by one or in a group, the mirror has become a trap, the castle a dungeon, and ourselves a beast imprisoned by our own projections. The joy of the happy soul lies in taking delight in an "other" which causes it to forget itself for a moment. We find a measure of peace when we forget our own affairs in a card game, the smell of a birch tree in fall or of wild ginger, the height of an imposing peak as the sun sets, the sound of a brass band, or the intricacies of a scientific puzzle. Knowing God, from Whom all things come, is by definition the ultimate fulfillment of the human soul. At the core of Christian morality lies no "cold Christs and tangled Trinities," but a romance with the inventor of all things. Let us not deny that there remains in that romance an element of mystery and even fear.

I think again of Elie Wiesel at Buchenwald.

In the face of holocausts and killing fields, a glib sketch of God in a sunny sky and all well on earth would be obscene. In the presence of such abominations, a utilitarian argument for worship alone, "because it makes us happy, because it gives us reason to live" would be sacrilege. Atheists may be wiser in their way to say there is no God. Others may reply that the Jews and Gypsies suffered in previous lives for sins they do not remember. The Christian, however, is not offered any such glib solutions. We can only say that God was there, (and many non-Christians, like Alexander Solzhenitsyn, even found him there) but for reasons beyond our knowledge, did not intervene overtly.

Yet in a particularly poignant moment, Wiesel did come close to sighting the Christian God in Buchenwald. He described watching the hanging of another child, a "sad-eyed angel," along with two adults who had been caught with weapons. Behind him, Wiesel heard another prisoner cry out in anguish, "where is God? Where is God now?" "And a voice within me answered, 'Where is He? Here He is—He is hanging here, on this gallows.'"[5]

That is where Christians find the God we worship: hanging on a gallows, an innocent beside two thieves.

Francois Mauriac, in his forward, explained his caution about pointing to that answer:

> "And I, who believe that God is love, what answer could I give my young questioner, whose dark eyes still held the reflection of that angelic sadness which had appeared one day upon the face of the hanged child? What could I say to him? Did I speak of that other Jew, his brother? Did I affirm that . . . the conformity between the Cross and the suffering of men was in my eyes the key to that impenetrable mystery? . . . This is what I should have told this Jewish child. But I could only embrace him, weeping."

This is the God whom the Christian worships. He is the God of galaxies that shine like jewels in the night sky, the God symbolically depicted on the Sistine Chapel reaching out his finger from heaven to make and empower man. He is also the man who died on the cross.

Jesus compared the servant of God to a seed of grain which falls in the ground and "dies" (John 12:24). Within a seed is encoded a genetic library of information, telling the seed what to become, given soil, water, and sunshine. When I was a boy, I often put corn and bean seeds in wet napkins in a dark cupboard. In a few days the seeds would begin to sprout. In a week, the stalk might stick out an inch, and the roots several inches. This was the height of its glory, as long as it stayed in the cupboard. Were it human, it might say, "Look at me! At this rate, in a few months I'll be as tall as a tree!" But a corn seed only has so much stored energy. Leave it in the dark, and in a few days it weakens as it stretches for light. Then it withers and dies.

Moral ideals—the code written on our hearts that tell us what it is to be human—are, according to Christians, not sufficient to make us what we are to be. Society reinforces and directs our instinctive yearning for justice through early childhood training, and we are further molded by heredity and the rough-and-tumble of daily experience. God is the Sun who pours moral energy into our lives, the soil in which we find security, the rain that brings dead things to life. But if God is on holiday from the universe, while "all things are permitted," that freedom is a temporary and sickly thing. As Augustine put it, "Our souls were made for Thee, Oh God, and cannot find rest until they find their rest in Thee."

A cloud blots out the sun. The believer is wrenched to his roots. One's child dies, one's wife has an affair, one is incapacitated by illness. "I know God's hand is not against me," we tells ourselves, or echoing Job, "though He slay me, yet will I trust Him." Such optimism may seem like whistling in the dark to unbelievers. And even for believers there may come a time when faith is little more than a cry in the night. Not even Job could maintain a high level of trust for long. Even Jesus suffered the full heartache and bewilderment of abandonment, crying from the cross, "My God, My God, why have You forsaken me?" (Matt.27:46).

Yet in that cry, many Christians find comfort. Pain need not reflect bad karma from forgotten sins, the arbitrary wrath of God, or even wrong choices in this life. Maybe we're on the right track after all. Here before us, on the ground, lie the footprints of our Lord.

I choke on some Christian songs. "He's got the little tiny baby in His hands, He's got the little tiny baby in His hands." And yet we know the first few years of life are the most dangerous. When I read the Gospels, I can believe that if Jesus is the Son of God, and Father is like Son, then God must be holding his hands back from the children who don't make it for some good reason. But here is a mystery which the Bible only addresses in hints. Is not silence better than banal or thoughtless praise?

And yet how can I look at the sky in the evening, after the sun goes down behind the mountains and the sky is lit up, and not thank the Creator? How can we see our children's faces light up when they see a banner on the wall, "Happy Birthday" and not praise him who gives life? Children themselves know how to praise. My five-year-old son, whose latest interests include space and cooking, suddenly exclaimed to me out of the blue, a few weeks ago, "God made this whole universe. I love this whole universe. This is a beautiful universe that God made. We need more rye bread."

The opposite attitude is typified by a book called *The Pessimists Guide to World History.* The book gives details of hundreds of mass-murders, wars, floods, and earthquakes, along with sarcastic asides on the foolishness of belief in God in the face of such events. Every detail in the book may be true, but nonetheless the book is a lie. It introduces people only to say they died; it forgets to tell us that they ever lived. Surely existence is more important and significant than non-existence? Suppose I said, "Yesterday I saw a purple phoenix on the telephone pole outside my house." Surely the existence of such a creature should be cause for wonder, even if it flew away. The world is full of creations every bit as wonderful, though getting used to them, and jaded by cynicism, we do not notice, or give thanks.

Russia and America pointed thousands of nuclear bombs at one another for forty years. General Lee Butler, who was responsible for all American nuclear forces for three years, once admitted, "We escaped the Cold War without a nuclear holocaust only by some combination of skill, luck, and divine intervention, and I suspect the latter in greatest proportion."[6]

Have we thanked God for that? If we curse God for holocausts people commit, should we not thank him for the greater holocausts he saves us from committing?

Worship involves cultivating gratitude towards the source of blessings great and small. "Give thanks, for He is good," the Bible affirms, though it admits this is not always obvious. Without faith, writes the author of *Hebrews,* it is "impossible to please God;" (Heb. 11:6) perhaps because it makes it impossible for us to be pleased by God, even in a world where apples grow on trees, lilies poke out of mud and the moon stares at us between clouds. Job asked, should we only thank God when things go well? It seems to me that the exercise of faith in a supernatural God, far from detracting from our humanity, not only provides an eye of peace in the storms of our lives, it also ennobles us by teaching us to forget ourselves, teaching us to attend to the marvelous things around us, without damning (or damming) our cries when we hurt.

Church: What Makes Hypocrisy Ugly

One often hears that, "the church is full of hypocrites." To call a person a hypocrite does not mean that his ideals are too high, but that he fails to live up to them while telling others they should. But what is the alternative to being a hypocrite? To be a saint? To have no ideals? Or to have low enough ideals that we can attain them without too much exertion? The world is full of good ideals and bad ideals, promises too easily broken, too easily kept, and which ought not to have been made at all.

What is special about the church first, is that hypocrisy is one of the things it teaches us to watch out for in its members. And second, the ideals of some ideologies are such that hypocrisy is a welcome relief, as with the monk who proclaims non-attachment but can't bear to part from his brother monk, or of the revolutionary who shelters his capitalist neighbor from proletarian justice. But Christian hypocrisy is always ugly, precisely because Jesus' ideas about love are truly ideal.

Picture a field of corn ripening on a summer day, exhibiting, on the one hand, what C. S. Lewis calls the "gift love" of the sun, and, on the other, the "need love" of the plants which receive its rays. What relationship do the individual plants have to one another? If distant, corn stalks have little to do with each other, except for breeding; if too close, they compete for light and soil. Human community vacillates between these two prototypes from the vegetable kingdom: distant, stoic, uncaring, like tumbleweeds in a desert, and smothering, nosy, competitive, like hemlock sprouts on a nurse log in a rain forest.

It is not hard to observe these extremes in the church. Some fellowships act as an assembly of autonomous philosophers that wave in a breeze of moral admonition once a week, then go separate ways. You go away thinking, "I shook some hands, basked in a few warm smiles, but did I meet anyone?" You can attend such a church for years without feeling you have made contact with the love of Christ or even really gotten to know another human being.

Step into others, and you feel smothered with attention and love, as if a force-field is sucking on you and draining away your soul. Celebrity preachers like bright yellow weeds stretch to outshine one another in a ruthless struggle for funds and followers, where the principle seems to be "survival of the gaudiest." God likes big numbers, it is assumed, and potential converts to the hive are welcome. But among the crowd in the pews, independent thought and even non-prescription holiness are suspect. One feels like the character played by Woody Allen in the movie *Antz,* a worker in a vast, urban colony of busily-organized insects in Central Park, whose ant psychologist tells him, "you've made a breakthrough today. You feel useless and insignificant? You are useless and insignificant!" In many churches, house-church advocate James Rutz notes, "you feel about as important as another drop of water going over Niagara Falls."[7]

Apart from the rare sage willing to do the hard work of negotiating a golden mean, these are the natural extremes between which human societies oscillate.

Rabi Maharaj tells how he grew up as the son of a Hindu guru who apparently took a vow days after marriage to never communicate to another human being. His father spent days and years in meditation and reading of the Indian Scriptures, without so much as nodding at him even once in his life. The Carmelite monks who lived on pillars for twenty years in the Egyptian desert, and the Buddhist master who came to China from India in the Tang dynasty and said not a word for ten years but only stared at a wall, also showed the extent to which religion can facilitate personal autonomy in the quest for the divine. Marxist critics might say such mystics were parasites on society. Admirers may boast of the cosmic aid their mystic battles with the forces of darkness bring humankind. As a Christian, I cannot help but admire the discipline such men show, but grieve with Rabi Maharaj that the Ultimate Reality these men pursued with such determination did not encourage them to channel that fervor more directly towards the good of those around them.

While some religions shut us up in ourselves, others submerge us into the life of the colony. If all are one, if in the end we "merge into the ocean of being," then what is more pernicious and illusory than individuality?

Isolation and conformity are the duel neurosis of civilization—which the Biblical ideal exists to oppose. And I think the development of civil society in the

West shows that the church, even in a fossilized post-Constantinian form, has been moderately successful at developing the grassroots basis for human liberty.

Thinkers in non-Christian societies sometimes speak enviously of the West's success in developing a "public market of ideas" independent of the state. Even in wealthy, cosmopolitan, democratic Japan, when I asked my students, "where do human rights come from?" They answered, "from the government," or more precisely from one student, "from the Constitution." But when I asked her, "where does the Constitution come from?" She could only reply, "from the government." If I'd asked where the government came from, the only answer could have been, "from MacCarthur." Japan became a socially progressive state with a Constitution allotting "rights" as a concession to America, the nation which became in effect its feudal lord at the end of World War II. Even after 140 years of economic growth and fifty-five years of democracy, there are few grass-roots initiatives against child pornography, political corruption, or even high prices. The attitude is still "the state giveth, the state taketh away, blessed be the name of the state," a holdover from the days when the emperor was a god. There is surprisingly little public debate. Newspapers are controlled by a cartel of shadowy king-makers, and journalists who speak out against abuse more likely to lose their jobs than win prizes. You get the feeling the Japanese will still follow whatever order comes next.

For government in the Western tradition of democracy, rights come from God.[8] Where else could they come from? Matter plus energy plus chance? An "ocean of being" in which cruelty and kindness remain undifferentiated? From deities flitting back and forth from Mount Olympus on personal whims? Apart from the doctrine of a personal and just God it is surprisingly hard to find a theoretical basis for individual freedom. (George Orwell, himself an atheist, showed this point very well in his novel *1984*, in the book's interrogation scene. His hero expressed hope that somehow, against all odds, the totalitarian regime, Big Brother, would some day be defeated. The villain asks him, "Do you believe in God?" To the hero's negative reply, the villain answered, "then what will defeat us?" Unable to find refuge in any principle higher than society, the hero ultimately succumbed and learned to love Big Brother.)

Modern secular ideologies have provided spectacular examples of the opposite tendency, creating societies in which it was mortally dangerous to wear a flower in your hair or whistle an old folk tune. Against that extreme have arisen individualists like Ayn Rand and Rush Limbaugh. Like ancient tyrants who buried jewels and wives in their tombs, they argue that the rich have no obligation to fork any of their treasure over to the envious masses. Both selfish individualism and depersonalizing conformity can be founded upon extrapolations from the natural and merely instinctive world, the world of *Antz*.

The Bible calls believers to something more complex, more difficult, and more human: to a society whose parts are distinct yet function as a unit, like the members of a basketball team, or the human body. Jesus went off to pray by himself, but returned to the collection of miscellaneous disciples he called his friends. If any man does not love his brother, wrote John, he does not know God (1 John 4). If a man does not take care of his family, wrote Paul, he has denied the faith and is "worse than an unbeliever" (1 Tim. 5:8). (That would spell trouble for many respected spiritual leaders.) The gifts of God, Paul wrote, are for the "building up of the body in love." "While all the numerous parts of the body compose one body," wrote Paul,

> "So it is with Christ. For by one Spirit we have been baptized into one body . . . If the entire body were an eye, where would the hearing come in? As it is, however, God has placed the members in the body, each particular one of them just as he saw fit" (1 Cor. 12).

Christianity provides a theoretical basis for the concepts of individuality and community in the doctrine of the Trinity. God is one, yet also plural.

Revelation gives a picture of heaven that also combines individual consciousness and organic unity. The saved do not lounge on private yachts while pretty girls drop grapes in their mouths. "There was a vast host no one could count out of all nations and tribes and peoples and tongues, standing before the throne and before the Lamb" (Rev. 7:9). Yet neither is the individual swallowed up by the throng or unmade by the bliss of knowing God. He who "overcomes" will be given a "stone," on which will appear a "new name . . . which no one knows except the recipient" (Rev. 2:17). Scottish writer George Macdonald wrote of this passage, "not only then has each man his individual relation to God, but each man has his peculiar relation to God. He is to God a peculiar being, made after his own fashion, and that of no one else."[9]

In theory, the Bible avoids the dangers both of totalitarian control and indifference. In practice, the structure of the church, especially since Constantine made Christianity fashionable, has often been perverted by power and respectability. While the same dynamics are capable of perverting fellowship on any level, and it takes work to encourage both group loyalty and individual autonomy in any group, I believe the recent popularity of "cell-group" gatherings in homes shows potential for realizing a more Biblical and holistic Christian community. In traditional churches, it usually takes some kind of commitment beyond Sunday morning—outreach to a local prison, building homes for the poor, involvement in influencing government for justice, work in the mission field—to experience the *E Pluribus Unim,* the unity in diversity, of the Body of Christ. The Biblical church is a church in action, not a personnel flow chart from the Vatican or a stone cathedral with rows of parallel pews facing front and center. After all, if sitting on a hard, unmoving surface soaking in nourishment were an adequate description of the Christian faith in practice, Paul would have compared the church to a barnacle or a lichen rather than a moving and active human body.

Government: The Grand Inquisitor and the Religious Right

In the early 1980s, Baptist Jerry Falwell created the Moral Majority to reform public morality in America. Among other things, he wanted to outlaw abortion, bring prayer into the public schools, and persuade the government to support Christian schools. About the same time a bearded Shiite Muslim named Khomeini formed a revolutionary government in Iran to reform the values of the Middle East. Islamic and Christian reform movements were soon followed by orthodox and highly politicized Hindu and Jewish movements which similarly reacted to the spread of Humanist values. Meanwhile, in Protestant churches there arose a movement called "dominion theology," which taught that believers ought to "take dominion" over every realm of social life.

In an article in the *New York Times,* Presbyterian pastor Robert Meneilly wrote an impassioned response to these trends entitled "Government is not God's work" in which he lambasted the "religious right."

> "We Christians must face up to the fact that Christianity has propagated, in the name of Jesus, devilish acts, bloody wars, awful persecutions, hate crimes and political chaos. We have seen this evidenced on television, with leaders of Operation Rescue harassing neighbors and demonstrating at women's clinics in the most detestable and criminal ways—in the name of Jesus! The hate that certain extreme elements of the Christian community have cultivated towards neighbors of a homosexual orientation resembles the environment of hell."

Meneilly concluded with words I quoted earlier, that the religious right "confronts us with a threat far greater than the old threat of Communism."[10]

Wars and inquisitions have indeed been waged in the name of Jesus. Who can deny that Biblical morality might be used as an excuse for oppression again? Or that even now the church is used to oppress and control? Christianity is hardly unique in this respect, however. As Burke pointed out, a certain quanta of power exists in every nation, no matter what its guiding ideology. "The mind will not tolerate a void," he said, noting presciently just as French revolutionaries were beginning to sharpen the guillotine, should Christianity be overthrown, "Some uncouth, pernicious, and degrading superstition might take the place of it."[11] As Chesterton put it, "I may, it is true, twist orthodoxy so as partially to justify a tyrant. But I can easily make up a German philosophy to justify him entirely."[12]

Human nature being what it is, tyrants can usually find a loophole in any set of rules or laws to justify themselves. How can an honest Christian, remembering the request of the apostles to send fire and brimstone on an unrepentant village, deny that the urge to bring about the Kingdom of God through superior firepower is perennially inviting to believers? But the darkest chapters of church history should be read as a warning about human nature in general, rather than Biblical values in particular. This can be seen in many ways. First, look at Jesus' response. Jesus not only denied his disciples' request, he rebuked and even hinted they were listening to the devil instead of God. He rejected every attempt to enlist him as a political candidate, and introduced a rather novel concept: separation of church and state. "My kingdom is not of this world," he said plainly (John 18:36).

Another fact to keep in mind in regard to the religious evils of the Middle Ages, is that while the era has been called the "Age of Faith," it was not especially an age of *Christian* faith. Many Christians agree that the church took a big step away from the spirit of the New Testament when it gained political power in the Roman empire. Charles Williams wrote:

> "In fact, it is doubtful whether Christendom has ever quite recovered from the mass-conversion of the fashionable classes inside Rome and of the barbaric races outside Rome . . . Christendom labored under its converts; they seized, colored, and almost ruined it."[13]

Political rivalry with Islam furthered influenced the direction of the church. Scripture had not yet been translated into the "vulgar" tongues of Europe, literacy rates had plummeted since the collapse of the Roman Empire, and the printing press had not yet been invented. Inquisitors banned the common people from owning any part of the Bible, and Bible translators, like John Wycliffe, and other believers who loved the word of God *too much* for their own good, were even burnt at the stake. (See Appendix.)

On one point the Inquisitors seemed to agree with modern communists and secular humanists: the Bible is a dangerous document. No wonder. The Garden of Eden represented choice. The covenant between God and the Jewish people was put to a vote. Jesus made the boast that many evil geniuses, from Alexander to Stalin, have longed to make: "I have overcome the world" (John 16:33). But rather than leaving an example of *jihad, coup d'etat,* or revolution, he was a conqueror who refused to be king, a "suffering servant" who quixotically taught his followers to "overcome" by forgiving their enemies. "Blessed are you when men revile you," he warned them plainly. "Pray for your persecutors" (Matt. 5). Jesus answered his disciples' request for ministerial positions in the new regime by explaining that the rules of power would work backwards in the Kingdom of Heaven: "Whoever among you wants to be great must be your servant" (Matt. 20:26).

It is true, unlike Buddhism, Christianity leaves room for believers to involve themselves in politics.[14] Was this a mistake? Would the world be safer if believers closeted themselves in mountain cells and meditated for peace?

In his futuristic science fiction novel, Arthur C. Clarke has a hero of the twenty-fifth century bring into the far reaches of space a tooth of Buddha, who founded what he called "the only faith that never became stained with blood."[15] Anyone who reads Asian history will realize that the truth is more complicated. As with any human history, the history of Buddhism illustrates the doctrine (on which Christians and Buddhists agree) that "power corrupts." The characteristic Buddhist ideal of renouncing power has an undeniable nobility to it, and individual Buddhists have sometimes reigned with wisdom and compassion, but the example of Buddha seems to have done little to contribute to the development of free societies.[16] If sages head for the hills, who takes the reins of government? The best commoners in Buddhist countries could hope for was a lay follower who had little ambition for enlightenment in the Buddhist sense, but had attained a measure of enlightenment in the European sense—an enlightened dictator, such as Ashoka of India or Shotoku of Japan. One could also hope that he was simultaneously influenced by the teachings of Confucius enough to know his limits, and his counselors to point them out when need be.

Buddhism has served as the conduit of tremendous philosophical and artistic development in much of Asia. It is also serving as the focus of much wishful thinking and naivete for people in the West who assume the grass is greener on the other side of the fence. In *Jew in the Lotus,* Roger Kamenetz noted approvingly the teaching of a Tibetan monk that "if people mix up their religion with politics, they are themselves the greatest enemies to the survival of the inner meaning of their faith."[17] He didn't seem to notice that this concept was a contradiction of the whole idea of a Dalai Lama. The present Dalai Lama well deserved his Nobel Prize for peace, and is a god to the Tibetan Buddhists. But the Tibetans have many gods, and some of the most efficacious adorn themselves with necklaces of human skulls. And how did the Dalai Lama obtained his political powers and status as an incarnation of the god of benevolence in the first place? By inviting the Mongolian army, fresh from genocide in the Northeast of China, to intervene in Tibetan politics. The history of Buddhism in Tibet, China and Japan has often been extremely bloody.

My point is not to belittle the achievements of Buddhism. My point is, rather, that any religion that achieves success will be used by unscrupulous people to oppress. It is unfair to blame Buddha for the evil deeds of those who ignore his teaching on compassion. It is equally unreasonable to blame Jesus for what happens when his teachings are not followed. No matter what religion or ideology a society adopts, even if it is the ideology of democracy, sooner or later tyrants will find a way to use it to justify oppression.

What, then, is our best defense? "All that it takes for evil to conquer is for good men to do nothing." Meditating, or praying, in the hills, while not nothing, is in the Christian (or Confucian) view an insufficient response if not combined with a prophetic willingness to stand up to oppressors on behalf of the oppressed.

Western idealists, having finally realized that Marxism was a dead-end street, sought inspiration in the East. The Dalai Lama, meanwhile, learned democracy from the West. And the West derived civil liberties from two sources: the Greco-Roman tradition, and Israel.

The importance of the latter can be seen by comparing the French and American revolutions. John Adams, sent to Paris as a representative of the new American state, bristled at the impiety and sexual immorality of the French ruling classes which fed the revolution. "As much as I love, esteem and admire the Greeks," he wrote in the margins of a book by an anti-Christian French thinker, "I believe the Hebrews have done more to enlighten and civilize the world."[18] Donald Treadgold, in his work *Freedom, a History,* argued that when it came to civil liberties, Adams was right: "Hebrew society was unique in the ancient near East in managing to avoid the techniques, devices, and institutions of despotism."[19] Treadgold showed how Medieval Christianity began to supply at least the beginnings of three elements found wanting in classical civilization: representative government, an economy not built on slave power, and liberty of conscience. These principles were present in implicit, rather than explicit, form in the Gospels, and the next two millennia saw them gradually take root and grow among the barbarian tribes of Europe.[20]

While no explicit theory of democracy can be found in the Bible, and the Christian Scriptures do not attack slavery outright, they lay out principles which are implicitly unfriendly to tyrants: choice, concern for the poor, and equality before God. The concept of "choice" is so deeply engrained that I think a mind that feeds upon the Scriptures should realize intuitively that conversion to goodness cannot be forced. The Old Testament also legislated steps by which the rich were required to help the poor and destitute. The poor were given special tax breaks, and laws guaranteed they could never lose their land permanently. Long before Karl Marx, the prophets thundered, "Wash yourselves! Purify yourselves! Seek justice; restrain the ruthless; protect the orphan; defend the widow" (Isa. 1:17). The rich were warned of judgment against "those who oppress the wage earner in his wages, and the widow and the orphan, and those who turn aside the foreigner" (Mal. 3:5), those who "sell the poor for a pair of sandals" (Amos 2:6). The prophets used apocalyptic language to describe the coming judgement. "The eternal mountains are scattered; the everlasting hills bow down" (Hab. 3:6). Nietzsche had a point when he complained that Christianity "obliterates distinctions between masters and slaves." This is why personality cults were toned down in the West after the Caesar-worship of ancient Rome, until the rise of anti-God ideologies beginning with the French revolution.

It was recently suggested to me that the Christian idea of sin is "fascist," because of the low view of human nature it suggests. The truth, on the contrary, is that the founding fathers of the American government self-consciously made awareness of sin one of the cornerstones of democracy. James Madison, chief author of the Constitution and a student of Presbyterian educator John Witherspoon, lucidly explained the theology behind the American system of checks and balances: "There is a degree of depravity in mankind which requires a certain degree of circumspection and distrust."[21]

The practical things in life are often unattractive, such as the parts of the body we stand and sit on, and the mud we grow our food it in. So it is with the unpopular but useful doctrine of sin, that may be the greatest practical check on tyranny of all. Here we find in embryonic form the seeds of all those troublesome political organs communism felt it could do without: an independent parliament and court, a free press, the veto.

The French revolution rebelled against the Medieval church not because it was too pious, but too worldly; to the degree it ceased to be the church, it ceased to act as a restraint on tyranny.[22] Charles Dickens wrote of bishops of the day who had "sensual eyes, loose tongues, and looser lives," who issued from their courts to "cringing and fawning . . . as to bowing down in body and spirit, nothing in that way was left for Heaven—which may have been one among other reasons why the worshippers of Monseigneur never troubled it."[23] Yet the church remained the church in name, a citadel of social prestige against which revolutionaries could rage.

One generation rejects the teachings of Jesus, scoffing at them in private, denying them in practice, but continues to go through the motions of religious ceremony. The next generation rises up in idealism against its parents, and marking hypocrisy and emptiness as the essence of Christianity, turns completely against it. The problem, as Chesterton put it, is not that the Gospel has been tried and found wanting, but that it has often been found hard and not tried.

The presence of hypocrites in the church, and the use politicians make of the church, does not prove Christianity wrong any more than the same phenomena proves Buddhism wrong. "Be on the alert!" Jesus told his disciples. "Many will come in my name and deceive many." He described believers as a remnant, a "people called out," in but not of the world, salt sprinkled on food, light in a dark room. He warned that while the church would change the world for the better, the world would not respond by becoming truly "Christian," but rather by turning against the Gospel in various ways, often in the name of God. Who can say Jesus was too starry-eyed in his view of the dangers of human community?

As the famous nineteenth century preacher Henry Ward Beecher (brother of the even more famous Harriet Beecher Stowe, author of *Uncle Tom's Cabin*) once pointed out in the context of the Civil War, "It has been found not difficult for men to repent of other people's sins."[24] The Crusades, Inquisitions, and religious wars should make Christians pause and reflect. But however often we repent of the sins of forefathers who, honestly or dishonestly, claimed to be followers of

Christ, we still face spiritual and political challenges of our own era which are equally complex and equally easy to mishandle. Religion can escape the taint of any positive action by denying reality and escaping inwards. It can also turn outward and try to change the world through force. Islam and Marxism attempted an almost complete identification of church and state, while some philosophical schools of Buddhism and Hinduism tended towards complete separation. Christians have done both, at times. Christianity does not offer a ready-made political program nor deny the need to make tough choices or the kind of existential anguish and uncertainty Abraham Lincoln felt at a critical point of the Civil War:

> "The will of God prevails. In great contests each party claims to act in accordance with the will of God. Both may be, and one must be wrong. God cannot be for, and against, the same thing at the same time. In the present civil war it is quite possible that God's purpose is something different from the purpose of either party . . . "[25]

Christianity, then, differs from some religions on the question of church and state in four regards. First, while Jesus had bigger fish to fry, he did not counsel us to withdraw from society or politics, like Buddha. Second, he never promised a utopian end to conflict, as did Marx. In fact he promised wars and persecutions of all kinds—not because Christianity hates humanity, but because people are ambivalent towards truth. Third, unlike Islam and other revolutionary religions, Christianity prescribes separation of church and state. And fourth, it provided the theoretical principles which served as a basis for modern freedoms: the doctrine of sin, legal equality, a special duty to the poor, and a special warning for the rich.[26]

Society: Why Tolerance is Not a Christian Virtue

When I conducted a poll of what Americans thought of various religions, one lady told me Christianity was "too exclusive," going as far as to define the whole point of Christianity as "to exclude those who do not believe, to impose beliefs on others." The best virtue, she said, is "to see commonalities among humans so that peace is maintained."

In fact, Christianity does admit a great many commonalities between believers and unbelievers. The highest common point is that we are all created in the image of God. Does not that viewpoint by its very nature give ground for a nobler peace than the primary competing view of humanity as a race that has evolved by killing off its rivals, like the tribe of monkeys in *2001 Space Odessey* which invented the club and slaughtered the neighboring tribe?

But pleasant words are not always enough by themselves to bring neighborliness. The prophet Ezekiel warned of prophets and priests who use peace for propaganda purposes, "Saying 'peace, peace' when there is no peace" (Ezek. 8:11). Indeed, the word was often used in bizarre contexts in the twentieth century. A missionary in Tibet noted that expressions of a desire for peace in the West were enthusiastically seconded by officers of Red Army he met there.'"We are struggling hard for peace,' was one of the first remarks made to me. . .to be thus addressed by a Chinese officer, engaged in the active invasion of Tibet, was baffling in the extreme . . . the desires expressed in the West for peace were being repeated in all sincerity by these young fellows."[27] Just as he overthrew the elected government of Russia in favor of a communist dictatorship, and prepared for Civil War, Lenin issued tracts using the words "peace," "democracy," and even "salvation" (*cna-cenue.*) Elsewhere he explained, "We must use what the peasants say, even if it is economically unsound or meaningless, as a hook for our propaganda."[28]

During NATO's attacks on Yugoslavia in 1999, I took a walk near my home in a suburb of Nagasaki, Japan, and found myself in a farming town on the far slope of a mountain. An election was coming up, and behind me a politician in a pickup truck had chugged his vehicle up the hill to ask the electorate of the town for its support over a loudspeaker. His risk-free method was to preach against NATO's war in Yugoslavia, which however irrelevant in the tangerine fields of a country on the other side of the world that did not support the war anyway, was not likely to be booed in Nagasaki. "Peace is the most basic necessity of life," he shouted. "Without peace, you can't have anything!" Almost the same day, after two high school students went on a rampage and murdered thirteen fellow students, the American president flew to Colorado. "We need to hammer into our children's heads that violence is wrong," he said, as bombs dropped on Belgrade.

It is easy to give simple solutions to problems you don't have to solve. It is easy to talk of "peace" when someone else is defending your borders, and the conflict is thousands of miles away, or when you are visiting someone else's school, and telling children how to solve adolescent dilemmas you no longer face.

When the Crusaders sacked Jerusalem and Byzantium and slaughtered innocent citizens of those cities, in the name of God, they were responding to a perceived threat. In the same way, when we were prepared to destroy the world in a nuclear holocaust, in the name of democracy, we were responding to a threat. They faced an ideology which joined church and state, which they found as frightening as we found the Red Army. It seems unfair to me that we who defended ourselves by threatening to blow up the planet, glibly ask what perversion of thinking led our forefathers to mere rape and pillage! Out of the heart come all manner of wickedness, said Jesus.

Christianity describes a low as well as a high commonality among humans. When I asked Americans "who is a sinner?" many non-Christians gave answers like "my boss," "Ronald Reagan," or "people who commit crimes." Christians, on the other hand, tended to say, "we all are."

This may sound like an insult, classifying you and me with Jack the Ripper and politicians of opposing parties. We don't want that kind of inclusiveness.

Yet, ironically, this "low" inclusive view of humankind—combined with the equally-inclusive "high" view of untouchables, sweating brown mobs, street children with social diseases, and gangsters, as children of God, and children of no lesser God either, but of a holy, loving, hands-on God, who designed DNA and put the pouch in the kangaroo and the nose on the elephant and flung pulsing stars into space—these two commonalities, at one so uncommon and so incredible, are in actual fact what helped create our political freedom. One nation, under God, with equal justice under the Law.

But it is also true that Christianity is exclusive. Jesus speaks unabashedly of children of darkness and children of light. Dualism is the inevitable fruit of freedom: we take different paths, and find ourselves in different places.

According to some, we are bound to reach Nirvana whether we like it or not. Come hell or high water (literally), in the end we are fated to join our consciousness to a state of Oneness. But is it more tolerant to say there is only on goal, than to say there is only one path to a particular goal?

Christians believe we have a choice about where we are going. We call one of the choices "hell," to discourage people from making it. But even in heaven we become more distinct, rather than less, and more human, rather than less. Christianity is about unity in diversity: a unity of unlikes, of distinct beings who are not one and therefore can love each other. To love means to love another; falling in love with yourself is boring and lonely. I am saddened at Shirley MacLaine's statement that, "the only person you ever make love to is yourself." Or Marx, that God was the sun we revolve around until we learn to revolve around ourselves. That dizzy and idolatrous revolution is close to what Christians mean by hell.

Living organisms require a liquid solution to move nutrients between organs. Sap and blood serve in multi-celled creatures as a substitute for the mother ocean in whose womb plankton float. Without some liquid solution, complex biological life is impossible.

It is often proposed that tolerance should serve as the ideal solution for human society. Like water, tolerance costs little, but is extremely valuable, floating the cargo of ideas and joining great belief systems. Tolerance keeps religions safely apart, while allowing a certain commerce of thought. The tolerant put up with the eccentricities of others, and drift free when fate pulls them apart.

The Gospel is the story of a God who sought to bind people to himself and to each other not with water, but with blood. He sent messengers into the world, and they were beaten and killed by a world which did not care for their "intolerance." Finally, he came himself. Having shed blood to bind his followers together, he told them, "go into all the world and preach the Gospel."

Jesus calls us beyond tolerance, not because he wants to be intolerant, or even nosy. The Bible admits that in the end, what one does with one's life is between oneself and God. But love requires that the standards of God not be "hidden under a bushel," because we are our brother's keeper.

The *Tao* is eternal, as Lao Zi put it. Those who try to "abolish all eternal truths" can't pull it off. Not the Zen patriarch Hui Ke, who burnt the Buddhist Scriptures, not Marx, Nietzche or Skinner, not the existentialists, not a single nihilist nor perhaps even the devil himself has succeeded in "abolishing" a virtue, even in his own heart. Ideals may be deconstructed, analyzed, refuted, smirked at, yet they are not destroyed, merely banished to the underground, where they pour out speech, day after day, and there is no one who does not prove in some way or another that he hears them still.

A Christian should not be surprised to find a Hindu risking his or her life to save a neighbor, anymore than a Samaritan stopping in a danger zone to bandage the wounds of a Jew. Christianity agrees the categories of right and wrong are common to all humanity. Burke put the matter in these terms, "we know that we have made no discoveries; and we think that no discoveries are to be made, in morality."[29]

Yet as eternal as is the *Tao* which unites humankind, the categories and competitions which divide us seem eternal. Ours is a world of competitions, alliances, ancient hatreds, and insolvable territorial disputes.

What the world needs no doubt is love. But we don't need a simplistic love which ignores the complexity of life, forces us into a single mold, or tells us to drop prior responsibilities and practice altruism in a hormone-free vacuum. True love, of necessity, affirms both the need for boundaries and the injustice and inhumanity of boundaries. Any reasonable approach to life must take into account our need for society and quiet, a secure home and a gate into the wide world, for order and freedom, for a sense of ego that allows individual humanity and also the occasional collapse of those boundaries that we call romance, patriotism or ethnic pride.

It is easy to climb a mountain, or found a monastery in which silence is the rule, or look at a blank wall, and brag that one has caused no sectarian warfare. It is easy to rule one's house with a rod of iron, and brag that unlike the neighbor's tykes, one's own children don't spray-painted graffiti on highway overpasses. (Maybe they can't paint?) But how do we arrange society to allow both unity and diversity, a complex and dynamic unity of unequal parts which is the meaning of the phrase, "*E Pluribus, Unim*?" How do we order families so that children grow up both responsible and happy? How do we organize spiritual community so as to benefit from the wisdom and intellect of our leaders, yet also from the spontaneity and simplicity of ordinary believers? How can the church influence society towards good without falling into a pharisaical sectarianism? These are not simple questions.

The central teaching of Christianity is the Incarnation, that God was willing to get his hands dirty to redeem humankind. The Christian church has gotten its hands dirty with a different kind of dirt as it sometimes foolishly ignored and sometimes even more foolishly tried to enforce Jesus' moral vision. Yet I believe that vision is still the most balanced understanding of what it means to "love our neighbor as ourselves."

In each case, the Bible picks what the modern world correctly perceives as the most difficult path: to submit to an unseen "Higher Power" and allow him to remake me in his image rather than simply manufacturing a god to look like myself. To stick with one love for life, and close my eyes to the rest, yet to encourage a healthy passion within that union and look at the body with gratitude. To confront other believers when I have to, never merely tolerating or indulging a brother's or sister's weakness, yet also avoiding a judgmental or self-righteous spirit. To neither overstep my authority, nor to run from it. To act as a check on government, yet also submit to it, and keep my eye on another kingdom. To allow myself neither the respectability and good will that comes with saying all religions are equally true, nor the gratification of holding all other religions as equally false, nor of exploiting eternal truths as a means to realizing political ambition or commercial gain. To forgive from the heart "up to seventy times seven," yet not sublimate anger into bitterness or gossip, or act like a wall flower, but honestly confront the person who has wronged you—in love. To lose all fears in the fear of God. In each area of life, to "die to self" without "acting like a martyr," and enjoy the resurrected life he brings even in this world.

The Bible spells out what I see as a reasonable but rather daunting rule for love. It shows a balance and a wisdom that sets it apart from human religions, including modern scientific ideologies, even as it incorporates insights that are perennial to humankind. Nor are these ideals arbitrary, but deeply rooted in the nature of who God is and what it means to know him. But they appear terribly difficult. As Chesterton once said, it is easy to fall down; there are many angles at which to fall, but only one at which to stay upright. But now let us consider what has helped the church to stand.

---

[1] Mozi, from Chen Jingpan, *Confucius as a Teacher*, Foreign Language Press, 1990, p. 296

[2] I am not saying this was the only or primary purpose of the dialogue, but I think taking Job's mind off his own troubles may have been his first need.

[3] An excellent essay on this subject, an aid to clear thinking as well as good writing and speaking, is George Orwell's biting essay *Politics and the English Language*, which can be found, among other places, in *Twentieth Century Literary Criticism*.

[4] Rudyard Kipling, *Jungle Book*, Signet Classics, Longman, 1961, p. 55

[5] *Night*, Bantom, 1960, p. 61-2

[6] *South Asia Pushes Nuclear Luck to its Limit*, Gwynne Dyer, *Japan Times*, April, 15, 1999

[7] *The Open Church: How to Bring Back the Exciting Life of the First Century Church*, Christian Books, 1992

[8] Note the similarity between the reasoning of the American founding fathers and that of Job. James Madison: "We hold these truths as self-evident. All men are created equal and endowed by their Creator with certain inalienable rights." Job: "If I ignore the rights of my servant . . . what shall I answer (God)? Did not He who made me in the womb, make him, too?" (Job 31:15).

[9] George Macdonald, *An Anthology*, compiled by C. S. Lewis

[10] Robert Meneilly, *New York Times, Weekly Review*, August 29, 1993 While some conservative Christians might have had this coming, Meneilly seemed rather selective and disengenious in his attack. For one thing, pastors in his wing of the church often did not see communism as a threat, but a promise. Paul Hollander details extensively in *Political Pilgrims* how many religious leaders supped with party chairmen and praised the revolution as a fulfillment of the ideals of Christ, while local colleagues dined on mouldy bread in prison cells. Gulag inmates Richard Wurmbrand and Alexander Solzhenitsyn give further examples. The short story *Buddha's Smile* in Solzhenitsyn's classic *The First Circle*, while dealing specifically with a political rather than religious leader, (Eleanor Roosevelt?), is a masterful description of the effect such complicity had on the morale of inmates. In any case, such comparison makes one wonder if pastors like Meneilly have even yet come to grips with what their friends on the other side of the Iron Curtain have wrought. In its first 150 years, Marxism put 100 million innocent human beings into the ground. Did the church claim its first victim that early in its history?

[11] Edmund Burke, *Reflections on the Revolution in France*, Pelican Classics, 1968, p. 188

[12] G. K. Chesterton, *Orthodoxy*, Doubleday, 1959, p. 125-6

[13] Charles Williams, *Descent of the Dove: a Short History of the Holy Spirit in the Church*, Pellegrini and Conalry, 1939

[14] People argue if it's feasible to "legislate morality." In truth, morality is all that is ever legislated: someone's ethical assumptions lie behind every law and even every new road. Christians differ about the extent to which we should try to enact our values into law. Personally, I think not too far. I favor laws against abortion, because (in the view that the American Constitution adopted from the Bible) it is the function of government to protect weak members of society. In the case of homosexuality, while laws in the past may have saved lives, and alleged Constitutional barriers to such laws seem a function of wishful thinking, it seems to me persuasion is the more Scriptural approach. In this and other cases, Christian principles influence me to a more "permissive" approach than would strictly judicial or utilitarian logic.

[15] Arthur C. Clarke, *The Songs of Distant Earth*, Ballantine Books, 1986, p. 285

[16] Donald Treadgold, *Freedom, a History*, New York University, 1990 p.81 Of

Buddhist countries, "free or clearly pluralistic institutions emerged in none of them before modern times, with the interesting exception of Japan."

17 Roger Kamenetz, *Jew in the Lotus*, Harper San Francisco, 1984, p. 166

18 *Christianity and the Constitution: The Faith of Our Founding Fathers*, John Eidsmoe, Baker, 1987

19 Donald Treadgold, *Freedom, a History*, New York University Press, 1990, p. 32

20 Ibid. p. 76-77

21 James Kennedy and Jerry Newcombe, *What if the Bible Had Never Been Written?* Thomas Nelson, 1998, p.96

22 For a lively and fairly objective study of French society a little before the revolution, including the relationship between church and state, see W. Lewis, *The Splendid Century*. For a more biased but dazzlingly insightful analysis of the errors of the revolution itself, much of Burke's *Reflection on the Revolution in France* still makes good reading.

23 Charles Dickens, *Tale of Two Cities*, p. 142-3

24 *American Sermons: The Pilgrims to Martin Luther King, Jr.*, Library of America, 1999, p. 649

25 Alonzo MacDonald, *The Spiritual Growth of a Public Man*, from *Character Counts*, p. 108

26 This latter is often misunderstood. Talmudic scholar Jacob Neusner interprets Jesus' words to the rich young man, "sell all you have and follow me," to mean that Jesus "demanded that to enter the Kingdom of Heaven I repudiate family and turn my back on home" (*Newsweek*, March 27, 2000, *A Rabbi Argues with Jesus*.) But while Jesus met many rich people, he said this to only one. There is no reason to assume it was or is normative for his disciples. Nor did the early church seem to think Jesus wanted them to keep away from their families; after all, Jesus visited his disciples at home and seems to have been on good terms with sisters and mother-in-laws. Mr. Neusner may be confusing Jesus with the Buddha; it is a common mistake.

27 Geoffrey T. Bull, *When Iron Gates Yield*, p. 117

28 See Vladimir Lenin, *To Workers, Soldiers, and Peasants*, and *Report on Soviet Power*

29 Burke, *Reflections on the Revolution in France*, Penguin Books, 1969, p. 182

CHAPTER 7

How Has Jesus Changed 👉
the World?

"THEN THERE'S Papa, who once said (Jesus is) God's Son all right, and that he survived the crucifixion just fine, but that the 2,000-year-old funeral service His cockeyed followers call Christianity probably made Him sorry He did."[1] David James Duncan

"My father was deported from Bessarabia by the Russians. We never had enough to eat. I was beaten in school, then put in jail for running away and joining the Iron Guard. I'd never met a single good, truthful, loving person. I said to myself, 'It's just a legend about Christ. There isn't anyone in the world like that today and I don't believe there ever was.' But when I'd been in prison a few months I had to say that I was wrong. I met sick men who gave away their last crust. I shared a cell with a bishop who had such goodness that you felt the touch of his robe would heal."[2] Valieriu Gafencu

The mid-day sun beat on the little party as it passed through the desert. One of the group suggested a stop, and they settled in the grudging shade of a row of stubby cypress trees. The leader of the band thought back to the shouts, dust, and blood of a day a few weeks before, as they dragged one of the cult's ringleaders out of town. The "elder" kept his cool to the end. "I see heaven open and the Son of Man standing at the right hand of God," blaspheming until his body hit the turf.

The leader stared moodily at an old snag. Isaiah wrote of a man who cut down a tree and used half of it for firewood, and carved the other half into an idol. Come, now, he mentally cross-examined the body. It had taken a thousand years to purge idolatry from our culture. Why are you so willing to throw away our heritage, everything that makes Israel stand out from idolatrous nations around us, for the pretensions of this Galilean magician? Was it any better to make an idol of a woodworker rather than the wood? "Let's be off!" he said. Picking up a rock, he gave a grunt as he took a strip of bark off the snag. "We're expected in Damascus. Better not keep the heretics waiting!"

Saul was no casual convert to the Christian faith. He was a living representative of Palestine's Moral Majority: "a Hebrew of Hebrews; in regard to the Law, a lay preacher, as for zeal, persecuting the church, as for legalistic righteousness, faultless" (Phil. 3:5-6). Saul was a fanatic, a fundamentalist in the worst sense of the word, empowered by the Ayatollahs of the day to cut a swath of holy terror through the ranks of the infidels.

Humanists of the old school used to tell us that what a person is, results from his genetic makeup and early childhood training. "The basic motivations which determine our values," Frederick Edwards wrote in *Humanist Magazine*, "are ultimately rooted in our biology and early experiences." One can build a good case for this interpretation from the failed attempts governments have made to reform criminals and drug addicts.

What role then does religion play in the development of morality? An even more depressing view, expressed by Nobel laureate Steven Weinburg, is that it socializes otherwise well-adjusted and talented men and women, like the young Saul, to mistreat those who fall outside boundaries set by their sect. "With or without religion," he said in debate, "you would have good people doing good things and evil people doing evil things. But for good people to do evil things, that takes religion."[3]

One can build a case for this theory, too, from the biographies of many ideological zealots ancient and modern, and the slow corruption bad ideas bring to eager young students like Mao Zedong. Faith in God taught Saul to murder. There is nothing new about that. The urge to kill is a universal part of human nature, and so it seems is the urge to sacrifice to gods, even if we call them History or Humanity. Yet what happened to Saul on the road to Damascus is also an oft-repeated part of the human story. What Saul met in the desert was not an ideology, a moral hypothesis, or a stone tablet, but a man. A few years later, we find this hate criminal, name now changed to Paul, facing drowning, stoning, snakes, whips, clubs, wild animals, and wilder men to preach the Gospel he once tried to destroy. The new passion within him expressed itself in a poem about love that 2000 years later I often heard on pop radio on the Buddhist island of Taiwan, set to a Chinese melody:

"Love is patient, love is kind. It does not envy, it does not boast, it is not proud . . . Love does not delight in evil but always with the truth. It always protects, always trusts, always hopes, always perseveres . . . Love will never fail" (1 Cor. 13).

Like most westerners, I grew up in an atmosphere of intense cynicism about the church.

Christ's teachings are good, most people agreed. Maybe even the most balanced and ideal the world has seen. Yet like the outcast in the Romanian prison, many wonder where the power is behind the law. When I meet Western Buddhists and Taoists, I often ask how they became interested in eastern religion. I've heard the words, "well, I grew up in the Catholic church . . ." so often I begin to suspect these words must be part of the new catechism. Having endured rather than enjoyed years of Christian indoctrination, many had come to believe the story of Jesus must be a legend, and the love the church preached nothing more than pious rhetoric. When I ask non-Christians what they think of Christianity, many give such replies as, "hypocritical: they preach love and acceptance, then view non-Christians as somehow less in the eyes of God," or "good ideals, but practiced with hypocrisy."

Many sensitive Christians, feeling with shame the failure of the church to live up to its calling, are willing to concede a great deal on this point. Philip Yancey and Paul Brand wrote:

"We who are His body have stained God's reputation by galloping off on bloody crusades, cracking bones and joints on torture racks, christening a slave ship The Good Ship Jesus, furthering racism in His name. God in Christ in human form is one thing; God in us is quite another."[4]

I won't say these arguments have no merit. How could I? I don't need to look further than my own actions and thoughts the past twenty-four hours to throw doubt on God's plan to reveal his love through believers. But nevertheless, looking with due humility at church history, and at my own life as well, I have to insist (however timidly at first, but with growing boldness) that this is the lesser story.[5]

A power surge of some sort flooded into Saul that day. Some say it was the sun. Others say the Son. But an energy of some nature rewired his spiritual circuitry, redirecting his gifts and passion from hatred to love.

The world is full of people like Saul, changed by encounters with Jesus. Over the past 2000 years, those encounters, along with Jesus' example and teachings, have changed life on this planet more than anything else. Gafescu found Christ in a Romanian dungeon. The light of Christ is often easiest to see in dark places—like the Walled City of Hong Kong.

The Walled City of Hong Kong

I lived in Hong Kong with young men and women from all parts of the globe who had come to the then-English colony to serve Christ and for cross-cultural excitement. Among the hundred or so students and staff in the abandoned hospital on the hill above Central and Wanchai, the friendly smiles of a couple young Chinese men stood out, and I often greeted them in the halls. They'd been drug addicts who had become Christians through the ministry of an English woman named Jackie Pullinger.

When Jackie first came to Hong Kong in the late 1960s, she was drawn to a district under the flight path to Kai Tak airport (anyone who landed at that old airport, especially at night, or like I did once, in a typhoon, will remember it well). Shaded by tall, skinny skyscrapers which defied all building codes, the Walled City housed 30,000 people in a few acres. With only two public toilets, the place was literally a cesspool. Also, for historical reasons, metaphorically: exempt from law enforcement as from building codes, the district had become a sanctuary for prostitution, organized crime, gambling, and drug addiction.

Were a person merely a product of his environment, there wouldn't seem to be much hope for drug addicts of the Walled City. Born as often as not to petty gangsters and prostitutes themselves addicted to heroin or opium, neither heredity nor nurture seemed to favor them. Should some wild idea of making oneself productive break through the fog of addiction, an addict's will was badly trained to discipline. Government-run rehabilitation centers, in which counselors made use of scientific methods and medicines, showed a recidivism rate of 90 to 95 percent.

Pullinger couldn't even speak Cantonese when she first came, and had no background in crime rehabilitation or treatment of addicts. But drawn to Hong Kong through a series of dreams and visions, she began haltingly talking to heroin addicts, murderers, and gang leaders about the love of God. One told her, "You have a power which I don't have. If my brothers get hooked on drugs I have them beaten up. I don't want them on heroin and I've found I can't make them quit. But I've watched you. And I believe Jesus can."[6] In her biography, *Chasing the Dragon*, Jackie told about a Triad leader named Ah Kei who became a Christian and went to visit relatives in China. At the border security guards recognized him. When he explained he was no longer involved in crime, they refused to believe him, since as Jackie put it, "The Chinese opium wars have proven that no one can escape from addiction." The entire family became Christians as a result of this change. Ah Kei's father celebrated with an exquisite feast (as only Cantonese prepare). He rose and gave a succinct reply to Weinburg's complaint that religion allows good people to do evil, "Once I was young and now I am old, but never before have I seen a bad man become a good man."[7]

I had the chance to meet such people in other contexts also. Men who had known violence, rejection, and deception since birth, and been addicted to drugs for years. Men with a past who, for the first time, had a future. The best word I can think to describe them is "cheerful." Like the hero in *Beauty and the Beast*, they'd learned to love, and it even made them *look* different.

While an attractive woman, Jackie did not claim it was her own beauty which changed these young men. Nor did she see herself as some sort of hypnotist. She argued,

> "Those who explained this extraordinary spiritual happening as an example of 'mind over matter' had to be ignorant of the facts. A drug addict facing withdrawal has a mind already half dead through continual drug abuse and is deeply fearful of pain. Most of our boys only begin to understand Jesus with their minds after they had already experienced Him in their lives and bodies."[8]

Jackie Pullinger was not the only Christian I met in Asia involved in helping drug addicts get their lives back together. Chinese Christians have a long history of successfully relying on prayer and discipleship to help addicts build new lives, from the ministry of a Pastor Xu in northern China at the turn of the last century, to a string of drug rehab centers throughout Southeast Asia run by the rugged characters of an organization called Operation Dawn. I often stayed with an American and Chinese couple on the beautiful east coast of Taiwan who discipled fifty drug addicts and prostitutes at a time in the Christian faith. I visited a center near the America military bases in the Philippines that helped 150 women leave prostitution every year. I found that some of the most successful Christian evangelists in Asia were once drug addicts and criminals. It dawned on me, as I met such characters, that in Asia, at any rate, Jesus was changing lives, not through ecclesiastical powers-that-be, but through powers that are not: simple, weak men and women whom God had called, like Saul on the road to Damascus.[9]

What Could Another God Do For India?

In the fall of 1984 some of us took a trip to Thailand and India, ostensibly for preaching Christianity, but probably as much to learn about the world as to teach it anything. India came as a shock to me: rats nearly as big as cats wandered into the library where I was reading my Bible to coolly look me over; and crippled beggars wheeled themselves laterally into traffic on skateboards to ask for a rupee. We even encountered what almost amounted to a religious civil war during our visit. I also met front-line troops in what appeared to be a small and disorderly army of Christians from around the world who felt called to an astonishing variety of service to the poor and outcaste. Mother Theresa is famous; but there are hundreds or thousands of Mother Theresas in India. I visited a center her order founded in Bombay, and talked with a man from the Brahmin class who had been rejected twice in his life: first, by his family, for embracing Marxism, and second, by his Marxist comrades, for developing asthma. He seemed overwhelmed by the love he experienced from the nuns who had picked him off the street, and wanted to know Jesus.

Bimal was a leper in Calcutta, a man whom passersby might have wondered what he had done in past lives to account for such an evil karma. His story may be the kind of thing radical Hindus have in mind when they accuse Christians of "bribing" the poor to convert. Taken under wing by an Assembly of God missionary and escorted to a leper colony, Bimal tried to work up his courage to throw himself under the wheels of the train. The missionary, however, kept watch all night through half-closed eyes. At the colony, Bimal became desperate, and began to pray to the God of lepers the missionary had told him about:

"Help me, Jesus. Help me, Jesus. You are the Son of God. You are the Son of God. Help me!"

"Bimal was suddenly overwhelmed . . . To this day he weeps when he describes the sensation . . . 'Leprosy suddenly meant nothing to me. In that moment, I felt stronger than leprosy. When days came that I weakened and became discouraged, I would pray again and that strength always came back to me.'"[10]

In many south Asian countries, lepers were among the first to become Christians. Why? Jesus gave his followers the example of one who reached out and touched lepers. Books like *Ten Fingers for God* and *City of Joy* chronicle the patient work of pioneer missionary doctors and scientists, and the gradual infusion of hope into leper sub-cultures through the efforts of those who followed the example of their Lord.

Rodney Stark suggests that the early church conquered Rome not only through the power of its courageous martyrdoms but also through equally courageous medicine. When the citizens of the capital fled the plague, and thus spread it, and when in their panic a philosophy of "abandon the sick and save yourself" began to grip the city, Christians risked their lives to feed, give drink and care for the sick. "Something distinctive did come into the world with the development of Judeo-Christian thought," he summarized, "the linking of a highly social ethical code with religion." "Christian values of love and charity had, from the beginning, been translated into norms of social service and community solidarity. When disasters struck, the Christians were better able to cope, and this resulted in substantially higher survival rates."[11] Stark noted that the anti-Christian emperor Julian complained that the "impious Galileans" took care of "not only their poor, but ours as well."[12]

Building hospitals has been seen as a pious thing to do in many religions: the Buddhist emperor Ashoka, for example, constructed hospitals around

India. The rise of modern hospitals in most parts of the world, however, can be traced less to the Enlightenment or the rise of Deism in the eighteenth century, but rather to "back to the Bible" revivals of the nineteenth century. Read the Gospels, and it is obvious why a renewed zeal for Scripture has always led to compassionate medicine.

> "Jesus went among all the towns and the villages teaching in their synagogues, announcing the good news of the kingdom and healing every disease and every illness. But as he looked at the multitudes He was filled with pity over them because they were like shepherdless sheep that are wearied and helpless. Then He said to his disciples, 'The harvest is indeed abundant, but the workers are few. Therefore pray the Lord of the harvest that He may send out workers into His harvest'" (Matt. 9: 35-38).

Jesus himself was the prototype of the "missionary doctor." Some think it more tolerant to do healing "without strings attached," with no effort to "convert" the patients. A Western disciple of an Indian guru who holds to this philosophy told me recently, "I view most missionary work with much disdain . . . to trade medical supplies in return for spiritual genocide (is) less than altruistic . . . My Master does much health and welfare work and neither our path nor our philosophy are ever mentioned. It is purely altruistic." One can find many secular organizations, such as Medicine Without Frontiers, the Peace Corps, and others, who bring tremendous physical aid to those in need around the world on these terms. Hats off to all those who do good out of sincere compassion. Yet how can they not get discouraged, fixing only that which is sure to break in the end? Jesus set an example of holistic medicine: not a spoonful of "chicken soup" platitudes for the soul to go with surgery on the body, but radical hope for the spirit as well. Bimal's body was not cured, though the progress of the *mycobacterium leprae* on his nerve tissues may have been checked by medicine, and he probably learned techniques to avoid flare-ups. But what good does it do to cure a patient's body if he has no hope? And what good is the hope if it is not based, ultimately, on reality? If Christ has not risen, Paul wrote, Christians are of all men most to be pitied.

Many Western doctors, who avoid getting too obsessed with work by recuperating on the greens of country clubs and the slopes of ski resorts, are not sure what to make of this crowd. Admiration might be granted, but after that, pity, or envy? When I travel to poverty-stricken corners of Asia, again and again I find Christian doctors and nurses who are not only bringing physical aid to the poor and minorities, but also showing the love of God in the tangible and infectious ways.

Christian compassion is based on the reality of the other, while Buddhist and Hindu compassion is based, in theory, on the denial of any distinction between self and others. However it is conceived in theory, the "field" (as Jesus described it) of the needy is "white to the harvest." The Japanese Zen Master Susuki noted once that Buddhists have "much to learn" from Christians about love; and learn they have. In recent years, Humanists, Buddhists like the Ci Ji foundation in Taiwan, and followers of Indian gurus, have spread out into the harvest field to apply modern medicine to the needy also. In a sense the compassionate, healing touch of Jesus is not limited, but multiplied, through such competition in good works.

The Fish That Made the Whale Vomit

As a boy, growing up in an America fighting a war in Southeast Asia against the Viet Cong, I felt a strange curiosity about the lands behind the "Iron Curtain." I began studying Russian in high school, and read the works of Marx and his followers in college. If the Soviet Union was, as Churchill put it, "a riddle wrapped in a mystery inside an enigma," the network of prison cells and work camps that made up the Gulag piqued my curiosity even more. So I read books written in communist prisons and labor camps. One elderly prisoner described how, whenever he turned to God, he felt renewal pouring into his whole being. Like Pullinger, he considered the psychological explanation and rejected it, feeling that this power came from outside of himself.

Modern psychology is ready to grant that faith may trigger what is called the "placebo effect" or the "power of positive thinking," allowing the mind to tap reservoirs of strength of which the individual is not consciously aware. When I have leaned on God in prayer, I also sometimes felt power from "outside of myself." And often I had objective reasons for thinking it did, which I will relate in a later chapter. Hindu sadhus who lie on beds of nails, Buddhist monks who burn themselves to death to protest injustice, or Jains who show mastery over the body by self-starvation, show an amazing power in the mind, which faith can release, to overcome suffering. The question is to what ends this power is channeled.

In China, I met older men and women who had been imprisoned for Christ. They seemed both humble and cautious; they had suffered a lot. Yet I noted fire in their eyes. And I sometimes got the impression the government was actually afraid of these poor and frail old people.

Alexander Solzhenitsyn, the great historian and one-time citizen of the Soviet Gulag, who as a Red Army captain had considered himself an atheist and a Marxist, found a special power in the lives of many believers he met in prison. He was not naive about the historical Russian church; he understood that much of it had been corrupt, xenophobic, and superstitious. But he found the power that changed a murderer into a minstrel of love on the road to Damascus was alive in the Gulag, where the guiding rule of life for nearly everyone else was "survival of the fittest."

"Christians went off to camp to face tortures and death—only so as not to denounce their faith! They were the only ones, perhaps, to whom the camp philosophy did not stick . . . There were a multitude of Christians: prison transports and graveyards. Prison transports and graveyards. Who will count those millions? They died unknown, casting only in their immediate vicinity a light like a candle."[13]

Richard Wurmbrand, a Jewish convert to Christianity in Romania who spent many years in isolation cells and prison camps, tells about the extraordinary heroism of many of those Christians in first-hand detail.[14] When I worked on a Russian fishing ship as a translator for a couple of months during the Cold War, I had the chance to verify some of the details of another story I read in my childhood. It was the autobiography of a naval cadet and KGB part-timer Sergei Kourdakov who tortured Christians in raids on underground churches. Confused by their gentle courage, his own complicity in murder, and an instance of apparent divine intervention, his book *The Persecutor* tells how he jumped ship off British Columbia and swam to Canada in a gale. The captain of the ship I worked on had often eaten with him, but now called him a "traitor."

The church is scorned, in Western Europe and America, as a den of hypocrites, haven of bigots, and a cradle of cold tradition. Perhaps Jesus would say the same to some churches, as indeed he does in *Revelation*. But candles can't be seen well until the sun goes down. Before the revolution, the Russian church, like ours, seemed divided between Pharisaical right and apostate left. War and tyranny, by bringing out the worst in human nature, gave opportunity for heroism. It also make simple virtue of the kind that in times of peace is mimicked by social politeness and smirked at by the avant-garde, glow with a beauty nothing else could match.[15] Christian morality has never been a flower that grows best in a hothouse. Jesus warned his followers they would be persecuted. (John 15:20). The twentieth century revealed a persecuted church of a beauty that should make any skeptic stop in their tracks. Solzhenitsyn, despite torture, Central Asian winters, beatings, starvation and cancer, saw that beauty and cried, "Thank you, prison, for having been in my life." Most people base belief on personal rather than communal experience, and any life, closely examined, can provide ammunition to a cynic. But after a century which has produced so many Christians of such a caliber, I will not join my voice to those who deride the church of Christ.

Jesus Comes to America

Christ also set a pattern that has been deeply influential in the social movements of the affluent Western world. This effect, however, has not always come directly, and usually not from top down. Henry Ward Beecher bemoaned the official Christianity of pre-Civil War America, which he said justified the oppression of Indians and slavery:

> "The pulpit has been so prostituted, and so utterly apostatized from the very root and substance of Christianity, that it teaches the most heathen notions of liberty; and why should you expect that the great masses of men would be better informed on this subject that they are? Do you believe that George Washington, were he living, would now be able to live one day in the city of Charleston, if he uttered the sentiments that he used to hold? He would be . . . swung up on the nearest lamp-post."[16]

Jesus treated the weak, foreigners, women, and children with a kindness which often scandalized sensitive religious observers, and did indeed get "swung up on the nearest lamp-post." His example and teachings eventually had a powerful, though never unchallenged, effect on Western society. This relationship is sometimes more visible from the outside. After an article entitled *"Two Thousand Years of Jesus,"* a Singapore Chinese wrote to *Newsweek Magazine*:

> "Your article emphasized the historical aspect of Christianity. Living in an Asian culture, I would like to add another perspective. Imagine a society where man is not made in the image of God and the dignity of the individual depends on his power and wealth. Imagine truth belongs only to powerful and influential people. Imagine a society where forgiveness is a weakness. These are still the conditions in many countries. What the United States and Europe have become are results of living out the very basic doctrines of Christianity. Don't shrug off Christianity and elope with secularism. It is your religion's greatness that has been slowly influencing the world for better."[17]

Most often these changes have not originated from the benevolent throne of ecclesiastical authority, but from simple men and women who wanted to follow Jesus.

Rudy Bridges was six years old, her parents illiterate farmers in the Deep South. The story of Jack and Jill was a tough enough nut to crack; the statutes of the Civil Rights Act might as well have been written in classical Sanskrit, as far as Rudy's ability to understand them went. Yet it was these documents that sent her, as the first black student, to a local elementary school, which previously had been all-white. No other students joined her in the classroom: the white kids stayed home. But every morning, crowds of adults gathered outside the gate of her school. As she walked in the door, escorted by federal marshals, they cursed and threatened her. Every afternoon when she returned home, a gauntlet of persecutors sent the little girl home with their jeers.

One day a young psychiatrist who was visiting New Orleans happened on the scene. Robert Coles, later professor of medical humanities and psychiatry at Harvard University and America's best-known child psychiatrist, was struck by the brutality and heroism of the respective sides of the mismatched confrontation. He began to visit Rudy at home, with her parent's cautious permission, to see how she was holding up under the strain. It was clear little Rudy felt helpless and fearful. Yet Dr. Coles also found, to his amazement, that by and large his young patient was doing well: eating, sleeping, playing, and learning to read, without any severe problem or complaint. "Now, how do you explain that?" he asked himself. "And I did not know how to explain that." He talked it over with his wife. Had he been in Rudy's position, they decided, he would hire a lawyer. He would write learned articles dissecting the pathologies of his enemies in the acidly analytical categories of social science. At least he would turn on them and given them an eloquent piece of his mind. But Rudy could do none of these things. She had no such defenses, yet appeared almost free of the ordinary stress of such a situation. Dr. Coles was mystified, until he found a clue in the girl's religious training, a simple approach to injustice that had never occurred to him in his years of psychological training.

In church Rudy's pastor talked about Jesus' crucifixion. On the cross Jesus prayed, "Father, forgive them, for they don't know what they are doing." Dr. Coles explained, "and now little Rudy was saying this in the 1960's, about the people in the streets of New Orleans." She prayed for her persecutors "because they needed praying for," and forgave them, like Jesus. And with that, hatred and fear slid off her like water off a duck's back. God not only "prepared a banquet in the presence of her enemies," but gave her stomach to enjoy it.[18]

What role has such forgiveness, modeled on the teachings and even more example of Jesus, played in the slow and incomplete reconciliation of races in America? Philip Yancey, who admits "I grew up a racist," and attended a church in Georgia which propounded a "twisted theological basis" for racism, described in his book *What's So Amazing About Grace* the heroic forgiveness of Martin Luther King, Jr. and his followers, and how it eventually conquered his heart. "Let us not seek to satisfy our thirst for freedom by drinking the cup of bitterness and hatred," King preached.[19]

What saved South Africa from large-scale interracial violence during the transition from apartheid? It once seemed everyone expected a bloodbath. In part, it was the statesmanship of De Klerk, Nelson Mandela, and Desmund Tutu. But even more, Yancey argues, and others have also pointed out, mutual forgiveness on a personal level prepared the way for national reconciliation.

True, the concepts of forgiveness and equality before God can be found in other religions as well. Mahatma Gandhi, after discovering the power of forgiveness in the *Sermon on the Mount,* (but less in the "Christian" South Africa of his day), poured over the Hindu Scriptures, and there found teachings close enough in spirit that he was able to draw upon native sources in his struggle for unity and freedom for the Indian people. But Hinduism is not *about* reconciliation. The *Bhagavad Gita,* which Gandhi chose (in his Christ-taught humanity) to integrate within his philosophy of ascetic non-violence, was *overtly* a call to accept caste responsibility to wage war. "If you are killed, you win heaven; if you triumph, you enjoy the earth; therefore, Arjuna, stand up and resolve to fight the battle!"[20] Buddha's teachings and example cut across caste lines, emphasize non-violence, and indeed even show a willingness to forgive sins. Theravada nun Ayya Khema, a Jew who discovered Buddhism after her family had been murdered by the Nazis, explained why she did not allow herself to be consumed by hatred by quoting Buddha: "No fire burns like greed; no grip grips tighter than hatred . . . "[21] But by denying boundaries in theory, in practice Buddhism was less active in breaking down social and political boundaries. If all the reconciliation that needed to happen had already occurred in one's heart, overt acts of forgiveness and reconciliation may seem less vital. Malcolm X spoke of a tremendous liberation he felt in arriving in Saudi Arabia and feeling the reality of the Islamic teaching that "all men are brothers." Equality under God was certainly a step forward for the Arabia of the sixth century, and will be for any nation whom class or race divide. But when wrong has been done, where do we find forgiveness? Or do we harbor bitterness forever, and pretend that the evil of our enemies does not already have some place in our hearts, too? This was the need which faced Malcolm X on return to a divided America, for which Martin Luther King Jr. and others found a solution in the cross.

Germany

Many Jewish survivors of the Holocaust feel, quite naturally, that it is impossible to forgive evil of such a magnitude. Christian literature is full of examples to the contrary, arguing that as Saul found the power to overcome his bigotry, even under the most terrible circumstances, God can provide power to forgive *anyone.* A communist party official in China murdered two men, father and son. When his own son became critically ill, the Christian wife and mother of the murdered men nursed him back to health. The two sons of a pastor in Korea were murdered by rebellious communist students. After U.N. troops returned to the area, the pastor snatched one of the guilty students from the firing squad and raised him as his own son. In East Asian culture in particular, these stories are almost unbelievable. In *The Hiding Place,* a survivor of the Ravensbruck concentration camp, Corrie ten Boom, who lost her father and sister in the German prisons, told how, after the war, she once met a brutal prison guard she recalled from the camp. Having become a Christian, he had a request. "Fraulein," he said, "Would you forgive me?" She had just been speaking about forgiveness, but now, recalling her sister's death, she felt no power to practice what she preached. She asked God for help.

> "Woodenly, mechanically, I thrust my hand into the one stretched out to me. And as I did, an incredible thing took place. The current started in my shoulder, raced down my arm, sprang into our joined hands. 'I forgive you!' I cried, 'With all my heart.'"

Ten Boom summarized, "I had never known God's love so intensely as I did then. But even so, I knew it was not my love. I had tried, and did not have the power."[22]

Jesus said that unless we forgive those who wrong us, we cannot be forgiven by God. But the New Testament also says, "we love, because God first loved us." The doctrine of the universal sinfulness of man has this practical application: it allows us to realize not only that we are sometimes our own worst enemies, but that our enemy is also like us. Even a Nazi puts his pants on one leg at a time. I suspect this truth may work subconsciously on all of us in different ways, depending on whether or not we embrace our own guilt. The lazy, unfeeling, or selfish acts of co-workers, spouses or children may seem more irritating because they remind us of our own unacknowledged shortcomings. In the recess of our souls, we know when we do not forgive, we condemn ourselves. Perhaps this is why Jesus' challenge to the men about to stone the woman caught in adultery, "let him who is without sin cast the first stone" silenced the crowd so completely.

Such anecdotes do not, by themselves, prove Christianity true. I am not denying that there are scoundrels among believers, nor suggesting that the church has a monopoly on heroes. It is also true that religious conversion of almost any kind can effect a dramatic change in a person's life, often for the better, and we can find many noble examples among other religions. But as much as the hypocrisy of the church has been used as an argument against Christianity, it seems to me, the true force of the argument flows strongly in the opposite direction. If a person could not find Christ in the twentieth century, he was not looking very hard.

Jesus in History

It is a commonplace among skeptics, and even among the general population, that the church has been "too heavenly minded to be any earthly good." The *Humanist Manifesto* argued that the Christian emphasis on "eternal life" drew the focus of humankind away from the practical work of improving life in this world.

> "Promises of immortal salvation and fear of eternal damnation are both illusory and harmful. They distract humans from present concerns, from self-actualization, and from rectifying social injustices."

To which it is only natural to reply, paraphrasing Confucius: "If you see and understand so little of this world, how can you presume to tell us what is illusory and what is real about the next?"

The ancient world was full of "social injustices" which no one dreamed of rectifying, even in relative outposts of civilization like the Roman Empire, until Jesus proclaimed the news of the Kingdom. Of 600 upper-class families studied at an archeological site in pre-Christian Delphi, "only half a dozen raised more than one daughter," while the rest were killed at birth.[23] Before Christ, Stark stated with a touch of hyperbole, "conquerors butchered for the hell of it." Pouring over Scripture and human history as well as Roman law, Augustine developed "just-war" principles which at least planted the idea of military restraint in the minds of Western warriors.

Will Durant says the world "never had seen such a dispensation of alms" as was organized by the Roman church. She "helped widows, orphans, the sick or infirm, prisoners, victims of natural catastrophes; and she frequently intervened to protect the lower orders from unusual exploitation or excessive taxation."[24] As we have seen, Stark argues it was precisely the "promise of immortal salvation" that caused Christians to care for those sick from the plague. And how else can one explain the actions of the monk who ended the gladiator fights by jumping onto the floor of the Roman Coliseum and being torn to shreds? Apart from eternity, how do you explain the return of St. Patrick to the island of his sufferings? He was one of the first cross-cultural missionaries, and Thomas Cahill claims he was also "the first human being in the history of the world to speak out unequivocally against slavery."[25] Cahill argues (with perhaps a touch of patriotic exaggeration) that Patrick's Irish converts almost single-handedly preserved Western scholarship and humanist traditions after the fall of Rome, providing a bridge for civilization to the modern era. What effect would Mother Theresa have had on the modern conscience if she had followed the model of social change given by the great humanist thinkers of our day? Had Alexander Solzhenitsyn continued in his earlier belief, expressed so well in the *Humanist Manifesto*, that the end of life is "self-actualization," would he have changed the world as he did?

Albert Camus wrote a dark novel about a plague in the North African town of Oran, which the town's priest said was a curse from God, while the town rationalist, a medical doctor, tried to combat with science. No doubt religious authority is by nature conservative and benefits from popular superstition; this will be the case no matter what the religion involved, even a secular faith. But if we turn from literature to history, again, we find that many of the scientists who brought the benefits of modern medicine to humanity were strong Christians. Seven of the ten founding members of what became the Royal Society have been specifically identified as Puritans. To men like Kepler, Pascal, Newton, Lister, and Faraday, science meant "thinking God's thoughts after Him."[26] Charles

Thaxton, a chemist and historian of science, notes that modern science arose in Europe after the introduction of printing made the Bible generally available.[27] He argued that the Biblical doctrine of Creation allowed Western thinkers to escape from idealist Aristotilian (we could add, Buddhist or Hindu) assumptions that stifled science. "People could discover for themselves that both the Old and New Testament regarded the material world as substantial, real, and good." Francis Bacon said the Greeks were wrong in their approach to nature because they didn't see it as created. Thaxton noted that many historians of science have described science as a "legacy" or even "child" of Christianity.[28]

Heavenly-minded William Wilberforce finished the work of St. Patrick by leading the fight to ban slavery in the British Empire. Few men in eighteenth century England tried harder to "distract" the English people with heaven as did the preacher John Wesley; he also opened England's first free medical dispensary. It was the "general next to God," William Booth, whose troops literally beat the drum in England, and then in Japan, to end forced prostitution.

Richard Nixon's "hatchet man," Charles Colson, had opportunity to effect reform through political sweat and arm-twisting, and with his office a door from the president's, he had a strong arm. After the Nixon presidency fell, thieves and swindlers were his new neighbors in prison. Upon release, Colson founded an organization, Prison Fellowship, that specialized in offering prisoners "promises of immortal salvation." Comparing his two careers, Colson felt he got more done in the Big House than in the White House, shaking the hands of car thieves rather than of prime ministers. Studying church history, he generalized the lesson: "The great reforms of history came about not so much because of political institutions, but as a result of God's power flowing through righteous and obedient people."

Colson's own autobiography might be taken as an example of the quixotic paths redemptive history sometimes takes. A political prisoner in the Philippines, a young opponent of dictator Ferdinand Marcos named Benigno Aquino, was given a copy of Colson's best-selling story, *Born Again.* Aquino experienced spiritual revival. Reprieved and exiled to America, after a few years Aquino felt a call to return to his homeland. "The Filipino is worth dying for," he explained, reading Scriptures to his family over the phone as he prepared to arrive in Manila.

Aquino was gunned down at the airport. Within a year, an angry nation, led by a Catholic archbishop and a vast throng of praying Christians, cast Marcos out of office and put Senator Aquino's widow in his place. Dramatic scenes of the "People Power" revolution were broadcast around the globe. Mass movements for democracy erupted in Burma and China, where they were brutally suppressed. But in Eastern Europe, copy-cat uprisings brought an end to communism.

On the last page of *People of the Lie*, M. Scott Peck quotes an "old priest" who says that "the only ultimate way to conquer evil is to let it be smothered within a willing, living human being." Peck argued: "A willing sacrifice is required . . . there is a mysterious alchemy whereby the victim becomes the victor." In an earlier book, Peck applied the same logic to his own practice, noting, "as I look back on every successful case I have had I can see that at some point or points I had to lay myself on the line."[29]

God may not play dice with the universe, as Einstein said, but he does seem to play dominoes. The heroic self-sacrifice of an individual who chooses to "lose his life" to gain it, sometimes knocks down systems of oppression across history like so many dominoes. Reform can I think be traced more often to prayer than to political or philosophical manifestos. In recent years, a Western church that still keeps one eye, from time to time, on eternity, has helped birth such movements as hospices for the dying, Alcoholics Anonymous, civil rights, Habitat For Humanity, homes for unwed mothers, and the struggle against abortion. But the most dynamic and revolutionary social changes in world history may have come in the nineteenth and early twentieth century when the church remembered its Master's call to lend the rest of the world some of the light.

Missions and Social Justice

Few events during my first year in Asia affected me more than my visit to the hill tribes of northern Thailand. As we drove into the Lahu village of Nong Kaew, I fell in love with the tidy bamboo huts, ears of corn hung from windows to dry, stalks standing twelve feet beside the road, stars twinkling between mahogany branches above. But peace was precarious. Each village was subject to what amounted to an ideological guerrilla war among competing world views: the drug armies of the Golden Triangle, an alliance of Buddhism with Thai nationalism, Marxist revolutionaries, KMT Chinese nationalists, and a few scattered Christians. In this contest, a dollar could be as deadly as a bullet. In Nong Kaew, children were educated in a building with a cross over the roof. The quaint Lisu village down the road was less tidy, and visitors needed to step carefully to avoid pig feces. At night they would be offered opium, a place to stay, and for a dollar or two, one of the girls. Earlier visitors received a less-commercial reception. But some tourists were happy to find natives uninhibited by western hang-ups about sex, and that a buck goes a long ways in the hills. Trekkers, mostly Westerners fascinated by native cultures unsullied by the West and indignant at missionaries for "ruining" native cultures, often had a hardening effect on village culture. By the time the Thai government began an aggressive campaign to halt the spread of AIDS, it was probably too late for those girls.

Missionaries made many mistakes in places like Nong Kaew, paying too little respect to native traditions and acting paternalistically in many cases. But the rest of the world has been far crueler. Isabel Kuhn wrote of her experiences in China and Thailand, "All the years I have been a missionary I have never known anyone to go to the tribes to help them except these two classes—Christ's missionary and the communist idealist."

In many ways communists were kinder to native tribes than western democrats. Anthropologists came to study native cultures, but didn't often "interfere" by teaching people how to better feed or clothe themselves. Tourists came to take pictures, among other things. Businessmen came to wrest oil, opium, emeralds or timber from the savages, allying sometimes with the national government, as in Indonesia, where in recent years Sawi tribesmen were forced to cut down their own trees as slave labor for Japanese timber companies. Soldiers came to tame them, then policemen to keep them tamed.

Christian missionaries, meanwhile, saved some tribes from extinction. They gave them medicine, empowered them by creating written languages, taught them better ways of raising crops, and showed them how to cope with modern technologies and temptations. Missionaries risked their lives to end blood feuds, cannibalism, and slavery to capricious spirits.

The contributions of Christian missions to the great literate non-Christian civilizations of Asia were almost as tremendous. Lyon Sharmon wrote a biography of the "George Washington of China," Sun Yat-sen, who like a high percentage of early Chinese nationalists, was a Christian. Though inclined to be critical of Christianity, she acknowledged,

> "The missionaries fostered scientific knowledge and translated scientific books. It was they who developed the humanitarian knowledge of healing and sanitation, and relief in famine and plague. One may safely say that there was nothing that might be done to stimulate intellectual progress or social betterment that some missionary somewhere did not undertake—from the better tanning of leather to the creation of a university. History may little care how many converts Christian missions have made in China, but it will never cease to reckon with the diffusion of western ideas, which seems now to have been only a by-product of the missionary penetration."[30]

I don't entirely agree with Sharmon. I think history will care how many converts missionaries made in China, just as they care about the converts Paul made. And the social values they "diffused" were not "western ideas," but that part of the Gospel that had been internalized by Western culture. She was right in saying social change was not the primary goal of most missionaries, however. The mission community tried to turn the world upside down only so it could see heaven more clearly. I don't think secular history has even begun to come to grips with the impact missions had, both directly and by spurring indigenous religion into competition in good works.

Christian missionaries gave India over 1200 hospitals and dispensaries, and eighty-six leprosariums. Followers of Jesus gave tribal peoples in East India the education and morale to adjust to the modern world without losing their sense of identity or control over their own institutions.[31]

The second and third waves of nationalists in many Asian countries, faced with a western mission network which tended to baby the new church and protected by Western gunboats, often became understandably suspicious of the "foreign" faith. Many regarded local converts as traitors to the traditions of their civilization, and interpreted mission work in cynical, sometimes paranoid terms. The missionaries were up to no good. Certainly they are acting as agents for their respective governments. Probably they were front-men for the forces of global imperialism. Perhaps they were even cutting up children in orphanages and using body parts for black magic.[32] As Asian nations have gained a broader perspective that comes with independence, some Asian scholars have become more objective about the work of missionaries in their countries than modern western analysts. The Shanghai historian Gu Weimin, for example, describes in detail how Christian missionaries not only introduced modern medicine, science, and education, but also a sea change in attitudes towards the poor and needy, hungry peasants in remote regions, addicts, children, and women. In an earlier chapter I noted how Hu She, one of China's greatest modern reformers and scholars, credited missionaries with teaching China to "look at women as human beings."

For all their earthly accomplishments these remarkable men and women often earn nothing but contempt from the world, which continues to crucify them as it crucified their Lord. The James Michener picture of narrow, uptight missionaries who, if they see fun happening anywhere, think they have God's mandate to stop it, or the psychotic missionary in the Harrison Ford star vehicle *Mosquito Coast*, is perhaps even more popular with the public today that the fat but helpless missionary in the cannibal's pot to an earlier generation. And no doubt there were, and are, bad eggs, and, as with all human peerages, a peculiar class blindness. (Though many of the most successful missionaries have been extreme individualists, showing an aptitude unusual in any circle to think for themselves. One might even use the word "pig-headed.") When I think of their mistakes, I also think of a church I saw in Bombay during my first year in Asia. All along two walls of the old colonial, western-style church were rows of Victorian memorials. "Beloved little Susan, age 5," one would read. "My dear wife Anabelle, age 25," another would record. In many countries of West Africa and South Asia, almost every member of the first wave of missionaries died of tropical diseases within a year or two of arriving in the field to bring the news of the Gospel. That did not stop a second, a third, and then a fourth wave of believers from casting their lives away upon the same soil. Unlike everyone else, they didn't come to take, but to give. Rather than casting stones at them for their foibles and sins, I wish I could sit at their feet and learn. In many of their faces, I see a reflection of their Master.

Perhaps it is as well that the world has not chosen its heroes from among this remarkable tribe. Were their often hair-raising stories written in the early Hollywood hagiographic style, as indeed some of them have been by overly pious biographers, we might get the impression that "God is looking for a few good men." The heroes of the Old Testament, on the contrary, look like they've come off a Puritan wanted list: a playboy, a man who tried to ditch his wife to save his own skin, another "hero" who gave away state secrets to hookers, and most famous of all, a king who had an affair and then covered it up by murdering the husband. Jesus' followers, too, put their pants on one leg at a time, and not in a phone booth. Peter, cocky and timid by turns, sheathed a real courage in a kind of romantic, half-cocked buffoonery. John the "beloved" was quick-tempered and ambitious. Saul began his career as an inquisitor, as we have seen, and ended it depressed, in prison.

Such is the cast of characters who "turned the world upside down." If you've been on the mission field, you may recognize a few of them.

In that sense, a recent hatchet job on Mother Theresa, in which the author proved to his visible gratification that the Catholic saint is "not heaven's agent on earth" but full of human flaws, only confirms Christian theology. If the world thought saints were people who were without sin, the man did the world a service. Jesus said all along there is a sinner in every saint, and true saints are the last to deny it.[33]

Christians should never forget the inquisitions, crusades, or tortures inflicted on slaves and Indians by "Christian" Americans. We have no right to avert our eyes from abuses perpetrated within our own churches, or pretend they have nothing to do with us. Yet at the same time, it would be dishonest to go along with the cynics. The church of Christ—that fellowship of sinners who love Jesus and try to follow him—appears even now dressed not for a funeral, as the cynic said in the quote at the head of this chapter, but for a wedding. The light still shines in the darkness, even that most opaque and oily of darknesses called prosperity, and still the darkness does not quite overcome it.

One might reply that Christianity has resulted in the conversion of many to a better way of life, but the same can be said of other religions as well. Buddhism brought a flowering of debate, scholarship, and learning to the deserts and mountain plateaus of Central Asia, culminating in a brilliant Tibetan culture. Japanese civilization practically began with the journey of the first pilgrim, Kukai, to China for Buddhist Scriptures. The Mormons built a society in the Utah desert which embodied the best American virtues of self-reliance, mutual aid, and social improvement. Millions of Marxists heroically gave their lives for the future of humanity. The Nation of Islam, flaky though it might be, taught Malcolm X to give up a life of petty crime, be faithful to one woman, love books, and become spokesman for the aspirations of his people. Even the People's Temple used religious commitment to help heroin addicts overcome their addictions in the early days.

I agree completely. Can man be good without God? If we define "good" in the usual sense of the term, my answer would be a qualified yes. I have lived three years in Japan, where Christians make up less than one percent of the population, yet good citizens, kind neighbors, and loving families, are probably closer to the rule than in the United States. If you ask, "can positive change in people's lives result from faith in persons who ultimately prove less than worthy of that faith?" Again, I think the answer is yes.

However, any honest historian would, I think, admit that if we look for positive, life-enhancing effect on human history, no other man or woman comes close the person Saul met on the road to Damascus. And no teachings have done as much to ennoble mankind than those of Jesus. John said that in Jesus the "*Tao* became flesh," and I think that love remains incarnate, first in his followers, and secondly in those he influences. Furthermore, while the good in Buddhism is seldom realized apart from "attachments" which cast doubt on the Buddha's central teachings, and while brotherhood within the Nation of Islam was only achieved by calling ninety percent of one's neighbors "devils," and while I doubt any German of the nineteenth century rose in the morning and thanked God to have Karl Marx as neighbor, the teachings and life of Christ are good and elevating from the core of who he is. The more a person is like Christ, the more enhancing his or her acquaintance will be to our dignity, though undoubtedly challenging to our self-image. But I do not claim this by itself amounts to a sufficient reason to believe in Christianity. The character and power of Christ to change history could be just a fortunate delusion, or an inspiring part of some higher paradigm. And for those who have experienced something else, these historical facts may seem hollow.

We have seen, I think, that Jesus has adequate claim to be the Way. Let us apply two additional tests to Christian teachings, corresponding to his claims to be "Life" and "Truth": the tests of happiness and of reason.

---

1 *But is He a Christian? Books and Culture*, Sept.-Oct. 1997, p. 32

2 Richard Wurmbrand, *In God's Underground*, 1988, p. 86

3 *Why Are We Here? The Great Debate*, from *International Herald Tribune*, April 26, 1999

4 *In His Image*, p.138. In their desire to be fair, or for rhetorical effect, Yancey and Brand are conceding a great deal here about who is a part of "his body."

5 Also, to literally give the devil his due, much of what is usually laid at the church was not the work of actual Christians. See Appendix B.

6 Jackie Pullinger, *Chasing the Dragon*, p.113

7 Ibid. p. 152

8 Ibid. p.160

9 I could have found the same closer to home in American inner city neighborhoods. In a review of a colleague's book, Princeton professor and activist John Dilutio argued that believers were virtually "the only people' who were really making a positive difference among the urban poor. "Although I doubt that any other card-carrying social scientist would even think to fault the authors for such a sin of omission, the most important missing endnote to *America in Black and White* is a reference to the Gospels according to Matthew, Mark, Luke and John." *Books and Culture*, June 14, 1999, Tim Stafford, *The Criminologist Who Discovered Churches*

10 Mark Buntain, *The Compassionate Touch*

11 Rodney Stark, *The Rise of Christianity*, Harper San Francisco, 1997, p.74

12 Ibid., p. 84

13 Alexander I. Solzhenitsyn, *The Gulag Archipelago, 1918-1956: an experiment in literary investigation*, translated by Thomas P. Whitney, Harper and Row, 1973

14 His most popular book is *Tortured For Christ*, but many of his other books are also thought-provoking and full of unexpected insights. He is a philosopher with passion who has seen, prayed, and experienced a great deal.

15 This may also have been much of the charm of Confucius' humble platitudes during the Warring States period in China, that so bewilders Westerners with a taste for exotic spiritualities.

16 *American Sermons,* Henry Ward Beecher, *Peace Be Still* p.659

17 George Chua, *Newsweek Magazine*, May 5, 1999

18 Robert Cole, *The Inexplicable Prayers of Rudy Bridges*, in Kelly Monroe, *Finding God at Harvard*, Zondervan, 1996, p. 38

19 Philip Yancey, *What's So Amazing About Grace*, Zondervan, 1997, p. 133

20 *Bhagavad Gita*, translated by Barbara Stoler Miller, Bantam Books, 1986, p. 34

21 Ayya Khema, *I Give You My Life: The Autobiography of a Western Buddhist Nun*, Shambhala, 1998, p. 140

22 Corrie Ten Boom with Jamie Buckingham, *Tramp for the Lord*, Fleming Ravell, 1977, p. 55

23 Newsweek, April 5, 1999, Kenneth Woodward, *2000 Years of Jesus*

24 For Durant's summary of this period, see *The Age of Faith*, p.72-78

25 Thomas Cahill, *How the Irish Saved Civilization*, Doubleday, 1995, p. 114

26 See *What if Jesus Had Never Been Born?* By James Kennedy and Jerry Newcombe, the chapter entitled *Thinking God's Thoughts After Him*, for details. The authors are prone to hyperbole, and some of their arguments are simplistic, but the evidence they give cannot I think be easily dismissed.

27 For that matter, Gutenburg invented the printing press so that more people could read the Bible. It is interesting that the person named the most influential person of the second millennia, became so because he wanted people to read the words of the most influential person of the first millennia.

28 Charles Thaxton, *Christianity and the Scientific Enterprise*, in Kelly Monroe, *Finding God at Harvard*, Zondervan, 1996

29 Peck, *The Road Less Traveled*, Simon & Schuster, 1978, p. 149

30 Lyon Sharmon, Sun Yat-Sen

31 For a poignantly ironic version of the conversion of one tribe in British India told from the standpoint of the tribesmen, see *Beyond the Next Mountain*, by Worldwide Pictures—also some nice scenery. The tribal hero gives a remarkable reply to common accusations that missionaries were imperialists and destroyed native cultures. See also *Wind Through the Bamboos* by Donna Strom, and *Eternity in Their Hearts*, Don Richardson, for more details about the remarkable process by which many tribes in that part of the world accepted Christianity.

32 These stories resemble the malicious rumors spread about the Jews during the European Middle Ages. In both cases the general population, under external threat (Islam, the West) reacted against alien cultures within almost like a body reacts against an implanted organ.

33 The Bible tells us that even people who think they are destroying the work of God are often actually doing his work for him, after all. But one does wonder about a person who takes glee in attacking an old lady who spent her life comforting the dying, and the squeals of delight (relief?) with which some people greeted the publication of that book—the jeering title of which does not merit mentioning.

CHAPTER 8

The Pursuit of Happiness

"I CAN'T get no satisfaction"—Mick Jagger and Keith Richards

"Hell is a state of mind. . . . And every state of mind, left to itself, every shutting up of the creature within the dungeon of its own mind—is, in the end, Hell. But Heaven is not a state of mind.'"—C. S. Lewis[1]

Nebuchadnezzar the Great, (625-561 B.C.) lord of a Fertile Crescent empire centered on Babylon, lived in a grand style. He out-maneuvered rivals, extended the borders of the state his father had entrusted to him, and sharply defeated superpower rival Egypt in a history-changing clash of armies at Carchemish, in modern Turkey. The wealth of conquered fiefdoms clinking in his pocket, Nebuchadnezzar hoped to be remembered as more than a blood-and-guts general. So he built a capital of startling magnificence, a city of enamel skyscrapers 650 feet above the plain and temples decorated with statues of gold, protected on all sides by a 56-mile long wall with a hundred gates and wide enough for the royal chariot to turn on. The king also had a green thumb. Before World War I, archeologists uncovered remains of his most romantic home-improvement project: the famed Hanging Gardens, built on a massive slab, cleverly engineered with internal plumbing, to comfort Amyitis, his homesick bride, with the greenery of her mountain land. Let ordinary mortals send flowers: this guy built a forest.

"He's the man," we might say, in the modern vernacular. "He's the god," said his servants. Expressing alpha-wolf status in the language of oriental despotism, they demanded that the peoples of the empire fall on their faces and worship him. And among statues, tapestries, beautiful women, flattering lackeys, and mockups of new architectural projects, it must have been hard to keep things in earthly perspective.

But not even a demigod could escape the heat of the Mesopotamian Valley. So on summer evenings, when the palace had soaked up sunlight all day, the king went strolling on the palace roof to catch a breeze off the Tigris River. Looking down he took stock of official Babylon: emissaries hurrying to and from the provinces, guards at the gate, fish merchants arguing with palace buyers, peasants returning from their fields. No sense in false humility. Each of these figures was a piece on his chess board. Each would jump when called, or even die when needed. As master player, he allotted to each according to his service to the greater good. And what was that good? What was the ultimate purpose of it all? One day, according to the testimony of a court official from a minor and sometimes troubling northern province, the emperor took a stroll on his palace roof in a contemplative frame of mind, and summed up the purpose he had found:

> "Is not this great Babylon, that I have built by my mighty power as a royal residence and for the glory of my majesty?" (Dan. 4:30).

The press in our day would not treat a politician who articulated such thoughts kindly. They would mutter under their breaths, while planning scathing editorials: "Who drew up your plans, oh Great One? Who cut the stones and hauled them down the river? Who plowed the fields that made the elite social bubble you live in possible?" From a Jeffersonian, Marxist or Tolstoyan standpoint, Nebuchadnezzar was a parasite, an aphid that climbed to the top of an oak, and stood swaggering and swaying to a cosmic breeze not of his making and not obliged to continue blowing his way. Yet we admire his swagger. Because in a democratic age, it is not that we don't believe in kings, as that we have all become royalty ourselves.

Several hundred miles away, another empire-builder, who also conquered nations, built palaces, and won an even larger place in history, also went for a walk one evening in a reflective mood. He did not look down, as a king on his serfs, but up, like a Bedouin. Above him, worlds made not for conquering, but for contemplating, twinkled at him. He took a deep breath and felt the affairs of state slip from his shoulders. He was a boy again, watching his father's sheep in the hills of Judea. Lord of sheep, perhaps, but servant to his father, youngest of eight brothers, and surrounded by a darkness from which the roar of a lion on the hunt or the lights of camping bandits might disturb his sleep. He spoke, naturally, full of wonder and hard-earned trust, to the Creator of the stars:

> "When I consider the heavens, the works of Your fingers, the moon and the stars, which you have created, what is man, that you should

take thought of him, and the son of man, that you should care for him?" (Ps. 8: 3-4 pph).

With a nod of their heads, Nebuchadnezzar and David defined the difference between faith in self and faith in God. Nebuchadnezzar looked down at what he had made, and staked his claim to fame on all he had accomplished. David looked up, and staked his life on the care of the one who created the splendor above him.

Both men, when they turned their heads, were of course searching for the same thing. Pascal wrote,

> "All men seek happiness. This is without exception. Whatever different means they employ, they all tend to this end. The cause of some going to war, and of others avoiding it, is the same desire in both, attended with different views. The will never takes the least step but to this object. This is the motive of every action of every man; even of those who hang themselves."[2]

Both David and Nebuchadnezzar sought happiness. But it would be hard to find two more opposite means to this end. Both men were successful, in worldly terms. One based his happiness on that success, the other on transcendent weakness and vulnerability, and trust in a God he could not see.

Does happiness come when I stand on my own two feet and take pride in my achievements? Or am I happier when I fall on my knees? What is the secret to success—the path of self-exaltation, or the path of humility before God?

Or perhaps best of all is a third path, exemplified by an Indian prince who left his palace entirely. Disillusioned at the fruits of materialism and disinclined to bow before God, many Westerners have begun to explore the paths of Eastern mysticism exemplified by the Buddha's great renunciation. Aldous Huxley, in a famous forward to the *Bhagavad Gita*, described a "perennial philosophy" that he said lies at the heart of all religious traditions, which involved an emptying of self in order to realize unity with Brahma or the God-nature. How does that relate to what the lady at the Light of Buddha Mountain said, "when I worship the Buddha, I'm really worshipping myself?"

And what of Jesus, the shepherd of the Christian flock? Which way did he look, and which way did he direct our gaze?

Life, Liberty, and Sleeping Pills Before Lights Out

Popular capitalist culture teaches us to count success the way Nebuchadnezzar counted it. *Lifestyles of the Rich and Famous* and *Entertainment Tonight* catechize the prevailing creed. Rock stars celebrate the "good life" of youth, money, and sexual vitality before shrieking audiences of adoring fans. Athletes and movie stars move in a world of fantasy where every day you are a lottery winner, every person you meet is young and restless, play is work and attractive members of the opposite sex knock on your bedroom door at night. If you really want to have a good time, a thousand movies tell us, you must throw off moral restraints. A few musicians cultivate an image of intrigue and mystery by singing praise to the devil, while movie witches dress hip and wink their eyes vivaciously. Advertising copy even encourages us to associate tasty food with sin, as in the comment, "that chocolate fudge cake is wickedly delicious."

Industrial society taught us not only to enjoy the good things in life, but to take pride in our godlike nature as well. Our ancestors believed that behind every tree, in every stream, on every mountain-top, a god or goddess might await. But after 300 years of Enlightenment philosophy, everything sacred seemed on the verge of being deconstructed: stars had become gaseous fragments of the "Big Bang," our ancestors had skeletons in their closets, the nobility had morphed into politicians with crooked smiles and insincere flattery whom we remove at whim. We "owe it to ourselves" to cultivate a "good self-image." Advertisers help. Ronald McDonald™ serves as court jester, while Nike™ helps us imagine ourselves in more hip poses. Prosperity, equality and the capitalist press reduce the category of the sacred to one: the omnipotent audience, who can create or destroy a television or world at the push of a remote or click of a mouse, or a political career at the drop of a piece of paper. Everything else is fodder for *Sixty Minutes*.

"Be still and know that I am God," says Psalm 46. Our servants in the studio call silence "dead time." We still contend with drivers on the highway, bosses, wives and children, and a few other ambassadors from mundane reality. But technology is freeing us of such intrusions: tele-commutes, high-tech start-ups, child-care, and the world's highest divorce rate help Americans raise lonely individualism to an art form. Even in church you don't have to meet anyone you don't want to. Mega-churches design services to raise spirits and achieve market share. Messages that impinge on that freedom Westerners thinks the key to happiness are few and far between.

But the church still does its bit to make people think the goal of the Christian God is to kill fun. Western theology, like the pews and organ in a traditional church, often seems an oddly confining and systematized approach to the inventor of the ostrich and the Tahitian sunset. The disciples saw Jesus in fields of flowers and on stormy seas, watched him heal the blind and face down angry mobs, and heard stories from him of camels going through needles and mountains jumping into the sea. By contrast, the church offers flannel boards, catechisms, and hard pews. People followed Jesus because they couldn't imagine what would happen next. Many go to church instead out of duty or habit. Having lost the habit, many young people look for aesthetic stimulation and community in the East.

Psychology since Sigmund Freud has had its own reasons for discouraging Christian belief. Faith was, if not an illness, a crutch. Those least able to make it on their own relied on a cosmic father-figure. M. Scott Peck notes that many psychiatrists, educated into a secular worldview, and finding that much of their business comes from men and women who grew up in the church and need help maturing beyond the need for external control mechanisms, concluded that "the church is the enemy."[3] Peck's more nuanced interpretation was to argue that while a strong religious community may serve, like the military, as a father to straighten out a wayward child, religious authority tends to instill a lower level of obedience. Leaving church may be part of a natural process of attaining a more mature autonomy and responsibility.

Freud blamed religion for a good share of the world's collective neurosis.[4] His disciple, Jung, on the other hand, openly acknowledged that people of strong religious faith rarely turned up among the cases he studied. But happiness, like religion, comes in many varieties.

Augustine tells how he was walking down a street in Milan one day brooding over a speech he had been composing in praise of the emperor in which "there would be a lot of lies, and they would be applauded by those who knew they were lies." He came upon a drunk beggar who was laughing and making merry. He felt depressed. Here he was, at the top of the world, a wealthy and talented young orator. Yet he was miserable, "spurred on by my desires and dragging after me the load of my unhappiness."

> "The goal of this was simply to reach a state of happiness that was free from care; the beggar had reached this state before us, and we, perhaps, might never reach it at all."[5]

Augustine came to a subtle conclusion. If asked whether he wanted to be cheerful, he would say, yes of course. While the beggar's merriment was not "true joy," it was "a great deal truer than the joy I was seeking." He was not better than the beggar for having more learning, for his misuse of that learning made him miserable."Yet still I know that the important thing is from what ground a man's joy proceeds."

Jesus said, "I have come so they may have life and have it abundantly." The question is not merely how to escape sorrow: we know drugs or television can help us do that. The question is, what approach to the universe allows us to achieve happiness as conscious and awakened human beings? What grounds of ultimate truth allows us to walk across the palace roof of our lives, in possession of our senses and realizing our full humanity, and smile?

The King Among the Cattle

Daniel describes what came of Nebuchadnezzar's boast:

"Instantly the sentence upon King Nebuchadnezzar was executed. He was driven away from other men, and ate grass like an ox, and his body was wet with the dew from heaven till his hair grew as long as eagle feathers and his nails as the claws of a bird" (Dan. 4:33).

The Master of the Universe went mad.

This has become a familiar story. In a documentary called *A Place Called Home*, Noel Paul Stookey, balladeer of the popular 1960's trio Peter, Paul, and Mary, reflected on the temptations of celebrity:

> "People would make special overtures, not on the basis of who I was as a person, but on the basis of my fame. And I would start to take advantage of it. 'Mr. Stookey, you don't have to wait in the line. You can go ahead and come in.' 'Mr. Stookey, do you want a table?' 'Mr. Stookey, I brought a girl to the party. Would you like to meet her?' I began to believe my own press clippings. And I was sick with it."

An epidemic of this sickness seems to periodically sweep the world of the stars: world conquerors barricading themselves in bunkers, divine teachers ladling out Kool-Aide, god-like celebrities washing their brains with chemicals. But we see symptoms of the same illness in daily life. "All problems seem to be reducible to one problem," wrote Earl Jabay, chaplain at the Neuro-Psychiatric Institute at Princeton.

> "The simple truth is that the self positioned as god is the most basic cause of the entire gamut of emotional problems in people. What we commonly call neuroses, psychoses, addiction problems, and behavior problems are the result of a life wrongly set up. All bondage impels us in the direction of death. The self in control of the self seeks to kill himself."[7]

Another psychologist, William Kilpatrick, made an equally categorical though more narrowly-defined observation in his book *Psychological Seduction*: "Extreme forms of mental illness are always extreme cases of self-absorption."

To our ancestors it would seem as if we had found our way back to the Garden of Eden. We want mangos, and they are on special for a dollar a pound, flown in from the Philippines. We want kiwi, and they wait in the produce department of the corner grocery. On the weekend, we can go hang-gliding, see multimillion-dollar epics for three dollars, or travel to island paradise on jet-powered magic carpets. Yet as we walk through the gate of utopia, flowers wither and fruit hardens into nettles. Chesterton pointed out in his biography of Charles Dickens that sincere pessimism was rarer than the mere "social virtue" of cynicism. But if you wanted to find it, it was easier to find among the privileged elite than among the suffering masses, the Augustines rather than the beggars.

Having attained more prosperity, leisure and fun than any utopian from

Plato to Marx thought conceivable, young men trade it all for a gram of transcendent dust or a night of pleasure, copying the bored aristocrats who invented Russian roulette. Young men in our ghettoes murder one another, victims not of starvation, but of *ennui*, having grown up without authority to constrain or discipline the natural god-consciousness of the infant. AIDS has become less a disease of the ignorant who have lost hope because they have nothing, than of the lonely who lose hope because they have everything material but have become slaves to excitement. Children in Ethiopia play on the ground with a stick and laugh, but Nintendo and Sega can't turn out alternate realities fast enough to stifle the yawns of many First World children.

Drs. Jabay and Kilpatrick had three things in common. (1) They began their careers thinking Christianity had little to offer their patients. (2) They became convinced secular psychology failed to accurately diagnose the fundamental human disorder: by prescribing autonomy, it aggravated rather than relieved the trouble. So they rebelled against their secular teachers. (3) They decided as Kilpatrick wrote, "although Christianity is more than a psychology, it happens to be a better psychology than psychology is," and became Christians.

Ernest Becker, while he seemed to notice the same things, did not become a Christian. He was a Humanist with a rare tenderness for the plight of humanity. His Pulitzer-prize winning book *Denial of Death* examined the beliefs of giants of psychology, like Sigmund Freud, C. G. Jung, Soren Kierkegaard and Otto Rank, with sympathy and intelligence. Everything we do, Becker argued, we do to deny our mortality. Our lives are marks in the sand, which we draw and pray the waves will not wash out.

Yet in the process of "making our mark" on the world we feel guilt. In our hearts, we feel justification must come from outside ourselves.

> "Now we see even further how guilt is inevitable for man: even as a creator he is a creature overwhelmed by the creative process itself . . . This is how we understand something that seems illogical, that the more you develop as a distinctive free and critical human being, the more guilt you have . . . what right do you have to play God?"[8]

One can see why, from a Christian point of view, success is particularly hazardous to the soul. It allows us to think we are self-sufficient, to create a world of our own from which we can shut out not only those who might hurt us, but those who might help us too. As C. S. Lewis pointed out, pain, such as Nebuchadnezzar's illness, or pleasure, such as the sight of the stars, have this in common: they direct attention away from the self. The beauty and pain of creation shatter our worldly hopes. We hear the sound of the wind on the prairie grass, or see trees bent with the winter's first snow. A CAT scan comes back from the doctor and our worst fears are realized. At such moments, an eternal thought, a hope or fear that lies beyond all we have built, crashes through the barrier of daily striving and renders it trivial. An immortal taste slips to our lips for an instant and we feel with an ache as if the secret to some life more real than we had known hovered like a hummingbird for a moment, only to fly away.

Where has it gone? Is it hiding in the next love, the next promotion, the next journey, in the woods or the stars? Will we find it when the world is at peace? When all the hungry are fed and the naked clothed? But then they will be just like us, and the world conquered by suburban malls and golf courses. When cancer is an ancient rumor, when we are genetically engineered to be healthy for 300 years? Even if we gain universal freedom, prosperity, and long lives—even eternal lives—can we be truly happy if our deepest hunger is left unfilled? Whether we realize it or not, that desire is to find an object worthy of ultimate praise.

Becker believed the feeling of guilt at assigning supreme value to our own creation arises whether or not the "artist" believes in God. If a person tries to prove his value through creativity, to "justify his heroism objectively," he feels a sense of exposure and inadequacy. (Which, so long as he has not "made it," he might attribute to lack of success.) "Who do you think you are?" something seems to ask. The effect is aggravated, it seems to me, if, as with kings, rock stars, football players, and movie stars, the artist cannot walk out of his studio without being mobbed by adoring fans who remind him that he *has* made it, and try to pilfer some of that godhood for themselves.[9] (This explains much of the famous "charisma" of successful gurus.) But in his heart of hearts, the hero knows the figure he has created for his public is hollow.

Becker quoted the great psychologists Otto Rank and Carl Jung on the danger arbitrary enlargement of ego boundaries carries. Then he noted, with surprise, that Danish theologian Soren Kierkegaard had beaten both to the punch:

> "Here Rank and Kierkegaard meet in one of those astonishing historical mergers of thought . . . that sin and neurosis are two ways of talking about the same thing—the complete isolation of the individual, his disharmony with the rest of nature, his hyper individualism, his attempt to create a world from within himself. Both sin and neurosis represent the individual blowing himself up to larger than his true size, his refusal to recognize his cosmic dependence."[10]

Genesis, describing a conversation between a woman and a reptile, described the progress of the same pathology thousands of years earlier:

> "'You will not die at all! God said this, because He knows that when you eat of it your eyes will be opened and you will be like God, deciding between good and evil' . . . She picked some fruit and ate it. She also gave some to her husband, and he ate it. When they ate the fruit, their eyes

were opened, and they realized they were naked; so they sewed fig leaves together and made robes to cover themselves" (Gen. 3:4-7 pph.).

The story of Adam and Eve has in it something of the quality of myth or dream. "Hey! Where are my clothes?" It's like the story of the original "spin doctor," the tailor who wove the king a set of clothes that were visible "except to fools and knaves." Nobody wanting to admit they were either, the ruse went, if not undetected, unannounced, while the emperor strolled naked through the streets. Finally a boy, the most naive and innocent person in the kingdom, pointed out the obvious.

So it happens again and again in the history of the human race. Our clothes are our pretensions. Humanity continually re-enacts this "original sin" of pretending to be God, and prances through the court asking the world to worship. And because we all have a stake in this game, often no one is naive and simple enough to call the bluff. The most desperate form of courage, someone once said, is the courage to stand in front of a crowd and affirm (in the face of enlightened public opinion) that two and two are four. "No, you are a human being, not a god. Nor are you a worm, dust in the wind, or a piece of trash. All things are not one: each is what it is, and is related to the whole in a fashion unique to itself. You are man. You are woman, created in the image of God. But not God."

Worship and Sanity

David, pondering the stars, asked, "What is man, that You take thought of him? And the son of man, that you care for him?" But then he continued: "And yet You have made him a little lower than the gods, and crowned him with glory and honor. You allow him to administer all that You have made, putting all things under his feet" (Ps. 8:3-6).

That "yet" is the point upon which two great truths find balance, the balance of a dynamic sanity. First, a scientific curiosity about realities external to ourselves which reveal that we are transient and dependent beings in a universe of awesome proportions. Yet at the same time, a realization that people *are* special, not because of what we have done, but because of what we have been given. David was called a "man after God's own heart" first of all because he was a *man*. He knew how to weep, how to dance before Yahweh; how to fight, and how to run. His was a grateful, humble, and cheerful humanity, like a child at Christmas who opens a present and jumps up and down with delight at a new puppy or fire engine.

One element in the genius of great Russian novelists like Tolstoy and Dostoevsky consisted in their ability to strip away layers of adult pretension, the "emperor's new clothes," in which we wrap ourselves. The heroes of their novels, such as Levin in *Anna Karenina* and Alyosha in *The Brothers Karamazov*, tend to be those who doubt themselves. Like King David, they recognized their cosmic dependency, though unlike him, not all find someone to depend upon. Tolstoy poured over the Sermon on the Mount and made its ideals the basis of his life. Yet he was not a happy man, and he ended his life in despair, because he did not know God as father, but, as Gorky characterized the relationship, "two bears in one den."[11] Tolstoy knew Jesus as guru, not as Savior.

Nebuchadnezzar, on the other hand, did find a measure of salvation:

"And at the end of the days I, Nebuchadnezzar, lifted up my eyes to the heavens, and my reason returned to me. I blessed the Most High and praised and honored Him, who lives for ever" (Dan. 4:34).

Nebuchadnezzar regained sanity by looking up and praising.

Praise is the greatest pleasure in life. We take a friend from out of town to all our favorite spots because we enjoy hearing other people speak well of what we see as good. We watch Sister Mary cavort through the museums of Europe and rhapsodize over the great art of the Western world, and when we hear enthusiasm about a work by an artist we love, we feel like we've found a friend. We step out of our tent on a crisp morning in the mountains and ask the first passerby, "isn't this beautiful?" It would not be nearly so much fun if there were no "other" to share it with us: we are glad that all things are not one at moments like that. We are happy to see beauty, and even happier to know others can see and enjoy it too.

G. K. Chesterton believed happiness depended on finding the true object for our highest enthusiasm.

"The man who cannot believe in his senses, and the man who cannot believe in anything else, are both insane, but their insanity is proved not by any error in their argument, but by the manifest mistake of their whole lives. They have locked themselves up . . . they are both unable to get out, the one into the health and happiness of heaven, the other even into the health and happiness of the earth."[12]

According to Jung, even healthy people have neurosis: emptiness, boredom, meaninglessness, loneliness, guilt, anxiety, fear of old age and of dying. We are frustrated when we lose control of our lives, as all of us will at one time or another. The world looks increasingly ominous as we age. Earl Jabay suggested that "healthy" people may even be in worse shape than his "sick" patients, because they lack knowledge of their need. Put in that perspective, Nebuchadnezzar's breakdown may have been the best break in his life: a turn with wild animals helped him realize his humanity.

Becker thought Christianity "naive." He was surprised to find Christians, like Augustine, Pascal, Chesterton, and most of all Kierkegaard, clinging to their ancient Scriptures, and describing humankind's deepest problem in ways similar to those described by the brightest stars of empirical psychology after a lifetime of clinical research. Christians say "sin," and psychologists "neurosis," but in either case pride was the root cause of human misery. Another Biblical term for the problem is "idolatry."

Gods in the Image of Man

An idol may be a physical creation like a block of wood carved into the image of a bodhisattva, a developed skill like figure skating, or a system of ideas by which to explain the universe, that we call an "ideology." It may be something I find in nature: a tree, a stone, the force of evolution, the laws of mathematics. It may be a heroic human being or noble ideal. Often it is something we park in the garage, deposit in the bank, or pretty up for the world in front of a mirror. It is that to which we assign transcendental value in an effort to create our own salvation, that to which we become attached in an ultimate (rather than temporal) sense, an anchor for the ego in something we like to think is "bigger than life."

If other people also see that object as especially important—whether a deceased benefactor to whom Taiwanese farmers address prayer, a hot new movie star, a software startup—the idol becomes a cult. Anthropologists have realized that the power that people perceive emanating from the deity is proportional to the fervency of worship it receives. The force of public opinion can elevate any trinket to cult status. Yet in the end, as David's son Solomon realized after he inherited his father's palace, and all the maidservants, mansions, and gold bullion that went with it, all of this (looking down, on the creations of human hands) is vanity (literally "vapor") and striving after wind.

What do we call a person who has found his god has legs of wood? A skeptic? A cynic? A freethinker? Whatever we call him, he might be right when he says the god he created, or (more often) the god his parents or society created for him, is a cheat. He may even be right when he says all gods are a cheat. But the need to acknowledge a higher power is so basic to human character that when stifled we nearly always find a substitute, a Mao, Rajneesh, even a Michael Jordan.

Jabay, Kilpatrick and Chesterton all came to the conclusion that men and women need God. Becker and Rank, as unbelievers, agreed. If we are to be whole all our deeds must find validation in the approval of one greater than ourselves, and greater than the idols we build and the ideologies we imagine. "(A creative individual) knows that the work is he, therefore 'bad,' ephemeral, potentially meaningless—unless justified from outside himself and from outside itself."[13]

Becker was nonplused to find the psychiatric science he admired dove-tailing so neatly with Christian theology. "Our hearts are restless until they find their rest in Thee," said Augustine, and secular psychologists, taking a deep and searching look into the human soul, found themselves voicing a loud "amen."

"Man is a 'theological being' concludes Rank . . . what makes it uncanny . . . is that these are the conclusions of a lifetime of a psychoanalyst, not a theologian. The net effect is overwhelming . . . Such a mixture of intensive clinical insight and pure Christian theology is absolutely heady. One doesn't know what kind of emotional attitude to adopt towards it . . . "14

Go Into All the World and Cure Neurosis?

Becker went a step further, and wished into being a piece of Christian theology many other unbelievers have tried to wish out of being. Even if a saving ideology could be found to rescue ourselves from both vanity and idolatry, would this ideal faith be confined to a few fortunate adepts of psychology? Were those in most need of liberation to have no chance of hearing it?

"Can any ideal of therapeutic revolution touch the vast masses of this Globe . . . the modern mechanical man in Russia, the near-billion sheep-like followers in China, the brutalized and ignorant populations of almost every continent?"15

After all the criticism that has been leveled at Christian missions, it is interesting to see a humanist of Becker's caliber re-invent Jesus' Great Commission from scratch. One wonders what Becker would say had he met those who prayed and found new reason for life in a Soviet Gulag. Or if he joined in a meeting in the countryside of Henan Province where faces that once screamed denunciations of neighbors were alive with the joy of worship? Or sat in on meetings like I've been to in Taiwan, Thailand, and the Philippines where most of the people who sang and pounded drums and guitars and prayed used to do drugs or run brothels?

True, the church often creates neuroses as well, as do all human associations. The church is like a doctor who manages to poison some patients, not because his medical books are in error or his medicines defective, but because he misuses them. I know a person who spent two years incapacitated by depression and guilt, hardly able to get out of bed, thinking that her relatives were all going to hell and it was her fault. But the compassion of Jesus flowed naturally in response to ordinary human needs, without compulsion or guilt. It is ironic that the person who really did bear the sins of the world showed no signs of a Messiah complex. But apart from the spirit of Christ, it certainly is possible to make the truth toxic.

The world admires Mother Theresa for her sacrifice. That sacrifice was real: Jesus repeatedly told his followers that no one was worthy to be his disciple if he didn't "take up his cross, and follow me." Jesus promised his followers an "abundant life," but part of that abundance, he warned, would be an abundance of trouble. Those who left home for the sake of the Gospel would gain a hundred mothers and sisters and brothers, "along with persecutions" (Mark 10:30). Paul modeled that richness:

"In measureless toils and imprisonments, in floggings beyond count and facing death frequently. Five times I received from the Jews 40 lashes minus one, three times I was shipwrecked, for a night and a day I have been adrift at sea. In my many travels I have been in dangers of rivers and robbers, of Jews and Gentiles, of city, desert, and sea . . . in hunger, thirst, and often without clothing. Besides these . . . there is the daily responsibility for the churches. Who is weak without my being weak? Who is led into sin without my burning with indignation?" (2 Cor. 11).

And yet Paul told believers to "be joyful in the Lord always," (Phil. 4:4), and indeed was known to sing praise choruses in prison. I argued in the last chapter that, in general, Christians who think they are on a "mission from God" are not a menace to society, but its greatest hope. As I read the story of modern missions, I see this is because they are the people who have the most hope to give. David Livingstone, who, as explorer and pioneer missionary to Africa, faced hunger, disease, and lions, once told an English audience,

"I have never ceased to rejoice that God has appointed me to such an office. People talk of the sacrifice I have made in spending so much of my life in Africa . . . Is that a sacrifice which brings its own blest reward in healthful activity, the consciousness of doing good, peace of mind, and a bright hope of a glorious destiny hereafter? . . . Say rather it is a privilege . . . I never made a sacrifice."[16]

So the world would also be right to envy Mother Theresa, as indeed the journalist Malcolm Muggeridge who made her famous did. Besides brothers, sisters, mothers—and suffering—the Sisters of Charity gain joy from their work, as do all who model true humility. (I do not want to deny that non-Christians can grow in a relative humility and love.)

On my first visit to Thailand, our hosts were planning to move out of the house we stayed in, and large stacks of magazines sat by the front door. I started leafing through one stack, and came upon a cover article in *Time Magazine* about "Modern Missionaries." The author, who told the story of a number of missionaries around the world, noted that he had never come across a group of people more cheerful. The story that most caught my eye was that of the Morse family. The article credited the clan with over 100,000 Asian conversions to Christianity. The patriarch of the clan had gone to Tibet in the 1920s. His children, Robert and Eugene, grew up in China, and before they learned English they spoke the language of the Lisu minority, one of the poorest and most oppressed ethnic groups of Asia. After being driven out of Tibet, then China, the Morse children, then their children, then finally the fourth generation of Morses, continued preaching in the hills of Burma and Thailand.   T h a t evening I attended a prayer meeting. A man of about sixty came in after me, spied an empty chair, and gave me a friendly smile. "May I have a seat?" he asked. "Hi, I'm Eugene Morse." He seemed genuinely curious about this 22-year-old stranger. Several years later, on a return to Thailand, I went with Eugene to visit his brother Robert as he was dying of leukemia in the hospital. I was impressed by the kindness and friendliness he showed me, and was surprised to learn later that shortly afterwards, he died.

I have run into some of the twentieth century's most famous missionaries by similar happen-stance, and often found the same humility and curiosity: A. J. Bloomhall, biographer of the China Inland Mission, David Adeney, pioneer missionary in China, James Taylor, president of Overseas Missionary Fellowship and great-grandson of Hudson Taylor, and Dr. Paul Brand, whose pioneer rehabilitation work among lepers in India was followed by a career drawing spiritual lessons about the human body. I know people like to be skeptical of saints. But I have never run across a group of elderly people with heads on straighter or eyes with more sparkle and purpose. (Except perhaps for some elderly believers who spent decades for their faith in Chinese prisons.) "Gloomy" or "unbalanced" are the last words I would use to describe these people.

Jesus once met a "rich young ruler" (professional athlete or internet billionaire, perhaps?) who asked his advice about what to do with his life. The Gospel says Jesus was not jealous of the man's riches, but "had compassion" on him. He did not express this compassion as is usual, however. He did not tell him about a tax shelter or a girl who would like to meet him. On the contrary, he told him, "Go sell all that you have and give to the poor. Then come, follow me."

Writer Philip Yancey's experience serves to put Jesus' counter-cultural advice in perspective:

> "My career as a journalist has afforded me opportunities to interview 'stars,' including NFL football greats, movie actors, music performers, best-selling authors, politicians, and TV personalities. These are the people who dominate the media. We fawn over them . . . Yet I must tell you that, in my limited experience . . . our 'idols' are as miserable a group of people as I have ever met. Most have troubled or broken marriages. Nearly all are incurably dependent on psychotherapy. . . .These larger-than-life heroes seem tormented by self-doubt."

Becker explained. "The more you develop as a distinctive free and critical human being, the more guilt you have. Your very work accuses you; it makes you feel inferior. What right do you have to play God? Especially if your work is great . . . "[17]

Yancey contrasted his experiences with those he calls "servants," medical personal working among out-castes, lepers, the homeless, the poor, relief workers in the poorest backwaters of the world, people with doctorates translating the Bible among tribes in the jungle. He concluded, "I was prepared to honor and admire these servants . . . I was not prepared to envy them. Yet . . . they possess qualities of depth and richness and even joy that I have not found elsewhere."[18]

It is possible to interpret the joy of the saints as some kind of placebo effect. The Nation of Islam also helped drug addicts escape addictions. Followers of the True Buddha sect told me they felt "calmer" and "more at peace" through meditation. Just as medieval doctors who bled their patients probably did them some good from time to time just by getting them to believe their methods, so it may be argued that priests of all religions occasionally do good simply by unlocking the potential of the human mind to trust in a Higher Power. Marx said religion is the "opiate of the people;" well for a person with no hope, opium has its uses.

But not all faith is equally healing. Marx was right about that, and proved it, too.

What Kind of Happiness does Eastern Religion Offer?

The modern world is off on a journey to "rediscover the sacred." Babyboomers are back in church, or in temples, yoga classes, and Zen meditation centers. Many have begun to feel that "man shall not live on bread alone" (Luke 4:4). By all of these paths, as Pascal pointed out, we hope to find happiness.

David called us to look up. Others say the solution is to look in, through psychology or so-called "eastern" religion. (I say so-called, because following Chesterton, I doubt generalizations about belief based on geography.)

Some psychologists tells us salvation comes through "knowing ourselves." This is the "perennial philosophy" Aldous Huxley believed found its most perfect expression in the *Bhagavad Gita*. The world of things and individual consciousness is a manifestation of the Divine Ground, the *Tao* or *Brahma*. The purpose of life is to realize the *atman* the "spark of divinity within the soul," the eternal self, that is the Godhood within each of us.

Christianity agrees this philosophy is perennial. But from a Christian perspective, union between *atman* and *Brahma* may act as a subtle form of the perennial delusion that we can be gods. Scott Peck argued that while Hinduism and Buddhism encourage us to give up our "ego boundaries" and attain enlightenment by relapsing to a child-like state, a mature experience of Oneness should not be confused with the "glimpse of Nirvana" that we attain through falling in love, sex, or drugs. "Nirvana or lasting enlightenment or true spiritual growth can be achieved only through the persistent exercise of real love."[19] But the love he talked about was based on an affirmation and acceptance of ego boundaries. This is what Hindus and Buddhists call dualism, and they tell us it is the fundamental illusion.

It would be untrue to say no religion besides Christianity can make people happy. It is possible to find peace and even exhilaration by embracing Zen, for example. Tucker Calloway, a Southern Baptist missionary, admitted as much in his surprisingly sympathetic study *Zen Way, Jesus Way*:

> "I, a Jesus-man, know the Myoko, the Mysterious-Joy, of walking the world the Zen Way. But I have chosen, and choose anew each day, to go the Jesus Way. If what I wanted was sheer, uninterrupted delight, freedom forevermore from tensions, struggles, the frustrations of failure, the aching load of responsibility, the agony of grief, the ache of guilt—if that is what I wanted, I would go Zen . . . Such benefits as these it does truly bring."[20]

We can find a measure of happiness in any religion, or in the pursuit of excellence in any field. But here we are back to Augustine's question. Where can we find a happiness that fulfills our highest calling as men and women?

Was Buddha himself a happy man? Buddhist art is, on this score, ambivalent. While some pictures of Siddhartha at the moment of enlightenment show an expression of unambiguous child-like delight, in many pictures from the caves at Dunhuang, in Central Asia, he strikes a ghastly smile, like someone who has read too many cynical editorials, but realized they were all a fraud, a man who sees through everything and realizes there is nothing left to see. If that is happiness, it is too proud to take delight in anything outside itself. One sutra does indeed picture Buddha in such a mode:

> "When shortly after his Enlightenment, Sakyamuni was going to Benares, he met the ascetic Upaka on the way and said to him: 'There is no master for me, no one is comparable to me; in this world I am the only fully Enlightened One; I have attained perfect and supreme Enlightenment; in this world I have overcome all and am omniscient . . . I am the Tathagata, the teacher of gods and men, omniscient and endowed with all powers."[21]

In the later esoteric tradition, Buddhism borrowed from Hinduism the idea that for the master, all things are permissible, because he has overcome the distinction between himself and external reality:

> "All the Buddhas replied: 'Son of a good family, (your Vajra teacher) is to be regarded by all Buddhas and all Bodhisattvas as the Vajra of the Thought of Enlightenment. And why so? The Teacher and the Thought of Enlightenment are the same and inseparable . . . He is the father of all us Buddhas, the mother of all us Buddhas, in that he is the Teacher of all us Buddhas . . . the merit of a single pore of the Teacher is worth more than the heap of merit of . . . the Buddhas of the ten directions . . . "[22]

Tibetan monastic scholarship can be a tough, competitive, and humbling career. Despite being worshiped as an emanation of the god Avalokitvara by the Tibetan people, the Dalai Lama has cultivated an attractive human curiosity and vulnerability. Clearly, it is possible to interpret the eastern traditions so as to encourage humility and human dignity. But the plainest reading of some sutras, and acquaintance with many popular "Living Buddhas" and "Realized Beings" suggests that "unity with the Godhead" may threaten our humanity and even our sanity. Lu Sheng-yen, founder of the True Buddha school, wrote:

"What is 'truth?' Truth is me. And what am I? I am Buddha, to speak simply, I am the truth, and heaven and earth and all things are an incarnation of me . . . I change shape into myriad objects and things, and thus enclose the entire universe, include the entire universe, and become a single body within the universe, eternally existing together within it."23

With such Masters, ego-implosion seems to merge into ego-expansion and fuse with common vanity. "Holy Red Crowned Grand Vajra Lotus-Born Master Lu Sheng-yen" loved to be photographed with the Dalai Lama and American politicians. He sits on a throne with his followers below him on the floor. His exalted position, mansion, and alleged womanizing, have been common in the esoteric tradition from the time of the Tibetan religious heroes Atisa and Milerepa.

This stance is, as I noted earlier, derived from the Indian concept of guru.

I invited a regional leader of one of the most tolerant and ecumenical Hindu sects to explain Hinduism at a seminar. He was a man of dignity and learning, who had served as the head of the state inter-religious council. His disciples spoke of the "swami" in a devotional tone. The woman who arranged his speaking engagement very reluctantly lent me his photograph, telling me, "I treasure it very much." Such photographs are worshiped in the Hindu tradition.

As I chatted with him at his ashram, and later at the seminar, he struck me as friendly in a dignified way, and he proved an excellent speaker. But I did not feel as if I were completely meeting him, as if he were partly withdrawn to some lonely and sad plane. Perhaps I am reading too much into a single short acquaintance, and perhaps this is partly a matter of personality. But one Western seeker who visited many ashrams in India later wrote of "deathlike serenity" and "austere severity" as norm among Indian gurus he met; so perhaps my impression of distance was not totally subjective or unique.

Can we argue, from a monist point of view, that self-centeredness in the normal sense of egotism as well as the literal sense of finding one's center within, is "against nature?" Flowers compete to bloom and rabbits to run. India is the land of gods and of men who have achieved god consciousness. Some of them express that consciousness by training fingernails to grow through the flesh of their palms, or by lying on beds of nails. The Tantric path to godhood, through "consort practice," the mystical union of male and female, or the accumulation of Rolls Royces, is in tune with a cheerier side of competitive nature. But modern, capitalist society has proven Nebuchadnezzar's discovery that to allow the impulse to ego expansion free reign is to court psychological ruin.

Popular and (in one sense) more healthy forms of "eastern" religion often encourage followers to place faith in some unseen "higher power." Cult movements like Hare Krishna and Seikyo Shokagakkai teach that we can save ourselves and reach a higher level of consciousness by repeating a holy name. Pure Land Buddhism, with its talk of savior beings, appeals to those who are humble enough to know they'll never make Buddha themselves. This is the Buddhism that caught on with Asians.

The concept of *nirvana*, extinction of desire and personality in an eternal rest of peace, which in theory lay at the core of Buddhist and Hindu doctrine, was always a white elephant as far as the masses were concerned. Most Asian Buddhists, if they knew about nirvana, show little ambition to go there. They preferred the intermediate heaven called Western paradise, a place more fit for human habitation. Likewise, the Taoism that really became popular spoke of a land of immortals. In the Chinese classic, *Journey to the West*, the uncouth and cheeky Monkey King raided the Garden of Immortal Peaches and gorged himself on ripe fruit. The Monkey King was a hero to the Chinese precisely because, monkey though he was, he retained a bumbling humanity even in the most exalted regions of heaven. As proud and arrogant as the "Great Sage, Equal to Heaven" could be, he was in this respect more humble than Kipling's pretentious simians, and many "Evolved Masters" of all traditions, East and West. The ordinary Asian did not want to extinguish consciousness, but make life "more abundant."

Yet according to Becker, in spinning prayer wheels, circling stupas, chanting magical vowels from another world, and chipping stone into the form of a god— or in preaching the Gospel—the ordinary person, too, may build a ziggernaut, worshipping the works of his or her hands, rather than the maker of those hands. The psychological inadequacy of the religions of man is that they *are* the religions of man. We could be happy about our gods, if only we could forget we made them. I know some say Christians have invented their God, too. We will see in later chapters this is not the case. But even if it were, Christianity would retain the psychological advantage that Christians have forgotten they invented him.

Gandhi And Saint Paul

Monistic religions often speak about human desire in strangely contradictory terms.

The *Bhagavad Gita* warns against "Triple Veda" religious devotion, by which the "righteous" attain a heaven of such exquisite pleasures that those who enjoy them use up all their good karma. Yet a few sentences later it promises "peace eternal" if the worshiper only "takes your delight" in Krishna, the highest God.[24] So it tells us to extinguish desire, but only in order to fulfill desire; for that is what delight implies.

If it is possible to attain a state of indifference toward avalanche lilies blooming on the fringe of a snow field in June, would such a state be pleasing to God? How would you feel if your children announced, "I am no longer attached to Christmas. I am indifferent to whether or not I receive presents this year?" I'd be crushed.

And how can one desire a state of desirelessness, anyway? Louis Fischer, in an afterward to the same edition of the *Gita,* admitted: "Mahatmas are rare. Desirelessness is an ideal to which few in India or anywhere attain or even aspire," but noted that "several times in his life Gandhi expressed the hope not to be born anew." He noted:

> "Desirelessness, or Hindu renunciation, it has been argued, leads to personal indifference and passivity and national poverty and stagnation. Gandhi contended, on the contrary, that to act while renouncing interest in the fruits of action is the best road to success. 'He who is ever brooding over result,' he wrote, 'often loses nerve in the performance of duty . . . he is ever-distracted, he says good-by to all scruples . . . he therefore resorts to means fair and foul to attain his end.'"[25]

I find this confusing. What does it mean to *aspire to* a state of *desirelessness?* Aspiration *is* desire. And can you *hope* to achieve that which can only come by renouncing *ambitions?* All of us need some kind of hope for the future, by whatever name, and all of us want our actions to yield achievement.

Christianity also tells us not to "brood" over results, but to do our best and leave the results in God's hands. Certainly Christians agree that good ends do not justify all means; in that sense, we should be "detached" from the fruit of our labor. But that is not the same as to "renounce interest" in the results of one's actions, which this passage itself proves, I think it poppycock to say Gandhi ever did.

It does not seem to me, reading his autobiography, that Gandhi was "indifferent" either to the results of his labor or to his own future. He moved India because he was moved by India. The *Gita* taught him discipline that aided him in the fight. But the *Gita* he carried around India was also a call to caste responsibility and Civil War. Around him others were heeding that call, and it killed him inside to watch. But perhaps in his concern for the fruits of his actions, Gandhi was more a disciple of Christ than of Krishna.

No one accused Paul of being indifferent about anything. He raved, shouted, broke into parenthetical paragraphs of rhapsody, grew ironic, called co-workers sons, and threw up his hands in frustration at their obstinacy. He said he would be cursed if that could bring his people to their senses. He embraced coworkers on partings, and spoke unabashedly of loneliness when he felt deserted. He endured tortures for the Gospel, but never courted martyrdom or asceticism for its own sake. When he got cold, he asked for a coat. When he got lonely, he asked for a friend. Yet with all his passionate sensuality and attachment to the fruit of his actions, Paul did not "lose nerve" or "say good-bye" to his scruples, as Gandhi assumed that a passionate person would. He remained as much a man of integrity as Gandhi, and perhaps more a man of contentment. Unlike Gandhi, he felt comfortable when he "had abundance" as well as when he "suffered want." The secret of this contentment was gratitude: the thankful accepting of all good things from the hand of God, even pain which, as ascetics know, brings its rewards, and even pleasure, which as children know, should never be scorned.

Buddha and Jesus

Buddha and Jesus both sought that balance which is the goal of all sages, but by different means. Buddha rejected all passions, in theory. Jesus embraced and exaggerated each emotion, playing the tune of his life with an exuberant emphasis, a Fifth Symphony of love. Jesus "endured pain and suffered grief" (Isa. 53:3 pph), but also "came eating and drinking" (Matt. 11:19). He showed up at parties with the wrong sort of people. He broke into spontaneous thanksgiving when his disciples came back from a successful outreach. Nor did he avoid those chords of emotion most taboo among Stoics, such as anger or fear. He drove merchants out of the temple with a whip. He wept at the hardness of heart of those who cared more about propriety than kindness. He poured out his sorrow and fear on the night of his betrayal till his robe was wet with the tears and sweat of his humanity. On the cross he cried out in loneliness and agony: "My God, my God. Why have you forsaken me?" (Matt.27:4).

Jesus said, "I have come so they may have life and have it abundantly" (John 10:10). The man most god-like in love, was most human in his feelings.

But each of these moments of intense humanity came while Jesus, like his ancestor David, was looking up. His agony came during prayer to his Father. He rejoiced in prayer. He threw money-changers out of the temple out of zeal for "his father's house." It was to God that he cried on the cross. Like David, the Son of Man found humanity in relation to God.

What began in humble and emotional prayer to God, tended to end in compassionate acts towards men and women.

Compassion means, "passion with." How can you be compassionate without passion? Feel as another person feels. Feed the hungry because you like food; don't tell them they are lucky to be saved from the bondage of lust for food. The nobility of great "Eastern" sages like Gandhi lies in the partial contradiction their lives give to their philosophy. To some extent, they resembled the Biblical heroes of the faith in being characters, men and women of distinct passion who to some degree escaped the trap of introversion and impersonality by caring about something or someone more than an inward-looking philosophy.

Nebuchadnezzar lost humanity through pride. Through pride, religious zealots (including many in the Christian tradition) throw humanity away as an encumbrance to spirituality. The fact that adepts approach God through great discipline and subtle reasoning only separates the spiritual and intellectual "haves" from the vast majority of "have-nots" more severely. If present reality is purely a result of past choices, as the doctrine of karma teaches, the fortunate can only pat themselves on the back and the miserable kick themselves. If reality is the result of heredity and the iron law of determinism, we are no better off.

Rabi Maharaj writes of growing up the son of a Hindu sadhu who took a vow a few days after marriage to never speak another word. Later, his mother deserted him to pursue religious training in India. For him, as for his father, the path to "autonomous creativity," to union with God, would lie in ascetic practice and the worship that simple Hindus increasingly offered. At the very moment of receiving worship from a neighbor, however, realization that he was not God, non-God consciousness, broke upon him. He went home and wept.

> "During those long, lonely hours I went back over the life that I could remember and wondered at my blindness. How could a cow or a snake—or even I—be God? How could the creation create itself? How could everything be of the same Divine Essence? That denied the essential difference between a person and a thing, a difference I knew was there, no matter what Lord Krishna and the Vedas said. If I were of the same essence as a sugarcane, then essentially there was no difference between me and sugarcane—which was absurd.

> "This unity of all things that I had experienced in meditation now appeared preposterous! Pride alone had blinded me. I had wanted so much to be Lord of the universe that I had been willing to believe an obvious lie."[26]

The Bible says God "sets Himself against the arrogant, but grants grace to the humble" (1 Peter 5:5). The sum total of that grace is the salvation God offers through the death of Jesus for our sins. There is nothing in the message of the cross for us to pat ourselves on the back. The cross reminds us that none of us is at a higher stage of evolution. All our good deeds are "filthy rags;" by comparison. As Paul said, this a hard blow to our pride. But while the pill of humility smells bitter, it sweetens in the stomach, and soothes our souls as it goes down. If, as Becker says, the burden of autonomous creation is too heavy for even the greatest geniuses to bear, then the burden of our own salvation would ground our souls to dust. Praise God, he does not make us bear it.

Worship and praise are not a magic potion, but a daily spiritual diet that heals the spirit. The Bible claims that either the disease or its cure will survive death.

Death is the ultimate frustration of human happiness. The first three levels of faith—in the mind, the senses, and other people—cannot tell us whether the breath of man, our *chi*—goes up or down, to Hades, nirvana, a peach garden beyond the world, the land of hungry ghosts, Western Paradise, or the place where the dot on the computer screen retires at night. We know what death looks and smells like, and we can verify it with fingers on a friend's wrist. But that's all we can do.

I think it is reasonable to trust Jesus on this point, because he said, "I have come so they may have life, and have it abundantly," and we can see that life in him and in those who "throw away" their lives to follow him. What makes such faith truly reasonable is the Resurrection of Jesus from the dead. There's life, for you. The question is, can we believe it? If God is real, and if miracles happen, and if the Gospels are reliable, then there is no reason to deny the strong evidence that the Gospels give. These are among the questions remaining to us to consider.

---

[1] C. S. Lewis, *The Great Divorce*, MacMillan Co., 1946, p. 69

[2] Pascal, *Pensees*, thought #425, from Piper, *Desiring God*, p. 15

[3] Peck, *Road Less Traveled*, p. 207

[4] Paul Vitz notes, however, that none of the case studies Freud published were of believers. (*Books and Culture*, Jan.-Feb. 1999, p. 32) Vitz made a more detailed study in *Sigmund Freud's Christian Conscience* (which I have not read), and generalized his conclusions *in Faith of the Fatherless*. (An excellent book.) Vitz proposed that, in a topsy-turvy fashion, materialists, including Freud himself, confirm Freud's hypothesis about God as a cosmic father figure. In many cases, atheists are not those who disbelieve in God, but those who rebel against the caricature of him their upbringing allowed them. Like any child in rebellion, they try to become that against which they rebel. "Freud . . . said we should all hate our father unconsciously and wish to replace him. If that is the case, why would we replace him with a supernatural father? In fact, Freud's theory clearly predicts that we should all . . . have an unconscious, irrational, and neurotic basis for atheism." I will consider this question further in the following chapter.

[5] *Confessions*, p. 145-6

[6] Historian Will Durant alleged that the Daniel account is "legendary and vengeful," but admitted the ruler was both proud and of doubtful sanity. *The Story of Civilization: Our Oriental Heritage*, p. 223. Simon & Schuster, 1950 My purpose here is to explore the relationship between these two qualities.

[7] Earl Jabay, *Kingdom of Self*, p. 81

[8] Ernest Becker, *Denial of Death*, Simon & Schuster, 1973, p. 172

9 Paul Hollander's harsh analysis of Western intellectuals who hob-nobbed with communist dictators is worth considering in this context: "Everyone found what he wanted most, and a sense of superiority into the bargain. It was easy to feel superior to the rabble who stood in lines, who were shoved off trains to make way for cash customers . . . The only place in the world where you could stand at the apex with dictators and merge ecstatically with the masses simultaneously; a synthesis of absolute power and absolute humility heretofore vouchsafed only to rare mystics and martyrs." *Political Pilgrims*, p. 61

10 *Denial of Death*, p. 196

11 Paul Johnson, *Intellectuals*, Harper Collins, 1988, p. 108

12 *Orthodoxy*, Doubleday, 1959, p. 27

13 *Denial of Death*, p. 172

14 Ibid., p.175

15 Ibid., p.281

16 John Piper, *Desiring God: Meditations of a Christian Hedonist*, Multnomah, 1986

17 *Denial of Death*, p. 172

18 Philip Yancey, *The Jesus I Never Knew*, Zondervan, 1995, p. 117-8

19 *The Road Less Traveled*, p. 97

20 Tucker Calloway, *Zen Way, Jesus Way*, Charles E. Tuttle, 1976, p. 227

21 Sanghabh, from Etienne Lamoutte, *The Buddha, His Teachings and His Sangha*, p. 43

22 David Snellgrove, *Indo-Tibetan Buddhism: Indian Buddhists and Their Tibetan Successors,* Boston, 1987, p. 177

23 Lu Sheng-yen, *Da Shouyin, Zhigui*, Taizhong, p. 15

24 *Bhagavad Gita: The Song of God,* translated by Swami Pradhavanda and Christopher Isherwood, 1944, Vedanta Society, p. 83, 85

25 Ibid., p.142

26 *Death of a Guru*, Harvest House, 1977, p. 110

CHAPTER 9

The Non-History of God

IN *A History of God*, Karen Armstrong argued that the "Western" concept of God was a pious invention. She noted that some of her ecclesiastic friends agreed. "Other rabbis, priests and Sufis would have taken me to task for assuming that God was—in any sense—a reality 'out there'. . . . God was a product of the creative imagination, like the poetry and music that I found so inspiring." While at times monotheistic religions exhibited a certain artistic flair, belief in God is naive and harmful in its "fundamentalist" phase. The book was warmly praised not only by organs of the secular press like *Time* Magazine, but also by a former Archbishop of Canterbury. No doubt she was thinking of persons in a similar position when she noted: "A few highly respected monotheists would have told me quietly and firmly that God did not really exist—and yet that 'he' was the most important reality in the world."[1]

While reviewers seemed to find Armstrong's book something of a novelty, it reminded me of *Evolution of the Idea of God* by Grant Allen, written a century before, and commented on by G. K. Chesterton. Chesterton said it would have been more interesting, if God had written a book on the "evolution of the idea of Grant Allen."[2] For one who has reason to doubt the assumptions with which Armstrong hamstrung herself—that God cannot write books, create stars or tell his own story—her book, while educational, seemed a little surreal. It was like reading a history of Western photography written on the assumption that Yosemite Valley was only a figment of Ansel Adam's imagination, not granite you can grasp and pine needles that burn over a fire. Armstrong narrowed her focus so completely that she missed God.

She was not the only one. Religion is often defined as man's search for God, but it could also be described as our attempts to hide from him. One could go a long ways toward understanding history by defining institutional religion as, "authority constituted for the purpose of keeping people from falling into the hands of their Creator." Yet everywhere you go, there he is. Francis Thomas' famous poem captures more truly the shared experience of all races:

> "I fled Him down the nights and down the days: I fled him down the arches of the years.
> I fled Him down the labyrinthine ways of my own mind; and in the midst of tears.
> I hid from Him, and under running laughter . . . From those strong feet that followed, followed after.
> But with unhurrying chase, and unperturbed pace, They beat And a Voice more instant than the Feet.
> 'All things betray Thee, who betrayest Me.'"[3]

I will argue that the Christian God, the God of the Bible, is not a Western invention, and in fact not an invention at all. Everywhere there are human beings, people know about him. When Christian missionaries arrived in cultures with no Bible, they found God there waiting for them. Often he told the locals they were coming.

Chesterton argued that in every age and at every time religion tends to exhibit four elements: "God, the gods, the philosophers, and the demons." When I went to Asia, I found Chesterton right and Armstrong, and other writers reluctant to find God (or the devil) outside of Western monotheism, wrong. The experts had pulled the wool over our eyes. The Creator is not just a Western tribal deity: he is also the best-kept secret of paganism.

I first came across this truth in two books by Don Richardson before I went to Asia. In the first, *Peace Child*, he told the story of how he, his wife and small children went to live among a primitive tribe in New Guinea that had the rare distinction of practicing both headhunting and cannibalism. This tribe, the Sawi, held traitors in highest regard, especially those who "fatted their foe with friendship" before turning on and cannibalizing them. When he told his new friends the story of Jesus, they saw Judas as the hero, and Jesus as the dupe. Ultimately he found secrets in the culture of this cruel and violent tribe that allowed them an understanding of the Gospel that, in some ways, was deeper and more profound than that of Western Europeans. They became Christians, and Richardson survived to write his second book, building on the insights he tested in the swamps of New Guinea.

Eternity in Their Hearts, attempted, in a series of remarkable narratives, to rewrite the history of world religions in general and Christian missions in particular.

Secular anthropologists had been teaching the "evolution of the idea of God" for over a century. In the nineteenth century, an anthropologist named Edward Tylor explained how "primitive" cultures developed a concept of the soul, then of many gods, then, paralleling the rise of royalist society and great empires, monotheism. The next step would occur when this process became self-conscious, and man realized he was alone in the universe and God was one of his creations. Marxist revolutionaries and Biblical critics leaped on these conclusions, the former to show why all religions should fade away in the wake of revolution, the latter to trace the "developed" monotheism of later Old Testament editors from a "primitive" god of war. Armstrong's thesis is one remnant of that theory.

But, as Chesterton seemed to grasp intuitively, and Richardson showed in detail, wherever missionaries and anthropologists went, they found God had been there before.

Anthropologists reasoned that if one wanted to study the origins of religion, one had better go to the most primitive tribes, assumed to be the aborigines of Australia. So a great deal of the debate swirled around the Outback. The first reports claimed aborigines had hardly any religion, certainly no concept as advanced as a Supreme God. Then reports came in from many directions of an omniscient being known as Bunjil, Daramulun, Baiame, or Nuralie. Tylor blamed missionaries for planting this concept among the aborigines. When that was no longer feasible, Emile Durkheim tried to tie the Aussie God to his theory of totemism, and to marginalize him by calling him "a high god," as Armstrong marginalized him by the term "Yahwism." But the fact remains, when they looked for the most primitive religion, this is what they found:

> "The characteristics of this personage are fundamentally the same everywhere. It is immortal and indeed an eternal being, since it is derived from no other . . . He is spoken of as a sort of creator. He is called the father of men and is said to have made them . . . At the same time as he made man, this divine personage made the animals and the trees . . . He is the benefactor of humanity . . . He communicates . . . the guardian of tribal morality, he punishes . . . he performs the function of judge after death distinguishing between the good and the bad . . . They feel his presence everywhere."[4]

Tribal peoples were aware of God, Richardson argued, yet did not know him. He seemed distant, like the sky with whom he was often vaguely (but only partially) identified. But in tribe after tribe, and in tradition after tradition, the apparent absence of God was thought due not to his negligence or lack of concern, but because their ancestors had, at some moment of crisis, turned their backs on him.

Some tribes identified a specific event in the past with this disaster. The Santal of Bengal told how their ancestors bowed to local mountain spirits while trekking across Afghanistan to the subcontinent.[5] The Karen, Kachin, Wa, Kui, Lisu, and Mizo of Southeast Asia said their ancestors had lost a book God had given them. The Lahu told how God's law had been written on rice cakes, the Naga, on animal skins which dogs had eaten.

Not only did peoples on every continent have the idea of a Creator who loved mankind and from whom they were alienated, Richardson noted that many of these peoples believed that one day a way would be found to reestablish intimacy with God. Missions succeeded because the people (often without the explicit awareness of the missionaries themselves) interpreted the new message about God's "Peace Child," as a fulfillment of the most sacred truths in their own tradition.

Richardson related tales from South America, Europe, Africa, India and the Far East. His stories of several hill tribes in the Golden Triangle, the foothills on the borders of China, Thailand, India, and Burma, particularly caught my attention. Many of the tribes in that region clung to archaic traditions about the Creator, whom they knew by various names: *Pathian* to the Mizo of India, *Gui'Sha* to the Lahu, *Karai Kasang* to the Kachin. Like other peoples around the world, these Southeast Asian tribes felt their ancestors had committed some irresponsible act by which God had been rendered unapproachable. Yet they believed one day he would send a book that would tell them how to know God again. In several cases, Richardson noted, legend specified this book would be brought by a white man.

During the nineteenth century, a prophet arose among the Wa named Pu Chan. He preached that *Siyeh*, the Creator, was about the fulfill the ancient promise of the lost book. One day, he told his disciples, "follow this pony. Siyeh told me last night that he white brother has finally come near! Siyeh will cause this pony to lead you to him."[6] The donkey in question did not stop to drink and lay down at the first watering hole, nor did it head home. Instead, it led the amazed tribesmen on a hike of 200 miles across mountain trails to the northern Burmese city of Kengtung. It walked into a mission compound, and headed for a well being dug in the ground. Out of the hole appeared the dirty face of a Baptist missionary named William Marcus Young.

Wa tribesmen crowded around him and asked, "Have you brought a book of God?"[7]

I had the opportunity, years later, to visit some of the churches that sprung up across the hills of Southeast Asia in response to the arrival of the book of God. I visited one beautiful wooden church started by Young's two sons, just across the Burmese border in China, which rests on a tree-covered hilltop above a small Lahu town in the hills, with a bell out front to call the people in the town below to worship. Millions of tribal peoples in that part of Asia are now Christians. Few if any became believers through colonization: when the British ruled India, for example, they sometimes bared missionaries from meddling with the hill tribes. These tribal peoples had been subject to centuries of exploitation and "missionizing" from their Buddhist and Hindu lowland neighbors. But they were fiercely independent, violent, and suspicious. Apart from Richardson's thesis, it would be hard to explain their quick and transforming conversion to Christianity. In China, these tribes were cruelly persecuted for conversion to "Western" religion under Mao Zedong, yet remained strong in their faith. I met a Chinese girl who had traveled through regions on the border of China where the Lisu live, and was so impressed by their spirit that she asked me many questions about Christianity.

A Christian anthropologist in Yunnan, the Chinese province bordering on Burma, told me that "pretty much all" the minorities of southern China had some prior belief in the Creator God. Later, an agnostic Taiwanese anthropologist in Japan affirmed, with some bewilderment, something similar about China's minorities in general. The Dai of Southeast Asia are known as a Buddhist people: it is part of their self-identification, and part of their tourist promotion. Imagine my surprise, then, when with my (lightly Marxist) Dai teacher I translated the title of their epic Creation poem and discovered it could be rendered, "in the beginning gods (or God; the Dai language does not distinguish between singular and plural) created the world."

Richardson argued,

> "One of the most amazing characteristics of this benign, omnipotent 'sky-god' of mankind's many folk religions is His propensity to identify Himself with the God of Christianity . . . He cheerfully acknowledges the approaching messengers of Yahweh as His messengers! He takes pains to make it very clear that He Himself is none other than the very God those particular foreigners proclaim!"[8]

I found such stories common in the "pagan" world, and a key to understanding how Christianity has spread over the last 2000 years. Tribal peoples in Taiwan told me how they had been vaguely aware of a righteous God even while they were still hunting heads. An elder of the Makah Indian tribe on the Northwest tip of Washington State told us how a Makah prophet predicted the coming of the first missionaries. The ancestors of the Hawaiians once worshiped the Supreme God as Io. Hewahewa, the high priest, admitted, "I knew the wooden images of deities could not supply our wants. . .My thought has always been, there is one only great God, dwelling in the heavens." He called the missionaries "brother priests."[9] I once heard a young Hawaiian man, raised in the neo-traditional worship of the volcano goddess Pele, recount in chant the moving story of how the Hawaiian princess Kapi'olani recognized the God of the missionaries as the true God, and defied Pele on the lip of the active Kilauea crater.

Europe

The success of Christianity in Europe apparently also owed a great deal to what God had done within the cultures of the continent before the Gospel arrived. Paul set the example when he preached his famous sermon in the cultural center of the Mediterranean world, Athens. He arrived a Jew from the alien metropolis of Antioch. When he started preaching, educated Athenians laughed and asked, "What is this babbler trying to say? He seems to be advocating foreign gods." These are familiar comments to missionaries. "Who are these people with their strange accents and uncouth ways? Why do we need this alien deity they bring us?"

How did Paul respond? "Open your Torahs to *Genesis*, and let me tell you idolatrous *goyim* about Yahweh, the True Hebrew God of whom you are totally clueless?" No, Paul knew more about Greek poetry and philosophy—and the Bible—than that.

Paul knew the Greeks had a name for the God whom he wanted to speak of—*Theos*. He had no doubt read Plato's plaintive thoughts on the Creator, and was probably aware that the Greeks were living with the expectation and hope of some further revelation of his character. (The rumor had spread "all over the east" that "it was fated for men coming from Judea at that time to rule the world."[10] Virgil spoke of "the birth of a child" of the gods with whom "the iron age of humanity will end and the golden age begin," and "the serpent too will die."[11] Paul did a day's field research. Arriving at Mars Hill, Paul reminded the Athenians that, in their zeal to cover all the bases in the spiritual world, they even worshiped at an altar "to an unknown god." Paul described that God not as a totally unknown quantity, but as the Supreme Deity whom Greek philosophers and poets had said, "'in Him we live and move and have our being. . .' and 'we also are His offspring'" (Acts 17).

Later Christian thinkers such as Clement and Augustine also realized God had never been a total stranger to the peoples of the Mediterranean world. Clement saw the Greek philosophers as "tutors" to point men to Christ. Augustine quoted extensively from Plato and philosophers of that school on the existence and character of the Supreme God. He perceptively noted that besides Socrates, Plato, and Pythagoras, and of course the Jews, "there may be others who perceived and taught this truth among those who were esteemed as sages or philosophers in other nations," such as the Indians, Egyptians, and Persians.[12]

The Gospel did not arrive in Scandinavia without peculiar forms of advance preparation, too. Like the Greeks, the Viking religion came with a clause implying engineered obsolescence—a queerly humble and desperate cosmology that hinted at some future and greater hope not yet visible, with qualities sketched roughly in legend. Lewis described the Norse mythology as "the irreversible, tragic epic marching deathward to the drum-beat of omens and prophecies."[13] The demons of disorder (Jotuns) had fought the gods to mutually-assured destruction. Historian Will Durant records, "in this twilight of the Gods all the universe fell to ruin: not merely sun and planets and stars, but, at last, Valhalla itself, and all its warriors and deities: only Hope survived—that in the moment of slow time a new earth would form, a new heaven, a better justice, and a higher god than Odin or Thor."[14] Durant, baffled, asked, "had the Vikings come to doubt and bury their gods?" Scandinavians even baptized their children "as a symbol of admission into the family."[15] It seems as if the Norse gods had spread a giant welcome mat out across Denmark for the Christian faith.

The same was the case in the Polynesian islands of the Pacific. A Supreme, benevolent, righteous Creator God, never worshiped with an idol, was remembered across the Pacific, but by the eighteenth century this worship was restricted to the upper class in Hawaii, who found crueler gods more politically useful. The Supreme God's name (*Io*) was "too sacred to be mentioned openly."[16] Prophets forecast, however, that the True God would speak from heaven in a way "entirely different from anything they had known"[17] and "the *kapo* of the gods brought low" (Kapo was a brutal caste system by which commoners had been enslaved for 500 years.) Indeed, a Hawaiian aristocrat overthrew the *kapo* within days of the time the first missionaries to Hawaii set out from Boston. When they arrived off the coast of Hawaii, according to Daniel Kikawa, a prophet named Hewchewa, seeing their vessel, told the king, "Here the true God will come," predicting the mission of the people in the boat, and the exact spot it would land.

How about educated, lowland Hindu, Buddhist, Taoist and Shinto cultures of Asia? Do we also find memory of the Creator among the so-called "pantheistic" civilizations of the East?

Tribal peoples usually prove more willing to accept the Gospel than rice-growing civilizations of Asia, which had more to lose from Western colonialism. Mountain tribes were more likely to see the "white brother" as a friend or at least neutral in their struggle against a local, lowland, and usually Buddhist or Hindu oppressor. The patriotism of early Christians in Korea contributed to the quick acceptance of Christianity among the Koreans, who had known God as *Hananim*.

But I have come to the conclusion that the great Buddhist and Hindu civilizations of Asia did not disbelieve in God any more than "folk" peoples, they merely tried harder to ignore him. In a very different tone from his sensitive address in Athens, in the book of *Romans* Paul described a peculiar religious pathology: "Whatever can be known regarding God is evident to them; for God has shown it to them. From the creation of the world His invisible qualities, such as His eternal power and divine nature, have been made visible. . ." However, people:

"Suppress the truth . . . Although they had knowledge of God, they failed to render Him the praise and thanks due to God. Instead, they indulged in their speculations . . . Claiming to be wise, they became foolish. They even altered the glory of the immortal God into images in the form of moral man and of birds, four-footed beasts, and reptiles" (Romans 1:18-23).

While these comments will not win any prizes for tactful religious dialogue, I think he could have said the same after a lifetime of studying Asian religions.

This is not to say Asia's (at least initial) rejection of Christianity was entirely the fault of Asians. The first wave of missionaries to reach Asia, the Jesuits, were very culturally-sensitive, and also enormously successful at first. However, as Europe began flexing its new muscles in the eighteenth and nineteenth centuries, its interaction with "pagan" peoples became increasingly arrogant and odious. Asians rejected Christianity to save their cultural souls. And what they rejected, more often than not, was a Christianity that truly was the tribal religion of Europe. In the process of rejecting that religion, the cultural elite often tried to exclude much of their own richest tradition and force a narrowly-defined national orthodoxy, called Hinduism or Buddhism among other names, upon their nations.

China

China has three religions, it is often said: Confucianism, Taoism, and Buddhism. None of them, as usually understood, are monotheistic, and so most people assume God is a foreign concept in China. This is not the case. In fact Confucianism began, in the ancient writings of China, as a moral reform with faith in a loving and just God at its core. What are called Buddhism and Taoism, and taught as such in Western schools and Western books on comparative religion, are very rarely of interest to most Chinese. Practical expressions of these religions appear, more often than not, as the cry of people looking for a personal Savior, for a heart of kindness behind the universe. Belief in a Supreme God was often drowned in a sea of idolatry, but was never quite absent from the minds of the people. It was acted out in annual sacrifices the emperor made to Heaven, remembered in popular proverbs, and even encrypted in some mysterious fashion into the very language. From before the time of Confucius, the Chinese have worshiped one whom they called *Tian* or *Shang Di*, the "parent of mankind," who rewarded good and punished evil, and was never worshiped with an idol. I found that even after centuries of anti-Christian propaganda and decades of education in which the only Western philosophers allowed to have a voice were atheists like Dewey, Nietzsche, and Russell, many if not most non-Christians in Taiwan believe, albeit vaguely, in a Creator God.

Chesterton wrote of the Greeks what could be said of the Chinese and many other pagan peoples as well:

"For them what was truly divine was very distant, so distant that they dismissed it more and more from their minds . . . Yet even in this there was a sort of tacit admission of its intangible purity . . . As the Jews would not degrade it by images, so the Greeks did not degrade it by imaginations. When the gods and goddesses were more and more remembered only by pranks and profligates, it was relatively a moment of reverence. It was an act of piety to forget God."

Yet even in the midst of paganism moments came when, "the motley mob of gods and goddesses sank suddenly out of sight and the sky Father was alone in the sky."[18]

The Supreme God was honored most often in China by silence. One of his names meant "Heaven," and to the Chinese he seemed distant as the sky. Only the emperor could worship him, annually at the magnificent Temple of Heaven, or periodically by offering sacrifices at the top of Mount Tai in Shandong Province. Of the fourteen emperors whom local chronicles list as having climbed the mountain in historic times, nine were among the most successful of all China's emperors.[19] Some were, indeed, violent and manipulative, but others were devout, integrating the worship of the Supreme God into various beliefs. Among the pilgrims to Tai were the founder of the Sui dynasty, Yang Jian, who seemed to seek in the worship of Heaven a cure for his own insecurities and violent temper; Wu Di, under whom the great Han dynasty reached its first glory; Ming Di, during whose reign Buddhism arrived in China; Gao Zong and Xuan Zong, under whom the Tang dynasty reached new peaks of power and influence, and the great Kang Xi and Qian Long rulers of the early Qing.

The Chinese made the worship of Heaven a test of a healthy humility—not only to God, but also to the traditions of their ancestors. Those who could not abide this act of humility on its own terms tended to be flamboyant and gifted, but with faults Chinese history magnified at the expense of their virtues. Qin Shihuang, builder of the Great Wall, expropriated the name of God for his title. Hui Zong, an artistic genius, bankrupt China in the face of Mongol invaders while entertaining the flattering theory that he was the son of the Jade Emperor. Zhu Yuanzhang, cruel founder of the Ming Dynasty, reverted to the ancient practice of worshiping his ancestors on a level with God. Hong Xiuquan called himself the younger brother of Jesus, and Mao Zedong abolished Heaven and the gods, both laying waste to China to save it.

The Chinese ruler who perhaps most exhibited that balance of strength and compassionate culture that is the ideal of Chinese leaders, the Kang Xi emperor, climbed Mount Tai twice, and befriended Jesuit missionaries. The worship of Heaven, he explained, "actually originated in the traditional respect for *Tian Zhu*" (readily accepting the newly-minted Catholic name for God, "Lord of Heaven.") His skeptical neo-Confucian advisors must have rolled their eyes at this foreign-inspired "anthropomorphism," but in Chinese history, denying personality to the Supreme God was the true innovation.

There also came sacred moments in Chinese history when for ordinary mortals, too, the gods and philosophies of man disappeared in a moment, and the Creator remained alone in the sky. One such moment comes in the *Dream of the Red Mansions*, when the heroine, in desperation, addressed prayers "directly to God rather than to Taoist and Buddhist gods." "Mighty Heaven, I, the unworthy head of the Jia Clan, humbly lay myself at your feet and implore mercy . . . I implore protection. Punish me and spare them."[20] At Mount Tai, Confucius gazed up at Heaven, and noted, "the world is small." A thousand years later, one of China's greatest poets, Du Fu, perhaps thinking of the temples to various deities that clutter the slopes of the mountain, echoed Confucius by saying, "At a single glance all the mountains grow tiny beneath," but in Mount Tai, "the Creator has concentrated all that is numinous and beautiful." One nineteenth century collection of Chinese proverbs listed about a hundred proverbs that show that the common man also looked to the Creator as court of last appeal.[21]

The Chinese people have practiced the absence of God in a very special way, remaining strangely deaf over twenty centuries to the atheism and pantheism of their official teachers.

India

The *Bhagavad Gita*, the most popular (though not most authoritative) holy book of India, appears on the surface as an argument to a warrior to fulfill his just obligations in battle. The *Gita* also purports to teach the potential unity of *atman*, the emanation of the divine within all of us, with *Brahman*, which translators sometimes render God, but who is "beyond" personality. "There are two kinds of personality in this world, the mortal and the immortal. The personality of all creatures is mortal. The personality of God is said to be immortal . . . . But there is one other than these; the Impersonal Being who is called the supreme Atman."[22]

And yet nothing is more obvious in the *Gita* than that this "Impersonal Being" is personal. While allegedly pervading all, he clearly has no truck with evil, and stands almost entirely on the side of the good. While claiming to aid the pilgrim in extinction of all desire, he repeatedly appeals to desire. "You are first and highest in heaven, O ancient Spirit. It is within you the cosmos rests in safety. You are known and knower, god of all our *striving*."[23]

You might argue the personal character of God in the *Bhagavad Gita* is a rhetorical function: the author is giving voice to Brahma in the person of Arjuna's charioteer, none other than Lord Krishna, much as the author of Proverbs gives Wisdom a feminine persona, or John Bunyan peoples his universe with personifications of abstract ideals. An educated Hindu may indeed understand this "emanation" to be a rhetorical convenience. But do most Hindus? Did Gandhi, who treasured the *Gita* above all books? In his autobiography, he talks repeatedly and reverently of a God whose will seems distinct from his own, who is wholly good and not evil, and who hears prayers. He never pretends too close an identification with this God. "I have never seen Him, neither have I known Him," he admits forthrightly.[24] "There are innumerable definitions of God . . . They overwhelm with wonder and awe and for a moment stun me. But I worship God as Truth only. I have not yet found Him, but I am seeking after Him."[25]

Did even the author of the *Gita* really conceive of God as impersonal? The Brahman of the *Gita* prefers good to evil. He speaks with the voice of a man. He says that some are worthy of immortality, and others are not: "Though a man be soiled with the sins of a lifetime, let him but love me, rightly resolved, in utter devotion: I see no sinner, that man is holy."[26] He is called creator, above all gods. (How can we talk of "above" and "below" if all are one?)

To say there is a God who created and knows all things is a clear statement. To say there is no such God is also a clear statement. But to say God is "in" all things and all things are "God" is to say I suspect nobody really knows what. If you say, "All things are God, including the chair I'm sitting on," I strongly suspect we are putting words together for the purpose of confusing ourselves. An "impersonal God" is a contradiction in terms not in Western thinking alone but in every thinking, and I sometimes wonder not only if anyone really believes it, but if anyone even knows what it means. I suspect the *Gita* "gives" God a personal voice not for stylistic purposes alone, but because nearly everything the *Gita* says about God would be meaningless otherwise.

The separation between God and self may be the great delusion that meditation aims to overcome. Yet the most popular and noble Hinduism seems in this case to be on the side of the delusion. It seems to me that what Gandhi found in the *Gita* was that dualism, that humility before God, which monism claims to conquer, but which made him and the greatest emperors of China, sane.

Don Richardson tells the story of the Santal people, a large ethnic group which inhabited the area north of Calcutta, India. When a Norwegian missionary named Lars Skrefsrud learned their language and began preaching the Gospel, he found them amazingly open. He heard a Santal sage explain to his fellows, "What this stranger is saying must mean that *Thakur Jiu* has not forgotten us after all this time!" Skrefsrud pricked up his ears when he heard this; "thakur" meant "genuine," and "jiu" meant "god." They told him how the "Genuine God" had made the first man and woman, who sinned and turned away from him. Later, after a world-wide flood, the ancestors of the Santal had been seduced into worshipping the spirits of the mountains. "In the beginning," the sage told him, "We did not have gods. The ancient ancestors obeyed Thakur only. After finding other gods, day by day we forgot Thakur more and more until only his name remained."[27]

Consider how the following passage in the most ancient Indian Scripture, the *Rig Veda*, parallels the Genesis story of creation:

> "The All-Maker is vast in mind and vast in strength. He is the one who forms, who sets in order, and who is the highest image . . . Our father, who created and set in order and knows all forms, all worlds, who all alone gave names to the gods, he is the one to whom all other creatures come to ask questions. . . .these things that have been created, when the realm of light was still immersed in the realm without light."[28]

What is the true history of God in India? India is composed of a wide variety of nations, tribes, and linguistic groups. To some Christians in the south of India, it is Hinduism, rather than Christianity or Islam, which is the ideology of the imperialists. Other Christians point to monotheistic elements in the Vedas themselves, and suggest that at an earlier stage, Indian religion may have involved a patriarchal monotheism, like that of the book of Job.[29] Some minority peoples of India, like the Santal, Naga, and Mizo, in their mountain redoubts ignored Hindu orthodoxy and the call for pure "Indian" religion, and stuck to their own ancient if somewhat vague and forlorn beliefs in a Creator they no longer knew how to approach, until news of the Gospel came and spread quickly among them. And even in the heart of Hinduism, the still, small voice of the "Genuine God" often seems on the verge of breaking through.

Japan

Paul argued, as we have seen, that God has made his existence and nature "evident" to mankind in some sense through nature, though mankind "suppresses" that knowledge.

Japan is perhaps the hardest test case for these theories, and consequently provides the clearest affirmation. Japan is generally described as a country that is Buddhist and Shinto at the same time: both religions, it is said, are so tolerant that Japanese see no conflict between registering birth at a Shinto shrine, marrying in a Christian church, and being buried as a Buddhist. But unlike India, which is the most religious of nations, in Japan, religion is something of a taboo subject. Japanese do not claim to understand even their own religions, still less anyone else's. A Japanese friend told me, "the only people who know about Buddhism are the priests." Monks visit homes, mumble chants, the meaning of which no one inquires about, and leave. Japanese are relatively insulated from talk about gods or religion in the family, are taught secularism in the schools, and grow up assuming Christianity is a foreign religion.

But where did the Japanese people come from? Wherever they came from, their ancestors must have known about God, because the literature and traditions of nearly every race within 2000 miles of Japan maintains clear references to the Creator. Nearly all the minority peoples of China, Southeast Asia, and the South Pacific had stories of a high, benevolent, yet righteous Supreme Creator. The Chinese are the people in this area whose records go back the farthest. Their earliest records, the *Book of Poetry* and the *Book of History*, speak of God, and genetic tests suggest that the Japanese may have come from Shandong, which was the center of the worship of *Tian*. A visitor noted in the thirteenth century that while practicing shamanism, the Mongols also "believe in a (supreme) god, the creator of all the visible and invisible," and source of reward and punishment.[30] Wherever the Japanese came from, their ancestors undoubtedly had knowledge of the Creator.

When Christianity arrived in the sixteenth century, some Japanese thought Christianity was just the latest fad in Buddhism from India (from whence the Catholics had embarked). The first missionaries fumbled for language in which to express the new religion, translating heaven as the "pure land," (*judo*), and calling priests "monks."[31] Some daimyos, or feudal lords, realized the trade benefits that came with the new religion, and ordered their followers to convert *en masse*. Christianity "became a kind of . . . ornamental accessory for the progressive samurai." But it seemed to have very shallow roots. One proof of this is that Francis Xavier and the other Catholic priests had difficulty even finding a name for God in the Japanese language: in 1551, Xavier realized that Buddhist terms they tried out, *Hotoke* and *Dainichi*, "did not indicate a Creator but some pantheistic notion." So they switched to the Latin term *Deus*, which unfortunately could be satirized by skeptics as "*Dai Uso*," the "Big Lie."

By the beginning of the seventeenth century, all the superficial factors that seemed to favor the Catholic mission had dissipated. The Japanese realized the new faith was not a sect of Buddhism, carried arms as well as Bibles, and came as the vanguard of a powerful foreign culture that had subverted many states. The great daimyos discovered that other Westerners were willing to trade without preaching, and commanded their followers to renounce the now-unnecessary faith. In 1597 twenty-six Japanese believers were hung on crosses on a hill about ten minutes walk above what is now Nagasaki train station. Within a few decades, tens of thousands more were drowned in the tide, boiled in hot springs, and hung upside down in pits of excrement. Every year officials made their rounds of the houses in Nagasaki, calling on inhabitants to trample on crosses and other Catholic icons to prove they had no part in Christianity. Japan was closed to all foreigners, except for a few feet of tidal flat in the Nagasaki harbor, for 250 years. Paul spoke of men who "suppress the truth" about God. In the case of Japan, "suppress" was not a term in psychology, but in law enforcement.

It would not have been surprising if Christianity had disappeared. A Japanese friend told me, "If someone told us to give up our belief in Buddha on pain of death, we'd give it up."

Some people talk as if Japanese Christians did give up their faith. "It is not a miracle that there were over 700,000 Christians, nor that the whole number could disappear overnight," two scholars argued, "The Western religion disappeared quickly because it had no root."[32]

But actually, Christianity "disappeared" only in the sense that it hid, and that thousands of Christians were martyred. Japanese Christians proved strangely stubborn about their new faith. Amazingly, after 250 years of brutal persecution, when Catholic fathers returned, believers streamed in from the hills and islands of Nagasaki. These were the "hidden Christians," who kept their faith from generation to generation. Some scholars make much of the fact that in some cases the content of this faith became steadily more peculiar, to the point that some of the hidden Christians failed to recognize the Catholic church when it finally returned and decided to remain independent. Yet as a Mexican priest in Nagasaki told me, most of the hidden Christians did come back to the churches, which are full to this day, and which contain an unusual percentage of people willing to go into full-time service. My wife, who grew up in Nagasaki, became a Christian partly through the influence of local nuns.

There is the outline of the story. Now consider how odd it is.

Strange-looking foreigners speaking improbable Japanese come preaching a Supreme God. At first they call him "Buddha," then change his name to an uncouth and awkward foreign title. People accept this faith because they think it is from India, for trade privileges, or because their lord tells them to. Then they realized it isn't from India, the merchants go home, and their lord is killed or tells them to stop believing. Those who don't listen are publicly tortured to death. (Living in Kyushu, I sometimes come across memorials to these terrible events. Just above the road outside the resort town of Mt. Unzen, for example, lies a boiling "hells," on the far side of which you can see a rough wooden memorial cross through the vapors.) And God, for his part, keeps what seems an inscrutable distance.[33]

The real question is why Christianity did *not* disappear. How could a religion perceived as completely foreign win such wide acceptance in so short a time—and keep it?

One lesson we can learn from this remarkable episode is the value Japanese place on loyalty. But that by itself begs the question, for the Japanese gods do not inspire such loyalty very often: why, then, did the "Big Lie?" Why did so many Japanese find Christianity so much more attractive than "native" Buddhism and Shinto that they were willing to die for the Christian God, and worse yet, be called traitors to Japanese culture? The only explanation that makes sense to me is they did *not* feel they were being traitors.

David Lewis surveyed hundreds of Japanese in depth about their religious attitudes. He found that hundreds of years of oppression and a century of ignoring the idea of God had not made it disappear. In *Unseen Face of Japan*, he pointed out that during the Sakoku, the period when Japan was closed to the outside world, Shinto priests twice invented a religion dangerously "verging on monotheism," based on a Supreme God they called *Ame-no-minaka-nushi*: "Lord of the Middle of Heaven." The first outbreak of God-consciousness came in the seventeenth century, the second in the nineteenth.

One Japanese scholar, Ikuro Teshima, claims the "Lord of the Middle of Heaven" can be traced a thousand years further back to Nestorian Christians who came to Japan before the Buddhists. He points out that in Kyoto can be found a unique "Shinto" shrine dedicated to his worship. Many Shinto shrines have symbolic gateways called *torii* at their entryways. Here a unique torii stands on three instead of two pillars, as if to symbolize the Trinity. "At the very center of the triangular torii, a pile of stones is placed, symbolizing the presence of Ame-no-Minaka-Nushi, the God who is the origin of the universe."[34]

It also turns out that many or most modern Japanese *do* believe in God. Lewis asked Japanese if they believed in a "Being above man and nature." Almost two thirds of the respondents said yes. Some commented, "Nature is so great there must be a God," "There are many things man does not know," "There must be something to keep things going," or cited personal healing as evidence of a "Greater Power." After reading Lewis, I conducted a poll of first-year students at Siebold University of Nagasaki. I asked, "Do you believe in the existence of a good spiritual being who transcends nature, is aware of mankind (*seikai*, the world) and created all things?" Seventy students turned in the ten-question survey. A plurality, thirty-one, answered yes to this question. Only twenty-six answered "no."[35]

Where do modern Japanese get their idea of God?

Oxford psychologist Olivera Petrovich did a study of preschool children in England and Japan. Her researchers asked children a series of questions about how various man-made and natural objects had come into being. She noted, "Japanese culture is very different from Western culture with a very different history of science and religious tradition. So I thought I should be able to get some interesting comparisons . . ." The results took her by surprise. "On forced choice questions, consisting of three possible explanations of primary origin, they would predominantly go for the word 'God,' instead of either an agnostic response (e.g., 'nobody knows') or an incorrect response (e.g., 'by people'). This is absolutely extraordinary when you think that Japanese religion—Shinto—doesn't include creation as an aspect of God's activity at all. So where do these children get the idea that creation is in God's hands? . . . My Japanese research assistants kept telling me, 'We Japanese don't think about God as creator—it's just not part of Japanese philosophy.'"[36]

Petrovich deduced that young children infer the act of Creation "on the basis of their own experience." She suggested on this and other basis that "spirituality" (apparently in the sense of belief in a Creator) was a "universal act of cognition." Three explanations for these findings occur to me: that young children do reason to the idea of the Creator on their own, that the idea was suggested to them by adults for whom Shinto or modernist ideology was less normative than even most Japanese realize, or that knowledge of God is "innate," an awareness that does not depend on authority, reason, age, or race. All three suggestions may find support in Scripture and in the data. What is clear in any case is that, as Paul said, all of mankind does show awareness of God, no matter what our teachers tell us. Or as an African Ashanti proverb puts it, "No one shows a child the Supreme Being."[37]

Nor do I think reasoning from creation to Creator is limited to children or primitive peoples. As I have spoken in churches around the Pacific Rim about God in Asian cultures, I have often been struck by how many of those who come up to speak with me afterwards are both scientists and enthusiastic Christians.

The late twentieth century has seen the discovery of what is called the "anthropic principle," the fact that, as it turns out, the universe is finely tuned in an extraordinary way for the support of astronomers and other forms of life. In addition, biologists and everything they study exhibit a complexity several orders of magnitude greater than anyone expected in the nineteenth century. Paley compared the universe to a watch finely tuned; if he had only known, he could have compared many of its simplest inhabitants favorably to computers. One can only laugh when one recalls that some nineteenth century biologists thought organic life so simple that even insects could "spontaneously generate" out of manure. The argument from design to Designer is by no means limited to the uneducated in the modern era. I have heard it expressed in various forms by scientists wherever I have gone, even some who grew up surrounded by atheism.

"Strong Feet Followed After"

King David, Saint Paul, Francis Thomas, and G.K.Chesterton were right, and the whole field of anthropology and comparative religion wrong. The heavens do declare the glory of God. Our hearts and heads know that heaven and earth contain more than is dreamt of in our official ideologies, that beyond matter must be person. The religions of man can act as the "labyrinthine ways" down which we flee from him. Psalm 139 seems to warn that even jet lag cannot ultimately provide an escape:

> "Where can flee from Your presence? If I ascend to heaven, You are there. If I hide in the underworld, You are there also! If I fly to where the sun rises in the east, or settle on the western side of the sea, even there You will lead me and You will take hold of me. If I should ask the darkness

to cover me, or ask the light to become night around me, to You, even darkness is not dark, for darkness and light are equally bright" (pph).

When I "ascended to heaven" at Mount Tai, I found at the top a blank stone obelisk, erected by Han Wudi. This rock, reminiscent of the "uncarved block" of Taoism, was perhaps a statement not only of Han's inability to translate his experience of the ultimate essence of things into words, (as was explained to me) but also an acknowledgment of ignorance. The worship of the High God, unlike common deities, was never represented by idols. While envisioned in corrupt later stages in China as everything from an old figure in a dragon robe, to a local chieftain under the bodhisattva, there yet remained something undefinable about a god for whom the only proper symbol was an empty blue sky. The offering to the unseen and only distantly recognized Ruler on High seemed to represent some psychologically-cleansing middle ground in Chinese belief, with a hint of Confucius' gentle caution about the gods, and the iconoclastic simplicity of Lao Zi and of Zen patriarchs like Bodhidharma.

"I Fled Him Down The Labyrinthine Ways of My Mind"

I am, by character, a skeptic, and at time I have doubted the existence of God. There also come moments when I doubt the existence of atheists.

In graduate school my least-successful paper was about the relative roles of Marxism and traditional Chinese culture in the development of the thought of the young Mao Zedong. At one point in my paper, I incurred a caustic note from my professor by quoting an anecdote of only parenthetical significance from a book by Richard Wurmbrand with the provocative title, *Marx and Satan*. My professor, a by-the-book scholar, wrote in heavy red ink, dripping with sarcasm, "might the book have a bias?"

Richard Wurmbrand did indeed have a bias against Marxism. He spent eight years in a communist prison cell in Romania, was beaten, and had rats driven into his cage. He did not know what became of his wife and son, "tortured for Christ" in another prison. But he was an intelligent and open-minded man who perhaps read Marx more thoroughly than my professor, and forgave more sins in his lifetime than the whole department. His book balances the picture we are fed of Marx given us by scholars who see him as a brilliant theoretician with much still to contribute to feminists studies and linguistics, and veterans of religious dialogue who never met a tyrant they couldn't embrace in Christian compassion. It's not a book for children, but one I think a scholar should be open-minded enough to consider. [38]

Wurmbrand's theory, which he admitted was based mostly on circumstantial evidence, was that the great Marxists were not atheists. They believed in God, but preferred the devil.

One does not have to assume that a person's true religious beliefs are present to his conscious mind, of course. Long before Freud described id and ego, the Bible and literature have explored the relationship between what a person proclaims in public and what he or she believes in the secret places of his or her soul. In a previous chapter, I talked about Paul Vitz's theory applying Freud's theories to atheism. R.C. Sproul examines this issue in depth in an exposition of Romans 1 called *The Psychology of Atheism*. The book is somewhat one-sided, overlooking the more sympathetic approach Paul took to pagan traditions in the city of Athens, for example, but Sproul's points are worth consideration, I think, since he emphasizes what the modern world tends to overlook. He argued,

> "According to Paul, religion is not the fruit of a zealous pursuit of God, but the result of a passionate flight from God. The glory of God is exchanged for an idol. The idol stands as a monument not to religious fervor but to the flight of man from his initial encounter with the glory of God."

Sproul noted that the great atheists of the nineteenth century did not really try to prove the non-existence of God. In a sense they were affirming the Bible by saying religion was man-made. They simply over-generalized by including the universal apprehension of God, and under-generalized by excluding their own theories.

I am tempted to define institutional religion as "that authority constituted by society to keep people from falling into the hands of the living God." This function is especially obvious in the case of religious elites in Japan, Big Brother in communist countries, and European inquisitors. Genesis tells how, after they sinned, the man and the woman sewed fig leaves for themselves and hid from God. Religion, including what might be called "cultural Christianity," is often not the record of our search for God, but of cover-ups and escapes down the "labyrinthine ways" of consciousness.

Iconoclasm

The command of the Christian God to forsake other gods seems notoriously intolerant to many. Karen Armstrong, for example, complained about the Old Testament showdown between Elijah and the prophets of Baal. Elijah was not content to pick a fight with the priests of Baal; after he won, he put all 400 of them to the sword. "These early mythical events," she sneered, "show that from the first Yahwism demanded a violent repression and denial of other faiths."[39] By contrast, "Paganism was an essentially tolerant faith . . . there was always room for another god alongside the traditional pantheon . . . in Hinduism and Buddhism people were encouraged to go beyond the gods rather than to turn upon them with loathing."[40]

What Armstrong is describing here, however, is not the tolerance of paganism towards people, but towards other gods. Occultism usually is tolerant towards the powerful, whether divine or human. This is why human sacrifice, which the prophets rebuked and put an end to in Israel 3000 years ago, remained a part of Indian religious culture until India was conquered by cultural Christianity. This is why, while Buddhism represented the triumph of a kinder ideal, the gods of Tibet wear necklaces of human skulls. Neither Hinduism nor Buddhism saw any profit (or prophet?) in confronting the demonic element in their cultures: in the formative myth of Buddhist Tibet, Phadmasambhava won the demons of Tibet over to his side, so that Buddhism could rule by means of their energies, chastened and converted (or at least chained) to good.

Paganism is not always even tolerant toward other gods, however. Tibetan Buddhism was popular in East Asia not because it preached pacifism, but because it helped kings win battles. Gang rivalry in Taiwan is also a rivalry of patron saints. Anyone who has read Homer knows that the gods themselves quarreled, and that their quarrels were reflected by colossal battles on earth. But it is true that when interests did not clash, Olympic society held to a principle of "live and let live."

That was balance of terror or indifference, not true tolerance. Pagan gods seldom if ever stood up to oppressors, human or divine, on behalf of the weak. That was the historical distinction of prophets of the true God, and what Elijah's confrontation with the prophets of Baal was all about.

A excludes non-*A,* and the worship of God does exclude the worship of non-God. To understand who God is, is to see this. That does not need to mean believers in the Supreme God will persecute unbelieving neighbors. Christians who force their faith down other peoples' throats, John Raskin argues,[41] are those who are unsure of what they believe. As Dostoevsky revealed, the Grand Inquisitor was a Great Idolater, or he would have realized that it is God who preserves and defends the believer, not the other way around.

Why did Elijah attack the prophets of Baal? First, he was fighting for the soul of his nation against a foreign tyrant—Jezebel—who with her religious allies had slaughtered the priests of God. Just as an American public official swears to uphold the Constitution, it was the job of Jewish prophets to remind the nation of their allegiance to the Constitution the Jewish race had made with God. The turn to Baal represented an act of treason against a covenant that allowed the Jewish people to survive 2000 years of exile and serve the modern world as one of the sources of our freedom.

Also, Elijah's opponents literally had blood on their hands. On this particular occasion, true, it was their own blood, but that was not always the case. They no doubt aided in the slaughter of God's priests, as well as in ritual sacrifice of children.[42] Elijah was not unique in using force against his religious opponents. What was unusual is that he was willing to strike against oppressors rather than bowing politely before gods they made.

One can see something of what was at stake for the future not only of Israel, but of the human race. The prophets of Baal were teaching the human race a dangerous lesson: "through self-mutilation, God can be forced to act. Gain the world by destroying your soul." Is not the whole theory of psychotherapy also an attempt to track down and destroy false gods, to release us from our bondage to neurotic constructs? God is likewise intolerant towards idols because he is loving towards men.

Suppressing the Knowledge of God

The Great Spirit was, Richardson said, felt to be distant. People needed a go-between, an emanation from the divine, whether because they wanted to find God or because they weren't sure they did. Across Polynesia, priests were under an oath not to speak the name of the Creator.[43] The only person in China allowed to worship Shang Di was the "Son of Heaven," the emperor, and he only once a year. In Africa, "The great celestial god, the supreme being, all-powerful creator, plays only a minor role in the religious life of most tribes. He is too far away or too good to need an actual cult, and he is involved only in extreme cases."[44]

We do not need to study primitive anthropology to understand. There are plenty of Americans, too, who involve God only in "extreme cases," which we call "foxhole conversions." But what could it mean that Africans felt God was "too good or too far away" to help? How can one be too good to help? What does goodness have to do with distance? Yet intuitively, I think we understand these statements, too. The distance we feel is a moral distance: we are not sure he will respond, because we are not sure we deserve his help, or whether we want to live by standards that a willingness to accept such help might imply. In Jesus' story of the Prodigal Son, son and father were separated, but it was not the father who moved.

The Apostle Paul described human religion in terms that are subtle and realistic. People have been aware of God through nature "since the creation of the world." But we turn from that knowledge in favor of speculation that allows us to make a show of profundity, preferring graspable falsehood over unseen truth, distancing ourselves from holiness. We "exchange the truth of God for a lie, and worship the created rather than the Creator."

In this way of looking at things, the Enlightenment did not represent the triumph of atheism, but a diversion of the instinct for worship from worthy to unworthy objects. Indeed, how else can one explain the elevation of a failed street artist to "Das Fuhrer," whose neurotic ravings drowned Europe in blood? How else can one explain the power Karl Marx still exerts in universities, a man whose historical predictions were no more successful than a street-corner soothsayer and whose ambitions ended in horror? Just as a person escapes addiction to cigarettes by drinking, the fall of Marxism led less often to enlightenment or repentance than the Dracula-like rebirth of old superstitions and territorial grudges.

The same process can, of course, be seen in the West.

Armstrong argues, "There is no one unchanging idea contained in the word 'God;' instead, the word contains a whole spectrum of meanings, some of which are contradictory or even mutually exclusive." But Christians don't worship the *word* God. Nor does any believer claim to comprehend the total reality behind that word. The word does not "contain a spectrum of meanings," it suggests a reality greater than we can know. The same is true of all nouns to a degree; how much more when speaking of the Reality who is source of all being?

God is by definition the one who is not what we think of him, but what he is regardless of human thought and projection. In this, the vague appellation "higher power" is helpful. What is the higher power higher than? If we mean One higher than our conceptions of him, then that is merely a modern name for the Sky God. *Yahweh* also involves an in-built agnosticism: "I am that I am." Lao Zi's term *Zi Zai Zhi* is similar: that which contains the basis of existence in itself. God is he who smashes idols.

Our God is not only he who must be described with a "Not Thus," nor even, in the more subtle mysticism on which Eastern and Western traditions occasionally converge, "Not not thus." While all concepts by which we imagine God may be flawed, it is more idolatrous to define God negatively alone, or even by negating negatives, when he always defines himself positively, as good, creative, joyful, holy and righteous.

Armstrong argues, "Each generation has to create the image of God that works for it." So we do. But worshipping that which we have made ourselves is counterproductive and neurotic—a symptom of rather than solution to our alienation. Like sexual fantasies, it joins us to an "other" whose "other-ness" we know ourselves to be unreal. By contrast, true worship, like true love, is full of surprises.

We have invented many tools for seduction, intoxication, and destruction in the modern era. Sometimes I think the most objectionable of all may be the lights with which we drown out the stars. It is not that, objectively, what we call "our planet" has become any less of a pinprick in the universe—we have learned about an infinite wealth of worlds beyond the night sky. Only now, when we go outside at night, we can't see them. Only the Big Dipper and a few other stars shine bravely through the haze of our street lights and neon signs. The vast cosmos has been rendered invisible so we can avoid mud puddles.

Just so, religion threatens to drown out the reality of God.

It is not surprising that some teachers of comparative religion haven't discovered God. They admit themselves they weren't looking for him. They were looking down, at the works of human hands, the "religions of man," creations of human imagination. They were watching pyrotechnic shows on the wall of the cave, never thinking to meet someone from outside it. They wanted aesthetics, not salvation, and got what they asked for.

Yet through the images tradition creates, God can reveal himself. All nations run from God, even the Jews ("It is hard for you to kick against the goads"; Acts 9:5). A dim awareness of the Creator remains in every nation. Yet at the heart of all humble religion lies a riddle. Who is he in himself? How can we know him and find his forgiveness?

Paul says that this God whom we worship, in vague terms, while tolerant in the past and "overlooking" idolatry, "is now summoning all people everywhere to repent" (Acts 17:30).

Paul wasn't only writing about atheists, pagans, or Jews. Cornelius Plantinga, Jr., asks a series of questions that touch the raw soul of every Christian as well:

> "How many believers really believe in God, as opposed to some deified image of themselves? How many, for example, really do attend to the counter-cultural images of God in Scripture—the ones that judge and condemn as well as the ones that affirm and comfort? How many of us would rather fashion God in our own image so that God's pleasures and peeves will merge conveniently with our own? Believers, not just secularists, exchange 'the glory of the immortal God for images resembling a mortal human being.'

> "Why else do new revised versions of God keep appearing? Why else does God emerge as racist, sexist, chauvinist, politically correct, legalist, socialist, capitalist? If we are intellectuals, God is a cosmic Phi Beta Kappa; if we are laborers, God is a union organizer (didn't His Son say, 'I must be about my Father's business?'); if we are poor, God is a revolutionary; if we are propertied, God is night-watchman over our goods. The god of the Persians always looks like the Persians. 'Unbelief is not the only way of suppressing the truth about God,' says Westphal.' 'It is only the most honest.'" [45]

And yet, to a Christian, God is all of these things. Mohammed didn't make up the 99 names of Allah; he got them from the Bible. God does reach down to save us, according to Scripture, with arms of compassion like the 1000 arms of Guan Yin, appearing in different guises according to our needs, "all things to everybody" (1 Cor. 9:22). He is the "parent of mankind," as the ancient Chinese Scriptures testify, comforting, punishing, saving, challenging, warning. All of these positive characteristics reflect more truly than any vague talk of "absolutes" the positive character of the God who created a universe that is other to himself.

The danger is when we substitute ideas about God for the presence of God. That is a mistake anyone of any or no religion can make.

The God Who Was an Atheist

The history of skepticism is in a sense also part of the history of God, for the God of the Bible is the father of Skeptics and Mother of unbelievers. If a boy grows up in a family in which a God of love is preached but a God of hatred followed, he may resolve the conflict by doubting God exists at all. The God he denies is one of the false gods the prophets preach against. A nation oppressed may turn on its oppressors and reject the God they preach and that clings like a bad odor to their forms of thought and speech and even clothing. In so doing they may in fact be rejecting a false, tribal deity. An astronomer is confronted by believers who tell him the world is only 6000 years old and all the lights he has spent his life studying were created by God a relative moment ago to fool his retina.

In turning from such a narrow conception of God to a search for unpolluted science, or Truth or Justice, the skeptic may in fact be laying his life on the altar of an "Unknown God" not so unlike that which Paul found in Athens. That is to say, so long as he is humble enough to know he doesn't know. It has always been the impulse of Biblical faith to confront oppressive and degrading conceptions of God. In doing so even apart from Scripture, perhaps we render a partial worship to the true God without realizing it. In shattering idols even the most savage critic continues the work that God set for his prophets. In the life of every Christian, faith does not mean clinging to pictures of God our imagination produce, but falling back upon God himself, who shatters all images.

Yet it is better to avoid the word "atheist." Affirmation of even the wildest positive claim, such as, "I saw a navy-blue lion walk across Main Street," can be humble. But almost every universal negative is inherently arrogant. Who knows the universe so well he can say what is not in it, let alone beyond it?

And let us also not call lack of knowledge "agnosticism" and raise ignorance to the dignity of a creed. People can be proud of anything. An alcoholic brags, "I can handle my drink." A tight wad says, "I never waste my money." A spend-thrift boasts,"No one ever called me a cheap-skate." But surely the habit of bragging about not knowing if God exists and claiming that *no one* can know (since I don't) is the most silly of all idolatries. As we focus our attention on progressively more complex objects, the initiative shifts from student to object of study, from the fox on the earth to the Hound of Heaven. A God who does not retain the initiative is by definition an idol.

Positive knowledge of anything is always iconoclastic. I form conceptions of a person over the Internet: meeting that person smashes the constructs I have built of him.(Though not entirely.) Of course meeting a person is not the end of the process, but the beginning. C. S. Lewis noted that the difference between a person in a novel and a real friend is that in real life a person never quite stays within character. He "always has another card up his sleeves." God smashes our images to save our souls. Yet he does not do so merely by saying "not that," nor even the more subtle "not not that." It is idolatry just as much to say God can't speak or to say all words must be his words as to put pet bigotries in his mouth. We insist on the right of people to say what they want to. If we are serious about hearing from God, we need to allow him the same freedom.

The question is often asked, "why should God speak exclusively through a single, sometimes irritating, nation, or through a church composed of sometimes even more irritating human beings?" Part of the answer is that he didn't, and doesn't, as much as people suppose. But why did he choose the Jews, and one Jew in particular, as the focus of his salvation? In the end we can only put this question in a category with, "Why did God make so many stars?" and, "Why do electrons have to be so hard to pin down?" The empirical method is to deal with realities as we find them, to let constructs be falsified by facts. In this sense the Bible is by contrast with other religions, even allegedly scientific religions like Marxism, stubbornly empirical: whatever guesses we might hazard as to the why, they do not change the what. And the what of God's revelation cannot be comprehended by a priori theories, but only be watching to see what he in fact does. This is the meaning of the saying that Christianity is a historical religion.

To this point I have argued that the life of Jesus has helped mankind become kinder and more sane. Furthermore, on several recent occasions, when that concept was vociferously rejected, it is no hyperbole to say, "All hell broke loose."

Now we have seen that some awareness of God is universal; if not in every heart, at least in every culture. People think of him as Creator. He is not worshiped with an idol. He is always good (read Greek or Chinese mythology and see how rare that is.) Yet he is known only vaguely and distantly. Humanity has a feeling of both alienation and immediate presence. We see him as judge of all. The Jews expressed these truths most dramatically, but people everywhere seem to perceive them.

Why is it that every people and tribe under heaven knows about God? How does he shatter the images we make of him yet still speak to us in a recognizable voice? Why is it that however much white noise the ideologies of mankind kick up, they cannot drown out the voice of the Creator, still and small though it is?

The idea of God (and, to a lesser extent, the devil) has I think been shown to be coherent. Let us now see if evidence of anything "out there" suggests that Hound of Heaven really is on our trail.

---

[1] Armstrong, *A History of God*, Ballantine, 1993, Introduction

[2] G. K. Chesterton, *Everlasting Man*, p. 24

[3] Francis Thomas, *The Hound of Heaven*, Fleming Ravell

[4] Emile Durkheim, *The Elementary Forms of Religious Life*, translated Karen E. Fields, The Free Press, 1995, p. 288-292. Durkheim tried to disassociate this sky god from the Christian God by linking him to legends of exalted ancestors. This seems to me to be begging the question: how can he be sure religious development did not proceed the other way instead? The oldest historical records of the Asia-Pacific region, those of China, show a Supreme God quite distinct from ancestors far back as you can look.

[5] Don Richardson, *Eternity in Their Hearts,* Regal Books, 1981_p. 41-47

[6] Ibid., p.87

[7] Ibid., p. 87, 102

[8] Ibid., p. 50

[9] LaRue W. Percy, *Hawaii Missionary Saga*, Mutual Publishing, 1992, p. 19

[10] Suetorius, from Paul Maier, *In the Fullness of Time*, Kregel Publications, 1991, p. 50

[11] Jaroslav Pelikan, *Jesus Through the Centuries: His Place in the History of Culture*, Harper & Row, 1985, p. 35-36

[12] Augustine, *City of God*, translated by Henry Bettenson, Penguin, 1984, p. 311

[13] C. S. Lewis, *Historicism*, in *Fernseed and Elephants,* Collins/ Fountain Books, 1975, p. 49

[14] Will Durant, *The Age of Faith*, Simon and Schuster, 1950, p. 508

[15] Ibid., p. 505

[16] Daniel I. Kikawa, *Perpetrated in Righteousness*, Aloha Ke Akua Publishing, 1994, p. 57

[17] Ibid., p. 162

[18] G. K. Chesterton, *The Everlasting Man*, p. 96

[19] Dwight Baker, *T'ai Shan*, 1924, p. 196

[20] Leslie Howard, *Expansion of God*, Orbis Books, 1981, p. 339-342

[21] Clifford Popper, *Chinese Religion Seen Through the Proverb*, 1926

[22] *The Song of God, Bhagavad Gita*, Vedanta Society of Southern California, 1944, p. 113

[23] Ibid., p. 95

[24] Mohandas K. Gandhi, *Autobiography: The Story of My Experiments with Truth*, translated by Mahadev Desai, Dover Publications, 1983, p. 246

[25] Ibid., Introduction

[26] Ibid., p. 84-5

[27] *Eternity in Their Hearts*, p. 43-44

[28] *Rig Veda, an Anthology*, translated by Wendy O'Flaherty, Penguin Books, 1981, p. 36, *Visvakarman*

[29] Robert Brow writes of the Vedas, "Whatever name they give to God, they

worshiped him as the Supreme Ruler of the universe. This practice is called Henotheism. God has several names, just as Christians today have several names for God, but the names do not indicate different gods. They are different aspects of the one God. Henotheism changes into Polytheism when the names of God are so personified that various gods are separated, and they begin to disagree and fight among themselves. The later Vedic literature has certainly become polytheistic by, say, 1000 B.C., but the earliest Aryans must have been Monotheists." From *The Case For Christianity*, p. 143.

30 Johann de Plano Canpine, from Bertold Spuler, *History of the Mongols*, p. 71

31 See David Lewis, *The Unseen Face of Japan*, Monarch, 1993

32 Aikawa and Leavenworth, from David Lewis, *The Unseen Face of Japan*

33 A book by a famous Japanese Catholic writer, Susaki Endo, about this period, is poignantly titled, *"Silence."*

34 Ikuro Teshima, *The Ancient Refugees from Religious Persecution in Japan*, at www.keikyo.com/books/hada

35 Eleven said, "I don't know," or "sometimes," or left the question blank. Two volunteered pantheistic reinterpretations of the "good spiritual being."

36 *Science and Spirit Magazine, In the Beginning: An Interview with Olivera Petrovich*

37 John Mbiti, *African Religions and Philosophies*, quoted in *Case for Christianity*, p.140

38 Amazing, the narrow-mindedness of Academia. As a young man Karl Marx wrote a poem about destroying the world. The movement born out of his adult writings came close to doing so. Most people in the world believe in the existence and influence of pernicious spirits. But because of a dogma about how the universe is set up, or perhaps a dogma about the right of thinkers to publish free from responsibility for the effects of their theories, it doubtless is out of bounds to ask about the relationship between the author of so much madness and the "Father of Lies."

39 *A History of God*, p. 26

40 Ibid, p. 49

41 John Raskin, *Power and Gender at the Divinity School*, from *Finding God at Harvard*

42 Few things are more unpleasant than the blasé reaction Western apologists like Joseph Campbell and Karen Armstrong give to human sacrifice. Even while Indian statesmen borrow Christian outrage, or at least accuse Christians of making such stories up, Campbell writes with tolerant equanimity about ritual murder.

43 Daniel Kikawa, *Perpetrated in Righteousness*, p. 57

44 From R. C. Sproul, *The Psychology of Atheism*, p. 68

45 Cornelius Plantinga, Jr., *Not the Way It's Supposed to Be: a Breviary of Sin*, p.108-9

CHAPTER 10

Miracles

"HUMANISTS STILL believe that traditional theism, especially faith in the prayer- hearing God, assumed to love and care for persons, to hear and understand their prayers, and to be able to do something about them, is an unproven and outmoded faith." —*Humanist Manifesto II*

"Dear God, how come you did all those miracles in the old days and don't do any now?" —Seymour, Richard Wurmbrand, *From the Lips of Children*

The Yagba people were troubled. The monsoon was late, and crops had been left unplanted. In the early twentieth century in rural Nigeria, one didn't hop in the station-wagon and drive to Safeway when food ran out, nor even, when the shortage became desperate, hope for relief from Oxfam. The spirit world was the people's only recourse. And so for a week, villagers beseeched the gods for rain. To no effect: the sun came up every morning like an enemy at siege. Having allowed the pagans an opportunity to show the impotence of their gods, the local Muslim community prayed to Allah for a second week. Still no response. Perhaps it was time to give the new cult a chance.

For the people of Yagbaland, where levitation and spirit travel were "old-time religion," an oracle of a New Age had appeared in the physically diminutive but spiritually commanding figure of a Canadian missionary named Tommy Titcombe. He had proven a one-man five-foot whirlwind of social revolution, pushing such radical innovations as sanitation, the humanity of women, (it was a Yagba chief who said "women are just animals") and the curious hypothesis that twin babies were human. Authority figures of Yagbaland, like authority figures everywhere, saw innovators as a threat. Like all revolutionaries, Titcombe knew that ultimately, authority for change derives from power. And power, as Mao put it, comes from a barrel—in this case, a rain barrel.

The night sky was filled with stars when the Christians gathered to test the power of their God. Half an hour after they began praying, they heard the sound of big, juicy drops "plunk-plunk-plunking" on the church roof. Soon prayers were drowned out in the roar of life-giving water from heaven.

Or so, at least, the story said.

Would God Do Miracles?

It is often said that a belief in miracles would undermine science. Some atheists feel the concept threatens religion, as well. Randel Helms objected to miracles on religious grounds in *Free Inquiry Magazine:*

"A miracle is an arbitrary interruption, by a deity, of the ordinary sequence of natural law . . . As Voltaire long ago pointed out, to hope for a miracle is implicitly to argue the non-existence of God's omniscience and omnipotence, implicitly to argue that God was unable to create a world in which He does not have to intervene miraculously in order to make things go as He wishes. A proper God would never need a miracle."

The idea that God or the gods might intervene in the world seems to people like Helms or Voltaire a kind of impiety. In classical Hindu and Buddhist thought the gods are helpless to change even their own karma, still less that of another sentient being. That which a person has sown, he or she will reap, and that is the end of the story. Deists of the eighteenth century, likewise, could conceive of nothing more grand than the great mechanism of natural law, which carried all before it and which God had set in motion at the beginning of time. Modern materialists, even more, see the connection between cause and effect as the firm and unassailable basis of scientific inquiry: the word "arbitrary" is a challenge to the committed scientist, whose premise is that he can explain anything, given access to all the significant data. Scientism, the theory that man with his logic and ruthless honesty could explain all phenomena, including how men love, war, pray, and worship, swept the world like a tide in the nineteenth century. Like other ideas that came in on the same tide, such as Marxism and the "History of God" fallacy, this skepticism about Christian miracles (at least) still rests in pools and pockets of ideology such as anthropology, linguistics, and Biblical criticism.

The *Humanist Manifesto* quotation at the head of this chapter expresses an empirical rather than a philosophical argument against miracles. Science has explained many phenomena once thought to be supernatural. Epilepsy is caused by malfunction of the central nervous system, not demons. Rain comes in response to atmospheric and oceanic conditions thousands of miles away, not to the clap of a god's hands from Mount Olympus. Science progresses by boldly confronting events that appear on the surface to be unconstrained by natural law, and discovering deeper laws which explain what had hitherto been mysterious.

My purpose in this chapter is not to argue philosophy with Voltaire, so much as empirical fact with the authors of the *Humanist Manifesto*. I will argue that miracles still do happen, Seymour, whatever we think of them. I will only give a few examples, not because evidence is hard to come by, but because those examples are so easy to come by that I think the reader is likely to have access to similar evidence. I will argue that God continues to work in the same way as he did in the Bible, through acts that reveal the character of the Creator. Supernatural works of God often lie at the center of history. In the following chapter I will consider how miracles differ from another category of supernatural or allegedly supernatural events which, for the sake of clarity, I will call Magic. And in the chapter after that, we will see that miracles undermine neither science nor Christian religion, but do throw a monkey wrench into unscientific and anti-Christian blends of the two that are popular in modern Biblical criticism and comparative religious studies.

As a child, I loved to read stories like that about Tommy Titcombe in Yagbaland. I think even then I was inclined to wonder if my faith was wishful thinking. I guess my native skepticism came less from the skepticism of the world around me, than from the fact I had never seen a miracle myself. After all, even the disciples, though they had never read Feurbach or Freud, stubbornly assumed fish are best caught by fishermen, water is not made to be walked on, and dead men tell no tales, until contrary evidence forced them to admit exceptions.

I read a book by C. S. Lewis as a teenager called *Miracles: A Preliminary Study,* that addressed the doubts of skeptics like Helms. Lewis began by carefully building a philosophical argument for the supernatural. Next he argued for the existence of God. Then he did his best to show that if there is a God there's no reason why he couldn't, wouldn't or shouldn't allow humankind an occasional recess from natural law. Only near the end of the book did he give a passing glance at specific historical events.

I found the book a typically brilliant product of Lewis' genius, and worth a read, but felt a bit let down. Lewis used most of the book to attack a position that seemed of marginal relevance. The question of whether a "proper God" would do miracles struck me as abstract and unreal. Had Helms and his deistic mentors ever read the Bible? Had they looked out their windows? The Bible said nothing about a "proper" God in a "proper" universe. It told the story of a cosmos out of joint and how it came to be that way. The miracles it described were all about putting things back in order: they were no more "arbitrary" than the way a doctor moves a patient's arm to set a broken bone in joint. And the arrogance of some of these enlightenment thinkers took my breath away. How did Helms know what a "proper" God in a "proper" universe would do? Was it not possible that the God who "flung the stars into space" might possibly have something in mind that even Voltaire hadn't thought of? (Perhaps Voltaire in particular hadn't thought of?)

My question was more practical, like the one Seymour asked or, in a less philosophical manner (in the form of *a priori* dogma rather than a question), the authors of the *Humanist Manifesto*. I did not doubt miracles were a good idea. My reason for skepticism was the opposite of Helms: not because I thought people so clever that they could out-guess God, but because I could see perfectly well people are liars, and can convince themselves of anything if they put their minds to it. I, for one, did not want to die and cease to exist. I had incentive to deceive myself, and so, I thought, must everyone else.

Like Seymour, I was attracted to stories like Titcombe's, but they seemed exotic, hypothetical, and a little too good to be true. The need for the supernatural grace of God was undeniable. I remember at eight calculating what percentage of my life I had already lived. I was afraid of the boogie-man, rats with rabies, cancer, and (to a much lesser extent) nuclear war. As a young adult, I sat in taxis in Bombay while Indian beggars wheeled twisted bodies into traffic to beg for a few rupees, half of which would be taken by a protector. I met young girls from mountain villages who called to furtive men in the streets so that they could fill their quota of tricks for the day and not be beaten by the thug on a stool out front. I traveled through parts of the world where people still went hungry when rain didn't come, and eagerly edged up to the bus with decrepit apples for sale, or scooted into a restaurant and finished my meal after I left.

From childhood I read stories of Christians who lived and worked "on the front lines" as missionaries. These believers, like some of those whose stories I told in an earlier chapter, staked their lives on the truth of the Bible. Some people mocked them, but I saw them as heroes, and I envied them their adventures. They set out alone, with a bag of medicine and a Bible, and tried to change someone's world. Often in the middle of the story there'd come a miracle: a healing in answer to prayer, food coming from an unexpected quarter at the last minute, or a rainstorm to quench a draught. The miracle thrilled me, but also made me suspicious. Was it thrown in to reassure followers and sell books? Had the hero omitted prosaic details that might provide a more mundane link between cause and effect? Was it a lucky coincidence? Did a timely storm in Africa really prove there is a God who cares? Selectively, it seems?

In my native skepticism, I did not even think to believe those instances of the supernatural that seemed to attract the fanfare from atheists. "Crowds flock to see mysterious figure of the Virgin Mary—did her eyes move?" "Preacher meets two hundred-foot Jesus." "Monks watch in amazement as the sun turns into a giant crystal ball." When the word "Miracle!" flashed from the human-interest story of the newspaper, or glared from the front pages of the tabloids, or was whispered to dramatic music for poorly-shot television documentaries, I turned away with a yawn. In reaction to the materialism of the modern world, some people flung themselves into a gaudy and disproportional supernaturalism that did indeed seem an offense to natural law. Two seemingly opposite currents raged side-by-side in the society I grew up in: a strict empiricism, which strained at gnats, and an increasing re-mystification of belief, which swallowed camels.

The stories that caught my attention were dramatic without being melodramatic. The plot was about ordinary human needs: famine, illness, a world that had come apart at the seams. Ordinary people dressed in ordinary clothes told in a calm voice about how God had called them to follow Jesus by trying to put broken lives together. At a dark moment, a divine hand seemed to break through the barrier between worlds, like light pouring through a rent in the clouds. A miracle occurred, beautiful, graceful and dramatic as a rainbow. But the story wasn't about the rainbow, it was about the storm, the rain, and the light from heaven.

Titcombe's story was one among many. I read other narratives in an exciting book called *God's Smuggler*, which told the adventures of "Brother Andrew," a retired Dutch soldier, in smuggling Bibles into Eastern Europe during the Cold War. Once, Andrew visited a church of 1200 people in Moscow with a friend named Hans and some Bibles to give away. Since it was illegal to tote "religious propaganda" into Russia, and each church had spies, the two men separated, each asking God to direct them to the man he wanted them to give their Bibles. Both felt drawn to the same person. Brother Andrew related,

> "This man was from a little church in Siberia, two thousand miles away, where there were 150 communicants but not a single Bible. One day he had been told in a dream to go to Moscow where he would find a Bible for his church. He resisted the idea at first, he said, for he knew that there were few Bibles in Moscow."[1]

Titcombe's rainstorm could have been a coincidence. And did the rain always come when he prayed? But stories like Brother Andrew's challenged the skeptic in me to find another explanation. Did the visitor stand out by a wistful or searching look in his eyes? Was he mentally unbalanced? People with emotional problems often seem to gravitate to foreigners. That might account both for the dream and the fact that both men noticed him. Or on nights when Brother Andrew told such stories, perhaps leaving out a few details, did he find the collection plate heavier?

The stories were not primarily about miracles. Yet the miracles drew me, like a rainbow.

My Western, scientific, middle-class background had imbued me with skepticism about rainbows. They slipped away when you got too close. Santa Claus turned out to be grandpa, a tall, gruff Norwegian longshoreman with a cotton beard over his face. Leprechauns were an advertising gimmick for a breakfast cereal company.

My faith in God was a faith in events I'd never seen, in places I'd never been, reported by people I'd never met.

I went to Asia as a missionary in 1984 in part to find out if God was real. In Hong Kong I shared sink space with people who said they'd seen the lame walk and the blind receive their sight in Jesus' name. A few times I seemed to be given a glimpse of the future.[2] I traveled on a team with an American woman, and later dated a Chinese woman, both of whom had been saved from suicide when Christians they had never seen in their lives walked up to them on the street and told them, "don't kill yourself. God loves you." I met people who had been healed of cancer and seen visions.

At the end of the rainbow I found a pot of gold: I liked these people. Most were down-to-earth, cheerful, and curious. They didn't give themselves airs or brag about what they'd seen or done—more often such stories might come in the form of a confessional told late at night, when we were alone with a few bowls of popcorn and the Almighty God. Some prefaced their stories by saying, "I hardly ever tell anyone about this. I know it's hard to believe." They told me because I was curious enough to ask, but I was also skeptical enough to cross-examine them. Thus, empirically, I came to the conclusion that some miracles, at any rate, probably do happen.

At the same time, I visited temples around East Asia, read ancient Indian sutras, and talked with ordinary believers in Asian religions. I saw that the supernatural is also a part of the religious tradition of other peoples. Stories are told of Buddha himself which some think similar to the Gospels. At key points in the history of Buddhism, such as the contest between early Zen and the esoteric teaching in Tibet, the winning of Japan to Buddhism, and in the Tang dynastic court of China, history and magic seemed to be similarly interwoven. I did research on Chinese folk tradition, and on a Chinese sect that blended esoteric Buddhism and folk Taoism with signs and wonders to attract millions of followers.

Two categories of supernatural events seemed to emerge fairly clearly. They did not strictly resolve themselves into "Christian" and "non-Christian." Many allegedly Christian miracles clearly belonged to the second category, what I will call "magic." Surely the Virgin Mary has better ways of revealing love than making statues bleed, for example.

Nor am I concerned to prove what I call "miracles" never happen outside the Christian tradition. How could I know that? Unlike materialism, Christianity suffers no injury if we admit an angel to an occasional pagan emergency room. So far as I know, the Bible never directly rules out the possibility that

God sometimes does miracles outside the Judeo-Christian tradition. It does come down hard on human charlatans. Nor does it naively assume, like many Western mystics, that the spirit world is free of deceivers. But as Confucius said, "to know what you know, and what you don't know, this is knowledge." The supernatural is, by definition, power: and as with all forms of power, whether electricity, gravity, or the atom, nothing is wiser than caution. If God should heal a Muslim or Hindu who has never heard of Jesus, whom am I to argue?

But while the categories of miracle and magic may overlap between religions, I found they do in such a way as to confirm the pattern set by the Christian Scriptures.

A miracle is not like a laser light show or a fireworks display set off for entertainment or applause. It is like the Biblical idea of the rainbow, a sign from God. What is a sign? A display, sometimes lit up at night, pointing travelers to a city. Miracles reveal God to humanity, not only telling us that God is, but showing us where to find him.

Pennies from a Beggar, Hamburgers from Heaven

"'Do you not remember when I broke the five loaves for the 5000, how many baskets you picked up full of leftovers?' They said to Him, 'Twelve.' 'When there were seven for the 4000, how many hampers of leftovers did you pick up?' They said to him, 'Seven.' And He said to them, 'Do you still not understand?'" (Mark 8:19-21).

One of my first clues that God might do something empirically interesting in response to my prayers came in college. I was short of money. One morning I prayed with some desperation, and a little faith (enough to move, perhaps, a small pile of sand) for a resolution to the crisis. After breakfast I caught a bus and waited in front of a downtown Seattle department store for my transfer to the University of Washington.

A thin, scruffy man came up to me in worn-out clothing and asked for "a dime."

"Did you hear that?" I prayed silently. "*He* wants money from *me!*" I pulled my pocket inside out. "I don't have any!" I said, perhaps a little truculently. "Look!" The beggar threw some coins into my hand. "Take this!" he exploded, and stalked off.

Later that day while my classmates were tackling Chinese grammar, an alarming question came to mind. If my pockets had been empty, how had I been planning to go home? I'd forgotten to bring change! Bus fare was about seventy-five cents. I checked my pockets. Sure enough, just a few pennies more! Apart from what the touchy beggar provided, I wouldn't have had enough for my return fare.

In Frank Capra's *It's a Wonderful Life*, the hero, learning at a discouraging point in his life that a bumbling, hobo-like character named Clarence is his guardian angel, remarks sardonically, "it figures." But if God sent a bum instead of an angel in response to my prayer, I interpreted it as gentle irony, rather than second-class treatment."You are worried about money? I can provide for your needs through a street panhandler, if I like."

My larger financial need was also met, I forget how.

Years later, I worked as a free-lance missionary in Taiwan. I tried to talk the church and government into taking more active steps to save girls who had been forced into prostitution. Sometimes it was depressing work. I seldom had the chance to see what, if anything, I was accomplishing, and felt like I was knocking my head against a brick wall of apathy at times, not to mention the community's fear of shadowy gangsters and corrupt police. One of my purposes in going to Asia had been to see if God answered prayer. If I thought prayer was a magic wand by which I could change the world and impress supporters, my years in Taiwan dis-imbued me of that notion. Yet I did see evidence that God was on my side, even when I was shaky.

At one point I ran out of cash. I wasn't being supported by any organization, nor had I asked anyone but God to support my work financially. (That was part of the experiment.) Having just received a check for $150 from home, I took it to the bank Friday afternoon, congratulating myself on how timely it had arrived and how easy the life of faith was turning out. They told me to come back on Monday. I felt a sudden depression, and went home to take inventory: a spoonful or so of peanut butter, no soap, no toilet paper, about a dollar and a half. Some of the cockroaches in our apartment probably had more set aside than that.

The next morning I blew most of my remaining funds on an "egg biscuit" and juice for breakfast, and a round-trip train ticket from the suburb of Panchiao to Taipei, leaving nothing for lunch or dinner or food the following day. I have gone through skeptical periods, but what is the good of doubt when you want to gripe? The week before I'd showed slides of mainland China at a small storefront church near my home. I reminded God that when the lady in charge for a song to close the meeting I'd chosen *Great Is Thy Faithfulness*. "Now how can I sing that song?" I pointed out. "I don't even have money to buy a hamburger!" I walked to a park a couple blocks in front of Taipei station, and paced back and forth between pagodas and bushes. Sure, I could borrow, or, if I was too proud for that, go hungry for a couple days and call it a fast. But why serve God if he had abandoned me? "I guess I'll go back to the States," I threatened. I knew the "punishment" would hurt me more than God; it implied a loss of hope. But I was feeling sorry for myself.

The cloudy skies offered no reply, and I started to leave. I passed a bench near the entrance of the park where a Chinese girl was reading an English newspaper. I was tired of talking to someone who didn't answer, and besides she was pretty, so I struck up a conversation. She asked me why I had come to Taiwan and I found myself grudgingly telling her about the God I'd been complaining to. Finally I started to leave, and she asked my name.

"*Ma Dewei*," I said, giving my Chinese name.

"*Ma Dewei? Ma Dewei?*" She asked with surprise. "You're not Ma Dewei?"

Two years before I'd found a wallet on the ground at National Taiwan University three miles away. I'd taken it to the campus Lost and Found, dropping a note with my name and the message *Shang Di ai ni*, "God loves you," inside. Out of four and a half million people in the Taipei metropolitan area, this girl was the owner of that wallet! To thank me she took me to McDonalds™, a few blocks away. It was only after I'd finished most of my cheeseburger that I remembered saying something about hamburgers to God.

That evening, I went to church for a meeting, but was told that the pastor wanted me at home. His wife, a bright and gracious woman, had prepared a tasty stew, the kind of western food I seldom tasted, and wanted me to share the meal with them. After dinner I hurried home to finish my slideshow at the little church near my house. Unexpectedly the church gave me a small honorarium. Then the woman who led the meeting suggested we close the evening by singing *Great is Thy Faithfulness* again.

> "Great is Thy Faithfulness, Oh God my Father/ There is no shadow of turning with Thee./ Thou changest not Thy compassions they fail not. / As Thou has been, Thou forever will be . . . All I have need, Thy hands have provide./ Great is Thy faithfulness, Lord, unto me."

Monday I rode a bus to the bank with a full stomach, clean skin, a chastened heart . . . and three cents in my pocket.

Bible stories like the ravens who fed Elijah with bread when he was hiding from King Ahab in the wilderness during a drought, or about the fish Peter caught with a coin in his mouth to pay his taxes may cause some critics to doubt. But many Christians who have been in dire straits have learned that often, God does provide—not magically, nor to stop all suffering, but in the context of a relationship, and often, to teach lessons, as Jesus did in the Gospels.

When we take our first feeble steps of faith, we learn not only *that* God is, but also something about *who* he is. We may find God is not only an artist, but also has a flare for drama. Miracles are in one sense the least "arbitrary" thing in the universe. Timed, tailored, and set up by Someone who knows everything happening on stage, even the stage of our minds, they bring order out of chaos, as the stars were brought out of formlessness, and life out of mud. Compared to miracles, natural law itself is arbitrary.

Miracles are often described as "irrational." What is truly irrational is to believe in a God who can do miracles, experience those miracles yourselves, yet continue to doubt. Like the disciples, and like myself, many believers are guilty of this form of irrationality.

Divine Healing

> *"Great throngs came to Him. They brought along lame, blind, dumb, maimed and many others whom they laid at His feet, and He healed them; so that the crowd wondered when they saw the dumb speaking, the maimed sound in body, the lame walking, and the blind seeing. And they glorified the God of Israel"* (Matt. 15:30-31).

It is a common-place that psychosomatic illnesses, ailments caused perhaps by bitterness or anxiety, can sometimes be cured by the power of suggestion. Critics often suggest that the healings recorded in the Gospels rely on such methods: they were "faith healings," physiological improvement deriving from a kind of placebo effect. The New Testament tells how Jesus cured people whose illnesses were clearly not just "in their heads," however, as in these cases. This is one reason many scholars reject the historicity of the Gospels.

If I had not met dozens, or hundreds, of people who have been similarly cured, in the name of Jesus, I might find such doubts fairly convincing. But many Christians tell how they were healed miraculously of diseases seemingly not "just in their heads."

Brother "Z" was head of a prosperous Chinese family in a village a couple hundred miles south of Shanghai, almost in sight of the coast. The area, which is called the "Jerusalem of China," is one of the focal points of the rapidly-growing church in China: walking around local villages, you see Christian calendars with red crosses above the doorways of from ten to twenty percent of the houses. I met Brother Z at a house church in Canton, where he'd come to look for Bibles. He was also one of the local leaders of a network of unregistered churches. He told me how he got involved in this dangerous work.

Some years before Brother Z had come down with cancer. The doctor informed him that without some very expensive medicine, he would die; the medicine would keep him alive for a few years, perhaps. Unable to afford the medicine, he went home and asked some Christian ladies to pray for him. He also began to pray. While in prayer, he said, a light shone on him and he saw Jesus. Jesus told him, "Go and preach the Gospel." The next morning he came downstairs to breakfast, his throat restored. Since then he has been obedient to this heavenly vision, investing the profits of his family business in preaching and praying for the sick in nearby villages and around China.

Brother Z took me to the top of a hill behind his house. There, on the far side of an idyllic valley of dark green rice waving in the breeze, and across a creek, lay a little hamlet of a few dozen homes. "Three years ago in that village there were no Christians," he explained. "We went there and prayed for a sick person, and he got well. Now there are many families in the village who are Christian."

So it went, in village after village. All along the rich coastal plain, and up into the mountains behind it, people were being healed and putting red crosses on their doors.

What did I find convincing about Brother "Z's" stories? He didn't have anything to gain by lying. He refused the money I offered in thanks for his hospitality, in fact he paid my way, and the only thing he asked for was evangelistic books he could use in preaching the Gospel. (He practically tore a book on Christianity and Buddhism out of my hands.) Many preachers in China like him have been imprisoned and even tortured for their faith. The first thing he wanted to do when I came in the door was kneel down beside a bed with me and pour out his heart to God. He seemed like a man in genuine submission to his Creator.

The social sciences have developed a number of interlocking explanations which can be made to cover just about any religious phenomena, including divine healing. You might say Brother Z was subject to the power of self-hypnotic suggestion. You might point out that cancer is unpredictable and subject to occasional spontaneous remission. It might be that the risks of the ministry were compensated for by social benefits he gained from a leadership position within the thriving new sect, giving him incentive to lie to enhance it. Or perhaps his faith tapped into some hidden reservoir of psychic power common to all who chant and meditate and pray.

But in cases such as this, suggestion and coincidence seem to pack too weak an explanatory power. I could see the man wasn't lying. The spirit of self-sacrifice and business-like practicality I noted in him seemed utterly inconsistent with any convoluted psychic or spiritual dynamics. Besides, there were all those red crosses. Apparently people who had been taught Marxism and Buddhism since childhood were encountering something that was giving them reason to turn to Jesus.

In China, I met some of the millions of Chinese who have become Christians in recent years. I found that often, it was miracles which drew them to God. I met people like a farmer from Anhui province, whose wife, he said, had been possessed by a demon which had gone out of her after long, concerted prayer. Raised in the environment of traditional Chinese folk belief, it may have been that what they interpreted as an evil spirit was really some kind of psychological malady. But neurosis is devilish hard to cure, and often requires years of patient work by trained and sympathetic workers to overcome. The fact remained that, whatever it was, prayer seemed to have done the job.

I asked a young man at a church in a small city in Central China what his friends said when he told them he was a Christian. "They laugh at me," he said. Then, looking at me with a serious expression, he added, "but I will believe in God until the day I die." He told me how, the day after she became a Christian, his wife suffered brain damage in an industrial accident, and how God miraculously restored her despite his unbelief.

Such incidents do not seem unusual in the Chinese church. Indeed, I have heard dozens or hundreds of even more striking stories told by people who were clearly not bragging or trying to expand their religious turf, but with a frank expression of awe. I have also heard miraculous stories told by people whom I regard with gravest suspicion, such as the popular tel-evangelist Nora Lam, who makes good money from naive American Christians. But the fact that some people may be telling lies and half-truths is no better argument against miracles than the fact that people buy fool's gold is an argument against the Alaskan Gold Rush. Researcher Tony Lambert, one of the most knowledgeable and cautious students of the Chinese church, says he is "very uncomfortable" with "orchestrated healing meetings" common in the West. "What is usually different about the Chinese accounts is that they record remarkable answers to prayer by individuals for themselves or their families when faced with real-life crises rather than in a hyped artificial atmosphere."[3]

Suffering and Miracles of Healing

What relationship did Jesus' guerrilla attacks on the rule of entropy in our lives bear to human suffering? Surely they did not end it. What they did was reveal the power of God against the forces of dissolution. They also reveal the compassion of God. But it often seemed Jesus healed people because he couldn't *help* himself. As passionate and unpremeditated as Moses' attack on the Egyptian slave-master, acts of healing frequently got Jesus in trouble, perhaps for the same reason: the Powers-That-Be interpret these acts of love as defiance. Perhaps rightly so.

Dr. Paul Brand describes how solitude and focus on grief increase one's perception of pain. The best way to overcome pain, he argued, is by a combination of physical stimulation and mental refocusing. He described how, when he was experiencing intense pain from gall stones, one evening he got out of bed and walked through the Louisiana night.

> "Frogs bellowed out their choruses in the pond, with crickets and other insects filling in the notes they missed. . . . I deliberately chose to walk on paths made of shell gravel dredged from southern beaches. These shells are very sharp . . . As I walked along, I also picked up small tree limbs and stones and fingered them. All these minor acts helped to combat the pain . . . I'm not sure when the singing began. I think I spoke at first, expressing aloud to God my wonder and appreciation for the good earth around me and the stars blazing overhead."[4]

As with Job, the New Testament does not present a complete philosophy of suffering, nor an instant panacea for the worlds' ills. Even Jesus' parable of the sparrow, which is meant to comfort us, troubles me sometimes. The Heavenly Father does not, after all, feed all the sparrows, and none of them lives very long.

Jesus' fundamental approach to suffering was, like the God of Job, practical rather than philosophical. Jesus did not merely help his patients get their minds off their problems, though his parables were as colorful as the speech Yahweh gave Job. Jesus was up-front about the role suffering plays in the growth of the spirit. Yet while he called his disciples to "take up your crosses," the fortunes of those on whom he had compassion were restored in a even more dramatic way than Job's.

One day, Jesus' disciples came across a beggar they seemed to recognize, at least, they knew enough of his case history to know he had been blind since infancy. They asked their teacher, "Who sinned, this fellow or his parents?" (John 9:2). I guess it was a theoretical question, such as doctrines like karma are invented to answer. Why is there suffering in this world? Why should the weight of the world's horrors fall upon the innocent?

Jesus did not answer the theoretical or universal aspects of his disciple's question, any more than God answered those of Job's. He gave a specific and practical reply. "This has not happened because he has sinned or his parents," Jesus replied, "but that in him God's work should be displayed." And then he cured the man. "God knows," the church has interpreted such answers. "For now, do something practical. Lay hands on a sick person and pray. Buy band-aides. Learn CPR. Relieve suffering where you can, and trust God the rest of the time."

I do not claim to have a better reply. Sometimes I lose sleep when I hear what men and women do to each other, and what nature does to all of us. Nevertheless, miracles of healing are evidence that God eventually will speak in a way that, even if it does not answer all our questions, will still the hearts of those who trust, and wipe away every tear from our eyes. "Death shall be no longer, nor mourning, nor crying, nor any further pain" (Revelations 21:4).

Miracles and the History of Christianity

I do not think divine provision and healings should be seen as sensational bids for fame and fortune on the part of a few flashy faith healers of questionable integrity, but as part of how God has related to people across the centuries. At key turning points of history events sometimes occur which are irreducibly miraculous. The greatest is the resurrection of Jesus.

Rodney Stark argued against historians who say the sudden rise of Christianity cannot be explained apart from miracles. Placing emphasis instead on Christian mutual aid, respectful treatment of women and children, and the courage of Christians martyrs, he compared the growth charts of modern sects such as Mormonism and found them similar. He argued, "The projections reveal that Christianity could easily have reached half the population by the middle of the fourth century without miracles. . ."[5]

No doubt it is soothing if one can find or imagine an explanation for a troublesome event that harmonizes with one's *a priori* theory of life. But that in no way renders incredible reports which assert (with great force of eyewitness testimony) that the actual cause of those events lay outside the scope of one's theories. The rise of Christianity was, as the *Acts of the Apostles* records in the first century, and Augustine records in *City of God* 300 years later from personal observation, accomplished not only by good works and preaching of a God whom Romans and Greeks recognized, but also by miracles. Cahill argues that conversion of the Irish a few centuries later "saved" Western culture during the Dark Ages. And the best he can make out, conversion of the Irish came down to the frankly supernatural flight of an English shepherd boy named Patrick from his slave master in Ireland, and God's later call for him to return.

Christianity has faced and continues to face intense suspicion and hostility in most countries of the world, some of which is the fruit of Western arrogance, some of which arises from the continuing need people feel to protect their cultural identity. A Thai who becomes a Christian may be disowned; a Saudi who believes in Jesus may be beheaded, or drowned in the family swimming pool. A Jew can study under the Dalai Lama or wage revolution with Lenin and find acceptance in his community, but be called a "traitor" if he or she converts to Christianity.[6] Even a Russian, Pole, or American who develops too direct a familiarity with the Scriptures, rather than as mediated through the self-appointed ecclesiastical guardians of orthodoxy, may endanger their status within their home culture. Missions made headway against the defensive prejudices people always build against "foreign" religion partly because God booby-trapped the cultures of the world with the time-released secrets of Christ's redemption, and partly because God spoke to individuals. Great sea-change conversions such as have occurred in recent years in Africa and Asia happened when local people saw Christianity as the fulfillment of their own cultural heritage, much like the old man waiting in the temple in Jerusalem for the Messiah who took the baby Jesus in his arms and praised God. It also happened because God then gave them further empirical demonstration of the truth of the Gospel.

Lutheran church officials did a study to determine what drew new converts in Ethiopia to Jesus. The study reported that between sixty and eighty percent converted through "direct experience or first-hand observation of the supernatural power of God . . . " Norwegian Lutheran Tormud Engelsviken wrote:

> "We thought they were responding because we were preaching the correct Lutheran doctrine . . . But now we know . . . It was the direct power of God in their lives that made the difference."

Missionary Peter Wagner went to South America also under the impression that sound doctrine was the key to successful preaching. But after years of observing what actually caused people in South America to convert, he came to the conclusion that miracles are among the most important causes for the thousand-fold growth of Protestant churches in this century.[7] Valson Abraham, director of India Gospel Outreach, estimated that nearly eighty percent of those in India who believe in Jesus are converted through miracles.[8]

The idea of a living God who acts in history is not welcome to everybody, and probably to no one at all times. Nevertheless, all facts, whether we welcome them or not, need to be taken into account if we want to understand the universe as it is, rather than constructing an idol for ourselves and demanding that reality reconfigure to resemble it. Observing history, I lose patience with theoretical arguments for or against miracles. When water runs down your back, theories of the aesthetic and social value of rain-making ceremonies become worthless; what you want is an umbrella.

The Tao that is spoken

"And they were all filled with the Holy Spirit and began to speak in other languages . . . And when this sound was heard, the crowd collected and were confused, for each one heard them speak in his native language . . ." (Acts 2:4).

The gift of tongues mystified the first people who heard it, and continues to confuse people. Although Paul laid out clear ground-rules for speaking in tongues, Christians still argue about what it is and who should or does use it and how. Some say if anyone speaks in tongues in the modern era, it must be the work of the devil. Non-Christian onlookers still wonder, as the Jews did in this episode, whether the people who use it are in their right minds, drunk, or hypnotizing themselves. Anthropologists readily classify the phenomena with the Jabberwocky of spirit mediums.

I've mentioned meeting some of the hundreds of drug addicts and gangsters who have become radiant Christians through the help of Jackie Pullinger. Pullinger insists that the gift of tongues has played a crucial role in this process. She says the first few years she helped seventy-five addicts withdraw from heroin and other drugs; each was taught to pray in tongues, and as they prayed, the pain of withdrawal left them. If the devil is behind the phenomena, he seems to be going to a lot of trouble to change idol-worshiping drug addicts into Bible-reading evangelists.[9]

I am impressed by the life of Jonathan Goforth, one of the most successful individual missionaries to China, as lovingly told by his co-worker, wife, and closest friend, Rosalind, in *Goforth of China*. To look at a picture of the couple, after fifty years of marriage and ministry, is to see the love, integrity and grit with which they conducted their ministry. If you can tell anything from peoples' faces, these faces seem to say, "Here stand a man and woman of God." Like the apostle Paul, the Goforths paid a high price for success: more than one of their children, exposed to the heat of the summer in Central China and disease, died in childhood. They lost everything during the Boxer Rebellion, Jonathan surviving an ax blow to his head during countless attacks and semi-miraculous escapes as they fled the Boxers. Far from getting a free ride from trouble, they went through almost as much as Job; yet God did reveal his love to them in many remarkable ways.

When he first went to China, Goforth had an experience with "tongues"—learning—trying to learn—the Chinese language. Goforth was a great optimist, as his name implies, but the tonal system was too much for him. One day he told his wife with atypical gloom, "If the Lord does not work a miracle for me with this language, I fear I will be an utter failure as a missionary." He picked up his Chinese Bible and left.

Two hours later he returned. "Oh Rose!" he said. "It was just wonderful! When I began to speak, those phrases and idioms that would always elude me came readily . . ."

Two months later Goforth received a letter from an old college roommate. The students had met one evening to pray, he wrote, "Just for Goforth." The date and time of that meeting, allowing for time differences, was just when Goforth finally cracked the nut of Chinese syntax. The letter noted that, "the presence and power of God was so manifestly felt by all in that meeting, they were convinced Goforth must surely have been helped in some way."[10]

Christian miracles don't insult the mind with demands for "arbitrary" faith. They not only submit to reason, they also fit into a larger pattern of redemption and mercy. They are not fully intelligible, in the sense of being explicable. Why were the Goforths saved from the Boxers, when equally saintly foreign missionaries and Chinese converts were slaughtered? Why did God not answer their prayers for their sick children? Rosalind Goforth did not claim to know the answers to these questions. God is not a tomato plant, that we can pick him apart in a lab, or a gerbil, that we can put him in a cage. God is not even a human being, whom we might get the better of in an argument. Faith in God may be based on empirical evidence, but it is a field of intellectual endeavor in which, by definition, He whom we seek retains the initiative. The proud, the Bible says, cannot know God; as Lewis explains, those who spend all their time looking down their noses at others cannot see what is above them.

It is reasonable to ask questions about miracles, including speaking in tongues, in all humility. Does this sound like a real language? Does the message, when translated, really say anything of value? Is that message consistent with the character of the Creator of all tongues? Can we find any evidence that something more than out-of-control emotion and imagination are involved? It may be that on some occasions, such evidence might be found.

Christians rejoice with scientists that matter is fixed in obedience to natural law, that in general we can take the principle of cause and effect for granted. In fact, some historians of science argue that after new translations of the Bible broke the stranglehold a more idealistic Greek paradigm had had on Medieval metaphysics, the Christian assumption of a "Law-giver" behind nature was greatly responsible for the rise of modern science in Europe. As one puts it, "The modern investigators of nature were the first to take seriously in their science the Christian doctrine that nature is created."[11]

Nevertheless, miracles are not a Christian dogma, which we must believe in the face of the evidence, but a part of the data upon with which all dogmas must come to terms. While not common, I suspect miracles happen more often than is usually supposed. The hand of God often works in a subtle way, however, which allows those not ready to see, to overlook them.

An American marine biologist named Pauline Hamilton went to China as a missionary, and then lived in Taiwan for some decades. She told her experiences in a book called *To a Different Drum,* some of which reminded me of my experiences on the same island.

Once Pauline's money, as well as funds for an upcoming student conference she was putting together, had been stolen from her house. She suspected her truculent housekeeper, Iu-lan, as the culprit, but lacked firm evidence. The morning following the theft, Pauline asked Iu-lan to make breakfast at 8:30. "Why should I set the table when there's nothing to eat?" the woman whined. Pauline related what followed:·

"When I came back, Iu-lan was still fussing and complaining. Just then—it was about 8:20—I heard someone knocking . . . . There stood my neighbor Mr. Li. He comes from Shantong, where the best steamed bread you ever tasted Is made, and what do you suppose he was holding—a great big platter of steaming hot bread! 'We know how much you like *mantou*,' he explained, 'so we made a specially big batch this morning . . .'

"When Iu-lan saw what I was carrying she asked with much curiosity, 'Where did you get that?'

"'The Li's down the lane made it,' I said simply.
'You can't just eat steamed bread,' she pouted.

'Well, lots of people do,' I replied quietly, 'and anyway, it will hold body and soul together.'

"Even as we were talking there came another knock, this time at the back gate, which we normally didn't use. On opening it, I was surprised to find little Mrs. Wang with a good-sized parcel in her hands. She was always a bit nervous and excited . . . with a quivering voice she explained, '*Wo zi ji sheng dé*' which literally means 'I laid them myself.' The parcel contained twenty eggs! When I took them into the house Iu-lan's eyes fairly popped. 'Who brought those?' she asked, her voice lacking some of its earlier scorn. 'Little Mrs. Wang who has the seven daughters. She said she laid these eggs herself. Rather special, I'd say.'

'Well, you still don't have any fruit or coffee.'[12]

Immediately afterwards someone else brought fruit on a bicycle, in the form of the "biggest papaya I'd ever seen." Iu-lan, forced to play out a bad hand, still had spunk to continue playing straight-woman to Pauline's guardian angel by pointing out they still lacked coffee. At that moment another friend whose husband worked for an airline walked up, still in time for breakfast, with a jar of instant coffee from overseas.

Iu-lan did not repent on the spot. It took a long while for her to admit the miracle, and longer to admit what it meant for her. While miracles provide empirical evidence of the existence of God, they are often more of an invitation than a summons to belief.

A piece of fruit, a hamburger, a beggar, thoughtful neighbors: the raw material of miracles may seem commonplace. As he did by feeding Elijah with ravens, or providing taxes for Peter with a fish that had snagged a gold coin, often God's provision seems to show humor: provisions from the same hand that designed the bill of a platypus and the hump of a camel. Is it not likely the first man and woman also laughed when they climbed a tree and discovered sweetness in an orange globe, or pried open bumpy white "rocks" at the beach and discovered sea food, or found God's hidden provision in the chicken egg and the rice stalk?

Christians are often asked, "Why is there so much suffering in the world? Why do some starve when the rains cease to fall?" Christianity arose not through an effort on the part of philosophers to find a solution to such problems, as did Buddhism. The Bible never pretends to provide an all-embracing theory, class warfare, racial oppression or *karma*, by which to explain all suffering. I think it suggests, on the contrary, that only those who need an answer and look for an answer, will find one, and that for their own suffering, not for the suffering of others. I do not know the reason for the pain I see around me. Sometimes I learn why I suffer, most often after the fact. The acts of God are at the far end of the spectrum from arbitrary: they give meaning even to suffering which they do not end, such as on the cross, and in the Gulag. By them, the world becomes a less-arbitrary place.

Exorcism

"And no one could ever bind him . . . All the time, night and day, he remained among the tombs and in the mountains, shrieking and cutting

himself with stones .... (Jesus said) 'Come out of the man!' . . . They came to Jesus and saw the demoniac, who had been possessed of the legion, sitting down, dressed and sane, . . . and they were filled with awe" (Mark 5:3-15).

But miracles are not always subtle. Some are frightening, like nature. Like the sea, they call us to silence ourselves. Like an earthquake they may shake without warning what had been firm and immovable. Like death they can bring us face-to-face with worlds beyond mortal experience. Like stars they remind us we are small. Such miracles also appear in history.

Spirit possession, or apparent spirit possession, is not a rare phenomena. The few possible cases I have come across personally were less terrifying (as movies would lead one to believe) than puerile.[13] The people involved reminded me of broken branches or limbs out of joint, or the random banging on a piano of a madman. The faculties of men and women made in the image of God had been turned to a futile and unworthy end.

World history often displays in a more public manner both the inhumanity and the vulnerability of the powers of darkness. The Aztec empire, protected by gods gorged with the blood of human sacrifice, fell like a house of cards, brought down by a plague of small pox carried by a handful of bold adventurers. The occult Marxism of Jim Jones ended in a pile of bodies, Jones among them. Adolf Hitler fell under the rubble of his Thousand Year Reich, 987 years early. The Soviet Union fell apart in weeks, not under assault of the West's high-tech, billion-dollar weapons, but a Gideon's army led by a Polish electrician and a Romanian preacher.

In retrospect, we can find social causes for each collapse. But if these kingdoms were built on spiritual power—and there is evidence the leaders of each appealed to occult forces—it is striking how quickly they crashing down, as if weighed and found wanting.

The Bible talks about a God who judges nations, with an often ironic justice. Egypt, the superpower of the day, worshiped frogs, until her homes were filled with toads. Hebrews worshiped Baal, god of the clouds, and the land became parched and the people pondered the impotence of the trendy new deity.

The same irony sometimes appears in our daily newspapers, if we have eyes to see. A general seizes power in the Philippines and welcomes a New Age sect to Manila which promises an "aura of invincibility" over the land. Within a few years, the country is struck by typhoons, earthquakes, revolutions, and a volcanic eruption. Finally the general is overthrown by nuns praying in the streets in front of tanks. A German tyrant goads his people to kill Jews. His top lieutenants are publicly hung, just as, and in the same number, as the sons of another tyrant who tried to slaughter the Jews 3000 years before. (Esther 9).

Devotions

I probably learned to say "grace" before I was three. The ritual seemed ordinary enough, like turning on a light switch. I asked God for daily bread, thanked him for it, and ate. But is it really likely that the Creator of nebuli, black holes and orbs of pulsing light spread for millions of light years in all directions, would listen when primates on a turbulent little planet close their eyes and address him?

"Let us make man in our own image," God suggests in Genesis 1:26. If we are an image of God, what is God like? My boys are always saying, "Look, Daddy!" or "Look, Mommy!" as they learn about the planets, the nutritional elements of strawberry shortcake, find a favorite character in a picture book, or put together a train track. The joy of invention is never complete until it is shared. The Bible says God wanted to show us what he made, too. He created *homo sapiens* to show us the fingerprints that are the stars.

We spend time with someone we admire, and begin to act like him. Christian faith means spending time with God.

Why are miracles distant and rare, rather than overpowering? Perhaps because, while an overwhelming demonstration of God's reality might force us to admit, in the abstract, to his existence and care, it is the joy and suffering of trying to do his will in a complex world that allows us to partner with him in the joy and suffering of creation. Over a period of nine months in the womb, he creates bodies which carry us through life. He forms our minds over many years. It should not surprise us, then, that spiritual knowledge of God does not usually come in an instant, like a Big Mac, but over time, like a work of art.

Recently I read an interesting article about the evolutionary scientist, Steven Jay Gould. One of his colleagues noted that he had an uncanny knack for finding the unusual, the artifact in a dig different from the rest, that held a clue to the meaning of the whole. Discoveries with enormous implications are often made by concentrating on tiny bits of evidence that don't fit into the old patterns: the unexplained wobble of a planet, an unusual color in the urine, a bit of off-color hair in the sink. In the same way, miracles are admittedly rare, seemingly less common than the inevitable facts of suffering and death. Yet they change the meaning of life.

Two opposing views of miracles seem at first to confront each other across a chasm of vastly differing worldviews in our day. The first is the idea that miracles never happen. The second is that miracles happen all the time, if only we have eyes to see them. But in fact, these theories represent two sides of the same coin. Those who say all religions are equally false, and those who say all religions are equally true, stimulate one another to deeper error, and miss the true drama of human history. For both ideas are essentially monism, which reduces all reality to a single category. But all drama arises from dualism in the literal sense, the idea that life contains real choices and real danger, and that the world itself and the human heart is the site of a duel between good and evil. So perhaps we should not be surprised that, for the most part, we are given space in which to allow that drama to develop.

---

[1] Brother Andrew, with John and Elizabeth Sherrill, *God's Smuggler*, Signet, 1967, p. 183-4

[2] I also met the kind of "prophet" the tabloids are fond of. A visitor to a Taiwan church I was attending tried to convince me, with great self-importance and impatience at my noncommittal response, that God had told him George McGovern was going to be the next U. S. president, and that Taiwan and Russia were about to join forces and go to war against China and the United States. This was in the late 1980s.

[3] Tony Lambert, *China's Christian Millions*, Monarch Books, 1999, p. 120

[4] Dr. Paul Brand and Philip Yancey, *Pain: The Gift No One Wants*, Harper Collins, 1993, p. 246-7

[5] Rodney Stark, *The Rise of Christianity*, p. 14

[6] In a contributing essay in *Smashing the Idols: An Inquiry Into the Cult Phenomena*, Elie Wiesel spoke of his "revulsion" towards Jews who believe in Jesus. Jews for Jesus are "hypocrites" who "use trickery and lies" to deceive Jewish youth and "repudiate their people and its memories." It is understandable that Jewish people would interpret the conversion of modern Jews to Christianity in terms of the long and sorry history of "Christian"—Jewish relations in Europe. (See Appendix.) But Jews have sometimes suffered as badly or worse under ancient and modern pagans, atheists, and Muslims, and Wiesel expresses no bitterness here towards Jews who convert to those theologies. The Holocaust was not invented by Christians, but by an evolutionary paganism that is more organically related to other modern ideologies, including Wiesel's atheism. While understandable as a defense mechanism against a dominant culture, such anger still seems a bit selective.

[7] Peter Wagner's book on South American Christianity has been published undere three different titles that, unfortunately, I have been unable to track down.

[8] Valso Abraham, *Charisma Magazine*, January 1993, p. 27, *The Holy Spirit Around the World*

[9] Even when tongues appear less complex than a true language, it would not follow that they may not serve as the vehicle for constructive and complex spiritual phenomena. See C. S. Lewis' essay *Transposition* (in *Screwtape Proposes a Toast and Other Pieces*, Fontana Books, 1965), directed to this subject, for stimulating suggestions on the overall relation between symbol and meaning, and in general, between brain and mind.

[10] Rosalind Goforth, *Goforth of China*, Zondervan, 1937, p. 88

11 M. B. Foster, quoted by Charles Thaxton, *Christianity and the Scientific Enterprise*, in *Finding God at Harvard*, p. 265

12 Pauline Hamilton, *To a Different Drum*, Overseas Missionary Fellowship, 1984. Note: I have changed the phoneticization of Pauline's Chinese quotation from Wade-Giles to Pin Yin.

13 C. S. Lewis portrays this quality masterfully in the science fiction novel *Perelandria*, in the character of Weston.

CHAPTER 11

Impractical Magic

HOW DO Christian miracles differ from the supernatural acts performed in non-Christian religions? Are pagan miracles an equally valid set of experiences by which people seek God? Counterfeit signs by angels of darkness eager to usher in a New Age of Satanic tyranny? A usually harmless but potentially psychosis-inducing exercise in delusional thinking? Or are supernatural acts all fraudulent, alike illustrating the suggestibility and gullibility of the human race?

The need to understand the difference between miracles and magic is urgent. Over the last couple centuries, old-fashioned skeptics like Darwin, Freud and Voltaire, and their heirs in the world of biology, social science, comparative religion and (increasingly) a computer science which threatens to merge all fields, have undermined belief in the miracles of God. Now, just when people hunger for a touch of the supernatural, we're flooded both with western witchcraft from before the "Age of Reason," and occultism from the undying traditions of the East.

How do we sort out authentic works of God from imaginary, faked or demonic acts? Some who claim to be part of the church have spread not a little confusion of their own, with stories about mysterious crosses in window panes or 600-foot apparitions of Christ ordering a preacher to raise more funds.

As a missionary and student of Asian religion, I've met people who prayed to non-Christian gods and gotten dramatic responses, seen ghosts, or experienced psychic healing. I've met gurus who relied on channeled messages to found new religions. Over ten years of study, I formed general impressions about the character of the occult and how it contrasted with Christian miracles.

The question remained in the back of my mind as I conducted two research projects on Asian religion.

The first was a study of the great pseudo-Christian Taiping Rebellion that almost overthrew China's Qing Dynasty in the mid-nineteenth century. Tai Ping theology mixed a bit of Christianity, mostly Old Testament images as filtered through the mind of an ambitious but dreamy young teacher named Hong Xiuquan, traditional Asian spirit trances, and Confucian ideology, into a single, dynamic, and surprisingly successful religion. In describing that great revolution, I found modern scholars often reflect a common assumption that, aside from petty doctrinal disputes, miracles in the Biblical and occult traditions draw upon the same psychological mechanisms. They depicted Tai Ping ideology as a "form of Christianity," distorted only by Hong's ignorance of orthodoxy, poor early translations of the Bible, and the intellectual limitations of the blue collar Christian whose pamphlet first introduced Western religion to Hong. One called Taiping faith "a version of evangelical Christianity"[1] which copied divine healing, speaking in tongues, and "fits of ecstasy" from Protestant revivalism of the period.[2] (In an entire book on the subject, however, he did not give any evidence that missionaries Hong met practiced these.) The most famous scholar who wrote about the Taipings, Jonathan Spence, implicitly stated the parallel between Hong and Jesus by entitling his study *God's Chinese Son*, trying to draw the two together in his introduction.

Yet Hong explicitly and deliberately rejected orthodox Christianity. Furthermore, it was not in the fundamentalism Hong had contact with that the most striking parallels to his movement could be found, but in early occult practices of the Mormon church, of all places. This was curious: it is very unlikely Hong ever heard of Joseph Smith. More curious still was the attitude of western scholars who, eager to reduce all supernatural events to a single category, overlooked the actual pattern of the evidence.

If for scholars all miracles ought to be equally false, and therefore explicable in terms of historical, social, and psychological influences, many ordinary believers would rather see them as equally true.

My second project was to research a popular new sect of esoteric Buddhism that grew out of Chinese spiritualism and emphasized psychic "response," a lot like the Fa Lun Gong sect whose suppression in China has been widely reported. Many of the followers of this sect also seemed to implicitly reduce all supernatural phenomena to a single category, which however they were eager to accept rather than reject.

Master Lu Sheng-yen, a self-proclaimed Living Buddha, came to America with the ambition of blending Taoism, the four main schools of Tibetan Buddhism, Chinese folk religion, and direct communion with spirit guides to introduce his Tantric "practical path to Enlightenment" to the world. His movement, described as "one of the most if not the most, dynamic and interesting contemporary Chinese schools of Buddhism,"[3] alleged four million followers around the world, and public appearances with up to 50,000 at one time.

Lei Zang temple, the sect's home temple in Redmond, Washington, (just down the hill from Microsoft) was a medium-sized building of conventional Chinese religious architecture, except for two Tibetan prayer wheels spinning out front. Colorful murals were painted on the walls of bodhisattvas and gods with fiery or round halos gathered around two thrones: on the right, one inscribed "Siddhartha mandala," and on the left, another inscribed "*Lian Hua Tong Zi* mandala." Master Lu himself occupied the central throne in the latter, with a brilliantly-colored cloth crown or mantle about four feet above his head. On the back wall of the worship hall more than sixty large idols and several vajras were arranged in three rows. On top sat tall golden Buddhas, each beneath a cloth "umbrella" about ten feet across hung from the ceiling with a Tibetan mantra written within. The gods and bodhisattvas of the lower levels were an eclectic marriage of heaven, hell, and everything in between: Indian elephant gods, Taoist patriarchs, gruesome Tibetan dharma protectors with garlands of human skulls, calm and compassionate bodhisattvas with dozens of arms uplifted to save all who call on them. The smallest figure in the Pantheon was the most incongruous: a six-inch statue of Jesus, set almost within the grasp of a fierce monster-god from India. Among the other figures, that of Master Lu himself— *Lian Hua Tong Zi*—was the most human and attractive, handsome, a bit portly, a trademark cheerful smile on his face. Lu seemed to bridge the many inhuman or supernatural figures and the mortals who come to worship them.

To the right of the temple, in a hollow against the fence that marked the boundary of the property, lay a little "dragon palace" where, on one visit, a monk and a nun were engaged in painting the multi-hued scales of a beautiful green dragon on a large yellow boulder, which had been moved from the original site of the temple. It edged incongruously against the unpainted picket fence of the neighbor's soggy and shaded Northwest backyard.

Master Lu was an artist, and lived close to the mountains and his beloved nature in an enormous, tastefully decorated Mediterranean style mansion about a half mile north of Interstate 90; to put it in Hobbit terms, the last habitable home going east from Seattle before you strike the Cascade mountains. There, surrounded by mountains of Twin Peaks fame, spruce and fir forests, and meadows of lupine where elk come to graze, Master Lu meditated and wrote. He had written over 130 exciting tales of his adventures in the spirit world by the time I did my research, of which many of his followers had read the entire corpus, sometimes more than once. When the weather cleared and "no thought" took him, (his disciples told me, "We never know if he's going to come"), he would suddenly appear at Lei Zang temple for the four o-clock

Tong Xiu Hui, mutual-cultivation meeting. News of his arrival swept through the temple, and worshippers dropped to the floor. (Leaving me standing awkwardly by myself, trying to look in-obtrusive.) When the meeting began, I got a taste of how Master Lu's Buddhism mixes philosophy and magic.

A young nun from Hong Kong nervously gave a simple and moving homily on the "Eight-fold path," in Mandarin Chinese with a Cantonese accent. Master Lu followed by launching into a seemingly irrelevant but intriguing story, full of humorous asides, about the "Dragon palace" outside the temple, and the reason temple workers had just painted it for the fourth time. The first dragon had been very sensitive; Master Lu yelled "rain," and it rained; he put his hands together, and the dragon god descended to meet him. But some people complained the green dragon wasn't sufficiently "Buddhist," so the former director of the temple painted in his place a "beautiful" but surly yellow dragon. American reptile that he was, the new dragon hardly ever came when called, and was cheeky and flippant in his crown and royal robes when he did show. "Don't blame me. Someday you'll understand," said the replacement third dragon when he, too, failed to act on Lu's commands. Finally Lu's voice, which had been the slow, modulated, naturally-articulate voice of a traditional Chinese story-teller, raised to deliver the punch-line, delivered by the third dragon. "You tore down the old dragon palace and built a new palace. But the money used to build this palace came from a person who *deceived people to get it.*" (I was dumb-struck. Was this all about a temple scandal? After a pre-emptive strike like that, who would dare accuse Master Lu of deception?) Finally Lu brought closure to the original theme of the lesson: "We were talking about the eight-fold path. If you take dishonest gains and do something good with them, does that have any merit?"

Master Lu's books were full of such adventures. In one, he told how, during a prolonged drought in the Northwest, the god of Mount Rainier appeared to him and bowed (thinking it proper etiquette when dealing with Asians), begging him to exert his psychic powers to save the trees and animals of the mountain. The narrative contained a dig at a Living Buddha across town, whom the god first approached with the problem but found to be "a blind teacher of the blind." Lu proved himself a true Living Buddha, and the Living Buddha across town incompetent, by bringing rain, killing with the kiss of his trademark Taiwanese humor.

Awe of the numinous and fear of the uncanny were both absent from the experiences Master Lu related about the other world. This was unusual among Taiwanese mediums. As one anthropologist noted, "Nearly all *tang ki* maintain that they tried every possible inducement to persuade the possessing god to select someone else," even at the risk of their own lives.[4] Master Lu, on the contrary, breezed through encounters with traditional Chinese ghosts, gods, and bodhisattvas with a swagger reminiscent of martial arts fighters or the Monkey King.

As a young man, Lu Sheng-yen had been a Christian for a few years, until he met a Taoist god in a vision. The next day he went to a temple in central Taiwan, where an old lady with crooked eyes commissioned him in the following terms:

> "Some wicked people have deliberately put on the coats of the Buddhas and gods to engage in affairs that harm others. Under the guise of psychic counseling, these people take financial and sexual advantages of their fellow beings. They use smooth talk and heresy to spread the fallacies . . . The Bodhisattvas know that you have a kind heart and that your behavior is proper; therefore they want to entrust you with their mission."[5]

Many would find that ironic. "Taking financial and sexual advantage of people under the guise of psychic counseling" were precisely the charges made against Master Lu in the Chinese community. A postal delivery man from mainland China, who told me he was an atheist, came to my house in north Seattle and, seeing a Chinese book on esoteric Buddhism in my hands, launched unbidden into a spirited attack on Master Lu. "I can't stand that guy," he said, telling me about a rich woman who offered all her money to the temple, only to have Master Lu tell her, "You need to have sex with me. I'm a god." Several people told me Lu was simply using religion to get rich. How could a real Buddhist wear a gold watch, drive a Mercedes, or demand that his followers fall on the floor at his feet? Nor was it only Christians and atheists who doubted the propriety of his behavior. One Zen nun told me True Buddha "might have some sense to it, but it's not Buddhism, and if he wants to preach it he should call it something else." She was especially offended by the fact that Lu's followers eat meat.

And yet it became clear, as I talked with people in the sect, not only that believers were sincere in their commitment to Buddhism, but that the reason they were attracted to this particular sect was because they experienced greater supernatural power in it than anywhere else. Not everyone in True Buddha experienced it, but in general the sect seemed to be boiling over with signs and wonders. The signs were similar to boasts by popular occult gurus, such as Sai Baba, Yogananda, Qing Hai, and Jim Jones. It appeared the most controversial cults are not less supernatural than more respectable forms of Buddhism or Hinduism, but more so. That is one of their attractions.

The Supernatural Attraction of Master Lu

For some, Master Lu's supernatural powers confirmed and developed psychic powers they had begun to realize on their own before meeting him.

"A lot of time I go by feeling," an American doctor raised by an Aleut grandmother in Alaska told me. His grandmother had taken him through the woods and taught him the deities of trees and plants. He practiced Gelugpa and Nyingma Tibetan Buddhism for a while but did not feel the same connection. "One dream that was really kind of telling, was after I had taken refuge," (i.e., submitted to the claims of Buddhism and Master Lu.) "I was in a kneeling position. Guru Lu held his hand out and light emitted over the crown (of my head.) It was as clear as you and me standing here."

Others joined True Buddha after finding spiritual power in his movement they had not encountered elsewhere. Master Lu combined *wu wei* (go-with-the-flow) of Zhuang Zi with the *wu chang* (impermanence) of Buddha in an optimistic blend that a mechanic from Brunei found attractive. He credited the school's meditative practices, and easy-going philosophy especially, with helping him sleep better.[6] His faith was enhanced four years before, when his car hit a house and was crushed, while he was thrown clear and saved from death. A more somber confirmation came the previous year: "My father-in-law was sick. My Grand Master said he would die in six months. Even the doctors didn't know. In six months, he died."

"I needed to go back to Thailand," a Cambodian woman told me as a small child slept beside her on the floor during a Saturday worship service. "It popped into my head to ask Buddha, the *dharma* and the *sangha* to help me and bam! I got the visa done just like that." Her first meeting with the Master had been enough to persuade her of his power. "I asked Master Lu about something no one would know—a certain secret that no one knew and I asked him, and he knew it. The following weeks I kept having dreams about him manifesting himself, telling me it was time to be awakened." While she had read those of her teacher's books that had been translated into English, she learned his other teachings telepathically, she said. "The majority of the teaching is transmitted to my mind."

A young Chinese Indonesian lady with a Catholic background told me, "I met him once and he told me to chant the guru mantra a million times. I said, OK, he told me to do it, I'll do it. Not very long after that, I began getting responses, the spiritual responses people had talked about before but I didn't believe in. Grand Master Lu would talk about the responses he saw and it was exactly what I saw." She noted two kinds of responses: feelings, and a general ability to make a success of her efforts. Sitting with me in the doorway of Lu's multi-million dollar mansion, she reflected that Buddha was a state of mind, and this state, while bound to bring earthly benefits along the way, was more important. "Our teacher teaches that whatever realm you are in, whether heaven or hell or human, if you achieve that state of mind, you are Buddha. You want to be successful, so you don't want to worry about money, you want to have more wisdom, be at peace—there are tons and tons of things along the way."

An older lady from Indonesia noted that "other Buddhism is all very good," but "our *mijiao* is *ling* (psychically powerful), very *ling*. Right away you feel it." She had read about twenty or thirty of the Master's books, and believed the stories in them "one hundred percent." When she joined the sect, she suffered from chest pains, and had an operation. "As soon as I read my Master's incantation, I immediately had *gan ying*.' (responses) It didn't feel as painful."

What did I conclude from my study of the True Buddha movement? Not that Master Lu was telling the truth about his visions. I can't guarantee Master Lu's visions were an invention, but after reading his stories, talking to his disciples, and seeing his magnificent home, the supernatural sign that would have seemed most fitting would have been to see his nose grow. The critics appeared right to this extent, anyway: Lu struck me as a scoundrel.

The True Buddha Sect was engaged in vigorous, even cutthroat, competition with similar sects combining Chinese spiritualism and Buddhist philosophy: Supreme Master Qing Hai, a Buddhist nun from Vietnam who offered salvation to five generations of ancestors through herself, "Modern Day Savior and Living God Almighty,"[7] Xing Yun, whose Light of Buddha network has also provoked controversy, and Lu's archrival Lin Yun, also from Taiwan and founder of Black Sect Tantric Buddhism, a mild-mannered gentleman in a tie who poses with movie stars and politicians, and much like Master Lu, offers his followers dream analysis, *mudras, feng shui*, visualization, *qi*, and Taoism, along with a blend of esoteric Tibetan teachings. Master Lu called that school the "five poison sect," claiming Lin engages in black magic.

I found the stories his followers told more compelling than Lu's own exotic adventures. You might put some of these healings and successes down to autosuggestion or wishful thinking, or the kind of statistical anomaly that turns up if you run thousands of people through a guru's hands, then interview just the few who stay. None of them compelled either belief in the supernatural or the need to call any of my informants "liars." Some seemed fairly convincing. Even a couple who left the sect and Buddhism when it began using human skulls and semen in its rituals told me they still felt spirits were "all around that place."

I came to the conclusion Master Lu was an entertaining but unscrupulous liar, who may or may not keep a few devils in the closet. He seemed to enjoy the miraculous mostly in private, and always in a way that affirmed the importance of the "Holy Red-Crowned Grand Vajra Lotus-Born Master Lu Sheng-yen." He was an artist, and I would have enjoyed his stories if I had not seen for myself the depth of faith his followers put in him, been inside his mansion, and met some of the people who paid for it. As with the Taipings, supernatural power seemed to charge the air of his camp like static electricity before a mountain storm, with signs and wonders discharging on all sides. But also like Hong Xiuquan's adventure, though doubtless more subtly, it seemed likely a great amount of human debris would be left on the ground in the end. If the figure of Jesus seemed odd among the idols of Lei Zang temple, the contrast between Master Lu and Jesus, and the signs they performed, could not be more complete. It is the contrast Jesus himself drew when he said, "The thief comes only to kill and destroy. I have come that they might have life, and have it more abundantly"(John 10:8,10).

That is the contrast I mean to describe by the words "miracle" and "magic."

While I tried to reserve the word "miracle" for events which demonstrate the reality of God and the fact that he answers prayer, not all of the events I described in the last chapter are conclusively supernatural in that sense. For example, the story of my "hamburger from heaven," or Pauline Hamilton's breakfast, could *conceivably* be a series of coincidences. (A Chinese proverb tells about a farmer who saw a rabbit run into a tree trunk. Picking up the stunned hare, he took him home and had his wife cook it for dinner. Then he went back and sat by the tree trunk to wait for more. If that method of obtaining meals works for you, then maybe we can call such provision as Hamilton experienced coincidence.)

By magic, I mean an event which claims supernatural origin but shows by its character that it is not from God. By miracle I mean an supernatural event whose character suggests that the God who created us may be involved. The two differ, I believe, in at least five ways, which can be verified both in Scripture and in the lives of our neighbors.

(1) Miracles ask to be verified: Magic insults the intelligence.

Several years ago, on a drive through Hawaiian Volcanoes National Park, I noticed a sign beside the highway: "Road Closed." It was a considerable under-statement, I found when I stopped my car and got out to look. The road in question was buried several feet in lava. I walked across a field of hardened magma and found only a few yards of road remaining, the yellow line down the middle leading incongruously and hopelessly to a heap of stiff black rock with a line of ferns sprouting around the edges.

The highway people know their business, and makes signs simple and sensible, to keep people on the road.

God knows his business, too. He formed the mind, as the government builds road, and his instructions are meant to keep us on the highway of good sense. God's signs, while an interruption of the natural course of events, are meant to guide us through life in control of the vehicle of our souls. (Paul says "self-control" is one of the "fruit of the Spirit"; Gal. 5:22,23, NIV). Miracles don't demand that we close our eyes, but that we open them. This is why, when the Old Testament prophets talked about miracles, they used verbs like "consider," "think," "try," and "test." John tells us Jesus did miracles "that you may believe Jesus is the Christ" (John 20:31). As if even the evidence of sight and hearing were not immediate enough, Jesus told Thomas, "reach your finger here" to touch. (John 20:27). As Christian apologist Bernard Ramm put it, a miracle in the Christian sense "must be a sensible event."[8] Intuition and psychic phenomena do not qualify.

True, those who believe without seeing are called "blessed." The Gospels are merely second-hand evidence for us in the modern era. But they are *good* second-hand evidence. Even as they recorded a sequence of astounding super-natural events, the authors show their commitment to truth in many ways: by basic agreement within differing points of view, attention to detail, an objective tone, by fairly recording the doubts and objections of unbelievers without trying to refute them at every point, and by laying down their lives as an affirmation of their testimony. Paul never asked his audiences to "take the Gospel on faith," or to pray God for irrefutable psychic experience. Rather, he spoke of historical events: "the king knows about these matters, . . . for they have not occurred in a corner" (Acts 26:26).

Verifiability—the idea that a claim is only good if it can be tested by facts—is what Christian miracles are all about. The man who said, "I believe because it is absurd" wasn't even talking the same language as the Bible.

This is the language of much of the more gaudy forms of paganism, ancient and modern. The occult is like a menu off of which you can order if you find nature too tame. Wild yarns, whether from Shirley MacLaine or a 2,000-year-old "guru" someone claims to have met in the Himilayas, may be accepted according to taste without a scrap of evidence. Lu's followers accepted his stories based not on external evidence, but on internal responses when they met the Master. This attitude is ubiquitous among monist gurus.

While I was researching the True Buddha school, at the front of the hall to the left, in a little glass case, stood a collection of bones from the body of the Grand Master's mother, who passed away a few months previously. Beside the case an explanation was written: the bones, most of them white but some a light green or yellow, were *shelizi*, sariras, which appear in the body of one who had attained enlightenment and passed to the world of the Buddha. A series of photographs about the funeral and auspicious internment of the deceased also appeared on the reader-board outside the temple. This is not the first time Master Lu made use of this form of apologetic. In 1992, he published a booklet called *Sariras—Buddhist Relics Among Executed Prisoners*, which described the conversion of four death-row inmates in Singapore who converted to True Buddha, quoting their effusively grateful letters, and the between four and thirty *shelizi* found in their bodies after execution. Lu concluded: "Therefore, beyond any doubt, Living Buddha Lian-sheng . . . is a true Living Buddha . . . the True Buddha Tantric Dharma is a Correct Buddhist Dharma. This is supported by the fact that people who cultivate this Dharma, even including death row prisoners, all will obtain great spiritual achievement. What can slanderers say about this?"[9]

What any objective bystander would say, of course, is that this is no evidence at all. What does the color of bones have to do with the direction the spirit flies on death? And what fool does not know chemicals you can buy in the grocery store could do the same thing in five minutes? Yet this kind of grotesque coroner's evidence, which was so popular in the Middle Ages in the West, but which is totally absent from the New Testament, has been a staple of Buddhist apologetics for thousands of years.

This is not to say magic doesn't try to explain things. In fact, it almost always tries to explain too much. It takes the mysteries of life—patterns in the crops, lights in the sky, curious passages from Scripture—lines them into an arbitrary but psychologically pleasing pattern, and says, "here is the explanation!" Magicians are averse to the words, "I don't know."

Magic posits a relationship between cause and effect which relies on the suggestibility of the audience. Perhaps this is one reason the law of *karma* is popular. A twelve year old Vietnamese girl whose life ambition is to be a doctor, has a disease which causes her to look like a shrunken seventy-five year old woman. A baby in a rural district in South Africa where the owners of the land kept the black population in subservience through drink, is found by the side of the road with a bottle filled with wine. Why do terrible things happen to the innocent? The doctrine of rebirth gives an airtight explanation. You reap as you sow. No person is punished except for what he or she has done in a previous life.

Three figures in the history of humanity's search for answers stand out by restraint. Socrates and Confucius knew the limits of their wisdom, and kept to them. Jesus knew the needs of his followers, and kept to *them*. When confronted by questions not relevant to his questioner's spiritual needs, he invariably changed subjects. "Where should we worship?" "God is looking for people who worship in spirit and truth . . . Go, bring your husband. I will give you living water." "Should we stone a woman guilty of adultery as the law requires?" "Let him who is without sin cast the first stone." "Give us a sign!" "I will give you no sign, except the sign of Jonah . . . " "Who sinned, this girl, or her parents?"

This latter question is not irrational. In fact birth defects do sometimes derive from the careless lifestyles of parents—alcohol fetal syndrome, AIDS, crack babies. But the doctrine of *karma* forces one explanation too far. Jesus answered by changing subjects from *cause* of disability to *purpose*. Stop standing around asking questions. Make yourself useful—that's what God wants you to do. And yet in healing those he encountered, he did provide reason to believe and give glory to God.

How the East was Won: Did Buddha Work Miracles?

The orthodox faiths of Asia tend to reject God or nudge him to the side, while the common people remain vaguely aware of him. But the religions of Asia are a fairly heterogeneous blend of the other three elements Chesterton said make up non-Christian religion: gods, philosophers, and demons.

The historical success of Buddhism owes more to the likes of Master Lu than most people realize. The history of Asian religion is not, as is often portrayed in the West, primarily a history of ideas, but of magic: esoteric teachers who wooed Tang Chinese emperors with the magical defeat of enemies, Phadmasambhava who conquered the demons of Tibet, and Japanese faith-healers.

What kind of holy man was Buddha? Was the historical Siddhartha a miracle-worker, magician, philosopher like Susuki, or a visionary statesman like the Dalai Lama? The wonders recorded of Buddha show a certain innocent and ungainly beauty more reminiscent of mythology than magic. It is said that from the body of the Buddha shown the rays of the sun. Buddha became a white elephant, and entered his mother's womb trumpeting loudly. Ten thousand worlds quaked at his birth and all musical instruments sounded on their own accord. His mother's mind had no sexual desire and did not suffer from exhaustion. When born, Buddha said, "The chief am I in all the world," and carried in his hand a medicine which healed all who sought it. Then he said to his mother, "Pray, mother, is there anything in the house? I want to give alms." His horse, twenty-seven feet long, neighed so loudly the gods muffled it and placed palms under its hooves. The devil threw rocks, live coals, or flaming mud at him, but they transformed into bouquets of flowers or celestial ointment. Elephants, horses, birds, and other animals gave forth melodious sounds when they saw him.[10]

It would be pedantic to say such stories, or those of Mithras, Ram, Osiris, or Guan Yin, are false, exactly. It would be churlish to deny their charm. What they are are poetic sketches of salvation. We want a savior who loves, heals, overcomes the forces of darkness, and acts in the natural world with that sagely mastery God intended for our race.

No one with sense would treat the miracles of Buddha and the Gospels as the same kind of thing. Even some Buddhist teachers frankly object to the attempt on the grounds that history is irrelevant to Buddhism. It does not matter whether these things happened to Buddha two and a half millennia ago. What matters is whether we today can reach a state of consciousness in which we experience the blooming of the flower, hear the trumpet of the elephant, or feel the healing touch of Buddha.

Asians and Westerners alike admire the goddess Guan Yin as a beautiful ideal of mercy, love and salvation. Hundreds of stories tell how she sacrifices herself to save anyone who calls on her name—like Jesus, many say—even during her incarnation in the person of several quasi-historical and divine or historical and quasi-divine figures, like the Dalai Lama.

Buddhists seldom, if ever, try to separate the Guan Yin of legend or invention from historical reality. Buddhist thinkers admit the history involved in these stories is dubious, and even make it work in their favor. "If we cling to the phenomena, we will lose the truth," argued the fifth century Buddhist philosopher Zhu Daosheng.[11] An American who wrote a book about Guan Yin said he thought he heard her idol speak, though he wasn't sure. "Thenceforth I was her devoted follower, which does not mean, however, that I quite believed in her."[12] And no wonder: one of the points of monism is precisely that separation between fact and myth, true, false, or useful, is impossible.

From a critical point of view, to compare such stories with the Gospels would be like comparing the *Journey to the West* with Lewis and Clark's field notes. The Gospels gives names, settings, dialogue, and plainly describe the doubts of opponents and of disciples. Not only do the Gospels set the life of Jesus set firmly in history—under a Roman politician we know, in villages archeologists uncover, judged by a priest whose bones have apparently been dug up. They also surround the dialogues and acts of Jesus with an atmosphere of questing and baffled uncertainty that it is hard to believe anyone would invent.

The New Age makes a virtue of "going out on a limb." Statues often show Buddha with his eyes closed, in the release of an enlightened death. But Jesus made even the blind see, because that is what God gave us eyes for.

(2) Miracles tend to be practical; Magic is often showy.

When I lived in Taiwan, God sometimes met my needs in remarkable ways. He provided a place to stay where I knew no one, home-cooked meals when I was lonely, money when I was broke, and as I related, a cheeseburger and a song as specific answers to two doubting, but specific, prayers. Another time I was out of money and worried about holes in the socks I had left. Just then I received a package in the mail, not from my mother, or aunt, but from the young woman who later became my wife: inside, I found several pairs of clean white socks. After we married, I asked why she sent such an unromantic gift. "I just felt like that's what I should send," she told me.

Like a thoughtful friend, God always sends those who trust him what they need. (Though of course, unlike our friends, he knows better than we do what that is.) Those gifts, practical as socks, never lose the elements of surprise and creativity.

The difference between God's ways and the ways of the gods was demonstrated in a way that has remained valid for 2850 years, since Elijah met the prophets of Baal on Mr. Carmel. In that contest, 400 magicians danced and cut themselves with swords for hours to awaken their god, until they collapsed, drained and disappointed. The man of God prayed for a minute, and got a simple, dramatic reply: fire from heaven. Elijah received what he needed, as directly as a man barbecuing chicken asking his neighbor across the hedge for a light. He didn't need to demonstrate his worthiness or commitment by violence against himself, artificial means unrelated to the task at hand.

I've watched young men in the spirit of those prophets parade idols through the streets and cutting their backs with swords. I've seen mediums sweat and shake as they waited for a spirit to come upon them. I've also seen Christian crowds "worked up" for miracles. I've watched preachers shout in peoples' faces and shake them to encourage ecstatic response. Once a Korean minister visited the tribal church in Taiwan in the dormitory of which I lived. When she led a special worship service, I watched her push worshippers over, apparently thinking the Holy Spirit wanted people on the floor but needed help getting them there. I seldom saw my tribal friends worship as boisterously as that evening—or laugh so hard as when they watched a video of the service later and saw how the visitor had hoodwinked them.

Tal Brooke, a Western disciple of the world-famous Indian guru, Sai Baba, related:

> "I became a collector of these miraculous accounts of young Sai Baba. If a fraction of them were true, I decided, then truly Baba was on a par with Krishna or Ram or, as Baba claimed, the returned Christ . . ."

> "Baba would perplex people. In the early days more than now, he would fall rigid and lie paralyzed and unconscious for days. He would leave his body. He would convulse. And once yearly he still insists on a particular ritual: he claims to grow in his stomach stone shiva lingams (sex organs) and then regurgitate them publicly. Large egg-shaped rocks . . . . Baba would assume illness, refusing help, then heal himself. He would 'take on' strokes and heart attacks. One of these episodes lasted six days."[13]

People often ask the wrong questions about such antics. "How did Baba do these things? Was it a trick? Or was it real?" Those are the wrong questions, because it is a silly show, whoever is putting it on. Miracles happen, as I think anyone who cares to can learn. But nothing more unlike miracles, especially the miracles of Jesus, can be imagined than such ugly vaudeville. Tal Brooke later became a Christian, and believed his former guru maintained real connections of an unpleasant sort with the spirit world. But from a Christian point of view, the exact nature and origin of the deception matters less than its obviously dysfunctional character. The question is not *how*, but *why*.

Time Magazine related how followers of the Thai Buddhist priest Phra Dhamachayo thought he had (in some sense) turned the sun into a "large crystal ball." Some astronomers believe they may have found one such body in close outer space: a small sun that collapsed on itself, forming a super-dense pack of carbon atoms, as if to make the old nursery rhyme come true. "Twinkle, twinkle little star, how I wonder what you are, up above the world so high, like a diamond in the sky." Only this diamond, big as the earth, doesn't twinkle, for it has lost power to give light. The sun is a practical as well as beautiful object as is: what would be gained by exchanging it for another distant piece of jewelry?

What if a statue of the Virgin Mary, which does not digest food or create wastes that need eliminating or require oxygen for metabolic functions, does bleed? Why sleep on beds of nails? Frankly, I don't see the point. Why walk on hot coals, call a cobra out of a basket, or bend spoons at a distance? If my son messes with the cutlery, I send him to his room. (Is that what Jesus was doing when he cast out spirits? Giving the devil "time out?") In one of his fantasies, C. S. Lewis described a devil as "the union of malice with something nearly childish" acting with "petty, indefatigable nagging as of a nasty little boy at preparatory school."[14] The God of the Bible speaks often in a "still, small voice" (I. Kings 19:17); the voice of these deities commend themselves to our reason in a shrill falsetto.

People through whom God does miracles are usually "down to earth" without needing to be pushed. They often show the same reluctance to advertise that Jesus displayed.

Jesus' works were simple and elegant: a word, a touch, an appeal to his Father. He didn't need potions or incantations or mantras and my impression is he seldom raised his voice. Philip Yancey notes, "When he did something truly miraculous, he tended to hush it up."[15] Paul, too, was practical and low-key when he performed miracles. In First Corinthians 15 he tells us prophecy and tongues should be exercised in an orderly manner. God is a Master Dramatist, but never a mere showman. Miracles are signs pointing us to him, not a laser-light show to make us OOOH and AAAH and throw dollars on the stage.

(3) Miracles enhance human dignity; Magic makes us more or less than human.

Miracles are verifiable and practical, while magic respects neither human reason, need, or taste. Nor does it respect human dignity.

I wonder how much that woman at the Light of Buddha Mountain had seen of Taoist spirituality. The occultism that goes by the name of Taoism in China, as distinct from the philosophy of Lao Zi and Zhuang Zi which it claims to be based upon, and some more principled sects, can be an ugly racket. More than two millennia ago, magicians taught China's cruelest emperor to murder thousands of innocent servants to lend him occult powers in the next world. The same logic continued to bilk the poor out of their earnings to assuage the potential anger of "dead relatives in hell," and old men to renew strength at the expense of young girls in places like Snake Alley.

What outsiders, including Buddhists, objected to in Master Lu—the exalted position, beautiful mansion, and alleged womanizing, are normal for the esoteric Buddhist tradition. (Tibetan Buddhists also eat meat, though as a Christian I have no objection to that.) The Indian founders of orders in Tibet all became wealthy from the gold they were paid to expound their doctrines. One of the most popular tales in Tibet, the popular and moving *Life of Milerepa*, has as its premise that only the rich can sit at the feet of a good guru. "I should get nothing from this Guru without a handsome present. . .nor from any other Guru for that matter, for such is the custom."[16] The great Atisa was offered the wealth of a nation as incentive to found his school.[17] So in a sense, Lu's self-acknowledged status as a "guru to the wealthy" was a traditional claim to esoteric orthodoxy. Use of semen and human skulls in rituals goes back to the beginning of esotericism in Hinduism. The ghastliness of some Tibetan idols in Lu's temple expresses the same thing: "The release from passion (being) achieved by means of passion is fundamental to tantric practice," as David Snellgrove pointed out.[18]

The Dalai Lama described possession in the Tibetan tradition. The chief Tibetan oracle is called a *kuten*. He channels a spirit being who is the essence of the heads of the five Buddha families to provide advice for the political leaders of Tibet. "The kuten's face transforms . . . puffing up to give him an altogether strange appearance, with bulging eyes and swollen cheeks. His breathing begins to shorten and he starts to hiss violently. Then, momentarily, his respiration stops." The oracle leaps around, making gestures "as if his body were made of rubber and driven by a coiled spring of enormous power," grabs a ritual sword, and bows to the Dalai Lama. Finally, he collapses into a "rigid and lifeless form."[19]

Buddhism, which began by denying the existence of a personal God, created a plethora of gods and goddesses whose worship lies at the center of most Buddhist practice today. Buddhism also borrowed, in later centuries, the frankly horrific cannibalistic rituals of tantric Hinduism. These schools taught that union of male and female was key to cosmic consciousness, sin a shortcut to salvation, and degradation of the body rendered a person fit for immortality. The new hybrid won Tibet through the machinations of Phadmasambhava, one of the heroes of Tibetan religious history, with whom Master Lu felt special kinship. Phadmasambhava conquered the savage demons of Tibet, then bound them as vassals and servants of Tibetan Buddhism, becoming the man-eating demons in True Buddha and other esoteric temples. The more appalling of these rituals were reinterpreted and toned down under influence from more orthodox Mahayana circles. But when a counselor to Tibetan political leaders hisses like a viper, one wonders who, in that confrontation between Phadmasambhava and the demons, really got the upper hand.

Roger Kamenetz noted that the man who served as Kuten "appeared somewhat haggard for his age." In reply to an inquiry, his guide noted how stressful the ordeal was. "He feels a great deal of painful energy in his body, then has no memory at all. When he's finished, he passes out and after that for several hours he has a great deal of pain in the chest."[20]

All of this is in keeping with spirit medium-ship in the East Asian tradition. As I realized when I saw videos of the two in succession, possession of the Tibetan *kuten* and the Chinese *tang ki* looks remarkably similar. Jordan describes how *tang ki* "jump around or have various kinds of convulsions" during possession, some vomiting or salivating.[21] Mediums cut their tongues and smear a paper with the blood.

"When it is noticed he is beginning to appear drowsy, a bench is set before the family altar, and here he seats himself, leaning over the table, as his shirt is removed. Shortly, perhaps within five or six minutes, he begins to shake . . . To this is added an occasional belch or gasp. Within minutes he is shaking violently and begins drumming his fingers hard and rhythmically on the table. Suddenly he breaks into loud, high-pitched, unintelligible 'gods' language, which turns into halting Hokkienese."

The word *tang ki* itself, which means "divining youth," derives not from the age of the medium, but from the expectation that his life will be short. "During the time he is in trance, his own personality ceases to exist and he becomes the tool of his god . . . the *tang ki* is not a free man." At special public ceremonies the medium demonstrates the reality of possession by hitting himself on the back or forehead with a ball of nails, a sword, the saw of a swordfish, or an ax. Jordan notes, "How many times was I told of the *tang ki* who was saved from splitting his head with an ax" when a bystander pushed his arm as the ax fell so "he only lost an ear?"

What is the difference between magic and miracles? Jesus *healed* ears, for one thing.

Jordan quoted the reaction of the Norwegian missionary Reichelt to similar performances in China a hundred years ago. Reichelt was a remarkably open-minded Lutheran who admired Mahayana Buddhism. But he was also a man with a heart, and called such spirit possessions "among the most unpleasant things one sees in China." What is even more unpleasant to me is the show of scientific tolerance and utter lack of compassion with which Jordan responded. "It is not clear how unpleasant they are to the Chinese. Their bloody exploits are recounted years after with an enthusiasm that does not altogether suggest revulsion." No doubt. And no doubt Romans engaged in enthusiastic "post mortems" after watching men ripped to pieces by lions in the Coliseum, until a Christian monk interrupted the fun by being ripped to shreds in protest. It is unfortunate that the objectivity of modern social science allows some scholars to return to a state of Stoic tranquility in the face of inhumanity.

Some non-Christian observers have claimed that channelers are doing the same thing the prophets of the Bible once did. One of the Jewish rabbis who went to Tibet, Zalman Schachter, was reminded of the experience of Daniel. After all, Daniel also lost his strength on meeting the angel of God, and was overwhelmed physically by his experience.

It is difficult to imagine two experiences more different that that of the *kuten* or *tang ki* and the Old Testament prophet. They differ in at least five ways. First, Daniel remained not only conscious, but intensely himself, throughout his experience. Second, Daniel felt an awareness of personal and collective short-comings. This consciousness is part of almost every encounter with the Holy Spirit or angels in the Bible. Third, the angel spoke *to* Daniel, not *through* him. Humans in the Bible who are given supernatural tongues or revelations are able to speak or not speak as they choose: "the spirits of the prophets are in subjection to the prophets" (1 Cor.14:32). God respects the human will; the Holy Spirit is no body-snatcher. Fourth, the prophets not only remember their encounters with God, they never forget them: one can see the profound impression Paul's encounter with Christ made on him, for example, when he repeats the account of the meeting on three different occasions in the New Testament.

Fifth, as I noted earlier, encounters with God enhance our humanity, while encounters with demons, detract from it. The spirit medium tradition is represented in the Bible by the priests of Baal, who also worked themselves into a frenzy, jumped around and cut themselves. Elijah, by contrast, prayed and waited with dignity for God's reply.

The animal noises the Dalai Lama mentioned are familiar to anyone who has studied spirit possession among Chinese folk religions. It is true, this phenomena has also been noticed in some "Christian" revivals. But in the Bible, the spirit of God never makes a person talk like an animal. The Holy Spirit does not degrade, but rather enhances, the intellect: on one occasion making a donkey talk like a human being, and on others allowing people to speak human languages they had never studied. Supernatural abilities, in the Bible, are called "spiritual gifts," because God adds to, rather than detracting from, our humanity.

We have also seen not only that many occultists don a cloak of religion to degrade followers sexually. Esoteric theory seems to explicitly justify and prepare people for such exploitation in several ways. It denigrates normal sexuality, putting it on a par with the grossest perversions. It requires disciples to obey the guru in all things. It teaches "consort practice." And it allows the Master who has transcended lower levels of reality freedom to do anything. So it should not be surprising that so many esoteric gurus have treated their followers in a beastly manner.

I also met or knew of three people in Taiwan who were suicidal after "hearing voices" of spirits, and I do not think this is a rare symptom in occult practice.

I have also mentioned the popularity of drugs in some such circles. Hallucinogens lend users a feeling of omnipotence, a lowering of ego boundaries that leads to a sense of being "at one with the universe." But if the God who created the human brain wanted to impart a message to humanity, it seems unlikely he would do so by means of drugs which corrode and destroy his creation! We should be suspicious when we are given the same picture of God by people who erase boundaries and attain a feeling of oneness with God by mystics who deny reason, and by drug addicts who destroy reason.

248   PART IV: THE TRUTH

"Be as Gods"

Are we mere animals? Or are we, on the other hand, gods?

Gentle waves lapped against the California coast on a warm and romantic evening. A man and woman walked along the sandy shore. They did not hold hands however or talk about love. They had more important issues to discuss.

"Say it!" Said the man. "Go ahead and say it!"

"I am God."

"Say it again!"

"I am God! I am God!"

Thus Shirley MacLaine declared herself one with the essence of all things on national television. The divine status Master Lu enjoys in the True Buddha school is no aberration: for the master, all things are permissible, because he has overcome the dualistic illusion of a distinction between himself and external reality. The Buddha himself is presented in similar terms in some early sutras, as for example the earlier quotation in which he said, "There is no master for me . . . I have overcome all and am omniscient."

In the Guhyasamaja Tantra, the same omnipotence is attached to one's teacher, for much the same reason:

> "All the Buddhas replied: 'Son of a good family, (your Vajra teacher) is to be regarded by all Buddhas and all Bodhisattvas as the Vajra of the Thought of Enlightenment. And why so? The Teacher and the Thought of Enlightenment Are the same and inseparable . . . He is the Father of all us Buddhas, the mother of all us Buddhas, in that he is the Teacher of all us Buddhas . . . the merit of a single pore of the Teacher is worth more than the heap of merit of . . . the Buddhas of the ten directions . . . the Thought of Enlightenment is . . . the repository of omniscient wisdom."

Humility has been defined as "being willing to be known for who you are," so if that truly is who Buddha was, one cannot blame him for saying it. (If he did.) Yet humility also involves a willingness to yield to the authority of those greater, to identify with the weak, and take an interest in others. The works of God lift up the humble and humble the proud, making all of us more human even as we draw near to the divine. The prophets, in the midst of unearthly visions, are continually reminding us of our prosaic duties to widows, orphans, the poor, and strangers.

This combination of unusual humanity with unpretentious supernatural powers is what so bewilders the unbelieving critic who tries to understand Jesus. Jesus made claims about himself that, in their own context, are more astounding than those of Master Lu. Yet the title he used of himself most often was Son of Man. His miracles challenged and humanized his disciples, enriching, healing, feeding, comforting, and setting free those bound by Satan. He washed his disciples' feet, preached to the poor, touched beggars and outcasts, and died on a rough wooden cross. Around the world, one meets men and women working in the name of Jesus to redeem prostitutes, drug addicts, lepers and orphans to full humanity.

Few of the servants of God I have met seem in danger of mistaking their efforts for the work of the "Buddha within" or "Christ consciousness." Perhaps this is because one part "inspiration" seldom comes unmixed with ninety-nine parts "perspiration," as Thomas Edison put it. There is something about studying languages, dealing with bureaucrats and gangsters, killing cockroaches and cleaning up vomit on the floor that keeps a disciple's head from swelling. Sometimes inspiration is mixed with blood, too: as C. S. Lewis noted, martyrdoms and miracles tend to occupy the same periods of history. Miracles come so often in the context of serving, worship, and suffering that the believer can learn humility even while he "co-labors" with God. For this reason it may be perilous to feed too heavily from the sidelines on a diet of triumphalism and signs and wonders.

The Creator formed the stomach to use hydrochloric acid without digesting itself. He made the cobra safe from the prick of its own venom. Like tissues that protect God's creatures from the power he puts within them, humility is the membrane that allows a person to do the works of God without getting hurt.

(4) Miracles point to God; Magic points elsewhere.

I think again of my trip to Hawaiian Volcanoes National Park. Half a mile past the end of the road magma poured into the sea. One or two hundred tourists from around the world gathered on black lava cliffs above a black sand surf and watched. At first we could see only steam, but as it grew darker the glow of the lava itself became steadily more visible. Hours passed as we stared, silently watching without commercial interruption. "Awesome!" I overhead one man say to a friend. "Did I say this was awesome?" "Only about five hundred times," his friend answered. "Awesome," the first repeated for the five-hundred-and-first time. Another stranger turned to me in wonder and said, "God is still creating."

Miracles are part of God's ongoing creation, too, and they also move people to spontaneous praise.

A miracle is like a rainbow, I have said. After a period of pain and suffering, at a dark moment light from heaven breaks through the clouds, revealing God's purity in complementary shades. In works of healing, exorcism, words of knowledge, prophecy, and so on, Christ shows his character as Creator, Wisdom, Logos, Suffering Servant, Almighty God. As in Job, God's glory revealed in miracles (directly or through witnesses), in nature, or in awareness of his presence at other times, makes us drop our mouths open and stare. Unlike at the moment of *satori*, or enlightenment, we laugh not to see that all is one, but to see that all is not one. Someone is up there, and aware of us. We are cleansed in a bath of humility and fear of the Lord.

If miracles are like a rainbow, magic can be like a tornado: dirty, noisy, dangerous, and in some ways neither natural nor supernatural. Cars levitate, spoons are bent by invisible forces, people fly in the sky with no direction.

The autobiography of the supposedly "Christ-like" Indian guru Yogananda subtly illustrates the centrifugal and antiChrist-like character of magic. Yogananda relates that his first two miracles were done out of sibling spite. In the first instance, his sister Uma was helping him with his homework and complained of a boil. He announced that a boil would also appear at a particular spot on his own arm. When she didn't believe him, he became angry. "By the power of will in me, I say that tomorrow I shall have a fairly large boil in this exact place on my arm; and *your* boil shall swell to twice its present size!" For the second miracle, Yogananda prayed to Kali to steal two kites from a neighbor.[22]

A few points can be noted from these rather typical occult episodes, or lies, as the case may be. First, in them Yogananda acted like the petulant and silly Jesus child of the apocrypha—but unlike the Jesus of the historic Gospels. Second, psychiatrists tell us that a child's first memories are often revealing. Yogananda, in some of his earliest recorded memories, portrays himself as liar and thief who works magic out of pride. Even more revealing is Yogananda's emphasis on the power of will. The "force" was with him, and it was up to him whether he used "it" for good or ill. Whatever these powers might be, and whether he ultimately chose to use them for good or evil, it appears their purpose was to glorify Yogananda, not his Creator.

In *Out on a Limb* one of Shirley MacLaine's friends explained that sometimes "Spiritual entities use human beings to channel messages." The beings Shirley met seemed concerned for her spiritual development. MacLaine sometimes doubted the existence of her own friendly guiding spirit, "Mayan," but never its chivalrous intentions. But what she ultimately learned through years of such experiences was that "the only person you ever make love to is yourself." This seems a pathetic and lonely outlook for a person who has been so free with the door to her bedroom and her soul.

To return for a moment to an earlier point: where are the gods of pre-Christian Europe? Was Mayan acquainted with the cosmic entities for whom the Mayan high priests bathed pyramids in blood? Have those spirits all retired or been reincarnated? Or enrolled in the devil's witness-protection program, changed their names, and learned a new dialect?

One should never underestimate the power of language. Tal Brooke suggested:

"What the cosmic circuit needed was an Enlightened master from the East, one who was convincingly in a state of super consciousness, teamed up with a Western adept who would bridge the gap and translate all of the concepts into colloquial, hip, avant-garde, and semi-scientific language."[23]

Donald Waters, follower of the Hindu guru Swami Kriyananda and a well-established New Age leader in his own right, was one who found such semantics attractive:

"And then I came upon excerpts from the Hindu teachings—a few pages only, but what a revelation! Here the emphasis was on cosmic realities. God was described as Infinite Consciousness; man, as a manifestation of that consciousness. Why, this was the very concept I myself had worked out . . . Man's ultimate goal, according to these writings, is to experience that divine reality as his true self. But, how scientific! What infinite promise!"

As for the Bible, it "seemed too anthropomorphic for my tastes, steeped as I was in the scientific view of reality." What Waters shared with Western social scientists was a taste not for the inductive method or rigorous testing of theories, I think, but for vague Greek polysyllables. What is "infinite consciousness?" Is it a person, thing, or idea? Does it think, watch, notice, get angry, laugh? If it is conscious and infinite, why not call it God? Or is that word too short and meaningful? If Infinite Consciousness does not notice things around it, is not aware of the difference between right and wrong, or between itself and others, why call it consciousness? And what does it mean to be a "manifestation" of such a consciousness? If Waters meant that a conscious being of infinite power is trying to show himself through men and women, that is what the Bible says also, with the qualification that God is good and none of us reflect that goodness very well. Why does this statement become more scientific by substituting longer words, and ignoring flaws in that manifestation which can be verified in five minutes by walking down the street?

Possession is Nine-Tenths of the Law

Rajneesh soothed,

"Don't worry about what fills you or enters you. Let it happen. Surrender. Lose your identity forever."[24]

Elliot Miller, a Californian who became involved with the New Age movement during the hippie era, felt as he advanced in occult studies that he was gaining real, verifiable psychic powers. He began to experience unity with "God," but felt misgivings. Later he described one point of crisis in his spiritual pilgrimage:

"Suddenly, my euphoria turned to alarm. I strongly sensed that my soul was in great danger, as though something evil was trying to consume me. I began to resist the entity taking possession of me, but then the thought crossed my mind: 'This is just your ego putting up its last fight for survival. God is good! He wouldn't do anything to hurt you.' Satisfied with this explanation, I yielded again. The negative sensation was now gone, and it began to feel as though I was fading out and something else was moving into my place."[25]

Tal Brooke studied the lives of several famous Hindu gurus. He noted,

"Curiously, when the heavy hitting gurus, the Riders, emerged from the Explosion, close associates and family usually used the term 'possession.'"[26]

The precise nature of the psychic disturbance involved in such stories may be of secondary importance. I think it was C. S. Lewis who called the devil the "spirit of unreality." Some might ascribe these phenomena to strange psychosis, mass suggestion, or some other illusion. I suppose it might be possible to explain almost all I have personally seen, and most of what I have heard from eyewitnesses, by some social or psychological formula like these, or others suggested by Durkheim, Marx, or Freud. There remains a bit I am not sure I could explain that way. But the Bible does not encourage us to concern ourselves about the precise relationship between human and demonic states of consciousness. The emphasis is rather on warning us away from such things. In doing so, it seems clear that the Holy Spirit has our best interests in mind. What is painfully obvious is that, in a world without boundaries or ultimate authority, spiritual tourists can get very lost indeed.

(5) Miracles come in response to requests; Magic to demands

Magic can be seen as an attempt to force the universe's (or God's) hand. This may be why magic often involves masochism, the deliberate infliction of pain and injury on one's self, or sadism, the infliction of injury on others. One is trying to manipulate God, as a child bends parents to his will by shutting himself in his room or refusing a favorite desert. And, indeed, those who gravitate to such exploitative cults do tend to be products of abusive or neglectful parentage.

The Bible forbids us to deliberately harm ourselves. The prophets waged a struggle of many centuries against the most ghastly expressions of this impulse, burning children to death, and offering daughters to fertility cults. In this struggle, revolutionary religions—Islam, Marxism, the Tai Ping revolution— often served as allies to Christianity.

Nevertheless, new forms of the same phenomena have a way of sneaking in under new guises, after the High Noon of paganism has passed: witch trials, purges, struggle sessions, or other attempts to co-opt God or the gods through the ritual shedding of innocent blood. Pogroms against Jews were launched in concert with crusades against Arabs—propitiation of the gods of war by sacrifice of a less-desirable member of one's own society. Russian communists raised ritual sacrifice to a science, giving officials a quota, a percentage of the population that must by hypothesis be counter-revolutionary. Psychologists note a similar insidious impulse at work within families. Probably a great deal of child abuse can be explained as a subconscious ritual attempt to manipulate the forces of the universe.

Christians also sometimes try to manipulate God, shouting, pushing, using "In the name of Jesus" as a mantra, working themselves into a psychological state so as to force an answer through the sweat on our brow or a loud voice. The Bible encourages honest emotion in prayer. "Let your petitions be made known before God" (Phil. 4:6). But he is Master, and cannot be bought.

Many are desperate for a touch of magic. It is comforting to interpret all supernatural events as equal, whether equally false, to keep to a materialistic interpretation of life, or equally true, to satisfy the tenets of democracy or monism. Many Christians believe miracles and magic must be different on principle, because they arise from different sources. Most non-Christians assume, also on principle, they can't be different because all phenomena ultimately arise from the same source.

I have attempted to show, not on theological grounds, but on empirical, why supernatural events do not all belong to the same category. When we rely not on principle but observation, miracles and magic appear even more different from each other than either are from "normal" experience. Miracles are different because they are more human and more real than ordinary life—"supernatural." Magic is less human and less real—"sub-natural."

I don't want to be too dogmatic. No mortal is an "expert" on God. But from what I have observed, the supernatural divides itself into two fairly clear categories. I don't claim these categories correspond strictly to "Christian" and "non-Christian," in fact, the Bible itself leads us to expect a more complex picture. The devil, according to Paul, masquerades as an "angel of light" (2.Cor. 11:14). Nor do I suggest a simple contrast between "genuine" and "apparent" supernatural events. Most magic may be based on sleight of hand, will to believe, or coincidence: on this point, there is more room for agreement between Christianity and anthropology than is sometimes recognized by either.

Nor am I concerned to prove that true miracles never occur outside the Christian tradition. In this as in other regards, it seems to me the Biblical view of the supernatural is uniquely subtle and true to life. So far as I know, the Bible never explicitly rules out the possibility that God may work through people outside the Judeo-Christian tradition out of hand. And it does allow—even insists—that not all miracles in the orthodox lineage will bare the light of criticism. "Many will come in my name, saying, 'I am the Christ,' and mislead many." "False Messiahs and false prophets will arise and show great signs and wonders to mislead, if possible, even the elect" (Matt. 24: 5, 24). But in general the Bible describes a contrast between "prophets of Baal," who may have spiritual powers or may be faking it (a question of lesser importance, since in both cases they show themselves heirs to the "father of lies"), and true messengers of God. Miracles are at the center of Biblical revelation. Yet the Bible teaches us to be aware of charlatans, human and demonic. Christianity is in this regard both more broad-minded and more true to the range of human experience than skepticism.

The theologies of Master Lu or Hong Xiuquan, like the sacred scroll literature of China, various letters from heaven in nineteenth century America, modern channeled messages such as *Conversations with God* and *A Course in Miracles,* are clearly products of their respective times and social origins. If they were hand-written by the devil, it is strange the devil could not come up with anything worse. If they came from an angel, it is even stranger that an angel could not come up with anything better. I conclude, therefore, that such revelations emerge from the minds of men and women.

Often "revealed" religions looks like a hodge-podge of diverse influences with which the spirit medium has come into contact. The God of Mohammed, as has often been pointed out, shows the virtues and vices of Arabia. Mohammed borrowed stories and ritual eclectically from the Jewish Scriptures, native Arab gods, and the Persians. The *Book of Mormon,* which purports to translate a story from "Reformed Egyptian" about events which occurred in South America, derived even its grammar (inaccurately) from the King James Version of the Bible. Joseph Smith's later revelations, in the eclectic style of such gurus, showed the influence of Native American stories, frontier legend, and Masonry. Hong Xiuquan's religion was a brilliant though erratic attempt to syncretize Christian theology, Confucianism, and Chinese folk beliefs, and almost everything in his visions appeared to come from one or the other of these three. Modern cults add new elements to the mix: no new sect is complete without a generous helping of scientism, though similar sects have existed for thousands of years without the gods bringing the subject up before. In many cases (as with Smith, Mohammed, and Hong) the divine spirit seems suspiciously concerned for the sexual and financial prosperity of the cult leader. All of this, I think, suggests a human rather than divine origin for most alleged messages from the other world.

The teachings of Jesus did not come down out of the sky from a rocketship, but reveal a more subtle and intriguing dialectic with the spiritual traditions of humanity. Jesus both affirms and negates the ideals of Taoism, Buddhism,

Marxism, Hinduism, and radical Feminism. Jesus stated the affirmation in the words, "I did not come to annul the Law and the Prophets, but to complete them" (Matt. 5:17). He stated the negation when he told his disciples "take up your cross and follow me." But in talking about the cross, he was not only calling each of us to give up our ideals, but also affirming a great mystery within each tradition.

We began this story in the cave of Plato, and saw how the Gospel acted as a door through which myth entered and transformed history. Later we saw Jesus as the world's greatest prophet of a liberating and empowering feminism. Then we looked at human spiritual ideals that resemble a sketch of Jesus. In chapter nine, we saw how the idea of a good and just Creator, a "Parent" of humankind, is universal. At the same time, something within us wants to keep him at a distance; and we feel the alienation of distance or of crossed purposes.

Let us now move outdoors, and look at a campfire where representatives of the religions of man gather, while diverse and conflicting strands of tradition come together on the cross.

The death of Jesus for the sin of the world, and his resurrection the third day, is the heart of the Christian message. It is also, one would think, the most peculiar teaching of the faith. The cross is the universal symbol of Christianity. Paul called it "a stumbling block to the Jews, foolishness to the Greeks." Surveying the attitudes of the world's major spiritual traditions, *Newsweek's* perceptive religion editor, Kenneth Woodward, observed that while other religions saw Jesus as a fulfillment of their ideals, they found the cross a stumbling block:

> "Nothing shows the difference between the Jesus and the Buddha better than the way that each died. The Buddha's death was serene and controlled—a calm passing out of his final rebirth, like the extinction of a flame. Jesus, on the other hand, suffers an agonizing death on the cross, abandoned by God but obedient to his will. Clearly the cross is what separates the Christ of Christianity from every other Jesus. In Judaism there is no precedent for a Messiah who dies, much less as a criminal as Jesus did. In Islam, the story of Jesus' death is rejected as an affront to Allah himself. Hindus can accept only a Jesus who passes into peaceful samadhi, a yogi who escapes the degradation of death . . . Thus the idea that Jesus can serve as a bridge uniting the world's religions is inviting but may be ultimately impossible. A mystery to Christians themselves, Jesus remains what he has always been, a sign of contradiction."[27]

In chapter five, we saw that Asian tribal peoples, the Chinese, as well as the Jews, did have a concept of ritual sacrifice for the propitiation of sins. Now we will see in more detail that the cross is in fact a bridge, not only between heaven and earth, but also between East and West.

In a sense, it is not surprising that people of other religions should find the cross a "sign of contradiction," though. Jesus' own disciples often expressed such doubts.

I wonder what they talked about that final evening over supper, when their Master sprung the ultimate surprise on them. He had brought it up before, but never with such immediacy. Tonight he would be betrayed. One of them would be in on the conspiracy. (Here's a twist on the typical murder mystery: the victim announcing the plot to the suspects before the crime occurs!) The blood he shed, symbolized by the wine in their cups, would be "for the remission of your sins." Furthermore (an even more unusual twist), that would not be the end of the story. The third day he would come to life again . . .

Did they discuss the price of psychiatric services in the Greater Jerusalem area? Did they stare daggers at one another and break into suspicious factions as in Da Vinci's famous painting of the Last Supper? Or did they feel too bewildered and fatigued by the triumph, confrontation, and mounting sense of peril of those days, added to these unsettling revelations one after the other, to really grasp what he was saying? After a full holiday meal, did a few begin to nod off even in the dining room?

What on earth did he mean? Why should the Messiah die? What about his miraculous powers? How could God allow such a thing to happen, and on Passover, of all times, a holiday celebrating God's deliverance? Where is Yahweh when we need him most?

Judas went out to make some purchase or other. The dinner wound down, and the rest of the company spilled outside, perhaps feeling their spirits revive a little in the cool night air. It was spring, and the budding of olive flowers filled the air as they made their way to the Mount of Olives. How could anything bad happen on such a night?

Then, as they were fighting to stay awake, the police arrived, Judas at their head, and took their teacher. The disciples ran down dark paths to escape. Two or three checked themselves in flight, hid in the shadow of the olives, then followed the arrest party at a cautious distance. One stopped outside of the high priest's courtyard and warmed his hands by a fire. I imagine the conversation that greeted him as something above the limitations of time and geography. Around the fire he found people from past, present, and future, and from nations around the world; a small selection of humanity not that different from himself.

---

[1] Rudolf G. Wagner, *Reenacting the Heavenly Vision*, 1982, p.103

[2] Ibid., p.12

[3] Tam Wailun, University of Hong Kong Department of Religion, personal communication, April, 1998

[4] Jordan, *Gods, Ghosts, and Ancestors*, 1972, p. 70-75. Jordan expresses doubt this fear is genuine, but given the horror stories he himself relates, it seems natural enough.

[5] Lu Sheng-yen, *Encounters With the World of Spirits*, 1995, p. 9

[6] He still had trouble sleeping, however. He told me he woke up at midnight and a *gui*, devil or ghost, was at the door. He interpreted this visitation as a test of faith, and hoped to overcome it through further meditation.

[7] Master Ching Hai, *News* No. 19, 1991, p.76

[8] *Protestant Christian Evidences*, Moody Press, 1953, p. 125

[9] Lu Sheng-yen, *Sariras—Buddhist Relics Among Executed Prisoners*, 1995, p. 5-6

[10] Kametani Uenu and Ohori Michihata, *Buddhist Priests Choose Christ*

[11] C. N. Tay, *Kuan-Yin: The Cult of Half Asia*, Tsai Tuan Fa Ren Hui Lu Publishing, 1987, p.5

[12] John Eaton Calthorpe Blofeld, *Bodhisattva of Compassion: The Mystical Tradition of Kuan Yin*

[13] Tal Brooke, *Riders of the Cosmic Circuit*, Lion Publishing, 1986, p. 25

[14] C. S. Lewis, *Perelandria*, Macmillan Publishing, 1944, p.123

[15] Philip Yancey, *The Jesus I Never Knew*, Zondervan, 1995, p. 23

[16] Ras Chun, *Life of Milerepa*, p.63

[17] See Hubert Decleer, *Atisa's Journey to Tibet*, in *Religions of Tibet in Practice*, Donald Lopez, editor, 1997

[18] David Snellgrove, *Indo-European Buddhism: Indian Buddhists and Their Tibetan Successors*, 1987, p.190

[19] Roger Kamenetz, *The Jew in the Lotus*, Harper San Francisco, 1994, p. 178

[20] Ibid., p. 178

[21] V. Jordan, *Gods, Ghosts, and Ancestors*, University of California Press. Details here are from chapter four.

[22] Paramhansa Yogananda, *Autobiography of a Yogi*, chapter 1, available on-line at www.crystalclarity.com/yogananda

[23] Tal Brooke, *Riders of the Cosmic Circuit*, Lion Publishing, 1986

[24] *Riders of the Cosmic Circuit*, p.

[25] Elliot Miller *A Crash Course on the New Age Movement*, Baker Publishing, 1989, p. 220

[26] *Riders of the Cosmic Circuit*

[27] Kenneth Woodward, *The Other Jesus, Newsweek*, March 27, 2000

CHAPTER 12

The Bonfire

"DO YOU know what the cross means to us?"

The cross? What did it mean? It was a symbol of the enemy's stranglehold over Israel. It meant being sprawled out in public by the Romans like a pig in a *goyim* butcher shop. It was a sign that said, "We can do this to you if you step out of line."

I picked up a twig and threw it in the heart of the flames. Whether joining to make the night pass or freeze the moment and keep the next day from dawning, or just to get warm, I'm not sure. The fire created a world of its own, and in the sparks that danced out of it I looked for anonymity, or warmth to melt the ice my heart seemed to have become.

The speaker was not one of the twelve (though there were about a dozen around the fire), nor one of the seventy. I think I had seen one or two of the others before. I noticed one with a rough woven tunic and sheepskin mantle like a shepherd, piercing eyes and a black beard sprinkled with white, like a patriarch out of the past, in shadows to my left. The rest appeared to be foreigners. Some were dark-skinned, others light-skinned; it was hard to be sure in the firelight. Long, flowing robes, bare chests, jewelry. A few women. Even on the darkest evening of my life, I felt a touch of anger. When did Passover become a Gentile holiday?

"I am a Seljuk Turk who grew up slave of the Emir's oldest son in Ghazni. My father helped conquer and rule Jerusalem, so from childhood I knew something about warfare. But these Franj were like no warriors we had never seen.

Coming down like locust from Antioch, they despoiled even the villages of the Rum, their Bynzantine fellow believers; and we quickly learned not to expect mercy. After they took Jerusalem, not only did they slaughter the inhabitants, they tortured the Greek Nazarenes in the city. For what? To learn where this symbol of death, this cross, that they idolized as a holy relic, had been hidden."

"You understand," he continued, "to us there was nothing holy about the cross. On the contrary, it meant everything noxious and unclean. The smell of bacon. Blooded swords. Fire and death."

We agreed on that, I thought. *The cross was nothing but a slap in the face of the Lord, a terror that subdued hope.*

Guards passed and the speaker fell silent. With crowds of patriotic Jews in town, the garrison had been beefed up with legions off the Egyptian campaign; tough customers. They passed, and then Ali, as he said his name was, spoke again.

"While we do not believe in the cross, we do believe Jesus was a great prophet. All my life I have read our holy book, and it speaks of him many times. It says he healed the sick and raised the dead. I wanted to see him and hear the Gospel that he preached."

"But then I saw the crosses above Jerusalem, where his enemies want to take him now. A true prophet would not die such a death. We have been taught that Allah will rescue him. But I am afraid. Allah did not save us when the Franj sacked Jerusalem. Will he save his anointed? And if not, who can hope for salvation?"

A few months ago, when he was followed by crowds of thousands who hung on his words, they wouldn't have dared to make a move, I thought. We all hoped he would overthrow the Romans and set up a Jewish state. That's where I'd seen these people! These foreigners were among the crowds in Galilee! When did they leave? When Jesus started talking about "eating his body" and "drinking his blood."

And wasn't that what Jesus was talking about tonight, too?

A tall, aristocratic man with deep eyes began to speak.

"My name is Satya. In my country, our feelings about Christians are more mixed. Many of us believe we have potential to be higher than the gods. But each of us is heaping up a debt that we repay over millions of lifetimes. Our teachers tell us how to leave this world of illusion and sorrow and enter a realm of bliss free of pain, sadness, and doubt. But when I walk the streets of our cities, it is hard to fend off doubts. I see old ladies bent with rheumatism till they are small enough to beg from the shadow of an umbrella on the ground. I see young women raising children in concrete pipes. Meditation did not make these visions go away. We have seen many Christians working to help people like that. We have also seen the good influence of Jesus on the lives of Hindus like Mohandas Gandhi."

"But even Gandhi admitted that he had a grudge against Christianity as a youth. He heard a missionary abusing the Hindu gods on the street corner.

Hinduism is a religion of tolerance: we believe that all paths lead to God, so such intolerance was most unpleasant. When a well-known Hindu converted, he was induced to eat beef and wear English clothing. Gandhi was offended and disgusted."

Satya faltered and spoke in a low voice, that I had to strain to hear above the crackle of the fire.

"I did not come to learn about English religion. I came to solve a deep riddle from our sacred books that I think may concern this man." He fell silent.

"I know what you are saying about mixed feelings, brother."

A short man stood up, dark, but with a less rounded nose than a Numibian, and a long scar down his left cheek.

"I am a Dani from Irian Jaya.[1] Muslims scold us, 'Why don't you believe in the true God?' Tourists come from around the world, and some of them scold us, too. 'You've sold out to the West. You have forsaken the way of your ancestors and the heritage of the jungle.'

"They fly in on 747s with video cameras and lap-top computers, and want us to pose in penis gourds and grass skirts so they can tell their friends back home about their adventure. He never treated people—beggars, politicians, soldiers, poor women—as cultural relics, photo props, slaves—he treated them as people. So did the missionaries. That's one reason we listened to them. Not the main reason, though."

"We were not sure the white man was human at first. Some people thought his skin was inside-out. Others said he had died and was baked white by cremation fires! We laughed when he tried to learn our language, though; he talked like a parrot with a cold."

"Then one day he opened his book and repeated the words of our ancestors. Just a few words, and they changed our world—from the inside. 'We have come to bring you *ki wone!*'"

"'Ki Wone.' *The words of life!*"

"I once took a long journey with my cousin. We hiked all day in the rain through thick trees. As we climbed higher, the wind grew colder, all day long. Then, suddenly, we were at the top. The rains stopped. The clouds parted, and below us was a beautiful valley, a land of emerald lit by the sun."

"It was like that when he spoke those words."

"Our ancestors told us, 'When immortality returns to mankind, those who learn its secret first will come over the mountains, and tell you that secret, the words of life. Their skins will be white, because they are constantly being renewed like the skin of a snake. Be sure you listen to them when they come, otherwise *nabelankabelon*—"my-skin-your-skin," immortality—will pass you by.'"

"The missionary's skin was white. He was from beyond the mountains.

When he told us he had come to bring *"Ki wone,"* it was like the rain suddenly stopped and a new world opened before us."

The speaker paused and looked around at each of us.

"We didn't follow a star or the words of any papers to Palestine. We followed the promises of our ancestors. But now he who brought *ki wone* is on trial for his life."

Words of life. I had said those words to him myself! He picked us as his chief disciples, so I figured he wanted a little fisherman's advice. Be careful what you say, I told him. These people wanted a winner. All this talk about drinking blood and carrying crosses was no way to start a ministry. And why be so pessimistic? With his powers, why should things end so badly? I have a thick skin; a fisherman needs one. But I could still feel the sting of his retort. "Get behind me, Satan!" But then when people started walking out, he asked us, "Are you leaving too?" "Where would we go?" I said. "You have the words of life."

It suddenly struck me. He had been winnowing his followers! That's what the Lord said to Gideon, too, "Let the others go." As if, for the work he was doing, too many were an encumbrance. We twelve had been chosen, selected from among the people, as our forefathers from among the nations, or as the army of Gideon from among Israel.

The crackling of the fire settled to an occasional pop and flurry of sparks. I realized I had been sitting on a knot, and shifted my legs. No one seemed to be looking for me. An old man with an intense expression in his eyes, light brown skin, a bald head, and a wispy white beard, had been stirring the fire with a long stick, as if doodling. When a bit of flame sprang up, he cast the stick in the middle, gathered some small branches and threw them in the center of the embers. Sparks leaped up, and flame sprang up to embrace the logs. He spoke gently, as if we were sitting by a meandering brook talking about a frog hunt.

"Our ideal was the fisherman. A poet of my country wrote of a retired magistrate who played the zither in the woods, his 'heart untouched by worldly cares.' 'You ask about the nature of success and failure: from the river, a fisherman's song drifts to shore.'"[2]

He looked at me with a smile. I knew I'd seen him before!

"Not a fisher of men who cast his net to save the world. We wrote poems about fisherman who did not even bate his hooks. Who knew the value of the moment lay in itself. Joy was the journey not the goal," the old man continued.

"Yet our teacher Lao Zi also spoke of a fisherman who would catch more than fish. 'The nets of heaven are vast, and though thin, they lose nothing.'"[3] Success is inversely proportional to the force expended to achieve it, that is. He who had the true Way would change the world through weakness."

"He was not bound by possessions. He had no program, money, or ambition. To illustrate a point on finances, he borrowed a coin. To pay taxes, he sent a disciple fishing. At each moment he was natural and human, yet also master of men, spirits, and storms. Even sickness obeyed."

"Time was no more his master than money or the will of man. He engaged in conversation with anyone who stopped him—prostitute, cripple, or mandarin. Without force, money, or trick, he seemed in control of each encounter. When a blind man called out, he asked, 'What do you want me to do?' 'Act without striving, and accomplish all things.' Just so, sleeping in fishing boats, talking with beggars, in three years he changed the world."

The old man had a point, I reflected. I had never seen feelings expressed, overwhelmed, and swallowed by courage as I did by our Master tonight. He was not ashamed to be afraid. He admitted he was lonely, and asked us to pray for him. I was amazed when I saw the sweat running down his face, shining in the torch-light. But when the soldiers came, he stepped forward with an awesome calm, like when he stilled the storm on Galilee. "I'm the one you're looking for," he said. "Let the others go." We were outnumbered twenty to one, but at that moment the fear in the eyes of the soldiers—they expected fire from heaven, I guess, like the soldiers sent to arrest Elijah—filled me with wild boldness. Maybe I expected fire from heaven, too. That's when I picked up the sword. And heard another rebuke. And I saw in his eyes and in theirs, the strength of weakness, and the weakness of mere human strength.

"Let the others go," he told them. As if for this battle, a dozen were still too many. He had whittled us once more, and went to face the rulers of the people and the Roman army alone. Is that the vast net of fine filament that loses nothing?

Or has our Master gone mad and hell come to reign on earth?

I looked into the fire and tried to silence the thoughts in my mind.

A young woman spoke in a low but compelling voice.

"Fisherman! Peace child! Messenger of God! Look around you before we are all swallowed alive!"

"Has ever such a coalition of forces come together as on this night? State conspires with church, liberal with conservative, occupying legion with local establishment. Not because our teacher likes to fish! Not because he talked about a God of love! Because he speaks for the masses!"

The woman faltered, and spoke more softly.

"'Strength through weakness' is a fine dialectical tactic, but what is your goal? And what price are you are willing to pay to reach it?"

"I am not so troubled by the fact that his teachings will be set up as instruments of oppression and patriarchy, as an excuse for keeping the proletariat in its place. What's new about that? All religion proves the ingenuity of human beings to trample on liberty. Yes, I admit, our revolution in Russia did even worse. And he warned such things would happen."

"The stake are high for me, though. The god of the proletariat is a god of swift justice: the party does not deal in mercy. We say we care for the poor. That makes him the competition. No one is more dangerous than a person who practices what others preach. Even popes and patriarchs hate him, though they conceal it! So do my comrades. If I follow him, some evening a knock may come on my door."

"And I am not sure my comrades would be wrong. He is the greatest revolutionary. Tonight he will become a martyr, and we honor martyrs. But was he really, in his heart, a rebel? Is it freedom that he offers, or bondage to the ultimate Patriarchy?"

A man with yellowish hair and clear glass over his eyes that reflected the reddish embers of the fire, coughed as a breeze blew smoke towards him, then looked at her and spoke as if to an old friend.

"You talk about freedom, Nadezhda. What have I ever cared about but liberation of spirit?"

He looked around at the rest of us.

"In our college days, we protested racial injustice, the social restrictions of our parents generation, and our crusade against communism in Southeast Asia. We flirted with Marxism, and were angry at our culture for its hypocrisy, but deeply influenced by its rhetoric: the American ideal of 'life, liberty and the pursuit of happiness.'"

"We talked a lot about freedom *to.* Freedom to make love without marriage. To wear long hair and listen to loud music. You know, sex, drugs, and rock and roll. The other day a group of Englishmen demonstrated for the right to appear in public without clothes on. That is the kind of freedom that would have provoked passion, of all kinds, on my campus."

"Then old classmates started coming into my office. Now they wanted freedom *from* the things we spent our youths saying we wanted freedom *to.* One whined that he 'felt tied down.' So he took off with some young lady, and left his wife and three daughters to cope the best they could. I wondered. Does freedom consist of the opportunity to obey base instinct? Or the ability to transcend instinct? It seemed to me our glorious vision was wearing thin."

"His teachings ran cross-current from any society I've ever come in contact with. Love those who hate you. The purpose of life is to 'bare good fruit.' Die to yourself, and live."

"Do not lust! How we laughed at that! But he seemed to see intuitively that the freedom that brings all other freedoms is the freedom of limits."

The speaker's eyes seemed to glow as he took a deep breath, and went on. "I remember a movie about a thirteenth century Scotsman. The hero led a rebellion against some English tyrant. Finally the English captured him and tortured him in public to make him recant. With a crowd watching, he gathered his strength for one last breath, cried 'Freedom!' so loudly the king of England on his sickbed could hear. Then he died."

"That made me think. What does a man in chains know about freedom? But somehow the cords around his hands led him to some deeper level of freedom."

"Our teacher has gained that freedom tonight. It is a freedom that chills me."

"Sanity lies in how well one orients oneself to reality. I find myself doubt-ing—I don't know. His sanity? My sanity? Maybe the sanity of the universe. My profession is enhancing and extending life. He said, 'Take up your cross and fol-low me.' As a metaphor for self-abandonment, for dependence on a Higher Power—there's a great deal to learn in that. But this has gone beyond metaphors."

"He took the deepest ideals of my national and professional identities and deepened them. Yet this evening is an affront to everything I stand for. If I fol-low him, I will be a traitor to the American idea of freedom. My life would be a slap in the face of colleagues and their scientific approach to the human spir-it. I would betray my patients hope for normalcy and adjustment to society. What should I tell them? Take up your cross? I'd become an outcast."

"Hah!" A lean black man with gray temples and a faraway look kicked a log onto the fire, breathed deeply, and glared. "What do you know about outcasts? I know how he is feeling right now," he said, punctuating his words with a long, bony finger. A chill swept over me at the emotion that rose on his voice. "He is standing where I stood. I was dead, and am now alive again, because of him. And since I know what that means, I am afraid for him, and for myself as well."

"Tell us your story, brother," came a voice.

"You can call me Lazarus. No, I'm not Jewish. But I've been to Sheol and back."

"I am from the Masai people of the Sudan. We measure wealth in two things: cattle, and courage. But there is one trial beyond the strength of any man to endure."

"You think the church is responsible for the idea of guilt? Hah! Let me tell you about guilt. She is a lion on the prowl. You never know where she will strike. And when she does, there is nothing you can do to escape her fangs. In our tribe, one man is chosen to bear the sin of the people. He is banished for ever. No one may ever touch him or live with him again. He bears the sins of the tribe."

"When I realized the scapegoat was to be me, I felt like I was watching a body being shoved into a hole."

Lazarus' face glowed with a strange light. His voice sunk.

"How I thirsted for a human face! How many times I thought of killing myself! What held me back? Fear? Stupid hope? I am not sure. But then one day a man came to my hut. He spoke to me as if I were human. He held my hand. You do not know what the touch of a human hand can mean!"

"We call the Creator 'The Unknown.' But he talked about God as if he knew Him, as if anyone could know him—even a man who is no longer a man! He said God had sent a man to be the scapegoat for all. The guilt of every village and tribe and language under the sun was laid on his back."

"I could go home! It was the news of this cross that made me a person again!"

Go home! Is that what Jesus was doing, when he said, "Let the others go?" Was he telling us we did not have to be scapegoats with him? I was sorry when he said it, but glad too, and sorry to be glad. I told him I'd die for him. And he said, "No." Did he mean salvation is too great a burden for us to carry?

"Yah!" Zhen Dao replied. "Zhuang Zi tells us not to fear the end of life. Death is only one of the workings of nature. We never believed it. The history of Chinese thought is a long obsession to find an escape from death. And no one has looked harder than we Taoists."

"My people have scapegoats too. We call those who intercede with the spirit realm 'divining youth.' They, too, are cut off from the people. They die early, as if they carry our sins. Maybe that's why Confucius said, 'Respect the gods but keep your distance.'"

A short, bald man in a loose orange robe stood up. He spoke with an easy but distant confidence, as if he were little used to talking, but as if each word came from a deep well of contemplation.

"My parents died of the plague, and I was taken in by a temple on a mountain near Kyoto. We were taught the Pure Land faith. Salvation cannot come through our own efforts, but must be attained through the aid of a bodhisattva. I often repeated a Scripture called the *Hokke-kyo*. We thought we could rid ourselves of sins by chanting: A-me-to-fo. A-me-to-fo."

A little smile played around his eyes.

"We also worshiped Kannon. She is a beautiful goddess who rescues merchants lost in storms at sea, saves people bitten by poisonous snakes, and gives sons to barren women. She is not like the black, scowling gods of many temples. We named islands after her, put her figure in hot springs and on rocky headlands and over our cities to protect us. Her legends won the Japanese to Buddhism long ago."

"When the *Katoliku* priests came to Japan with their stories of Jesus and his kindness, they preached against our gods, but I think that bothered my fellow monks less than the fact that they undercut our prices. We were amazed at how they treated the lower classes. They founded hospitals for lepers. They saved babies of poor women from the elements. The Shogun, Nobunaga, noticed their good works, and got suspicious. He asked, 'Who ever heard of a a temple that gave alms to the people?'"[4]

"Kannon appeared as duck to save ducks, as thief to save thieves, as monk to save monks. These priests, on the other hand, gave their converts odd new names like Mi-ge-ru and Mi-ka-ru, and dressed them strangely. Then rumors came of a fleet of *Katoliku* soldiers ready to sail from Manila. The Shogun made common cause with Buddhist monasteries and expelled all foreigners. These *Katoliku* brought the compassion of Jesus to Japan. But they came in strength rather than the weakness Lao Zi and Jesus spoke of. Crosses were raised in the southern island of Kyushu, and it became a capital crime to worship God."

The priest sighed, and adjusted his robes.

"One night, many years ago, I dreamed that priests came from India to preached the true way of salvation. It was the next day that I heard of the arrival of Francis Xavier in Yamaguchi. This is why I believed and was baptized."[5]

"Now I am accused of betraying my ancestors, my family, and our culture. But in its essence, if not in its outer appearance, the teaching of Jesus is the fulfillment of what I have sought all my life."

"Now I am troubled. But why would anyone crucify a bodhisattva?"

An answer came out of the dark. "No change comes without bloodshed."

No one replied. The fire sputtered as if muffled by the darkness. A cricket sang under the stump of a fig tree outside the circle of light cast by the fire, that Zhen Dao had been renewing. Bats swooped near the flames to catch mosquitoes.

Suddenly there was shouting within the courtyard. A deep and familiar voice addressed the crowd, at first with confidence and even pomposity. I knew that voice; we had grown used to obeying and fearing it. But now it sounded hesitant . . . a hesitancy that chilled me. We heard a rhythmic throb of voices.

"Crucify! Crucify! Crucify!"

One voice suddenly rose above the others. "If you are this man's friend, you are no friend of Caesar's!" Then the crowd stilled as the first voice spoke again, this time with his anger too subdued to distinguish the words.

There came the sound of distant laughter and catcalls.

"Let's see you turn the other cheek again, Rabbi!"

"Prophesy where I'm going to hit you!"

Each sound cut me like a whip.

We sat motionless. It was as if each became a world to himself, imprisoned in his own thoughts, rooted to the spot. The crowd began to break up, some glancing with loathing as they passed, as if they had only just whet their appetite for bloodshed and despised the presence of foreigners in the middle of the city almost as much as they despised the "Galilean sect."

The night became quieter, though some were still milling around and talking excitedly.

"What does it mean?"

For a moment, I hated Satya for asking. What are you doing here, foreigner?

I thought. What does Jesus have to do with you? This is between us and our countrymen.

"It is a cornerstone of Brahmin philosophy that a man pay for his own sin,
and realize Godhood by his own efforts. Karma is the law that each of us must suffer in full the penalties for our own sins, both in this life and in every previous life."

"I am not sure we ever believed it, though. For thousands of years, Indians
have practiced ritual bathing in the Ganges or in the sea. We wash, or make
cakes that represent the body of a god, or sacrificed animals, for the same reason. From a strict point of view, it is hard to see why such ceremonies would
get rid of *karma*. Yet we felt instinctively that the bad karma had to be gotten
rid of by the aid of some external cleansing agent. We knew in our hearts we
could not pay for, obliterate or just ignore our sins."

"Gandhi hated the sacrifices. He was very tender-hearted. But he was not
able to stop those sacrifices. Perhaps because his wisdom was not the whole
wisdom of India."

Satya paused and looked around the circle at the fire.

"The *Rig Veda* is the oldest of our Scriptures. Some say it goes back to
before the time of Abraham. For most Indians, the Vedas are just mantras that
pundits quote without understanding. In fact, much of the *Rig Veda* is about
sacrifice. It says, 'Sin can be effaced by means of sacrifice.'"[6] "The *Rig Veda* calls
sacrifice the chief duty and the 'mainstay' of the world. It speaks of people who,
by the sacrifices, have been freed from their sins. It notes, 'Oh noble Kuru,
there is no place in the world for him who does not perform even a single one
of these sacrifices; how then shall he obtain heaven?' It says even gods attain
heaven only through sacrifice.

"Yet the *Rig Veda* also warns, 'The timbers of the bark of sacrifice are
unsound.' In one place it says, 'It is a sacrifice that saves. What is being performed, is the shadow of sacrifice.' So it seemed there was a greater Sacrifice of
which our customs, and I guess those of the Jews, were 'shadows.' Another passage from the Rig Veda says 'God himself is the sacrifice.'"

"How can God be a sacrifice?" Ali protested. "He is not a man, that he
can die!"

"Well that is the mystery." Satya held out his hands. "The sacrifice is usually an animal in India, as in Israel, though men have been sacrificed. The Vedas
have very specific and mysterious instructions about how the sacrifice is to be
performed. It must be a goat without blemish. A '*balusu*' bush must be placed
round its head. The animal must be bound to a post. Nails must be driven into
its four legs till they bleed. The cloth covering the goat should be divided among
the four priests. None of its bones must be broken. It should be given a drink of
soma juice. Then (and this is the hardest to understand) after the animal has
been slain, it is supposed to be restored to life. Yet its flesh should be eaten."[7]

"A perfect sacrifice, with branch draped over its head, nailed to a post. A cloth divided among four priests. Break none of the bones. Kill without mercy, but give soma to dull the pain. Then, give it life again! I came to Palestine with these riddles in my mind."

"When I came into the city, I saw a row of crosses on a hill. I thought, here is a land where they kill men like sacrificial sheep. Suppose an *avatar* were to appear in this country, an incarnation of God in human flesh such as is said of Buddha or Krishna? Just so God-in-man might die, as the *Rig Veda* says."

"Here I am, in this land of the iconoclastic God, who slays deities and tramples on our ancient traditions. And I have found the key to our ancient Scriptures! But here is my question: if God is going to save us by the death of a man, does that spell death also to my culture? Will all the thousands of years of philosophical insight and deep mystical experience go up in smoke when an avatar is nailed to a cross for the sins of the world?"

He stoked the coals with a half-burned faggot. Smoke and sparks leaped into the sky. My hopes of the renewal of Israel seemed also to be one of those sparks. Is this the fire that will consume the world? I asked myself. Satya was speaking again.

"Something just occurred to me. If our Jewish guru taught more people to worship Allah than any Muslim prophet, not only would his death save the souls of men, but also the lives of millions of sacrificial lambs. I wonder if Gandhi ever thought of that?"

"Did you know that Passover is actually a Chinese holiday?"

Zhen Dao laughed, and everyone stared at him.

"We also felt that sacrifice was the key to keeping in harmony with the cosmos. The most awesome ceremonial spectacle in China was the annual sacrifice that the Emperor made to Heaven. And each family made sacrifices, too."

"Every year at New Year's we stay indoors, like the Jews did on the night of the Exodus from Egypt. We say that some evil creature—an angel of death?—will kill those who stray outside. We bake unleavened bread and eat bitter herbs, just like the Jews did. And every New Year, some kill chickens and daub their blood on both sides of the door and over the entrance. In most of China we simply write characters in red, and past them on the door posts. So our doors look like the door-posts of the Hebrews on the day of Passover, when they fled Egypt. Many of the messages on the door-posts have to do with blessings from God, or speak of the hope that some day we may find freedom from death. For example, on one side, *"Let spring fill the cosmos and happiness fill this house"* and on the other, *"God (Tian) adds years and man increases the length of his life."*

"The old word for "come" in Chinese is a picture of a cross with a person on it, with another person on each side of him. In our language, 'person person'—*ren ren*—means 'all people.' It is as if the inventors of our language were telling us that a reconciliation for all, a coming to God, can only be brought by a man on a cross."

"An ancient Chinese word for 'world' was a picture of three crosses. In one form, the cross on the left curves towards the bottom of the central cross without touching it, then drops down. The cross on the right curved at the bottom to touch the central cross, as if to show that some reject the man on the central cross and sink, while others link themselves to his death."

"You think I am letting my imagination get away from me? Perhaps."

"But there is another character we often write on our doors at our Passover. 'Spring.' Somehow we always hoped that someday, a time of new life and hope would come to all the human race. We told of a 'peach garden beyond the world.' If you ate the fruit of that garden, you would live forever. We pasted 'spring' over our doorways as a symbol of that hope."

"When Jesus started talking about rising from the dead the third day, it all made sense."

It sure didn't to us, I thought. In fact, that made people leave, too.

Zhen Dao had picked up a burning faggot and brushed the ground clean, and began sketching a series of strokes in the dirt: side to side, and up and down.

"These three horizontal lines, left to right, mean 'three.' The box below, with the horizontal stroke in the middle, means 'day.' It was originally rounder, because it also represents the sun. These two strokes at the top signify 'man' or 'person.'"

"'Three' 'days,' and 'person.' For three thousand years, we have been writing a code we could not interpret over our door-posts. Spring seems to have something to do with something that a person will do after three days."

The patriarch in shepherd clothing spoke in a husky voice that carried easily. "I know another who died on one of these hills and came to life again: my grandfather."

"I was troubled at first when I saw you foreigners following Jesus. We've been used as an highway by many armies: Egyptian, Assyrian, Babylonian, Greek, Roman, Arabic, Turk, French, English—you name it. So we're a little shy. Sometimes we asked, 'Is this what God meant by promising us we'd be blessing to all the peoples? That they could loot us on the way through?' When we were scattered to the nations, it grew worse. We purged ourselves of foreign concepts out of self-preservation as well as respect for the holy other-ness of God."

He stopped and looked at the stars above us. The fire was dying down again, and it was as if the sky was full of angels at a great and comfortable distance.

"But tonight, it seems, we are united under heaven by our differences. Is this what your gurus mean when they say all roads lead up the same mountain, Satya? I am afraid the mountain he will climb tomorrow will be Moriah, where my grandfather went to the brink of death and came back again."

I shuddered. This cross, this terrible cross spreads out its hands like claws in all directions and joins even our ancestors in some horrible fellowship of suffering.

"Moriah?" Satya asked. "I do not know the story of that mountain."

"It is where the Romans take criminals—the place of the skull. I don't think we had a name for it in my day. But I am pretty sure that is where my grandfather almost died. It was a place of sacrifice then, too."

"Are you talking about father Abraham?" Forgetting to keep quiet, I blurted my questions out without thinking. "Who are you, anyway?"

"Reuben, the first-born. Our grandfather only told us it happened 'in the region of Moriah.' The Roman place of execution is nearby, and could be the same spot."

"I am not sure how Great Grandfather Abraham understood that he must do this deed, for he never spoke of it. But somehow he came to the conclusion God was demanding he sacrifice his only son, for whom he prayed a hundred years.

"My grandfather was terrified, but he trusted his father. At the last minute the old man saw a vision of some kind. Then he found a goat caught in briars. Yahweh spoke to him there once more. 'You have not withheld your son, your only son. So I will bless you and make your descendants like the grains of sand on the seashore and the stars in the sky. And all nations shall be blessed through your descendants.'

"God gave this promise on Golgotha?"

"It had to be within a few hundred yards."

It seemed each of us saw the events of the evening in terms of his or her tradition. But we all felt as if we were judged for betraying that tradition by following Jesus. Each of us fears to be Judas to his own people. Other peoples, too, were waiting for his salvation. Did that make it any easier?

I picked up a large and misshapen branch, and tossed the corner of it on the embers. Sparks flew up. I noticed many newcomers in the dark on the edge of the fire now. But I could no longer keep quiet.

"Don't you think I know? Yes, I see him in the Jewish Scriptures. I see him in the skin of the animal God killed to cover Adam and Eve. I read his death in the story of Moriah. I see him in the sacrificial animals, in the Passover lamb. I see him in the righteous servant who was 'pierced for our transgressions.' Yes, our prophets warned us that the Messiah would be a 'light to the Gentiles,' and that the world would be blessed through Abraham's seed."

"But what about my people? We have been crushed and oppressed for a thousand years. How much longer must we serve as doormat to the Gentiles?"

As the crowd grew and became more tense, I should have closed my mouth. But that was never my greatest skill.

"You *goyim* hate us now, and you will hate us after you call yourselves Christians. You will shut us up in ghettoes. You will call us Christ-killers till we hate his name. You will take that cross and run it through our hearts. In his name you will crucify my people. And then they will curse me. And even among your people, I will become a scapegoat for those who do not want to believe. Our Master will stretch out his feet and hands to be nailed to the cross, but I will be hung face to the ground!"

My throat went dry. I felt foolish, and fell silent. A girl looked scornfully at me.

"Haven't I seen you before? You're one of his followers!"

"No . . . I'm just a fisherman . . . Here to celebrate Passover. I'm not with these foreigners, and I don't know who you're talking about."

"I recognize that accent! This is one of the Nazarenes!"

Lazarus spoke with a dry, husky voice. "What will happen to Jesus? Will you crucify him?"

A man in a priestly robe replied.

"We'll do nothing of the kind. What do you take us for? We will honor his memory. He was a prophet. He was put to death by narrow-minded people who hold an exclusive vision of God and could not recognize true greatness."

"But you! You are traitors to you cultures. Reuben, have you forgotten 2000 years of persecution? Satya, where is your loyalty? Your people have been struggling to throw off the shackles of Western and Islamic imperialism for more than a thousand years! Nadezhda, have you forsaken your comrades in their hour of need to join this rag-muffin band of losers?"

"Truth is not meant to be tamely conformed to. Truth and value are something we create for ourselves. Religion is the highest expression of human ingenuity, it is not something that God does. Idols are works of art. You will put artists out of work!"

"You give people hope. But it is better to travel hopefully than to arrive. You steal the joy of the journey. God does not send sons. The dead cannot rise. We understand the principles by which the universe is run and it is dangerous naivete to suppose they allow room for a God who is anything more than an expression of the human spirit."

"You, Peter, are worst of all. You and your friends are the source of all the confusion and misplaced hope that has upset the natural order for the past 2000 years. You made this Jewish peasant Son of God. You invented his miracles. And you will lie about this night as well. If you live, you will not allow him to stay dead, but will cause the trouble he gave us to increase to no end."

"Seize them!"

A streak of dawn touched the horizon. A rooster crowed.

We turned and fled into the night.

The Cross and the Religions of Man

Huston Smith argued, "If God is a God of love, it seems most unlikely that he would not have revealed himself to his other children as well."[8] Thich Nhat

Hanh warned against rendering people "rootless" by cutting them off from their own religious tradition in favor of a foreign import.[9]

The love of God must touch all of the world. Faith needs to find its root in each culture. Both these two popular objections to the exclusive character of the Christian revelation sound reasonable. A follower of an Indian religion was probably thinking of both of these when she complained to me that Christian missionaries practice "spiritual genocide" by asking natives to give up their religions.[10] How do we reconcile this need for connection with our ancestors, and for a revelation of God through the known and familiar, with the need for universality, to believe what is true everywhere, rather than simply the arbitrary construct of our own culture? Could God reveal truth in a way that is consistent and yet allows for diversity of expression within that unity?

A third objection skeptics often give to the Gospel holds the key to solving both these problems.

The first Christians, like Peter, were Jewish. For them, the life, teachings, miracles, death and resurrection of their Savior was not a foreign teaching, but was prefigured in hundreds of ways in the Hebrew Scriptures. They saw him in the skin of the animal God killed to cover Adam and Eve, and in his warning to the snake, that: "He will crush your head and you will crush his heel" (Genesis 3:15). They saw him in the story of Abraham on Mount Moriah. They saw him in the sacrificial animals that alone could make us right with God, yet as in the Rig Veda, were not enough. He was the Passover lamb. He was the bronze serpent lifted up on a pole, to which the Jewish tribes looked and were healed. He was the righteous servant of Isaiah, "pierced for our transgressions" (Yet who would "see the light of life and be satisfied.")

The first followers of Jesus saw that the Jewish Scriptures did not pretend to be complete in themselves. They seemed a series of riddles waiting for an answer, a catalogue of pictures of a figure yet unseen, a list of leading questions, as well as a book of overt prophecies. Who was Job's intercessor who will speak to God as a man speaks to a friend? Who was the fourth man in the Babylonian fiery furnace who "looks like the son of God?" In what sense does David's descendent, the Messiah, subjugate all peoples of the world? What was the blessing God promised the world through the seed of Abraham? Such questions were pregnant in the text itself; one could only avoid them by careful ideological training.

How do skeptics respond? One popular retort is that the Gospel writers must have falsified events in the life of Jesus to fit Messianic elements in the Old Testament. A. N. Wilson pictures how he thinks this happened:

> "Like John, (Matthew) believes that all the things which occurred in the life of Jesus took place to 'fulfills' the Scriptures. That is to say, he has been through the Scriptures cheerfully lifting details, and then

inventing the 'facts' to fit the 'prophecies.' . . . Mark has equally ingenious ways of making history interpret prophecy, rather than the other
way around . . . "[11].

There are many things one might say in response. Were the writers of the
Gospels really in a position to falsify Jesus' manner or time of death, the reaction of the crowds, or his influence on subsequent history? I'll have more to say
about this kind of criticism in the following chapter. But the doubts skeptics
feel about Old Testament prophecies, as well as the dilemmas regarding the universal and personal character of God's love, are turned on their head when it
appears that Jesus fulfills archetypes and prophecies of religions other than Old
Testament Judaism. Obviously one has a harder time picturing the authors of
the Gospels "cheerfully lifting" images and doctrines from modern psychologists, Norse mythology, the *Rig Veda*, Chinese script, or from the ceremonies of
tribes in sub-Saharan Africa, and writing *them* into the New Testament. And if
the Gospel writers did not invent the ways that Jesus fulfills other cultures, why
accuse them of making up Jesus' fulfillment of their own traditions?

Jesus once told his accusers, "You search the Scriptures, because you think
that in them you have eternal life; and it is these that bear witness of Me . . . If
you believed Moses, you would believe me; since he wrote about me" (John
5:39-46). Paul wrote that Jesus "emptied Himself as He took on the form of a
slave," and "humbled Himself and became obedient to death; yes, death by the
cross." God "lifted Him up . . . so that at the name of Jesus every knee should
bow" (Phil. 2: 8-11).

Indeed, even teachers and Scriptures whose overall message is opposed to
the Gospel, often point in surprising ways to Jesus and his sacrifice on the cross.

The *Qur'an* bears witness to Jesus. It says Jesus preached the Gospel and
"heals the blind and the leper, and brings to life the dead." It praises him more
highly than Mohammed:

> "We sent our Messengers with the clear signs, and We sent down with them
> the Book and the Balance so that men might uphold justice . . . and We
> sent, following, Jesus son of Mary, and gave unto Him the Gospel. And we
> set in the hearts of those who followed him tenderness and mercy."[12]

Mohammed suggested that Jesus did not die on the cross, but that God
rescued him from that disgraceful fate. But the *Qur'an* points to the salvation
Jesus brought through his death on the cross in two ways. First, it clearly states
that the Gospel is the "plain command of God," and that no one can alter the
words of God. If these two statements are true, it follows that the Gospel has
not been altered. In that case, the Gospel records that tell how Jesus died for
the sins of the world and came to life, must be true.

Secondly, the *Qur'an* calls Jesus "Messiah." What does Messiah mean? It means the anointed one, the Savior promised in the Old Testament who would establish God's kingdom on the earth and be a "light to the Gentiles." This term points us again to the Messianic symbols and prophecies of the Jewish people that came true on the cross.

Confucius pointed to Jesus in a less overt, but equally significant, way.

Confucius spoke of a *Sheng Ren*, a holy person. It is often assumed Confucius idealized the past, yet he did not know anyone who had ever met this high ideal. "A *Sheng Ren* is not mine to see," he noted poignantly. (Maybe Jesus was thinking of Confucius when he said, "Many prophets longed to see what you see, but did not see it.") Confucius denied that he himself could be described in such exalted terms. Like the seed of Abraham, the *Sheng Ren* would bring a blessing to the common people of all the world. A *Jun Zi*, a noble person, would stake his life on the promises of heaven, and be willing to die to fulfill God's mission.

Confucius' greatest disciple, Mencius, wrote that a great sage would be born once every 500 years, arguing that his master was a sage. This saying of Mencius' took on a life of its own in Chinese Messianic literature. Much later, the great epic *Journey to the West* may have retroactively satirized one pretender to the throne, Wang Mang, who tried to overthrow the Han dynasty five centuries after Confucius, by having the Monkey King wage a buffoonish war against heaven during his usurpation. Modern revolutionaries like Hong Xiuquan and Mao Zedong also mentioned this 500-year interval. I think Jesus, who was in fact born 500 years after Confucius, fulfills the criteria of a *Sheng Ren* better than anyone else in history. His death on the cross did bring blessing to all the peoples of the world, even in the temporal sense Confucius no doubt had in mind.

Lao Zi also bore indirect witness to Jesus. He also spoke of a *Sheng Ren*, though his meaning was slightly different from that of Confucius.

A couple years ago a well-known Chinese philosopher named Yuan Zhimin wrote a book called *Lao Zi vs. the Bible*, that I mentioned in an earlier chapter. Yuan argued that Lao Zi's term *Zi Zai Zhi*, "The One whose existence is from Himself," a synonym for the *Tao*, was remarkably close in meaning to the Biblical name *Yahweh*. Lao Zi's *Tao*, he argued, has life, cannot be reduced to any image, (Zen Buddhism borrowed this from Lao Zi), and even, he suggested, less persuasively, showed signs of a triune character. People follow the *Tao* by overcoming strength through weakness. This is the main message of the *Dao De Jing*, and is echoed by many passages of the New Testament. This *Tao*, *Logos*, or Word, Yuan argued, is incarnate in the life of Jesus. By Jesus' humbling himself "even to death on the cross," the divine Word spreads out its fine filament like the great net of heaven, bringing up all who believe. Yuan made a bold claim:

"Do you know the Tao of Lao Zi? You think you know it, but are not quite sure, perhaps? Let me tell you a mystery . . . Lao Zi was a great prophet of God. And what he preached was the true Tao of God: the 'holy person' he wrote about was in fact Jesus." [13]

As we saw, the Rig Veda also seems to witness to the death of Jesus on the cross. It is true the idea of sacrifice has been opposed by some sensitive Indians. Horrified by a visit to the temple of Kali in Calcutta, Mohandas Gandhi said he would be unwilling for a lamb to die even to save a human life. Most Indians did not feel this way, however. And even Gandhi did understand and approve of the idea that the great might sacrifice themselves for the weak. After his visit to the temple, he wrote, "I must go through more self-purification and sacrifice, before I can hope to save these lambs . . . "[14] Yet at times, Gandhi seemed to recognize his inability to save even himself. But consider this also: wherever the "lamb of God who takes away the sins of the world" is worshiped, there are no more temples to Kali, no more animal sacrifices. Nor are there human sacrifices that Kali also long exacted.

Indian Scripture and practice bear witness that even people who are taught they are a part of God do not feel that they can save themselves. Mr Mandapaka, the Indian Christian whose analysis of the *Rig Veda* I have relied upon, argued in his tract *Sacrifice*:

> *"The logical conclusion from these passages in the Indian Scripture is that the sacrifices themselves do not confer salvation, but they are the type and the shadow of some great sacrifice which does. The true and great redeeming sacrifice would be the one performed by the Sovereign Lord of this world. He would put on both mortality and immortality and becoming incarnate as God-man, and somehow become the sacrificial animal and offer Himself as a sacrifice to redeem mankind from their sins.'"*

> *"Thus, it is said that God himself must become man, and then become a sacrifice to save sinners. But we do not read any such thing written about the incarnations of our country, nor in the sastras."*

Furthermore, if Mr. Mandapaka was right, the Rig Veda gives us a remarkable description of that sacrifice: tied to a post, nails driven in feet, branch on head, cloth divided among priests, soma to drink, no bones broken, flesh eaten, restored to life. No one who reads the Gospel records can fail to recognize these images.

Marxists such as James Cane also give testimony to Jesus,

> *"By North American standards Jesus could be considered neither a successful person, nor could he be considered morally respectable. He identified with prostitutes and drunks, the unemployed and the poor. Not because he*

felt sorry for them! But to reveal God's judgement against social and religious structures that oppress the weak."15

An American poetess found revolutionary inspiration not only in Jesus' teachings and identification with the oppressed, but also with his sacrifice:

"Thanks to St. Matthew, who had been
At mass-meetings in Palestine,
We knew whose side was spoken for
When Comrade Jesus took the floor.

Where sore they toil and hard they lie,
Among the great unwashed, dwell I: —
The tramp, the convict, I am he;
Cold-shoulder him, cold-shoulder me.'

By Dive's door, with thoughtful eye,
He did tomorrow prophecy: —
'The kingdom's gate is low and small;
The rich can scarce wedge through at all."

'A dangerous man,' said Caiaphas,
'An ignorant demagogue, alas!
Friend of low women, it is he
Slanders the upright Pharisee.

Ah, let no Local him refuse!
Comade Jesus hath paid his dues.
Whoever other be debarred,
Comrade Jesus hath his red card." 16

The term "red card" reminds us of a concept that Marxism and Christianity share in common: that there can be no forgiveness apart from the shedding of blood. We might choose to think of this as a "primitive notion," but modern history shows that it can work powerfully on emotions even when "superstition" is scorned. Thus human sacrifice reached a pinnacle of achievement in the twentieth century. But for Christians, the blood of Jesus is enough.

This should also be good news to Chinese spirit mediums who cut their backs or tongues while in trances, or hit themselves with axes:

The tang ki is "deliberately flouting, or somehow outside" the normal Confucian rules which consider it evil to damage one's own body. "We recall that he is considered to be a man who would normally die at an early age, but whose life has been 'artificially' extended by a god so that he may serve as the latter's mouthpiece. His mortification is said to be caused by the god as a sign of this status. It seems to me that the reason this is an appropriate and powerful sign is that it is a directly unfilial thing to do and represents the tang-ki's being cut off from the world of ordinary mortals."17

We've seen how the Chinese characters *world, come,* and *spring* hint at the cross and the resurrection of Jesus. The ideographs that make up the most popular character, *fu,* or happiness, are like an illustration of the Biblical story of how God once "blessed" or "gave *fu*" to the first man and woman. Like spring, this character is also pasted to the door-post during the New Year festival. *Fu* was originally a picture of a vessel used in sacrifice. The Chinese have felt for thousands of years that happiness could not come apart from sacrifice.

Tribal peoples testify to the same truth. Sawi headhunters on the coast of New Guinea saw Jesus as God's "Perfect Peace Child," who allowed them to end a tyranny of warfare and live in harmony. The Asmat believed communal life could only come through new birth. When children came of age, they passed them under their legs, as if through a communal birth canal. When a missionary repeated the words of Jesus to them, 'You must be born again,' they knew exactly what he meant. Because the message of the Gospel met such felt needs among them, in fifteen years, 150,000 tribesmen of New Guinea became believers.

About Masai outcasts, an African pastor said,

"One of the sweetest things I have ever done is to tell an outcast about Jesus. I cannot tell you the joy that comes over these men when they learn that the Savior has been the scapegoat for all mankind, that the sins of all generations have been paid for already by a man named Jesus."18

Psychology also points to Jesus, both to the fact that he was perfectly sane and suffered from no Messianic complex, and to the fact that his death on the cross is what we need from a Messiah. The following are two well-known quotations on the subject, that I think sum up fairly what we have seen in history and what we find in the Gospels.

"(The character of Jesus) . . . has not only been the highest pattern of virtue, but the strongest incentive to its practice . . . The simple record of three short years of active life has done more to regenerate and to soften mankind, than all the disquisitions of philosophers and than all the exortions of moralists."19

"If you were to take the sum total of all authoritative articles ever written by the most qualified of psychologists on the subject of mental hygiene—if you were to combine them and refine them and cleave out the excess verbiage—if you were to have these unadulterated bits of pure scientific knowledge concisely expressed by the most capable of living poets, you

would have an awkward and incomplete summary of the Sermon on the Mount. And it would suffer immeasurably through comparison."[20]

Scott Peck saw that in his practice, sacrifice was needed in order for healing to occur.

"The individual must allow his or her own soul to become the battleground. He or she must absorb the evil . . . I do not know how this occurs. But I know that it does. I know that good people can deliberately allow themselves to be pierced by the evil of others—to be broken thereby yet somehow not broken—to even be killed in some sense and yet survive and not succumb. Whenever this happens there is a slight shift in the balance of power in the world."[21]

Even an unbelieving psychologist can see the need for God to do something radical about human sin. When confronted by simplistic arguments that guilt was simply a hang-up resulting from immaturity, Ernest Becker let this slip out, (a Freudian slip?):

"Guilt is not a result of infantile fantasy but of self-conscious adult reality. There is no strength that can overcome guilt unless it be the strength of a god. . . ."[22]

So Becker seemed to see the very same thing that the writers of the Rig Veda saw: that guilt was real, unavoidable, and could only be overcome by some incomprehensible divine act.

The Dalai Lama called Jesus a "bodhisattva." In *True Son of Heaven*, I showed at some length how Jesus deepens and fulfills the Buddhist myth of the bodhisattva known in East Asian as Guan Yin or Kannon.

Christians call the basic human problem "sin," psychologists "neurosis," while Buddhists use the words "karma." In some ways, this latter is the most frightening concept of all: a train of guilt trailing behind us like the chains of Scrooge's ghosts, a million lifetimes long, that no one can break, and must be undone link by link.

While meditating in a Zen temple, a Jewish doctor I know named Steven Schachter realized that Jesus came to break those links for each of us.

After having looked into just about every other religion, he realized that if he wanted to go further in the Zen he had been studying for some years, he should try to figure out how the suffering of Jesus on the cross was "one" with what appeared to be its opposite, Buddha's calm release from suffering. How does one know what an apple taste like except by biting? So he tried as a koan the phrase, "Jesus, I accept you as the Messiah of Israel." When he said that, he realized, completely without preparation, that it was true. And if it weren't, Jesus would have to pay karmically for dragging him off the path. So Jesus paid for his sins, one way or the other; and he realized that he was done with his need for meditation. The karma was already gone.[23]

Let me go to Central Asia for my final example.

The Jiang are the oldest aboriginal people of China. They have lived in Sichuan Province for thousands of years. There is one town, called Oir, 10,000 feet above sea level, near the tree line. It was surrounded by an old defense tower that looks like crosses on a hill. Like the Jews, the Jiang in that village kept a day of atonement. One goat was slaughtered at an altar in a sacred grove, and the other let go.

In the mid 1920s, a missionary and his son visited the village. When the missionary heard of this custom, he read the Jiang priest the 16th chapter of *Leviticus* to him, which contains records of the same rite. The old priest leaped up, excited, and said that the book the missionary was reading must be the lost Jiang Scriptures! The son, later professor of Christian Dogmatics at the University of Edinburg, recalled what happened next:

> *"(The priest) went on to explain that they carried to their sacrifice a sacred roll of white paper or a scroll which stood for 'the Word of God' (although it had no writing on it) for it was the Word that was the real sacrifice and Savior—that was symbolized by a skull (usually that of a monkey because it was small) placed on top of the Scroll to indicate the death or sacrifice of the Word or Savior, a heaven-sent sin-bearer. Each year a fresh piece of white paper was rolled around the scroll to indicate the purity of the Word or Heaven-Sent Sin-Bearer which they termed variously Je-Dsu, Nee-Dsu or Rih-Dsu, meaning 'Saviour.' On hearing this my father then read the first chapter of St. John's Gospel which tells of the Word of God made flesh in Jesus Christ, the Lamb of God come to take away the sin of the world. He told the Chiang that they had been tucked away in such a remote part of the world that they had never heard that the Word of God had come in Jesus Christ to be the Lamb of God that bears away the sin of the world. As he announced the Good News to that little company the priest and all his household believed and were . . . baptized."[24]*

Some feel the idea that Jesus died for our sins shows the cruel or arbitrary nature of the Christian God. Many are offended by the idea that we are sinners who need the salvation of God. Others see the cross as a symbol of foreign oppression. The cross is indeed an offense to all of us on some level. Yet on a deeper level, it meets our needs.

> "One would hardly die for a righteous person; but still for a good person someone might perhaps bring himself to die. But God proves

His own love for us by Christ's dying for us when we were still sinners" (Romans 5:7-8).

Like awareness of God, and knowledge of right and wrong, the sense of guilt and need for a Savior is universally felt, though not universally acknowledged or acted upon. What's more, our many images of that savior bear a striking resemblance to Jesus and hint in amazing ways at what God has done for us on the cross. Grafting the Gospel onto other cultures does not leave them "rootless" as Thich feared, nor is it like putting a sheep's head on a yak's body, in the Dalai Lama's phrase. Rather, the message of redemption through the cross of Christ can be a seed planted in each culture that brings new life from the spiritual nourishment within that tradition. But Jesus warned that that would also be threatening.

---

[1] The following story is adapted from Don Richardson's *Peace Child*, p. 287-8.

[2] Wang Wei, *For Vice-Magistrate Zhang*, from *100 Tang Poems*, translated by Bruce M. Wilson and Zhang Ting-chen, p. 33

[3] *Dao De Jing*, 73-4

[4] From a paper in which Nobunaga gave reasons why he was considering proscribing Christianity in Japan, Otis Cary, *A History of Christianity in Japan*, p. 249

[5] Ibid. p. 65 Cary tells the story of a monk in Kyoto who had such a dream and converted.

[6] All these quotes are from *Sacrifice* by Adhyaksha Anubhavananda Kesava Raya Sarma Mandapaka. (Translated from Telugu by H. Kaveribai. Gospel Literature Service, Bombay, India.) He gives his original sources in the Rig Veda as follows: *Prathamani Dharmani, Yagnovai Bhuvanasya Nabhih, Yagnakshapitakalmashah, Nayam lokostyayaghasyah kutonayah kurusattama, Yagnena Va Deva Divangatah*, and *Tadya Maha Brahmanam.*

[7] Ibid.

[8] *Religions of Man*, p. 353

[9] *Living Buddha, Living Christ*, p. 197

[10] She was also asking people to give up their beliefs to embrace her idea of God, but saw that in a more positive light.

[11] A. N. Wilson, *Jesus, A Life*, W. W. Norton & Co. 1992, p. 62

[12] *The Koran*, p. 567 (Iron)

[13] Yuan Bujia, *Lao Zi Yu Ji Du, (Lao Zi and Christ)*, Chinese Social Science Publishing Company, p. 1

[14] *Autobiography: The Story of My Experiments With Truth*, Dover Pub., 1983, p. 208

[15] James Cane, *The Challenge of Liberation Theology*

16 Sarah N. Cleghorn, *Comrade Jesus* from *The World's Great Religious Poetry*, Edited by Caroline Miles Hill, Macmillan Co. 1923, p. 345

17 Jordan, *Gods, Ghosts, and Ancestors*, University of California Press, 1972

18 from Paul Eshleman, *I Just Saw Jesus*

19 William Lecky, *History of European Morals from Augustine to Charlemagne*, 1903, Vol. 2 p. 8, 9, quoted in Josh Mcdowell, *More that a Carpenter*, Tyndale House, 1977, p. 28-29

20 J. T. Fisher, from John Montgomery, *History and Christianity*, Intervarsity Press, 1964, p. 65

21 M. Scott Peck, *People of the Lie*, Simon and Schuster, 1983, p. 269

22 *Denial of Death,* p. 262

23 He tells the story in Ruth Rosen, *Jewish Doctors Meet the Great Physician*, Purple Pomegranite Productions, 1998

24 Thomas Torrance, *Two Missionary Expeditions to Sichuan and Wenchuan, China, in 1986 and 1994, Rejent Chinese Journal*, Volume III, No. 1, 1995. The word used here for "word" was no doubt *tao*, as they were presumably reading from the Chinese Bible.

CHAPTER 13

Jesus and the Religions of Man

"JESUS WAS Representative Man, Archetypal Man, Man as he might be if he could become that which in his essential nature he really is: or, as a Hindu would put it, if he could realize his Greater Self." —F. C. Happold[1]

"He was either a fully enlightened being, or a bodhisattva of a very high spiritual realization." —the Dalai Lama[2]

"Mary, God gives thee good tidings of a Word from Him whose name is Messiah, Jesus, son of Mary; high honored shall he be in this world and the next, near stationed to God." —*Qur'an*[3]

"And now I, Mormon, make an end. . .woe be unto him that will not hearken unto the words of Jesus . . . " —*Book of Mormon*[4]

"Do we not say rightly that you are a Samaritan and have a demon?" —Anonymous, First Century Palestine (John 8:48)

"But what about you? Who do you say that I am?" —Jesus

We have seen that the Jesus of the Gospels meets the needs, and even fulfills the prophecies and riddles of various traditions in a remarkable way. But this does not prove that the writers of the Gospels, the early Christians who took their lead from Peter and his friends, were telling the truth. Some describe the figure who fills the Gospels as the "Jesus of faith," as opposed to the "Jesus of history." The early Christians were embellishing the truth, representatives of other traditions sometimes say. The real Jesus was—take your pick: Zen mystic, Hegelian Humanist, magician, prophet who foretold the coming of Mohammed, Joseph Smith, or Karl Marx, "peasant Jewish cynic." Or he never lived at all—the stories were fabricated out of whole cloth by Peter, Paul, or Mary.

The most influential such reply in the modern era is a humanist portrait called the "historical Jesus." Scholars began to undertake the famous "search for the historical Jesus" in the nineteenth century, and it continues to fill bookstore shelves to overflowing. Most people assume this quest is unique to the modern world, the fruit of an impartial spirit of scientific curiosity. On the contrary, we will see that this search has been driven by the same motives that inspired other apocryphal writings about Christ. The muse behind these tales did not say, "Let us find out what Jesus was *really* like." Rather, she whispered, "Something must be done about this man. If he goes on like this, we may lose our place. Offer him the ideological kingdoms of this world, a spot of honor on our altar, if he only bows his knee to our theology. If not, we'll have to kill him or his followers, or at least discredit their testimony."

Buddhist Stories About Jesus

The student activity center at Cultural University on the mountain above Taipei was a distinctive round building about nine floors high. Saffron-colored drapes marked out the sixth floor as forming a distinct social environment even from the ground below. Inside, I met a group of young students.

"I came to learn about Buddhism," I told them.

"Here, read this!" One replied, "This is the true story of Jesus."

It seemed an odd answer. Perhaps he assumed that, as a Westerner, the most effective apologetic for his faith would begin by showing me that the Western Savior was a follower of Buddha. Or could it be a Zen koan, replying to a question about Buddha with a book about Jesus? If so, the cover might have been designed to bring a Christian to *satori*: *The Riddle of the Lost Steps of Jesus*, read the title, as a Semitic figure with a halo strode in a white robe across a map of the subcontinent like a giant.

I have heard the story of that journey many times since, in various versions. Swedish scholar Per Beskow, in his even-handed description of modern apocryphal Gospel stories, *Strange Tales About Jesus*, described its origin in some detail. In the late nineteenth century a Russian war correspondent paid a visit to South Asia. On a trip to the reclusive monastery of Hemis on the border of Tibet, he discovered a long-lost manuscript about the visit to the subcontinent of one "Saint Issa." The book described how this Issa, whom Notovich quick-ly ascertained was none other than the young Jesus during the years before he began his ministry in Israel, learned magic from Asian Masters.

Notovich's book created a stir when it was first published, but was soon exposed as a fraud. The head lama of the monastery swore no European match-ing Notoviches' description had visited them, and that the monastic library held no such volume. Notovich had, however, been treated for toothache at a Mora-vian hospital in India. After Notovich was exposed by a leading English Asian scholar, Max Muller, the stir caused by his "discovery" died down for a few decades. But later, the same theories resurfaced in the stories of a traveler to Ladakh named Nicholas Roerich in the 1920s, who quoted much of the same material, along with alleged Indian folklore of equally dubious value. More recently, popular books by Elizabeth Claire Prophet and an "autobiography" of Jesus by Richard Paton (sic) have incarnated the same story in a new corpus of works. One earlier version describes the training of Saint Issa in India as follows:

> "The white priests of Brahma . . . . taught him to read and understand the Vedas, to heal by prayer, to teach and explain the Holy Scripture, to cast out evil spirits from the body of a man and give him back human semblance."[5]

Why, having been asked about Buddha, did the young student give me a fraudulent account of the life of Jesus? Buddha said there were 84,000 paths to enlightenment; Jesus' way must, by hypothesis, be among them. I once asked one of Master Lu's disciples about the figurine of Jesus on the god shelf of the Lei Zang temple, smallest of about sixty idols, that looked vulnerable and out-of-place. "We have a great deal of respect for Jesus," she answered. Handing his image over to an Indian monster seemed an odd way to show respect. Yet many Buddhists feel more comfortable with the story of Jesus in a manageable and familiar form, like that of the bodhisattvas and the Jakata tales of the Buddha in prior lifetimes. It would not be safe to let the Jesus of the Gospels, with his authority, iconoclasm, anger at oppressors, and ability to outwit deceivers human and divine, loose on such a collection of entities.

Jesus is often made safe for Buddhism in more subtle ways.

Thich Nhat Hanh, in *Living Buddha, Living Christ*, gave a more subtle spin to the same attempt to requisition the Gospel stories for Buddhism. Not-ing that Pope John Paul called Jesus, "absolutely original and unique . . . the one mediator between God and humanity," Thich responded:

> "This statement does not seem to reflect the deep mystery of the one-ness of the Trinity. It also does not reflect the fact that Christ is also the Son of Man . . . Of course Christ is unique. But who is not

unique? Socrates, Muhammad, the Buddha, you, and I are all unique. The idea behind the statement, however, is the notion that Christianity provides the only way of salvation and all other religious traditions are of no use. This attitude excludes dialogue and fosters religious intolerance and discrimination."[6]

Thich's argument merits reply on several levels. First, one notes that as a Buddhist priest, he presumes to lecture the Pope on a proper understanding of Christianity. Now perhaps the Pope is guilty of misunderstanding his own religion. Raised in the Protestant tradition, I certainly I do not want to deny anyone, after an honest search of the Christian Scriptures, the right to differ with ecclesiastical authority. Yet surely it would be arrogant indeed to publicly rebuke the Pope on his understanding of the Gospel apart from very clear evidence that he is in fact wrong? But secondly, Thich is wrong. Not surprisingly, the Pope does know more about Christianity. Jesus is the "one mediator between man and God" is simply a quotation from the Bible (1 Tim.5), and the assumption of all the New Testament. Thirdly, while Jesus clearly thought of himself as "providing the only way of salvation," neither Jesus, nor the Pope who claims to follow him, extends the argument to say "all other religious traditions are of no value." In fact, the New Testament describes the Jewish law as a "tutor" to prepare the way for the Gospel. Jesus said, "I did not come to abolish but to complete" the Law and the Prophets that were the basis of Jewish tradition (Matt. 5:17). And while I gave more detail in the last chapter than is commonly known, my view that other religions can be of tremendous value to those who are sincerely seeking God is not heresy, but the traditional teaching of Christian thinkers from Paul to Augustine to Chesterton and C. S. Lewis. Nor do I think the Pope is a stranger to the concept.

Confronted with Jesus' claim to be "the Way, the Truth, and the Life," Thich is free to frankly differ. Instead, he looks for a way to take the sting (i.e., the point) out of Jesus' words:

> "When Jesus said, 'I am the way,' He meant that to have a true relationship with God, you must practice His way . . . we must distinguish between the 'I' spoken by Jesus and the 'I' that people usually think of. The 'I' in his statement is life itself . . . "[7]

Thich has been called the second most-respected interpreter of Buddhism to the western world, after the Dalai Lama. A great deal of wisdom is evident in his writing. But the essence of tolerance is to allow a person to speak for him or herself. Thich's idea of tolerance seems to consist of projecting his own worldview on Jesus. In truth when Jesus said "I" he meant himself, as do we all.

Thich Nhat Hanh has spent a life working for peace and practicing dialogue.

Yet even as he criticizes the Pope for an attitude which does not "foster tolerance and dialogue," he does not allow Jesus to speak for himself, nor allow Christians to define their own faith. In my opinion, that is the attitude that truly does exclude, or at least greatly impede, dialogue. How can we talk with each other if we begin by denying the other?

Thich's approach seems accepted among even many of the most admirable teachers of "Eastern" religion. (The Dalai Lama, who warned against "putting a yak's head on a sheep's body," is a conspicuous and welcome exception. While seeking, and finding, common ground with Christians, he seems to admit both his ignorance and also real differences.[8]) For many, Buddhism and related philosophies may be caught in a conundrum between the idea of monism and the actual nature of life in a world of differences. All is one; but all is not one. It is tempting to reinvent the "other" in terms of oneself. Even in defining Buddhism in a way meant to be free of dogma, Thich revealed an unexamined and therefore potentially hypocritical dogmatism:

> "For a Buddhist to be attached to any doctrine, even a Buddhist one, is to betray the Buddha. It is not words or concepts that are important. What is important is our insight into the nature of reality and our way of responding to reality."[9]

This argument seems like a linguistic ruse to have one's dogma and eat it too. What do "insight into reality" and "way of responding to reality" mean, if not what are called, in the context of Christianity, "doctrines" and "dogmas?" Is Master Thich really "unattached" to Buddhist teachings? Or having called them "insights," does he cling to them as stubbornly as any committed member of a faith community? It may be reassuring to call the belief that "all is one" an "insight" rather than a "doctrine" or a "concept," precisely because doctrines can be debated and concepts can be challenged, while "insights" cannot. If I say, "I think A," then of course you can argue with me. But if I say, "I see B," then no further argument is possible, nor any real meeting of minds in a common environment of objective reality. By defining itself as subjective, philosophical Buddhism may "stop the course of the heart" and "cut off thought" in a way that removes it from hope as well as danger.[10]

Jesus tells us to "love God with your whole mind" (Matt. 22:37). This is why the Christian faith, while it also incorporates psychological insights, is ultimately built upon history, not psychology. Many Buddhists avoid a true encounter with Jesus by clinging to doctrines that tell them not to cling. They quote the words of Jesus, not caring what Jesus really said, because truth is something one "sees" rather than proves.

Christians should realize, when they engage in religious dialogue with Buddhists, that "tolerance" of this kind is the kiss of death. The bottom line becomes, not "agree to disagree," but rather (as Chesterton quipped), "Buddha and Jesus are very much alike, especially Buddha." Yet the teachings of Buddha, that we should save ourselves by concentration and asceticism, that the end of life is to dissolve individual consciousness and escape joy as well as pain, was a weight too heavy for ordinary Asians to bear. The people of Asia were looking for a savior, a loving and personal emanation of the divine, who would hear their prayers and respond to them as human beings. One who would fulfill the ancient need of a sacrifice. One who would bring us to a personal God. No wonder Buddhist teachers are hesitant to allow their followers to take the Gospel records at face value, and, instead, send Jesus off to Tibet to study Buddhism.

Hindu Stories About Jesus

The Gospel of the Holy Twelve and the *Aquarian Gospel* do not bring Jesus to the border of Tibet, but only as far as the western reaches of India. According to the first, in his youth Jesus traveled to Assyria, India, Persia, and Chaldea. His disciples confessed their belief not in Jesus, but in reincarnation. Echoing the language of Luke's version of the Beatitudes, the Jesus of the *Holy Twelve* thundered:

> "Woe to the strong who misuse their strength. Woe to the crafty who hurt the creatures of God. Woe to the hunters, for they shall be hunted."[11]

Per Beskow commented,

> "We are dealing with a modern and rather clumsily made forgery. There is virtually nothing at all in this 'Gospel' that has the slightest ring of authenticity."[12]

In the *Aquarian Gospel*, Beskow wrote, "Jesus is given the features of an Indian guru." And, one might add, a new set of hooves:

> "Jesus taught the common people of Lahore; he healed their sick . . . He said . . . 'If you would live the perfect life, give forth your life in service for your kind, and for the forms of life that men esteem the lower forms of life.' But Jesus could not tarry longer in Lahore; he bade the priests and other friends farewell; and then he took his camel and he went on his way."[13]

Donald Waters (otherwise called Swami Kriyananda) added to the evolving New Age-Hindu story of Jesus' youth. His guru, Paramahansa Yogananda, explained to him that three legendary Hindu teachers (Babaji, Lahiri and Sri Yukteswar) were in fact the three wise men who visited Jesus in the manger. As a grown man Jesus had the decency to return their visit. Unfortunately, "the account of his trip to India was removed from the New Testament centuries later by sectarian followers."[14] In fact it was Babaji, still alive in the Himalayas after all these centuries, who sent Yogananda to the West on a mission to interpret the Christian Bible and the Bhagavad Gita so as to show that their teachings are one."

This practice of blaming "sectarian followers" for qualities in the Gospel one finds but wishes were not there, or does not find but thinks ought to be there, is standard among apocryphal accounts of Jesus' life, as we will see when we look at the supposedly objective "historical Jesus." More recent manuscript discoveries, of which Donald Waters was, apparently, unaware, have proven that the Gospels were complete or (in the case of John) probably complete by the beginning of the second century, however. Gospel fragments have been found from within a hundred years of Christ, so it seems unlikely that "sectarian followers," (i.e., Christians) could have removed accounts of Jesus' Indian pilgrimage "centuries later."

Yogananda said he was called to "reinterpret" the Bible to show its teachings were identical with those of the *Bhagavad Gita*. Apologists for pantheism have tended, in their reading of the New Testament, to take a few ambiguous passages out of context and emphasize a meaning which cannot be supported by the documents as a whole. The most popular such text is undoubtedly Luke 17:21, "The kingdom of God is within you." (But other translations say, "among you.") This is usually interpreted, against everything Jesus taught, the context of the discussion, and historical probability, to mean "salvation comes through realizing the *atman*, one's own identity with Godhood."

As bizarre and historically indefensible as tales of Jesus' training in India may be, they have become quite popular in New Age circles in the West. New Gospels have also been produced by automatic writing and other mystical arts that some Westerners find convincing, though they have been a mainstay of sectarian forgery in Asia for millennia. Others claim to have met "Jesus of Nazareth" in the spirit realm, reporting that he now holds to (in an undisguised form) a monistic New Age rather than dualistic Christian understanding of God.

Even Mahatma Gandhi was willing to "re-interpret" Jesus' words to correspond better with his interpretation of the *Bhagavad Gita*. I do not take issue with Gandhi drawing on the spiritual strength of diverse traditions in his campaign for the freedom and moral uplift of the Indian people. Nor do I wish to pour cold water on the commendable desire to look for the good in other religions. As you can see from the last chapter, I even think it is legitimate to mine the Scriptures of other religions for confirmation of what one takes to be a fuller synthesis. But tolerance means acknowledging the Other. To say, against a straightforward read of the records, that Christ and Krishna teach the same doctrine, a "perennial philosophy" which (it turns out) ultimately reduces to one school or another of Hinduism, is not tolerance. It is a kind of religious imperialism.

On a visit to the book store of the Vedanta Society in Seattle, I found a painting of Jesus, surrounded by books about Hindu mystics and the sweet smell of incense. The picture was tilting to one side in the frame, and Jesus had a deathly sad expression on his face, very unlike the joyful art of the early Christian church. The Vedanta Society prides itself on tolerance and commitment to inter-religious understanding. But I had to wonder, have the leaders of even the most open-minded sects of Hinduism had the courage to really look at the picture of Jesus given in the Gospels? Or have they created a Jesus, an idol in their own image, a Western savior safe for Hinduism?

The Bible tells of one who, like Gandhi, touched the untouchable. A man who, like Mother Theresa, loved those who had been cast aside. He healed cripples, fed the hungry, and warned people to put away everything which kept them from God; he confronted those who oppress and swindle not with an inward-glance, but with fire in his eyes and a whip in his hand. He spoke to those they oppressed not with promises of salvation and sin for a season in exchange for the keys to a Rolls Royce, but with a call to give up self to gain self. The Gospels describe someone who fulfills in remarkable detail hopes contained within the Indian Scriptures, and felt keenly by Indians, for a divine sacrifice for human iniquity.

Muslim Stories About Jesus

About the beginning of the eighteenth century a copy of an old document in Italian was purchased in Amsterdam by Prussian official J. Cramer. This document, purported to have been stolen from the library of Pope Sixtus V while he was asleep, was printed by British publishers.

Beskow describes the *Gospel of Barnabas*:

> "Throughout the Gospel Jesus constantly denies any divine status in his teaching. There is also a sternness in his rebuking of the Pharisees with frequent curses, which seems strange to the Jesus that we know from the canonical Gospels."

In this book Jesus says to Mohammed,

> "Oh Mohammed, God be with thee, and may he make me worthy to untie thy shoelaces, for obtaining this I shall be a great prophet and holy one of God."[15]

The *Gospel of Barnabas* is still popular in the Muslim world, for obvious reasons. I have been advised by Muslims, eager to spread their faith, to read this book for the "truth" about Jesus. In it, Jesus plays John the Baptist to Mohammed, who it refers to as "Messiah" (A term the *Qur'an* reserves for Jesus alone.) Other modern apocrypha, also popular with Muslim apologists, have Jesus escaping from the cross and living out his (exceedingly long) days in India.

Muslims often claim Jesus foretold the coming of Mohammed. (Just as the Mormon church interprets an obscure Old Testament passage about the fate of Judah and Israel as a prophecy of the *Book of Mormon*.) In the abstract, I think this kind of argument is not unreasonable. Were the Creator of all to reveal his salvation to all peoples, is it not likely he would prepare us for his revelation? If the supernatural is possible, I see no reason to reject the concept of prophecy out of hand. But these particular examples seem contrived. A prophecy which appears thirteen centuries after the events it foretells is not very convincing.

The *Qur'an* presents Jesus as a sinless, miracle-working messenger of God. The term it uses, "Messiah," is simply the Hebrew word for "Savior," though Mohammed probably did not realize that. One Christian Arab scholar stated,

> "Islam recognizes Christ Jesus to be far more perfect and sinless than any human being ever has been or could be. The *Qur'an* does not give to any of the prophets, not even to Mohammed, any of those special characteristics pertaining to Christ."[16]

However, I don't think there is any Muslim country in the world where it is safe for a Muslim to follow the Jesus of the Gospels.

Marxist Stories About Jesus

John Crossan's *Jesus: a Revolutionary Biography* is a more sophisticated work than the forgeries we have discussed so far, in that Crossan really does know something about first century Palestine. He also paints an attractive, if largely imaginary, portrait of his hero. While he did not go as far as the poet in the last chapter who said "Jesus has earned his red card," or James Cane's black revolutionary, his Jesus precipitated a non-violent social revolution, or in Crossan's words, was "a hippie in a world of Augustan yuppies."

> "He looks like a beggar, yet his eyes lack the proper cringe, his voice the proper whine . . . That ecstatic vision and social program sought to rebuild society upward from its grass roots, but on principles of religious and economic egalitarianism, with free healing . . . and free sharing . . . It did not invite a political revolution but envisaged a social one at the imagination's most dangerous depths . . . What he was saying and doing was as unacceptable in the first century as it would be in the twentieth. . . "[17]

The Italian filmmaker, Pier Paolo Pasolini, a Marxist, once made a movie called *The Gospel According to St. Matthew*, which, in the revolutionary 60s, "had the power to hush scoffing crowds" of student radicals by its depiction of a counter-cultural Jesus.[18] Practicing revolutionaries seem to have realized that with the KGB, they didn't need to be so subtle and artistic, however. Rather than damn Christ with the faint praise of a revised Gospel, they found it simpler to put his followers in Gulag, and their Scriptures in the flames.

Recently, I heard a professor from one of China's top universities speaking to 400 scholars from around China studying in the United States. He was speaking about a Marxist figure with whom everyone in the audience was familiar: Lei Feng, whose face and story has been among the government's chief weapons in the war for public virtue for two decades. Lei Feng was a soldier who died in a traffic accident, and whose diary, recounting his (most likely doctored) good deeds and self-sacrificial spirit was published by the millions. The professor asked a question I think many in the audience found poignant: "Is Jesus the real Lei Feng?"

Jesus was a revolutionary who accomplished more than other revolutionaries, yet without ever taking sword in hand. The New Testament records describe a solution he found to oppression that involved shedding blood—not of tyrants behind iron gates, soldiers who guard those gates, or capitalists who build them, but his own.

The Search for an Historically Plausible Jesus

Sophisticated skeptics may find some of the solutions to the problem of Jesus described above repugnant. Writing fraudulent Gospels! Torturing believers! Burning books! Some pause to note that "Christendom" has not been guiltless on these accounts, either.[19]

Many who defend the Humanist position feel towards the figure who dominates the New Testament the same ambivalence as do followers of other religions. This Zen story-teller, healer, prophet, rebel with a cause, is an attractive figure. But surely there is something baffling about the records. Would a sensitive young Jewish rabbi really claim to be "One" with the Creator? His mother would have had a fit. And do you expect us to believe these stories about him calming storms on large inland lakes, taking a boy's lunchbox and feeding a hungry crowd, or erasing years of neural and tissue damage from the virus *mycobacterium leprae* by a touch or a word? A martyr's death is more than likely for a charismatic preacher in the politically-charged atmosphere of first century Palestine. But much of the rest of the story must be explained by the gullibility of Palestinian crowds, fervent Messianic expectations, or the influence of pagan fertility myths in which a dying god comes to life. The resurrection was "cognitive dissonance reduction," Farrell Till, a former pastor who has gained popularity among critics as a debater, explained. "When something traumatic like that happens to people who put a lot of trust and confidence in an individual . . . they try to rationalize."[20] The early Christian community, crushed by the death of their Messiah, and eager like all religious communities to emphasize the importance of their founder, retroactively inserted tall tales and extreme claims into the records.

Skeptics admit it was not new historical evidence, nor even a more objective standard by which to judge empirical evidence, that caused them to challenge the only records of the life of Jesus. Rather, it was a paradigm shift, a twisting of the winds of philosophical opinion.

In a *Humanist Magazine* article, Kerry Temple, editor of *Notre Dame Magazine*, explained the origin of the "historical Jesus." European theologians, "spurred by the new naturalism, sifted through the evidence for the man behind the Christ."[21] Temple said these efforts were set in motion by the popular new sentiment that all phenomena must have a natural cause. The most famous nineteenth century skeptical scholar, Rudolf Bultmann, was up-front about his prejudice against miracles:

> "The continuum of historical happenings cannot be rent by the interference of supernatural, transcendent powers and, therefore, there is no 'miracle' in this sense of the word. It is in accordance with such a method as this that the science of history goes to work on all historical documents. And there cannot be any exceptions in the case of biblical texts."

Till cited Thomas Paine to argue that this is the only reasonable way to read history. "We accept from history those things that are ordinary, and we reject those things that are extraordinary." The world is full of legends and miraculous tales, so "if someone says something that our common sense tells us can happen, then we're willing to accept it," but not "when people want to talk about angels coming down and delivering golden plates, or angels coming down and rolling stones away from tombs."[22]

Temple explained how a person operating by these principles interprets the Gospel stories. When the Gospels say Jesus healed the sick or cast out demons, the stories "may have been added later. Or maybe not, since these kinds of miracles were fairly common in Jesus' time. While scholars agree Jesus was doing extraordinary things, other miracle workers . . . were performing similar deeds."

As for miracles which are more difficult to explain by psychological methods, such as the stilling of storms, Temple quoted John Collins:

> "Anything involving changes of nature we are more inclined to regard as theological fictions."[23]

Walking on water, feeding the 5000, raising the dead to life, are "simply legends" which have been "projected backwards." Jesus' claims to be the Messiah were also added by later believers. If we want to reconstruct an "objective" life of the founder of Christianity, we must begin by separating mundane fact from supernatural fiction. Matthew alone relates 150 miracles. If all this was added later, the records lie in ruins, and the Gospels become, as Temple concluded, "hardly dependable as historical sources."

But even so it is still possible to discern and admire a remarkable figure behind these myths. Having disarmed him of divine powers and authority, many skeptics find Jesus even more attractive. Temple summarized the new interpretive model:

> "Jesus was a teacher, a charismatic storyteller who conveyed truths in parables that were sometimes enigmatic but always rich in meaning. His stories often contradicted conventional wisdom or challenged the status quo. And in his teachings he emphasized the spirit and not the letter of the law. He spoke in favor of an individual spirituality, a personal relationship with God, even if it meant disregarding bureaucratic authority.

> "He was a radical—partial to the poor, the downtrodden, the outcasts of society . . . It was for these teachings, and for speaking with such startling authority, that the teacher was considered dangerous. It's not clear now which felt more threatened by him—the Jewish religious establishment or the Roman political structure."[24]

That is the Jesus with whom Humanists have to do: a teacher creative and heroic enough to contradict conventional teachings, even at risk to himself; an empathetic and admirable man who cared for the downtrodden; a Messiah, created not by finding any new evidence—almost all the evidence we have has been on the table for 2000 years—but by tilting the evidence we have and looking at it from a new direction; a safe and sane Jesus. This Jesus may have shocked, amazed, and angered the people of his day, but can do nothing to offend a modern, democratic Humanist, cause him to take a fresh look at his world, or disturb the course of his life in any significant way.

Temple hit the nail on the head when he said it wasn't clear who was most threatened by Jesus. When I read his arguments and those of the scholars he quotes, and other re-constructions of the life of Jesus, I often wonder the same thing.

Critics and the Evidence

I will not argue against the "historical Jesus" in detail here. Against those thousands of pages of historical reconstruction and ingenious conjecture, I suggest only that the reader read a pair of short essays. The first, a paper of about ten pages entitled *History and Faith*, was written in the early part of the century by J. Gresham Machen.[25] The second, even shorter at four pages, *Fernseed and Elephants*, was written in the middle of the century by C. S. Lewis.[26] If you read and internalize their arguments, you may perhaps "pick up snakes" of twisted New Testament exegesis with little danger. While of course they do not cover everything, what may be most remarkable about these two papers is that they refute arguments that have been advanced against the New Testament records decades *after* the deaths of Machen and Lewis. On reading them, the tremendous flood of "new scholarly theories" in the past decade seems to mark a pretty pathetic ebb in the stream of modern scholarship. It seems the critics have not even bothered to read, still less adjust their arguments to refute, two of the most famous Christian scholars of the century. After reading those essays, perusing new "historical Jesus" theories feels like watching lemmings plunge over a cliff.

But there is no denying these skeptical theories have become exceedingly popular. The "historical Jesus" is the most popular and widely-read apocryphal Gospel of all, and other religions have begun to rely on the arguments of this school. (I saw Crossan's revolutionary biography at a book store in communist China last year, for example.) For this reason, let me briefly discuss some of the most common errors the critics make in regard to the Gospels. Many parallel those made by the writers of other "strange tales about Jesus."

"Forty years is a long, long time"

One characteristic of skeptics is that they always want to impress you with the vast amount of time between the life of Jesus and the writings of the Gospels. Some of them speak of centuries to begin with. When you call them on that, they try to convince you forty years (one common fall-back position) is a long time. Crossan refuses to pay much heed to material he dates later than 60 A.D.

In the nineteenth century, scholars were able to say the Gospels were written "centuries" after the life of Christ. Recently-published New Age and Jewish attacks on the Gospel records continue to claim the Gospels were written "a century to a century and a half" or even "centuries" after the fact. But most scholars are aware that if they want to accuse the early church of doctoring the records, they just have decades, rather than centuries, to work with. Yet I do not think I have ever read a skeptical attack on the New Testament accounts which did not imply that the Gospels could not have been eye-witness accounts, because they were written so long after the life of Jesus.

Now, as a matter of fact, the book of *Acts* seems to have been finished before Paul's death, and that probably occurred in the early 60s. Luke came before that, and Mark no doubt before that, so it's probably only about twenty or thirty years after the events that the our accounts of them were written. But even if we go along with forty years, or make it fifty to be generous, so what? Jesus followers were without a doubt younger than he; all revolutionary movements consist primarily of young people. A follower born in 10 A. D. would only be fifty by 60 A. D., and seventy by 80 A. D. If the church was a small as Stark claims, that would mean that every fellowship would undoubtedly contain eyewitnesses to the events of the Gospels. Even if the church were larger, many of these people would still be around, as Paul said they were.

As I write this, Nagasaki was bombed fifty-five years ago. If I wanted to write an account of that day, it wouldn't be hard for me, living in a suburb of that city, to find people who remember it. I know several people who I am sure could give clear first-hand accounts—if I wanted to ask, and they wanted to talk. Some of them are still relatively young; there seems no particular need for urgency. And yet we've already passed Crossan's silly deadline for reliable accounts of the life of Christ by two decades.

Arguments that make much of the passage of time made more sense in the nineteenth century, when critics could still plausibly date the writing of the New Testament to the late second century. Even then, as has often been pointed out, the Gospels enjoyed a considerable advantage in this respect over all other ancient literature. Now these arguments are only impressive to the degree that they reveal the pigheadedness and lack of common sense of many of the critics.

"The Gospels are faith testimonies, not historical documents"

Critics often tell us that the Gospels are "not historical records, just faith testimonies." The Dutch theologian Edward Schillebeeckx, considered one of the world's leading authorities on the Gospels, argued that "The only texts that we have show Jesus already proclaimed as Christ by the church and by his first disciples. The New Testament is the testimony of a believing people, and what they are saying is not history but expressions of their belief in Jesus as Christ."[27] Critics often point to John's explanation of why he wrote his Gospel as proof of this contention: "These things have been written that you might believe, and that believing, you may have life in his name." "See!" they tell us. "John is far from an impartial witness. He and the other Gospel writers had an agenda!"

How would the critics expect an honest report of the life of the Messiah to read, I wonder? "I have carefully and impartially sifted the facts so that I could give you an unbiased historical account of what has occurred in Palestine over the last three years?" Turn to the *Gospel of Luke*, and that is in fact what you find, almost word for word (Luke 1:1-4). The critics don't pay much attention to Luke's account of the character of his testimony, nor to Paul's, because what they said doesn't fit the case they're making. But even taking John's forthright testimony, and pretending that it works *against* him, makes me wonder if such critics would know evidence if it bit them.

I have only testified in court once in my life. I had been walking back from Lincoln Park in West Seattle, when I saw young man whose red convertible was parked on the side of the road, locked in heated argument with a tow truck driver. The argument came to blows. The tow truck driver seemed to be the aggressor, but the other man managed to disarm him even after his opponent had fetched a crow bar from his truck. Then a police officer arrived and, refusing to listen to anyone's explanation, (he seemed to be friends with the tow truck driver) arrested the other man. He used unnecessary brutality, among other things, hitting him on the head with his nightstick so blood poured down his head. The man was placed in the back of the patrol car, at which point he went a little crazy, and began kicking the upholstery.

Why did I volunteer to give my testimony about this affair? Not because I was (any longer) a neutral party. I had an agenda. I wanted it known that the arrested party was not the primary aggressor, and that the police officer had acted improperly. Did I select the facts I told to fit my agenda? Yes and no. I tried to tell my story as forthrightly as I could. I had witnessed an event of interest to The People, and had taken an oath "to tell the truth, the whole truth, and nothing but the truth, so help me God." And so I admitted the kicking in the back seat as well as the blow to the head. But I may have underlined and emphasized those portions of my testimony that tended to further my "agenda." Did the judge find my "faith testimony" credible? He seemed to, for he let the defendant off with a slap on the wrist, citing my account as one of his reasons.

Now of course John and the other Gospel writers were more involved in their stories than I. They had been with their Master for three years, or had made a commitment to this illegal new sect on the testimony of those who had. I'm sure their hearts were beating more wildly than mine in the court while they wrote; they could have been killed for their testimony. They had an agenda: as John forthrightly stated, they wanted us to know Jesus was the Son of God, and they wanted us to "have life through His name" (John 20:31). But that does not mean they were prepared to lie.

The Gospels are not faith testimonies, they are testimonies of how and why the followers of Jesus came to faith, and what they realized that faith implied. In the process they reveal hundreds of odd, irrelevant and often even incriminating details that show their authors were trying to tell the "truth, the whole truth, and nothing but the truth." I went into some detail on this point in my comparison of the *Analects* of Confucius with the *Gospels* in *True Son of Heaven*, and do not want to beat the point to death. I do not think anyone would read the Gospels and think otherwise, if they did not have some strong ideological motivation. The fact that the Gospels sometimes seem to conflict on minor points does not disprove this point, as many critics argue, but rather underlines it all the more.[28] Obviously these men felt constrained to tell the amazing story of what had taken place in their midst as best they could, with all its jolts and jumps and unexpected twists.

"Modern, scientific scholars can see around corners"

It never ceases to amaze me when a critic recites with simple faith his creed that miracles "don't happen" in one breath, then in the next tells me exactly what Jesus was thinking or even how he would have thought. For example, (one of many) Robert Funk said Jesus "would have been appalled" if he'd known people were going to start a new religion in his name. Summarizing the view of the remarkable collection of scholars called the Jesus Seminar, he argued that Jesus did not think himself divine, "although he felt very close to God."[29]

Surely this uncanny ability to read the mind, emotions, and hypothetical reactions of a man who lived long ago in flat contradiction to the only records that tell of his life, explicating from accounts by people you call liars enough data to psychoanalyze a man you've never met, beats all the miracles of the New Testament! What need have we of science, scholarship, or a psychologist's couch, with such brilliance loose in the streets? Yet this attitude seems ubiquitous among skeptics. The Gospels become, in the hands of arrogant scholars, the modern version of Joseph Smith's peep stones or the "hidden treasures" of the Nyingmapa sect of Tibetan Buddhism. C. S. Lewis, who watched modern reviewers guess (wrongly) in a similar fashion about the origin of his own books and those of friends like J. R. R. Tolkien, is particularly insightful on this subject.

"Miracles Do Not Happen"

As noted above, it was an unwillingness to accept reports of miracles which prompted the "search for the Historical Jesus" in the first place. But if miracles do happen, then the entire basis for the search is a simple mistake.

Bultmann called the presuppositions he brought to the study of the Gospels "science." But the first principle of science is not naturalism, it is honesty. It is not, at base, a commitment to find a certain *kind* of cause, but to find the *true* cause. And so when Bultmann said that study of the New Testament documents could only begin with a presumption against miracles, this was an amazing admission. He meant that no matter what the evidence, no matter what the cost to historical truth, he would not find a miracle. He was saying he had ruled out the possibility that any religious interpretation of life could possibly be true before he did any research at all. And many other such scholars begin with the same presupposition. This is called "begging the question."

Lewis noted that, "Scholars, as scholars, speak on (the question of whether miracles occur) with no more authority than anyone else. The canon 'if miraculous, unhistorical' is one they bring to their study of the texts, not one they have learned from it."[30]

The first principle of science is objectivity, an empirical determination to submit to raw fact and adjust theories accordingly. I can understand why people would doubt the miracles of Jesus: in fact, the disciples themselves had a terribly hard time believing what they had seen. But surely it is more honest to say, "I don't know what happened" than, as G. K. Chesterton put it, tell "natural tales that have no basis" because one refuses to accept "supernatural tales that have some basis." This effort to suppress or throw out evidence based on philosophical prejudice is a betrayal of the best instincts of science.

"Miracles were common in those days"

Jesus' apparent ability to work miracles "just didn't mean the same thing" in the first century as today, many argue. By the lax critical standards of premodern thinking, miracles were small potatoes. Emperor Vespacian did them. Sabattai Sevi did them. Joseph Smith did them.

How, then, does one explain the reaction one reads in the New Testament to Jesus' miracles? "Amazement gripped them all" (Luke 5:26). "A great prophet has arisen among us" (Luke 7:16). "Through the ages this has never been heard of, that someone opened the eyes of one born blind" (John 20:25). "Unless I put my finger in the mark of the nails and thrust my hand in His sides, I will not believe" (John 20:25).

No, magic was common then, as it is common now. And miracles happened then, as they happen now. But when you read the reaction of the disciples, the crowds, and even Jesus' enemies to his miracles, it is obvious they didn't happen often then, anymore than now.

"There are many Messiahs like Jesus running around"

Skeptical scholars often compare the Gospels either to classical mythology or to popular supernatural cults. Temple for example noted how the Persian god Mithras was also said to be born of a virgin, called "good shepherd," and many other points of resemblance. Till implied that the Gospels were partly inspired by the pagan tale of Osiris, who is called Krishna in India. Several writers have commented on the schematic similarity between the Gospel stories and some of the legends about Buddha. Joseph Campbell talked of a "hero of a thousand faces," whose appearance in the Gospels echoes the mythology of peoples around the world. "This is all Jesus was," they implied, "just another incarnation of Krishna, just another face from our collective unconscious."[31]

What these similarities cannot prove is that, as many scholars have claimed, the writers of the Gospels were influenced by pagan mythological types. Campbell notes, for example, the discovery of a "Temple of the Cross" in Mexico that dates before 900 A.D. "So this can't have been brought by the Christians. The cross is associated with Kukulcan and Quetzalcoatl . . . You have a virgin birth, departure, a second coming, you've got the works."[32] Obviously, the disciples could not have borrowed these ideas from the Mexicans.

I think Lewis' ideas on this score explain such hints of the Gospel as I gave in the last chapter better than any vague notion of a collective unconscious. Professor of Medieval and Renaissance Literature in Cambridge, Lewis was a man who loved and knew books as well as anyone in the twentieth century. Even a critical biographer (A. N. Wilson) noted that a contemporary called him the "best-read man" of his generation, and seemed to substantially agree. Lewis wrote works of literary criticism which still stand out for their common sense and clarity of thought. He understood the process of imaginative creation from the inside, as well: aided by an imaginative and analytical turn of mind, books he wrote in science fiction, Christian apologetics, semi-confessional autobiography, children's stories, and literary criticism, have all become classics of their respective genres. His brilliant and subtle retelling of the myth of Psyche and Cupid, *Till We Have Faces*, has been called the "sleeper" novel of the twentieth century.

To Lewis, "myth" was neither insult nor reductionist category, but a form of literature suited for describing the human condition in a particular way. He became a Christian in part because he found in the Gospels the recognizable theme of great mythology, yet the stories were clearly not myth. Lewis wrote of *John*, in his day considered the most "mythological" of the Gospels: "I have been reading poems, romances, vision-literature, legends, myths all of my life I know what they are like. I know that not one of them is like this."[33]

Anyone who enjoys fairy tales or any form of fiction should be able to see what Lewis is talking about. Even when one reads the "Jesus myths" of Buddhism, Hinduism, the New Age, Mormonism, Marxism, and Islam—and the "Historical Jesus" of Humanist mythology—one finds the same difference. Per Beskow, after dispassionately analyzing twenty or thirty popular modern and ancient apocryphal stories of Christ, found that none could compare to the canonical Gospels.

> "A reflective reader will also soon be struck by the realization that none of (these non-canonical) Gospels gives us a deeper knowledge of Jesus. They do not attribute to him any qualities—divine or human—that might enrich our image of him. On the contrary, we get throughout a superficialized, sentimentalized, and seemingly modern image of Jesus, which some may find attractive for a while, but which will soon reveal its lack of substance. In the long run, most of these apocrypha make exceptionally dull reading.

> "Say whatever you like about the stories of Jesus in the New Testament—has their freshness, their power, and their ability to move ever been matched? Is it likely that they ever will be?"[34]

It is an odd, but indisputable fact, that not only are the Gospels unparalleled in the ancient world, as Wilson admits, 2000 years of forgery have also been singularly unsuccessful at recreating a believable Jesus. People of every religion have had a stab at it. Hundreds of manuscripts have been produced. Yet it is true not just of the dozen or so Beskow reviewed, but of the early apocrypha as well, that nobody with discernment would mistake the copy Jesus' for the original. The words of Jesus truly have proven (through unparalleled trial and error) to be "inimitable," as the editors of the *National Review* once described them. The *National Review*, when it called his words "inimitable," and the crowds around Jesus, when they said, "no one has ever spoken like this man before," were making the same point. Later fraudulent Gospels have driven it home.

How is it that on four separate occasions in the first century, presumably unknown Christians produced, by a process that must have been (in the views of the Jesus Seminar scholars) almost as fraudulent as automatic writing, these inimitable texts? How did they succeed in inventing a personality no one else has managed (with centuries of leisure) to copy?

Lewis was student of ancient Greek and Norse, as well as Medieval and Renaissance literature. Wilson was writing in reference to ancient Middle Eastern literature. Beskow made his remarks in the context of modern apocryphal literature.

I have noticed the same thing in studying Asian messiahs.

As a Christian who researches comparative religion, I feel I have more freedom than either a materialist or a New Ager. I am not only ready but eager to look into the claims of other Messiahs, have researched the lives of many of them, and even met a few in person. I am free to admire the founders and followers of other religions. I feel free also to confront the evil, and even the devil, in every religious tradition, even my own, and even myself.

Whenever I look into such alleged parallels, rather than finding another Jesus, I find: a woman who smokes too much and gestures nervously as she tells me her house is the New Jerusalem; a monk who lives in a big mansion and tricks women into giving up all their money by telling wild stories about spirits he has met; a troubled young man who thinks of jumping in front of a car and manipulates people around him by saying he has a spirit inside of him, or a dreamer who thinks the Manchus are evil spirits and God has a long white beard.

Meanwhile, historical figures who come closest to resembling Jesus in profundity of thought, honest example of their lives, and positive influence, do not make such claims about themselves, nor exhibit such powers. Gandhi made no attempt to hide the sins of his youth, claimed no miracles in the strict sense, and did not even seem sure of the existence or his understanding of God. The Dalai Lama pretends to neither the ability to remember past lives nor godlike wisdom and authority to guide his nation in the present.

I class the "historical Jesus" as just another apocryphal Gospel, an imaginary Christ introduced to ease the introduction of a new faith. This is no conscientious sifting of facts to come to an honest verdict: it is a kangaroo court, with verdict rigged and facts selected to reach that verdict. We who have followed our Master to this point wait outside the court of the Sanhedrin, warming our hands and trying to summon courage. Within, defenders of high and noble traditions betray their own best principles, because they are afraid that in this case, trouble may come of the true historical Jesus and they'd better do something about him fast. One can almost catch snatches of their dialogue:

"What shall we do? For this man performs numerous miraculous signs. If we let Him go on this way, everyone will believe in Him, and the Romans will come to take away from us our holy place and our nation" (John 11:48).

Reviewing the various versions of Jesus favored by various ideologies, one is reminded of the story of the blind men and the elephant: each person, touching a different part of the same animal, came to different conclusions about that with which they were in contact. One thought he was touching a horse, another a snake, a tree, a broom. Each, by limiting himself to that which is most familiar and lacking a perspective from which to apprehend the whole, interpreted the whole by the part with which he was familiar.

But the variety of the formulas ought to warn us that none of these apologists for a simple sketch of the life of Jesus have grasped the whole of their subject. We often speak of mysterious phenomena in a similarly reductionist short-hand. When bull elk meet in the forest to a thunder of antlers, we say, "That's their hormones at work." When a team wins a championship despite a lack of prominent players, we say, "They have good chemistry." Thus also we reduce Jesus to the known, familiar and manageable: an Essene, a Pharisee, a wandering magician, an Eastern mystic and teacher of the "One." Revolutionary. Socratic sage.

"Who do men say that I am?" Jesus asked his disciples.

"Elijah," "Mohammed," "Krishna," "Che Guaverra," "Gandhi," the world replies, as Jesus' disciples replied.

Yet a bystander who feels they have begun to apprehend an outline of the person behind these emanations of the collective unconscious, these tattered and symbolic fragments of mortal hope, is likely to feel a certain impatience with such theories, flattering and broad-minded though they appear. What all of these have in common is they kick Jesus upstairs, as it were, disarming him of the unmistakable authority and incredible self-identity which is the first thing any open-minded reader notices in the Gospels.

The religious leaders of Jesus' day were aware of that authority, and it angered them. "Blasphemer!" they cried. "Being a man, he speaks as though he were God. He's a madman and in league with the devil!" Several times they tried to stone him, and in the end spooked a Roman governor into sponsoring his execution.

Even today, on occasion you encounter a touch of the same desperation over the problem of Jesus. Philosophy professor and well-known humanist writer Paul Kurtz wrote of Jesus, "Anyone who believes that he was sent by God to save mankind is, in my judgment, clearly disturbed." Bertrand Russell, and many communist propagandists toyed with the idea that Jesus never lived at all, as do contemporary critics like Michael Martin and Farrell Till.

Our teachers find Jesus attractive, yet threatening. In response, each recreates him in its own image: a Jesus who studied magic in India; who visited South America and preached to the Indians; who died in Kashmir, or at the age of 110 in a small town in Japan.

Man of Myth

He is a welcome addition to any ashram. His temple would fit splendidly among those dedicated to Guan Yin, Lao Zi and Krishna on the holy mountain we would climb together. But the Jesus of the records, the Jesus of the "fundamentalists," is dangerous. Humanity's chief model, teacher, guru, prophet, bodhisattva, psychoanalyst, rebel, and avatar, is an offense to the religions of man. He said, "I am the Way, the Truth, and the Life. No man comes to the Father except by Me." He is not content to echo, or even debate, our philosophies. He has come to "fulfill," as if the most splendid artifacts of human civilization were merely prologue or epilogue to his death on the cross and the empty grave. And so religions teachers, individually and collectively, find they must write a more plausible end to the tale.

They do not say, "Crucify him." That has already been done. They say, "Let the dead stay dead." They wrap him with a thousand yards of parchment like a mummy, seal him in the infinite cave of natural causation, and roll the stone of dogma across the entrance. "Miracles do not happen." Or, just as well, "Everything is a miracle." "God would not come to earth as a man." Or, equally acceptable: "All people are aspects of God." "Karma cannot be reversed; each person must reap what they sow." Or, as affably, as desperately, "Actions have no consequences and no one holds us accountable."

God cannot be seen and, therefore, appears to us as conjecture. We can believe that the Ninety-Nine Names of God reflect various aspects of his holiness, admitting however that our rough sketches remain inadequate. But some try to persuade us, "God is the sum of our collective imagination." With Jesus, the situation is otherwise. We can open our Bibles and see for ourselves what kind of person he is. He is the figure of dreams, but also a figure who steps into the darkness of this world and taps us on the shoulder. His death and resurrection are not only a part of history, they part history in two. History itself is sundered by his life, and also joined, for that is the nature of a cross. It brings together what it separates.

A blood-red comet appears in the sky in the year of Caesar's assassination. A president who kept his nation together through a terrible Civil War has a dream in which he is walking through the White House and finds his own coffin and a nation mourning his assassination shortly before he is in fact gunned down. A senator returns from prison and exile with a premonition of early death, and phoning his wife, tells her "the Filipino is worth dying for." A slave hears a voice calling him to the sea where he finds a ship that takes him home. In obedience to that voice, he returns to the place of his slavery to preach Christianity and change the course of western civilization.

What do we do when legend enters history? How do we react when myth, like a sleepy Centaur, lies down in our path across the center lane of history?[35] The wise historian, having ascertained the facts as best they can, may shake his head, but will walk around.

What does the resemblance Jesus to religious myths prove? You might say it is a coincidence. You are bound to find such things if you look hard. Or perhaps they arise from a universal image in the "collective unconscious." Perhaps it merely means that people invent stories of supernatural saviors who sacrifice themselves for humankind because they are desperate and fear death. Or maybe we all share Christ-conscious, and others can also do what Jesus did, if they get in tune with it. (Though many cases put forward resemble instead what John might have called "anti-Christ consciousness.")

What do you get when you add all the images that the various religions have made of Jesus together? It took the church a few hundred years to define it all theologically. But I think their conclusions were implicit in the personality, authority, and deeds of Christ as we find him in the Gospels. The term "Son of God" is no more astounding or inherently polarizing than Jesus himself was.

What do we do when legend comes to life? When myth walks into history, and tells us to follow him?

Lewis described the reasoning that led to his conversion,

> "The question was no longer to find the one simply true religion among a thousand simply false. It was rather, 'Where has religion reached its true maturity? Where, if anywhere, have the hints of all Paganism been fulfilled?"[36]

Hans Christian Anderson told of a young man and a young woman who wandered in the forest until the maid was captured by a witch. The witch turned her into a nightingale and imprisoned her in a castle, along with many other enchanted maidens in similar state. The distraught boyfriend worked as a shepherd nearby as he sought a way to set her free. (He could not approach the castle without being frozen to the spot.) Finally, one night, the young man had a dream of a blood-red flower in a field. After days of searching, he found this flower. He approached the castle with it in hand, and the gate swung open and let him inside. Touching his beloved with the flower, she became a woman again, as did the other captured maidens.

The world is changed, and our humanity recovered, not in dream or fairy tale, but in history, when the shepherd with blood on his hands touches the walls of our prison. Faith in Jesus does not mean closing our eyes to the truth about the path he blazed, but opening them, and following them all the way to his father. The evidence I have given here is part of the reason I think it is reasonable to believe him when he says, "I am the Way, the Truth, and the Life. No man comes to the Father but by me."

What it amounts to, I admit, is evidence, not proof. I have focused attention in the direction of a set of phenomena. You might even say I have stacked the deck. This evidence, while strong, does not compel absolutely. God could have written "E=MC squared" in the text of *Leviticus*, or inscribed predictions about continental drift or world series baseball on Mount Sinai. Farrell Till once suggested that if God wanted him to believe, he might instantly create a fifty story building next door.[37]

It appears that, for most of us, he has chosen a more subtle (and, I would add, tasteful, adventurous, natural, and human) course. Faith, while I think reasonable to any seeker after truth, remains "assurance of things hoped for, a conviction of unseen realities" (Heb. 11:1). Therefore the trials and thrills of life in this earth remain ultimately a test not of God, but of each of us.

---

[1] Colin Chapman, *The Case For Christianity*, Wm. E Eerdmans, 1981, p. 258

[2] *Newsweek*, March 27, 2000, *The Karma of the Gospel*

[3] *The Koran*, translated by Arthur J. Arberry, Oxford U Press, 1955, *House of Imran*, p. 51

[4] *The Book of Mormon* (the rest of ch. 13 footnotes)

[5] *The Unknown Life of Jesus*, chapter 5, from Per Beskow, *Strange Tales About Jesus*, Fortress Press, 1983, p. 457

[6] Thich Nhat Hanh, *Living Buddha, Living Christ*, Riverhead Books, 1995, p. 192

[7] Ibid., p. 55

[8] Dalai Lama, *The Good Heart*, Wisdom Publications, 1996, p. 105

[9] *Living Buddha, Living Christ*, p. 55

[10] *Buddhist Scriptures*, Penguin Classics, 1959; Rosen Takashina, *Controlling the Mind*, p. 139

[11] Per Beskow, *Strange Tales About Jesus*, Fortress Press, 1983, p. 69

[12] Ibid. p. 71

[13] Levi, *The Aquarian Gospel of Jesus the Christ*, Devorss Publications, 1907, p. 60

[14] One might also blame the Nicean Council, perhaps, for blotting out records of Lahore, which does not enter history otherwise until the seventh century. J. Donald Waters, *The Path*, chapter 9

[15] *Strange Tales About Jesus*, p. 14

16 Dr. Anis Shorrosh, *Islam Revealed: A Christian Arab's View of Islam*

17 John Crossan, *Jesus: A Revolutionary Biography*, Harper and Collins, 1994, p. 198

18 Philip Yancey, *The Jesus I Never Knew*, Zondervan, 1995, p. 15

19 Nor has Jesus been the only victim of the spin doctors. One is reminded of books that recount the death-bed repentance of prominent atheists. (Though of course, such repentances probably do occur, just not as often as rumor might claim.) Pious Taoists in China produced records in which Confucius was presented as praising Taoism in a manner very like Jesus praising Mohammed in the *Gospel of Barnabas*. During the Tang Dynasty, Taoists also argued that Buddha was actually a disciple of Taoism whose teachings had been garbled by the Indians. The book they produced to prove this theory was correctly dismissed as a forgery.

20 From Till-Horner debate at Seattle Pacific University, www.infidels.org/library/modern/farrell-till

21 *The Humanist*, May/June 1991, p. 8

22 Till-Horner debate

23 *The Humanist*, May/ June 1991, p. 12

24 Ibid., p. 13

25 This essay can be found in *American Sermons, the Pilgrims to Martin Luther King, Jr.*, Library of America, 1999

26 *Fernseed and Elephants and other essays on Christianity*, Collins/ Fountain Books, 1975. (Actually not all of the essays in the book are on Christianity, but they are all worth reading.) This essay can also be found as an appendix to Josh Mcdowell's More Evidence that Demands a Verdict.

27 Kerry Temple, *Humanist Magazine*, May/ June 1991, *"Who do Men Say That I Am?"*

28 After a pair of students attacked a school in Littleton, Colorado, in 1999, there was some debate over whether one of the students had been asked, "Do you believe in God?" before the assailants shot her. Three eyewitnesses affirmed they had heard this encounter, though there was some difference about where. Others said they had not heard it. Jefferson County investigator Gary Muse noted, "Any time you have a traumatic situation, even if only one person is killed, every testimony is different" (*Christianity Today*, November 1, 1999) Superficial differences between first-hand accounts of a traumatic event is no reason to dismiss them. In fact, Paul Maier argues that "variations in the resurrection narratives tend to support, rather than undermine, their authenticity," by showing that they are based on more than one account, and that the early church was too honest to iron the story out. (Paul Maier, *In the Fullness of Time*, Kregel Publications, 1991, p. 180)

29 *China Post*, March 7, 199

30 *Fernseed and Elephants*, p. 113

31 In addition to the errors above, critics:

1. Tend to quote the same facts. For example, of all the things Jesus told his

disciples would happen in the near future, I know of only one that has flagrantly not come true, and in some ways that is the most equivocal: the promise to return before "this generation" passed. That is the one the critics always mention; they seem not to have noticed the others, that have come true, at all.

2. When they discuss a disputed passage, they invariably give it only that interpretation that puts it in the least-favorable light. In this example, the term in question must be translated "generation," not "race," and it must refer to the present generation of Jesus' contemporaries, rather than the final generation.

3. They shift the burden of proof from themselves to the Gospels. Arguments from silence figure large in these works: "There is no extra-biblical reference to this incident. Surely Josephus would have mentioned an earthquake at the death of Jesus if it really happened," one of the weakest of all arguments, and properly considered in this context a logical fallacy.

4. They tend to ignore facts that work against their contention. For example, the fact that Jesus said the Gospel must be preached to all races before the end.

5. And then, to add insult to injury, they admit they'd come to a verdict before the case was tried, anyway. Miracles can't happen, and that's the end of it.

[32] Joseph Campbell, *An Open Life*, p. 45

[33] *Fernseed and Elephants*, p. 108

[34] *Strange Tales About Jesus*, p. 110

[35] That one such instance was the birth of Jesus has been confirmed by astronomers. Every 805 years, a spectacular repeat conjunction of the planets Jupiter and Saturn takes place. Two years before the birth of Christ, such a meeting occurred in the constellation Pisces, the Fishes. To the ancients, Jupiter was known as the "King's Planet," and represented the "highest god and ruler of the universe." Saturn was looked upon as the "shield or defender of Palestine." Pisces, for its part, was associated both with Palestine and Syria, and also with epochal events. What would have been more natural for an observer, as the Gospels say a group of star-gazers from the East did, to travel to Jerusalem at such a time in search of a newborn "king of the Jews" who would bring about some great change in the course of human history? See Paul Maier, *In The Fullness of Time*, Kregel Publications, 1991, chapter 7

[36] C. S. Lewis, *Surprised By Joy*, Harcourt Brace & Co., 1956, p. 235

[37] What made this image almost painful was that he said this while in debate at the Seattle Pacific University campus, which is covered with a magnificent canopy of tall softwoods. I once spoke at the church across the street, and remember looking out at the window at those trees and meditating on the beauty of Creation. To me, those trees spoke more eloquently of the Creator than any sterile skyscraper.

APPENDIX: *Crusades, Inquisitions, Pogroms, and Witch-hunts*

The writer of the epistle to the Hebrews gives an inspiring image of a "great cloud of witnesses," men and women of the past who accomplished great deeds and now are in the stands, as it were, watching us run our races. In chapter seven I told a series of stories, showing how the Gospel has changed the world for the better, by the efforts of just such ordinary, and often deeply flawed, "heroes of the faith."

Some may object that I have neglected the other side of the balance sheet. What about crimes committed in the name of Jesus over the centuries? What about the rape of Jerusalem by "Christian" Crusaders? What about Jews tortured to convert? Or people burnt at the stake as witches? It is as if there were another great cloud of witnesses, this one for the prosecution. In what sense is the Christian message liable for these terrible crimes?

Discussing these topics, a critic told me, "You'll say they're not real Christians. But you have to take the bad with the good. Christianity has changed many lives for the better, but it has also done a lot of harm." Farrell Till took a harsher line. He argued that the Bible was "unique" in the harm it has done, and complained that apologists for the Gospel simply try to avoid such topics.

I agree that we shouldn't engage in pious cover-up of crimes committed in the name of the Christ. (Nor in the name of Krishna, Buddha, or Karl Marx.) But I also think we should try to find out what really happened, and what role the fundamental teachings of each faith played, before pronouncing judgement. It is just as escapist and unreasonable to accuse the fellowship of believers of crimes before looking into the facts as to whitewash the Church after crimes have been discovered. Actually, more so, because one who brings accusations always bears the burden of proof, and also because these events are long ago, and it is easy to misunderstand them.

What follows will not be an attempt to whitewash Christian history, still less to excuse oppression. Rather, it represents my own preliminary attempt to come to grips with what really happened during these episodes, and how Christ's Gospel of Love came to be abused for such terrible purposes.

The first thing I notice is that none of these things took place in the first thousand years of Christian history.

The Crusades

Islam, on the contrary, like Marxism, justified aggressive warfare from its inception. Muhammad himself is said to have led his followers personally on twenty-seven "major" raids. He promised his troops booty to fight, and took it himself, and forced slaves to go into battle. "When the sacred months have ended, slay the polytheists wherever you find them."

"Muhammad several times asserted that Allah would make the religion of Islam prevail (or conquer, *zahara*) over all other religions. This was a program of conquest. . . . The Muslims thus set for themselves, almost from the outset, the task of Islamizing the whole world by force of arms."[1]

For 400 years, Islam was in a state of nearly constant warfare, aggressive and expansionist, with all its neighbors, except where those neighbors were too strong to defeat for the time being. Force of arms swallowed the Persian empire and half of the eastern Roman empire, and created a new empire from India to the Atlantic ocean. Huge Muslim fleets attacked Constantinople. Muslim armies fought their way across Spain into France, finally being turned back at the Battle of Tours in 732. In 846 Muslims sacked Rome.

It was a bit like having the Borg at your doorstep. Mohammed promised those who died in the cause would automatically go to heaven, no matter what evil they had done. "The way to Paradise is lit by the flash of the swords!"[2] What Islam conquered, it assimilated. Pressure was slowly put on non-Muslims to convert. From the time of Mohammed to the present, the penalty for converting the other way was death. "Apostasy means turning away from or abandoning Islam, and the penalty for such turning away on the part of responsible adult Muslims was generally agreed to be death"[3]

How should the West have reacted to such a threat? When the Red Army was on our eastern border a few years ago, the West told Brezhnev, in effect, "If you try to impose your values on us, we will turn the world into a ball of radioactive dust." The West of a thousand years ago, instead, went on crusades, and did a fair amount of rape and pillage along the way. They sacked Jerusalem; we lined up missiles to nuke ten thousand Jerusalems. And we accuse them of barbarism.

At the same time, I am also hesitant to accuse them of Christianity. In my view, their religion was one part pre-Christian paganism, one part imperial Roman cult, one part Islam, and one thin slice of the Gospel.

The composite and extremely unorthodox nature of eleventh century "orthodoxy" becomes clearer when we consider the general history of ideas.

When one worldview is threatened by the arrival of a strong opponent, it generally competes by adopting some of the qualities of its opponent. Consider the reaction of indigenous East Asian religions to the arrival of a cosmopolitan Buddhism, for example. Modern Bon religion in Tibet has less in common with the pre-Buddhist religion of Tibet than it has with Tibetan Buddhism, especially of the Ngingmapa school. Shinto, in Japan, adjusted to the rivalry of Buddhism by becoming very like Buddhism in many respects. Taoism in China also adjusted to its rivals, both Confucianism and Buddhism, in the same way. And Buddhism also changed, as it adapted to native beliefs, as it continues to change.

Christianity went through similar stages of what you might call, speaking positively, development, or negatively, corruption, or more neutrally, syncretism. By the tenth century, Western Christianity was hardly the Gospel Jesus taught and we find in the New Testament. Jesus warned that the wheat and the tares would grow together in the church; this proved true of society's understanding of the Gospel as well as of each individual's commitment to it.

Christianity was influenced by three other religions. First, in the fourth century, the church became the official religion of Rome. This was a big step backwards, in some ways, a crushing defeat for the Gospel, even a second crucifixion. Christianity began to merge at this point with the emperor cult.

Second, for several hundred years, the Gospel continued to spread north, among barbarian kings of Europe. These kings idolized warfare. They carried bear and bull gods before them to battle. When they became Christian, often for political purposes, of course they tried to retain as much of that power as they could, often just baptizing old habits. Christianity made a difference in some places even at this stage, I believe. The Irish stopped slave-trading, according to Cahill, and became a much more peaceful people, for example. But the effect of Christianity was already being weakened by compromise in most of the former Roman empire.[4] Among the upper classes in France, Durant writes, "Conversion to Christianity had no effect." They used the church as an "expensive" instrument of control, and continued in "assassination, patricide, fratricide, torture, mutilation, treachery, adultery, and incest."[5]

The third stage in the evolution of the new syncretistic European religion came with the pressure of the Muslim empire. It took a few centuries. Then, after attacks and raids throughout the Middle East and forays into Europe from the east and the west, Muslim armies sacked Rome. Pope Leo IV, elected right after this visit, "Promised the Frankish forces that whoever died in this war would not be denied entry into the kingdom of heaven," copying Mohammed's promise to his troops of a couple hundred years before. But the West was still relatively cautious and guilt-ridden about fighting, feeling there was some inherent contradiction between the commands of Christ and even defensive warfare. "Before the late eleventh century, no one had worked out a doctrine whereby fighting itself might be considered a penitential and spiritually meritorious act."[6]

In 1085, Pope Urban II issued a call for a general counter-offensive against the Muslims to recapture Jerusalem ("the navel of the world") and the Holy Land. The "accursed race" of the Persians "has invaded the lands of those Christians and depopulated them by the sword, pillage and fire; it has led away a part of the captives into its own country, and a part it had destroyed by cruel tortures; it has either entirely destroyed the churches of God or appropriated them for the rites of its own religion . . . What shall I say of the abominable rape of the women . . . The Kingdom of the Greeks is now dismembered . . . "[7] He spoke not only of going to the aid of the "Greeks" and recovering what had been lost, but of revenge.

The Western forces gathered and set out. The "faithful" were a mixed lot, to put it generously. What St. Bernard noted of later crusaders was probably true, perhaps to a lesser extent, of the first as well:

"It is really rather convenient that you will find very few men in the vast multitude that throngs to the holy land who have not been unbelieving scoundrels, sacrilegious plunderers, homicide, perjurers, adulterers, whose departure from Europe is a double benefit, seeing that people in Europe are glad to see the back of them, and the people to whose assistance they are going in the holy land are delighted to see them!"[8]

On the way, one lot stopped off to massacre Jews in Germany. This was a horrible and bizarre affair. Albert of Aachan is one of the people who described these massacres, which were instituted by a feudal lord named Emico. "I know not whether by a judgement of the Lord, or some error of mind, they rose in a spirit of cruelty against the Jewish people and slaughtered them without mercy." After butchering them, men, women, and children, they took all their money and even clothing. Some local bishops tried to protect the Jews, while some townspeople joined in the attacks. Albert noted that this "foolish and insanely fickle" crowd not only committed wholesale murder, they also got it in their heads that a certain goose and a certain goat were "inspired by the Holy Spirit," and "worshiped excessively" these beasts. But the whole crowd got wiped out even before they got out of Europe, which Albert took as the judgement of God on them. "The Lord is a just judge and orders no one unwillingly, or under compulsion, to come under the yoke of the Catholic church." Unfortunately, a lot of people failed to understand that over the next few hundred years. (As I said earlier, the fact that conversion to truth cannot be forced, seems obvious in the New Testament. But how much did the New Testament have to do with these people's religion?)

The rest of the Crusaders went on to Jerusalem. On the way, they conquered many cities, most of which had recently been taken by the Turks. Some they gave back to the Greeks who had them in the first place, others they kept for themselves. In the city of Ma'arra, short of supplies, they were not content to massacre the inhabitants, but cannibalized them.[9] Finally they got to Jerusalem which, in the face of great opposition, they conquered in 1099. They murdered almost everyone in town, even people who begged for mercy. "Some of our men (and this was more merciful) cut off the heads of their enemies, others shot them with arrows; others tortured them longer by casting them into the flames." Then everyone in the blood-soaked city "rejoiced and exulted and sang a new song to the Lord! This day marks the justification of all Christianity, the humiliation of paganism, and the renewal of our faith. 'This is the day that the Lord has made, let us rejoice and be glad in it.'"[10]

What it really marked was a third crucifixion for Jesus. It may not have been the absolute low point in world history (there have been hundreds of such massacres), but was with little doubt the low point of "Christianity" up to that point.

I am not sure we can afford to criticize the tactics of the Crusaders with too much detachment, however. Up until 1989, the Western powers had nuclear missiles pointed at major cities across Eastern Europe and Asia. All of those cities held civilian populations much larger than Jerusalem. Had we bombed them, the nuclear fallout would have spread across the Northern Hemisphere. Here were our terms: cross the frontier into Western Europe with your troops, and in a few hours, we will destroy every living thing but the cockroaches. And we were prepared to carry out this threat.

What should we say of the overall concept of the Crusades?

By the end of the eleventh century, Europe had been under siege from Islam for 400 years. People tend to forget that, in the broader scheme, the Crusades were a counter-offensive, like the UN action in Korea. Islam had conquered by the sword. While the Egyptian Fatimids ruled over Christians with a relatively civilized hand, the proximate cause of the first Crusade was the rise of the more cruel Seljuq Turks, who renewed earlier images of terror—as Mao's Cultural Revolution did in the West while the United States became more involved in Vietnam. The Byzantines were weakening; if Greece fell, that would leave the road to Europe open. The chief function of government in any age is to provide for the general security. When a civilization can afford to do so, it will naturally prefer to carry the battle to the enemy's turf. This logic was as clear to infidels in the twentieth century as to "orthodox" Christians in the eleventh.

I am not sure it was immoral for Europe to go to the aid of Byzantium, or to try to win back some of the ground the Turks had conquered from them. And I am glad I didn't grow up speaking Arabic or Russian. But many of the people sent out to fight seem to have been superstitious thugs who thought the cross was a magical talisman. I wonder if they were influenced by New Testament teachings much more profoundly than a Mafia boss who crosses himself when he survives a hit by an opposing gang? I have my doubt.

Anti-Semitism

The pogroms that some of the Crusaders instituted along the way against Jews, and that continued for the next few centuries, had, as we saw, a bizarre beginning. The first really bloody attack was begun by a crowd following (and "worshipping") a goose. Where do you suppose they got that? What it sounds like is the golden calf the Jews worshiped, or the pagan animal emblems that pre-Christian German tribes followed into battle. It could have arisen from a deliberate repudiation of Biblical faith, as fanaticism partly inspired by the memory of paganism in European culture, or by some common psychic well of superstition, but they certainly didn't get the idea from the Bible.

Over the next two centuries, an odd trend could be discerned. Often, it was popes and other church officials who tried to defend the Jews against "Christian" mobs. One Jewish historian says that without that help, the Jews "would not have survived the Middle Ages" in Europe.[11] At times it may be that the church helped because the Jews were prosperous, and the bishops (being men of the world) wanted them around. It is also true the priests were about the only people who could read, and knew Augustine's authoritative advise to leave the Jews be, or what the Bible said, for that matter.[12]

The Church mistreated Jews in the name of Jesus for many centuries. Skeptics who complain that preachers never talk about such things are right: Christians should remember those crimes. I have never been able to figure out how anyone could derive the basis for anti-Semitic persecution from the Bible, however. I don't think anyone ever did, unless he or she brought that prejudice to the study. Jesus and his followers were all Jews, and seemed to revel in their Jewishness. Paul said he would be willing to be damned if that would save his people. Nowhere in the New Testament does anyone suggest violence against those who don't convert.

True, there are passages in the New Testament in which the Jewish leaders are rebuked in pretty strong terms. But there are more such passages in the Old Testament, and many seem stronger to me. I think we need to distinguish between internal and external criticism in this regard. The Jewish people have always had lively internal debate. The authors of the New Testament were Jews who saw themselves as participating in a prophetic tradition within Judaism which went back a thousand years, and has continued to this day. Within that context, such reproofs are like a mother rebuking her kids for running out in the street. I find it a perverse misunderstanding for an outsider to take those rebukes and convert them to hatred of the Jewish people.

So where did anti-Semitic feelings in Europe come from? Anti-Semitism existed in societies untouched by the Christian message—in Muslim, Indian, even far-Eastern circles. It existed in the Roman empire before Christianity, and it reached its climax of viciousness after Christianity lost ground to modern atheistic ideologies.

Small, successful minorities tend to be hated by the majority. The minority then withdraws from society (and it may have done so from the beginning to a degree) encouraging a vicious cycle of mutual prejudice. When there are outside pressures, and the majority is fairly homogenous, the majority is likely to look for a scapegoat in the minority. And when the majority attacks a minority, of course it will appeal to whatever the dominant values happen to be to justify itself. The same process can be seen in Southeast Asia with the Chinese minority, for example.

You can explain it in sociological or psychological terms. You can invoke Old Testament covenant curses to explain the Jewish race's bad fortune. I personally would be willing to entertain the suggestion that anti-Semitism is the work of demons out to destroy God's chosen people. But to blame the New Testament seems to me the most improbable solution.[13]

Inquisitions

Faced with an expansionist military ideology, a society must militarize itself or be destroyed. The temptation is to adopt the methods and ideology of your opponent, both externally and internally. In the same way, during the Cold War, Senator Joe McCarthy used "show trials" like Stalin to "protect democracy." And during World War II, Roosevelt put Japanese-Americans in camps, as if in imitation of our enemies.

So it's not surprising that the next low point in "Christendom," an internal repression that mirrored external expansion, came soon after the Crusades: the Inquisition.

According to Durant, "The number of those sentenced to death by the official Inquisition was smaller than historians once believed."[14] In an entire career, prominent inquisitioners sentenced a few dozen people to death each. More probably died in prison. This is not to downplay the atrocities; but it is important to get our facts straight, preferably from a writer who doesn't have an ax to grind. Durant, a skeptic, is probably not biased in favor of the alleged Christians.

But what is more significant is to look at the motives that led to the inquisitions, and see what, if any, role Biblical teaching played in those.

The Inquisition was an outgrowth of the Crusades. The ecclesiastic authorities, having found that their spiritual powers could be united with the secular powers to attack a foreign enemy, increasingly tried to make it work against domestic enemies as well. Several sects arose in the thirteenth century that caused the Roman authorities anxiety for one reason or another. The most popular was called the Cathari, or Albigenses. They were kind of like a semi-Christian Gnostic or Manichean cult, with a program rather like Gandhi's. They frowned on sex and eating meat. "They made the Sermon on the Mount the essence of their ethics. They were taught to love their enemies, care for the sick and poor, force was never moral . . . "15

How did these people get in trouble with the official church? They argued that, in Durant's words, "The popes were the successors to the emperors, not to the apostles." Christ was penniless; the priests rich. Therefore, "the Pope was the anti-Christ." And they denounced the Crusades.

Which side were the Christians, and which the heretics? Undoubtedly there were sincere believers in the official church, and the Cathari teachings had its theological flaws. But it certainly seems to me the latter were more in tune with the spirit of the Gospel and the person of Jesus than their persecutors.

The reaction wasn't immediate. But then Innocent III came to power (poor choice of names) in 1198. Durant admits he had some valid gripes with the movement: "How could any continuing social order be built on the principles that forbade parentage? . . . Could any economy prosper on the idolatry of poverty?"16

Innocent fired and excommunicated church leaders who didn't want to take violent actions against the Cathari. He carried out a purge, and bribed nobles with the promise of lands, and they still refused to budge. Finally he called for a crusade. After years of slaughter, Durant sums up the results:

> "A treaty of peace was signed at Paris in 1229, and the Albigensian wars came to an end after thirty years of strife and devastation. Orthodoxy triumphed, toleration ceased; and the Council of Narbonne (1229) forbade the possession of any part of the Bible by laymen."17

An orthodoxy that forbade people to own any part of the Bible? One wonders what to call that. It seems a bit of a stretch to call it Christianity. Far from being caused by too much Bible-reading, the inquisitions arose in part in reaction against the effect the Bible was having upon the masses.

Where did the religious authorities, having established their power in Europe and bent on enforcing conformity, find legal precedent for the Inquisition?

> "The revival of Roman law at Bologna in the twelfth century provided terms, methods, and stimulus for a religious inquisition; and the canon law of heresy was copied word for word from the fifth law of the title, *De haereticis,* in the Justinian code. Finally, in the thirteenth century, the

Church took over the law of its greatest enemy, Frederick II, that heresy should be punished with death."

It's not hard to see where the Cathari got the idea that the pope was the successor of the emperor or that he might be the anti-Christ.

Were any real Christians guilty in these matters? Undoubtedly some were, as a few real Christians may also have been caught up in the rape of Jerusalem or the massacres of the Jews. (Martin Luther certainly was guilty of contributing to virulent anti-Semitism, for example.) But during the inquisitions, people who really cared about the teachings of the New Testament were often the victims instead. Owning the Bible being criminalized, and most people illiterate, it seems to me the "Age of Faith" could only have been an age of superstitious belief in a religion that often bore only a tenuous relation to New Testament teachings.

Witch Trials

The Salem witch trials were a somewhat different matter. The Puritans, after all, knew their Bibles. And the Old Testament does prescribe the death penalty for practicing occult arts. So is Christianity to blame for those?

When you take a close look at the events of seventeenth century New England, again the picture becomes more complex, and the crimes committed seem to have less to do with Christianity than one might think.

How did the Salem witch trials get started? A group of young ladies got together and decided it would be fun to learn magic. So they asked an Indian slave woman to teach them. Before long, these girls started acting a little crazy—speaking blasphemies, cursing people, showing bite marks on the skin. They accused unpopular members of the community of being witches and having cursed them with the devil. After hysteria began to triumph over sense, they took on more popular targets.

When I read about this, I noticed three odd points that I'd never heard anyone bring up. First, the girls really did practice black magic. So why were they on the witness stand, and the other people on trial? Second, the outlandish stories they told have no parallel in the Bible. The Puritans must have got them from popular folk tales, whether European, African, or Native American. There is no suggestion in the Bible that the devil can do the things ascribed to him in those trials, though those are common ideas in most of the pagan world. In fact, the New Testament always looks on demon-possessed people with a therapeutic, rather than a criminal justice, approach. They are people to be pitied and healed, not put to death. Fourth, the Bible demands eyewitnesses in capital cases. So why didn't the Bible-loving Puritans follow the Biblical commands on that matter either, but accept so-called "spectral evidence?"

We find, then, that the Salem witch trials were not caused by people reading the Bible too much, but too little, and listening to pagan superstitions instead. I admit that real Christians were involved in this one. But the most guilty parties were the girls, who one admitted were just out to have some fun, and who also should have been identified (if anyone) as the real witches. They really did have an interest in the occult, and used black magic to gain at least psychological power over and harm other people. The Puritans bought their lies because they were too deeply influenced by pagan beliefs and not enough by the Bible.

What can people in general, and Christians in particular, learn from these episodes?

First, again, none of these things took place in the first thousand years of Christian history.

If you want to understand the true spirit of a belief, you should look primarily to its earliest adherents, and also to those in later periods who are in a position to understand it best. You can also trace the historical effect that the fundamental ideas of a religion have on cultural norms. Not trivial or accidental effects. It would not be reasonable to blame Islam if someone hits his head on a bookshelf while bowing to Mecca during prayer. But if he hits his wife, and quotes Mohammed's words about beating one's wife to justify it, I think that is a more fair complaint.

If you want to understand the true spirit of Christianity, I think it is more reasonable to look to two periods. First, the three or four hundred years when the teachings and life of Jesus and his first followers were still fresh and had created a church with a spiritual environment that, while not free of impure influences (as Jesus and Paul often pointed out), was animated by the direct influence of Jesus' teachings. After Christianity became the official religion of the Roman Empire, that direct influence became more and more diluted. Since it was politically useful to be a Christian, vast numbers of people with less than pure motives joined the church (including its upper ranks) and diluted it with pagan and imperial beliefs. Furthermore, literacy fell off dramatically, so people had less access to the Bible. (And then reading it or preaching any part of it was criminalized.) The second period in which the true spirit of the Gospel can most easily be observed in action is after the Bible was printed and made available to the public. (Actually, Gutenburg invented the printing press to help people read the Bible.) The Reformation and Counter-Reformation led by Erasmus, the Revivals of the eighteenth and nineteenth centuries, the Biblically-inspired reforms of the last 200 years, and the modern missions movement, are a better answer to the question: "What effect does Christianity, in a relatively pure form, have on society?" That is why I emphasized those two periods in earlier chapters.

Secondly, let us not be too strongly influenced by public opinion about past eras or distant places until we have looked at the primary sources. When we do so, we often find (as did Durant) that those periods are less dark in terms of human oppression than more recent and "enlightened" periods. (What will the twentieth century look like when it is telescoped from the perspective of several centuries in the future?)

Thirdly, society needn't worry when Christians reach for their Bibles, so they are looking for moral direction, rather than to justify what we have decided to do on other grounds.

Some who genuinely desired to serve Christ probably did take part in these crimes, but I think they got the idea that this was to deal with opposition not from the Bible, but the superstitions, bigotry, and legal chicanery of the society around them. They were swept along on the tide of popular prejudice, and used the Bible (like Adam and Eve used fig leaves) to cover up, allowing their attention to be diverted by the spirit of the Age from the clear admonitions of the New Testament to love, win by gentleness, forgive enemies, and walk the second mile. Enthusiasm is sometimes misplaced in the same way in the modern church. Skeptics perform a service to us all when they direct our attention to such instances.

Stalin and Mao called themselves "democrats." More people, then, have been killed in the name of democracy in the last hundred years than any religion in the last two thousand. French sociologist Jacques Ellul pointed out that in each period people appeal to the defining ideals of that generation, "Or no one will listen to them." In the twentieth century one of those ideals was Democracy, in the thirteenth, Christianity. Which is to say, "Christianity" happened to be what they used as an instrument of social cohesion and (not incidentally) to justify their power.

Bad people always justify their actions by the highest ideals available. Of course the Inquisitors, trying to regain control of society, quoted Scriptures. But I do not think the teachings of the Bible caused the Inquisition, witch-hunts, or pogroms. Each of these is a common social phenomena, which you can find at least in embryonic form in most societies at most times. Christ did not wave a wand over the West and turn people into angels; nor did he promise to do so. Nothing that has happened in subsequent Western history should come as a surprise to anyone who reads the Jesus' warnings of "wars and rumors of wars" and "false Christs who will deceive many" and "when they kill you, they will think they are doing God's work." All these things came true in the Middle Ages, and also in the modern era.

At the same time, the Church can also learn several lessons from these episodes. First, the church creates its own sub-culture, with folk tales and mythologies, that we tend to relate to Bible, even when they derive in fact from other sources. Believers should always beware of faddish interpretations of texts, allowing our understanding of the Gospel to be informed by exposure to the wise Christian teaching of many different times and cultures, as well as a skepticism about titillating new theories.

Second, with all the talk about spiritual warfare, and with the increased popularity of the occult, let us remind ourselves that we "wrestle not with flesh and blood." Let's remember Jesus' words to Peter. Any of us can act as the mouthpiece of Satan. Christians should not demonize communists, humanists, New Agers, or gay rights activists, and even while we oppose the work of Satan they may do, we should look to ourselves, lest we fall too. And we should be especially careful about attempts to pretend the devil's powers are physical in nature.

Third, if we forget these truths, Christians can become a part of the problem. Tyranny can happen here, to us.

One of the most gripping books of the century, William Golding's *Lord of the Flies*, tells the story of a group of boys who are stranded on an island in the Pacific. Though they try to cooperate at first, before long rivalries break out, and most of the boys follow the lead of an older boy named Jack, who leads them in hunting wild pigs, and then finally, in hunting down and murdering two of the other boys. The moral of

Golding's story was obvious, even, as he admitted, a truism, but one he felt an increasingly complacent Western world needed to be reminded of. After all, "a truism is true." The truism in question is that people like to kill. Nazism, Marxism, and the Inquisition were not aberrations. Evil systems do not create evil; they merely channel and encourage a latent potential for meanness that lies buried within each of us, suppressed by culture and custom, but waiting like Belzabub, lord of the flies, to emerge.

Golding was a Christian. While the moral of his story was not unique to Christianity, the form he gave it was a Christian fable. In fact, *Lord of the Flies* can be looked at as another remake of the story of Adam and Eve in the Garden of Eden. "It can happen here, too," was Golding's point. No Christian should disagree.

Finally, perhaps there is a silver lining to the increased paganism of Western society. "Power is perfected in weakness" (2 Cor. 12:9). Christians might even welcome the success of modern paganism, (apart from its harmful effect on individuals) not only because truth is easier to see against a backdrop of error, and not only because (to quote a French general) because now we can "attack in every direction," but also because the secular world works harder than it used to, to keep us humble. And that may be God's grace.

---

[1] Peter Partner, *God of Battles: Holy Wars of Christianity and Islam*, Princeton U Press, 1997, p.38

[2] Ibid. p. 51

[3] Ibid. p.43

[4] To be sure, Christianity has never been pacifist. It is reasonable to look for a way of balancing "turn the other cheek" with the responsibilities of protecting a nation from enemies. That's the question Augustine tried to work out with his just war doctrine.

[5] *The Age of Faith*, p. 94

[6] *The First Crusade, The Chronicles of Fulcher of Chartres and Other Source Materials*, edited by Edward Peters, University of Pennsylvania Press, 1971, p. 8

[7] *The First Crusade, Speech of Urban*, p.27

[8] *God of Battles*, p. 105

[9] *The Crusades Through Arab Eyes*, chapter 3

[10] Raymond d'Aguilers, *First Crusade*, p.260

[11] *Age of Faith*, p. 389

[12] Leonard B. Glick, *Abraham's Heirs: Jews and Christians in Medieval Europe*, Syracuse University Press, 1999)

[13] See Leonard B. Glick, *Abraham's Heirs; Jews and Christians in Medieval Europe*, for the sad story of the relations between Jews and Gentiles in Medieval Europe, looking at the story from a Jewish perspective.

[14] *Age of Faith*, p. 783

[15] Ibid., p.772

[16] Ibid., p.773

[17] Ibid. , p. 776

Speaking:

*David Marshall speaks to a variety of audiences, Christian and secular,
about Christianity and other religions or world cultures,
such as colleges, churches, mission fellowships, youth groups, and seminaries.
To contact him about a visit to your school or church, please send e-mails to*:

d.marshall@sun.ac.jp

Or write: David Marshall,
Siebold University of Nagasaki,
Nagasaki, Japan 851

Book orders:

To order additional copies of *Jesus and the Religions of Man*
please send $13 US + $1.50 for shipping and handling to:

KUAI MU PRESS
6765 37th SW
Seattle, WA, 98126

For quantity or ministry discount information,
please call (206) 932-9032
Or e-mail: d.marshall@sun.ac.jp

To order *True Son of Heaven: How Jesus Fulfills the Chinese Culture*,
please send $12 plus $1.50 shipping and handling to the same address.